SHIN YOSHIDA

Yuto, Yuri, Yugo, Yuya, Reiji, Kurosaki, Sawatari, Sora...
They're all cool and good-looking, aren't they? Which one
do you like? As for me, well... Heh heh heh... ♡

NAOHITO MIYOSHI

Foreshadowing explained! The mystery of Yuya and
company! And G.O.D. makes an entrance! Volume 6 is
packed with content, but I had to make a lot of corrections,
so it was a rough volume on a personal level... (I sweated
blood.) Thanks to everyone who pointed stuff out!

MASAHIRO HIKOKUBO

Eve has journeyed through all sorts of times in all sorts
of parallel worlds, and she controls legendary monsters...
Does that mean she has fought legendary Duelists?! Hmm...
Pretty exciting, yeah? ♡

3

6

SHONEN JUMP MANGA EDITION

ORIGINAL CONCEPT BY
Kazuki Takahashi

PRODUCTION SUPPORT: **STUDIO DICE**

STORY BY
Shin Yoshida

ART BY
Naohito Miyoshi

DUEL COORDINATOR
Masahiro Hikokubo

TRANSLATION + ENGLISH ADAPTATION
Sarah Neufeld and John Werry, HC Language Solutions, Inc.

TOUCH-UP ART + LETTERING **John Hunt**

DESIGNER **Stacie Yamaki**

EDITOR **Mike Montesa**

Printed in the U.S.A.

Published by VIZ Media, LLC
P.O. Box 77010
San Francisco, CA 94107

10 9 8 7 6 5 4 3 2 1
First printing, September 2019

VIZ MEDIA
viz.com

SHONEN JUMP
shonenjump.com

Challenge the Legends!!

ORIGINAL CONCEPT BY **Kazuki Takahashi**

PRODUCTION SUPPORT: **STUDIO DICE**

STORY BY **Shin Yoshida**

ART BY **Naohito Miyoshi**

DUEL COORDINATOR **Masahiro Hikokubo**

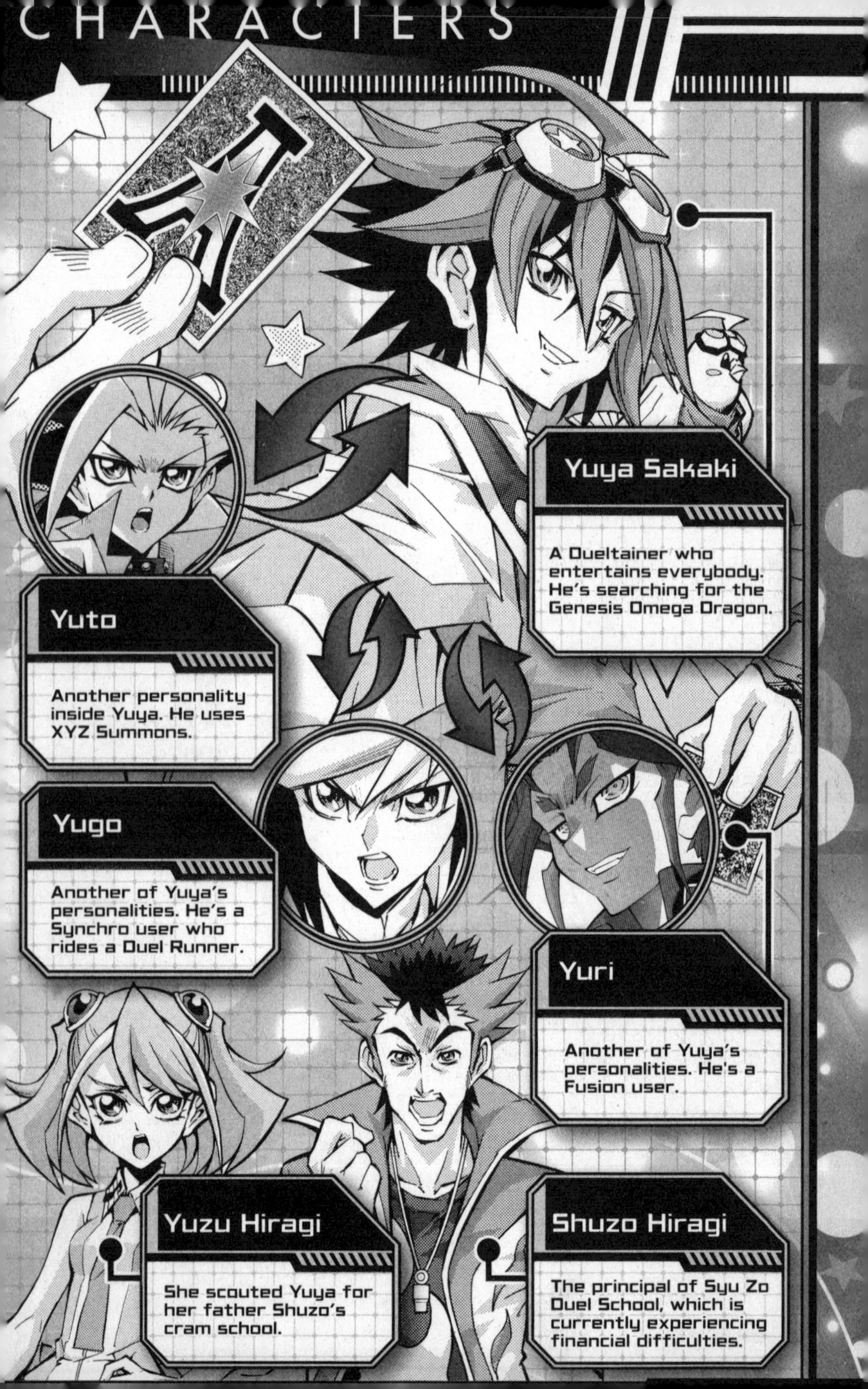
CHARACTERS
Yuya Sakaki
A Dueltainer who entertains everybody. He's searching for the Genesis Omega Dragon.
Yuto
Another personality inside Yuya. He uses XYZ Summons.
Yugo
Another of Yuya's personalities. He's a Synchro user who rides a Duel Runner.
Yuri
Another of Yuya's personalities. He's a Fusion user.
Shuzo Hiragi
The principal of Syu Zo Duel School, which is currently experiencing financial difficulties.
Yuzu Hiragi
She scouted Yuya for her father Shuzo's cram school.

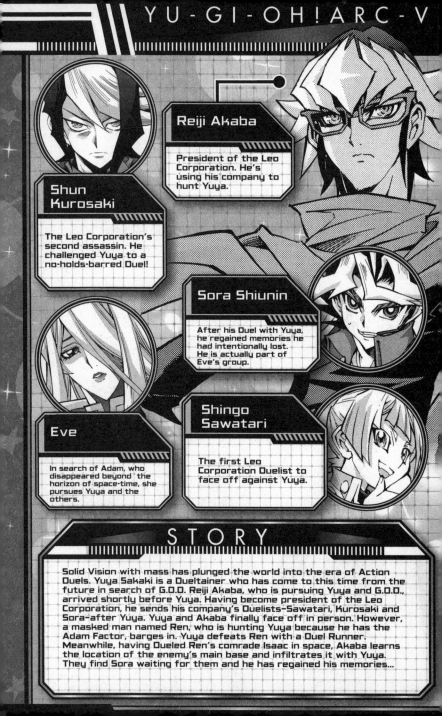

Reiji Akaba

President of the Leo Corporation. He's using his company to hunt Yuya.

Shun Kurosaki

The Leo Corporation's second assassin. He challenged Yuya to a no-holds-barred Duel!

Sora Shiunin

After his Duel with Yuya, he regained memories he had intentionally lost. He is actually part of Eve's group.

Eve

In search of Adam, who disappeared beyond the horizon of space-time, she pursues Yuya and the others.

Shingo Sawatari

The first Leo Corporation Duelist to face off against Yuya.

STORY

Solid Vision with mass has plunged the world into the era of Action Duels. Yuya Sakaki is a Dueltainer who has come to this time from the future in search of G.O.D. Reiji Akaba, who is pursuing Yuya and G.O.D., arrived shortly before Yuya. Having become president of the Leo Corporation, he sends his company's Duelists—Sawatari, Kurosaki and Sora—after Yuya. Yuya and Akaba finally face off in person. However, a masked man named Ren, who is hunting Yuya because he has the Adam Factor, barges in. Yuya defeats Ren with a Duel Runner. Meanwhile, having Dueled Ren's comrade Isaac in space, Akaba learns the location of the enemy's main base and infiltrates it with Yuya. They find Sora waiting for them and he has regained his memories...

YU-GI-OH! ARC-V

6 Challenge the Legends!!

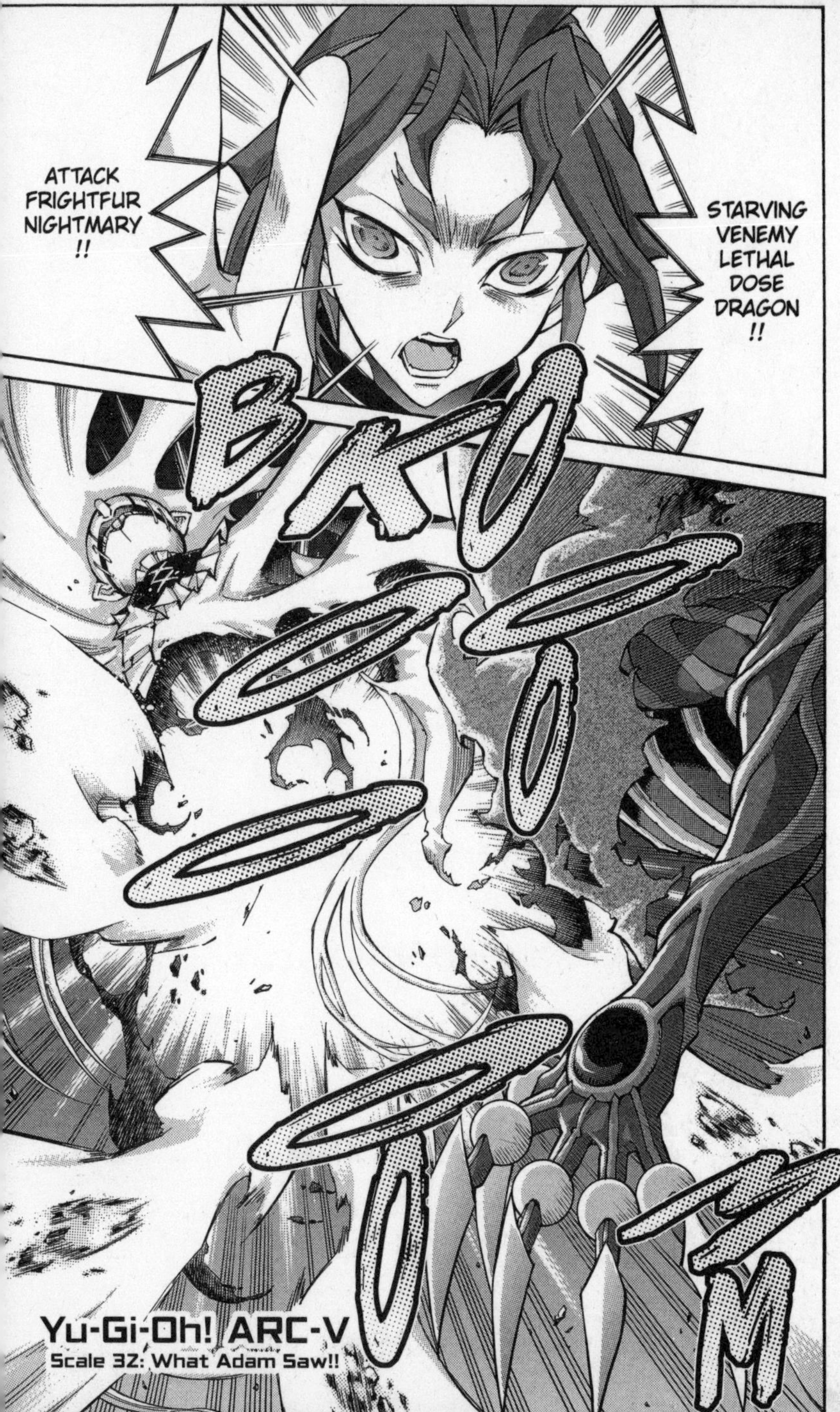
STARVING VENEMY LETHAL DOSE DRAGON !!
ATTACK FRIGHTFUR NIGHTMARY !!
BKOOOOOOOOMM
Yu-Gi-Oh! ARC-V
Scale 32: What Adam Saw!!

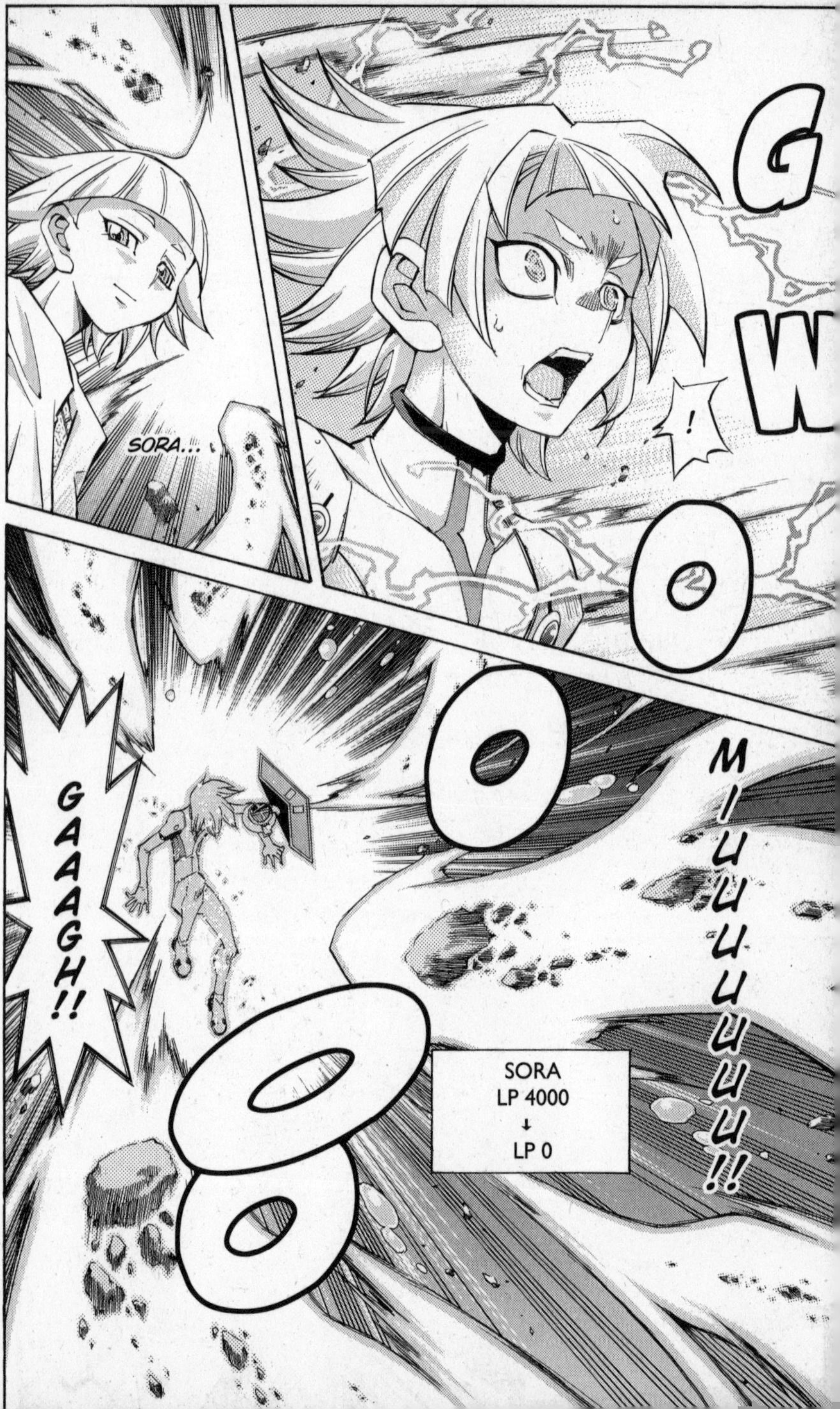
!
GWOOOO
SORA...
MIUUUUUUU!!
SORA
LP 4000
↓
LP 0
GAAAAGH!!

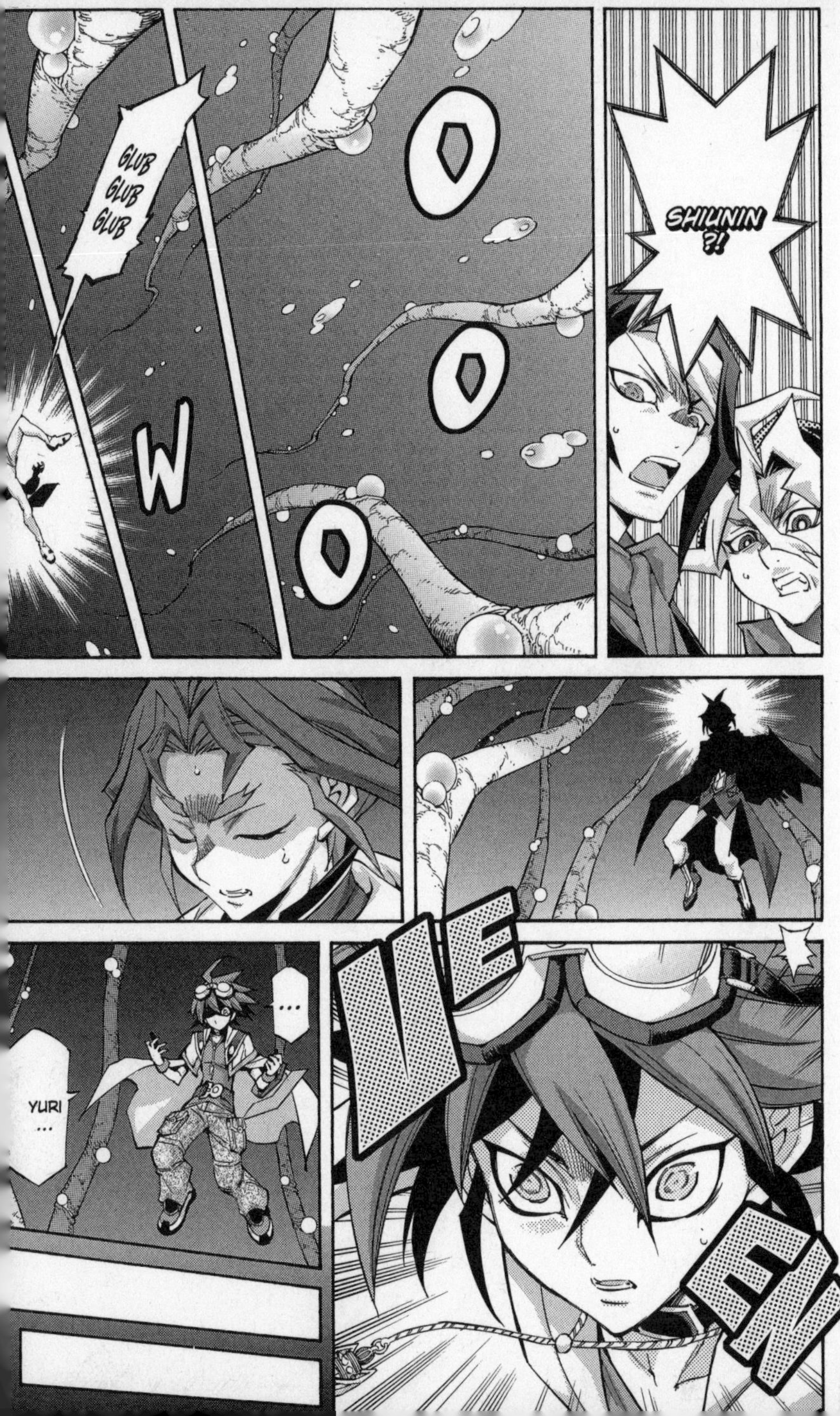
SHIUNIN ?!
WOOO
GLUB GLUB GLUB
WE
EN
...
YURI ...

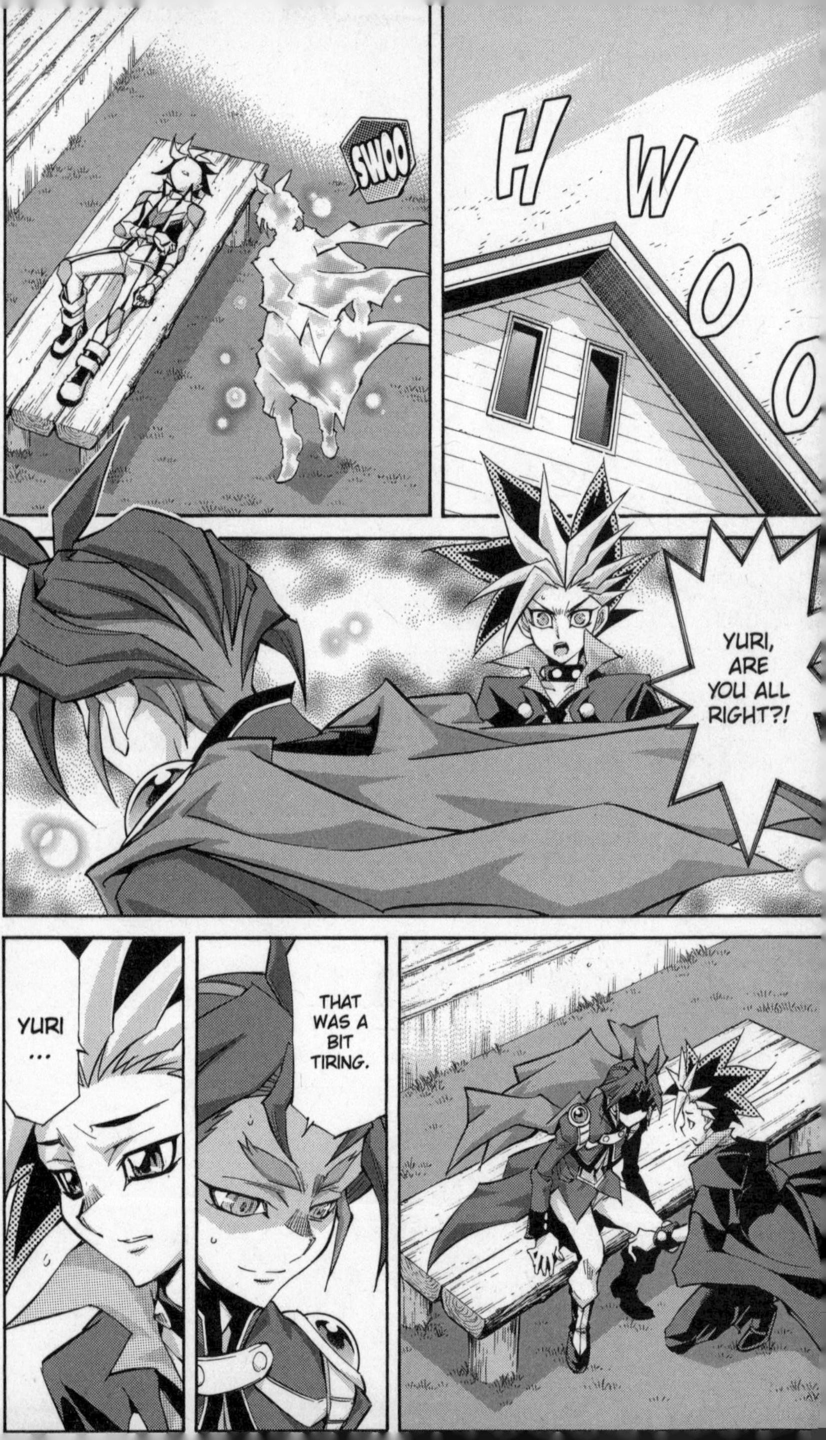
HWOOO
SWOO
YURI, ARE YOU ALL RIGHT?!
THAT WAS A BIT TIRING.
YURI ...

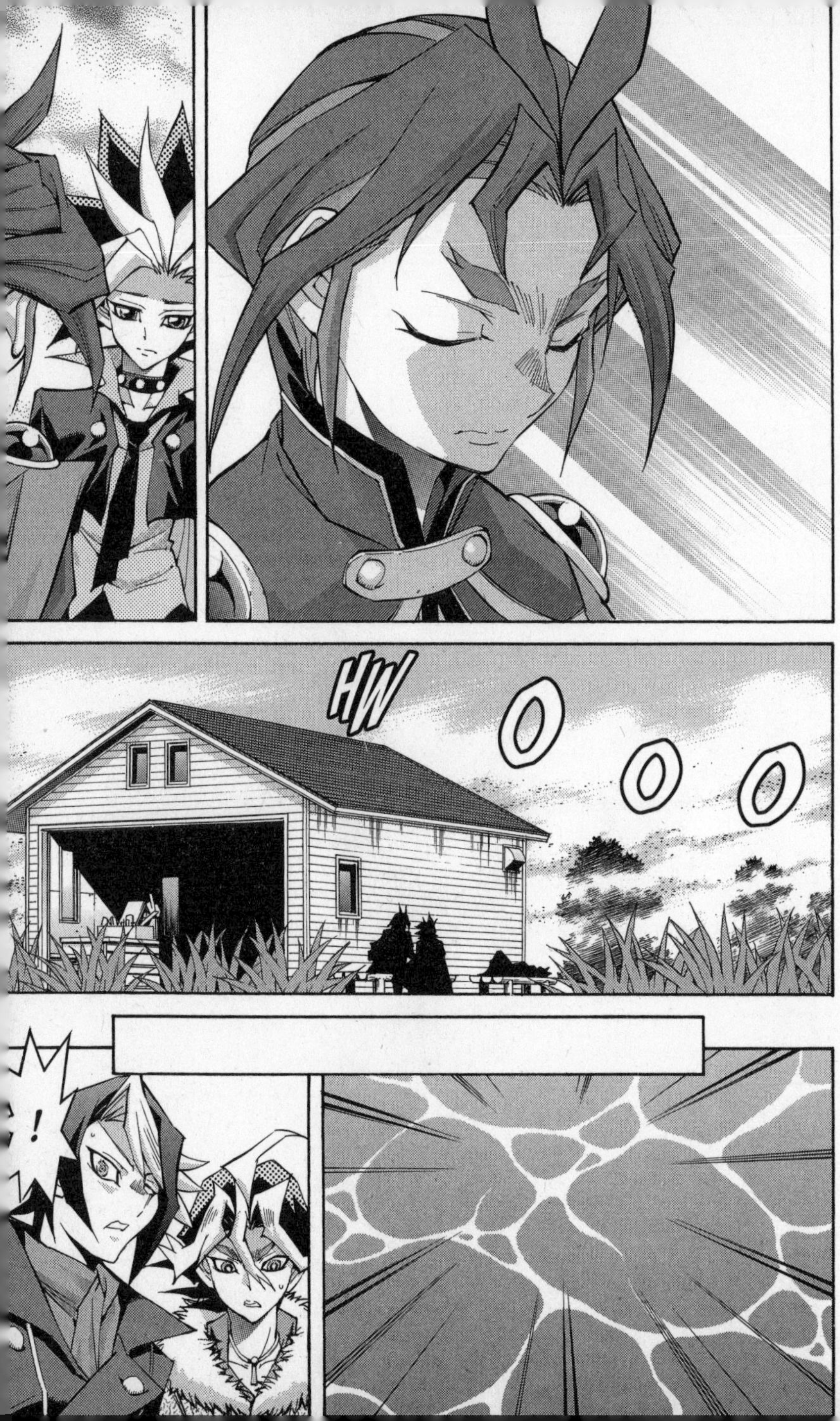
HWOOOO
!

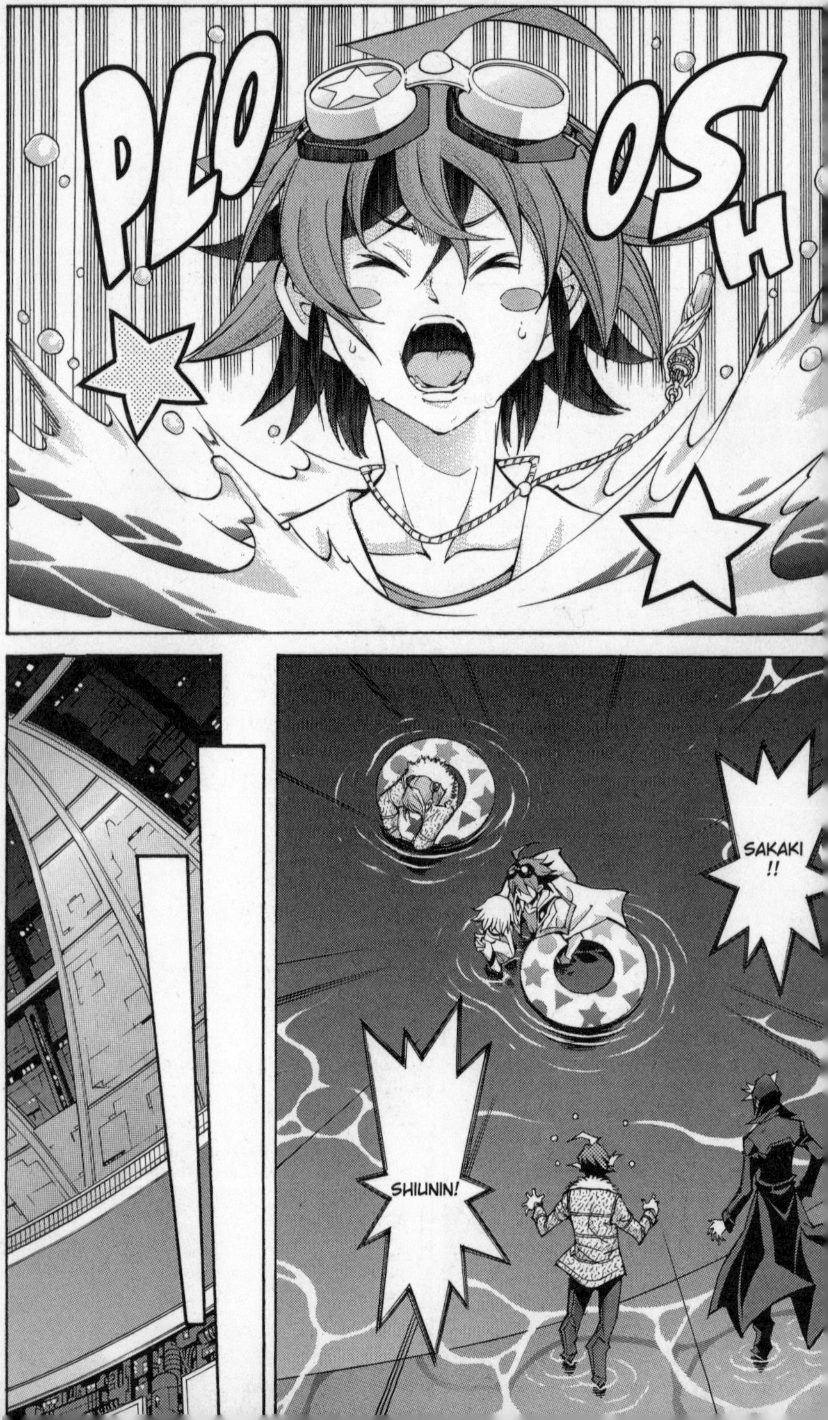
PLOOSH
SAKAKI !!
SHIUNIN!

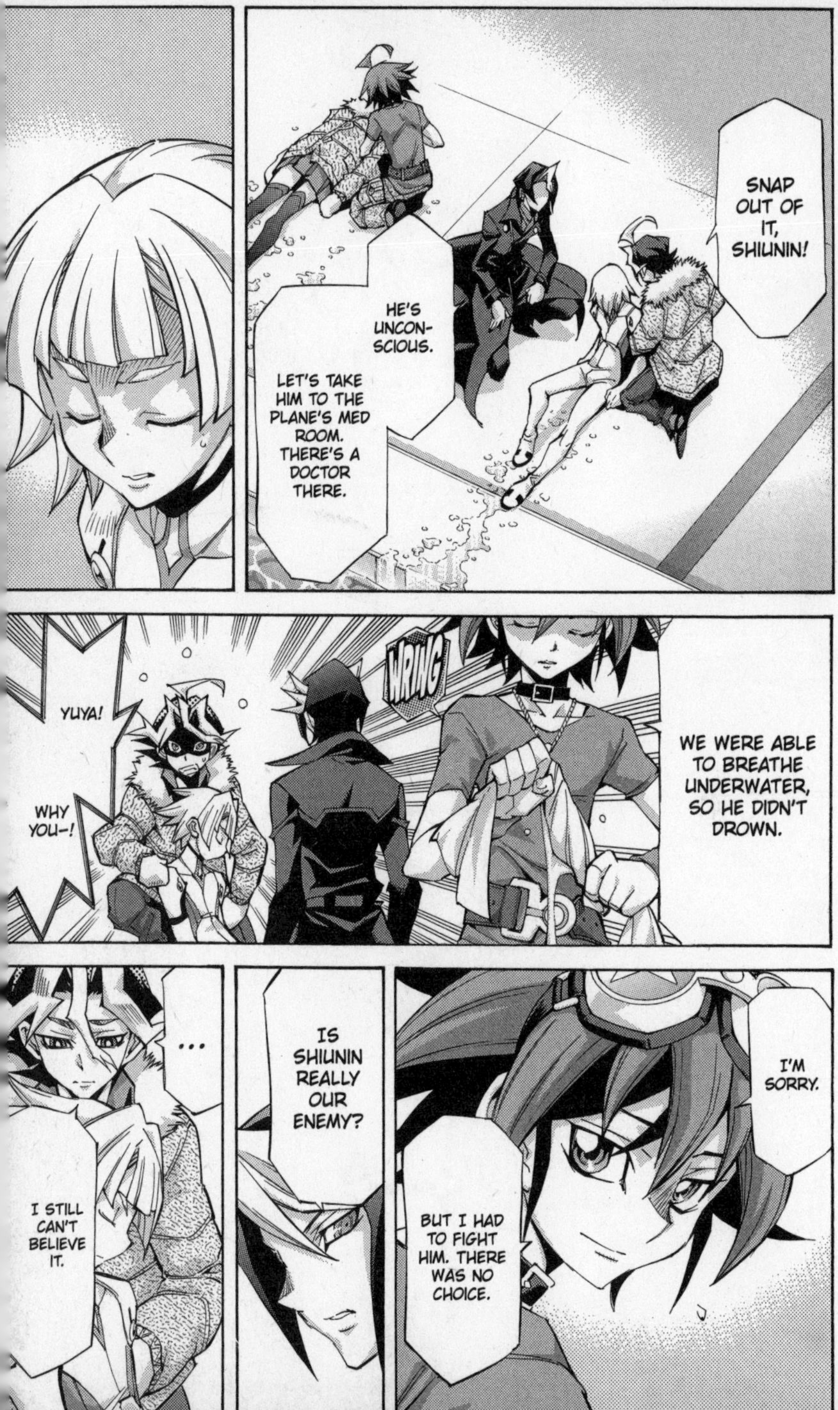
SNAP OUT OF IT, SHIUNIN!
HE'S UNCONSCIOUS.
LET'S TAKE HIM TO THE PLANE'S MED ROOM. THERE'S A DOCTOR THERE.
WE WERE ABLE TO BREATHE UNDERWATER, SO HE DIDN'T DROWN.
WRING
YUYA!
WHY YOU-!
I'M SORRY.
BUT I HAD TO FIGHT HIM. THERE WAS NO CHOICE.
IS SHIUNIN REALLY OUR ENEMY?
...
I STILL CAN'T BELIEVE IT.

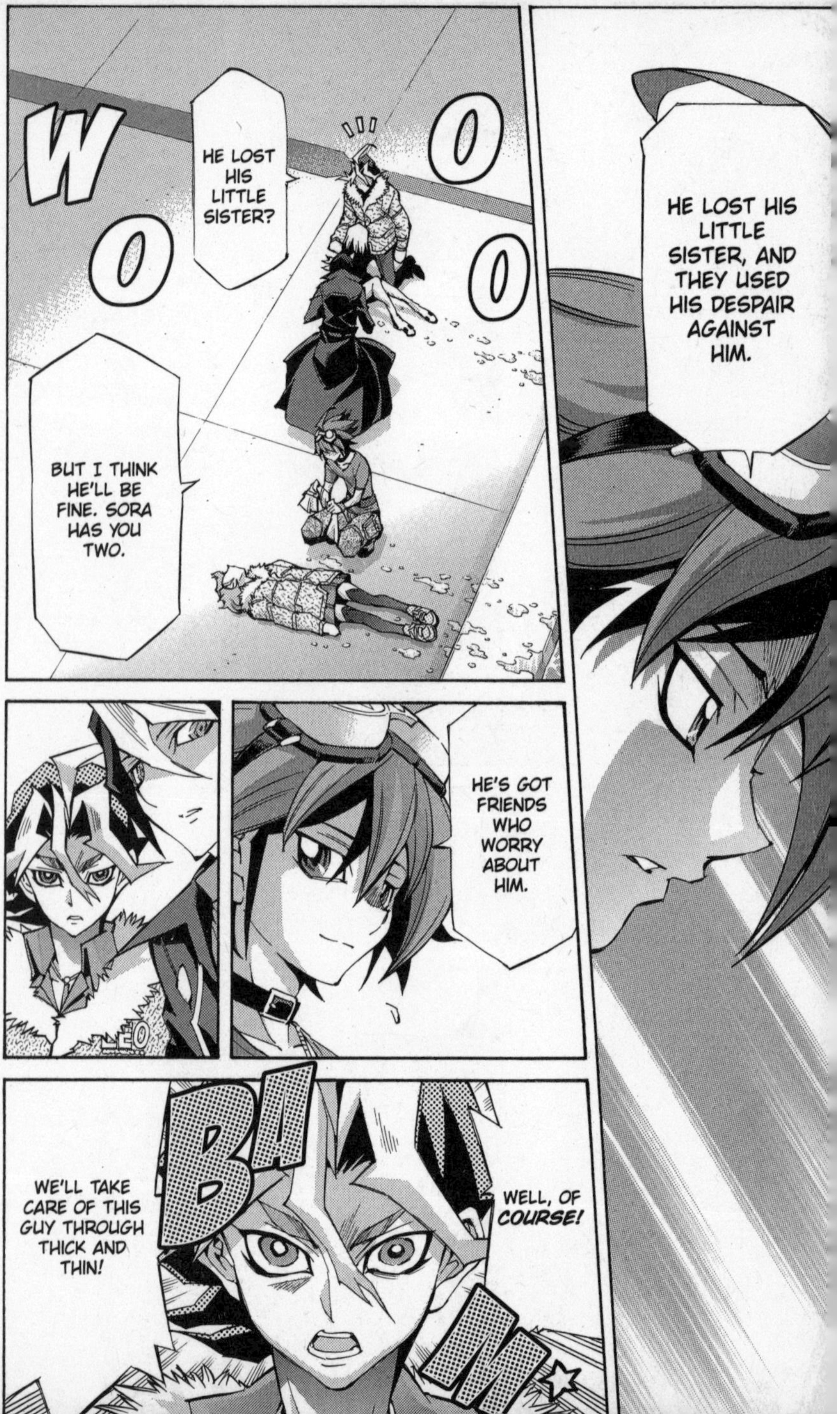
HE LOST HIS LITTLE SISTER, AND THEY USED HIS DESPAIR AGAINST HIM.
WOOO
HE LOST HIS LITTLE SISTER?
BUT I THINK HE'LL BE FINE. SORA HAS YOU TWO.
HE'S GOT FRIENDS WHO WORRY ABOUT HIM.
BAM
WELL, OF *COURSE!*
WE'LL TAKE CARE OF THIS GUY THROUGH THICK AND THIN!

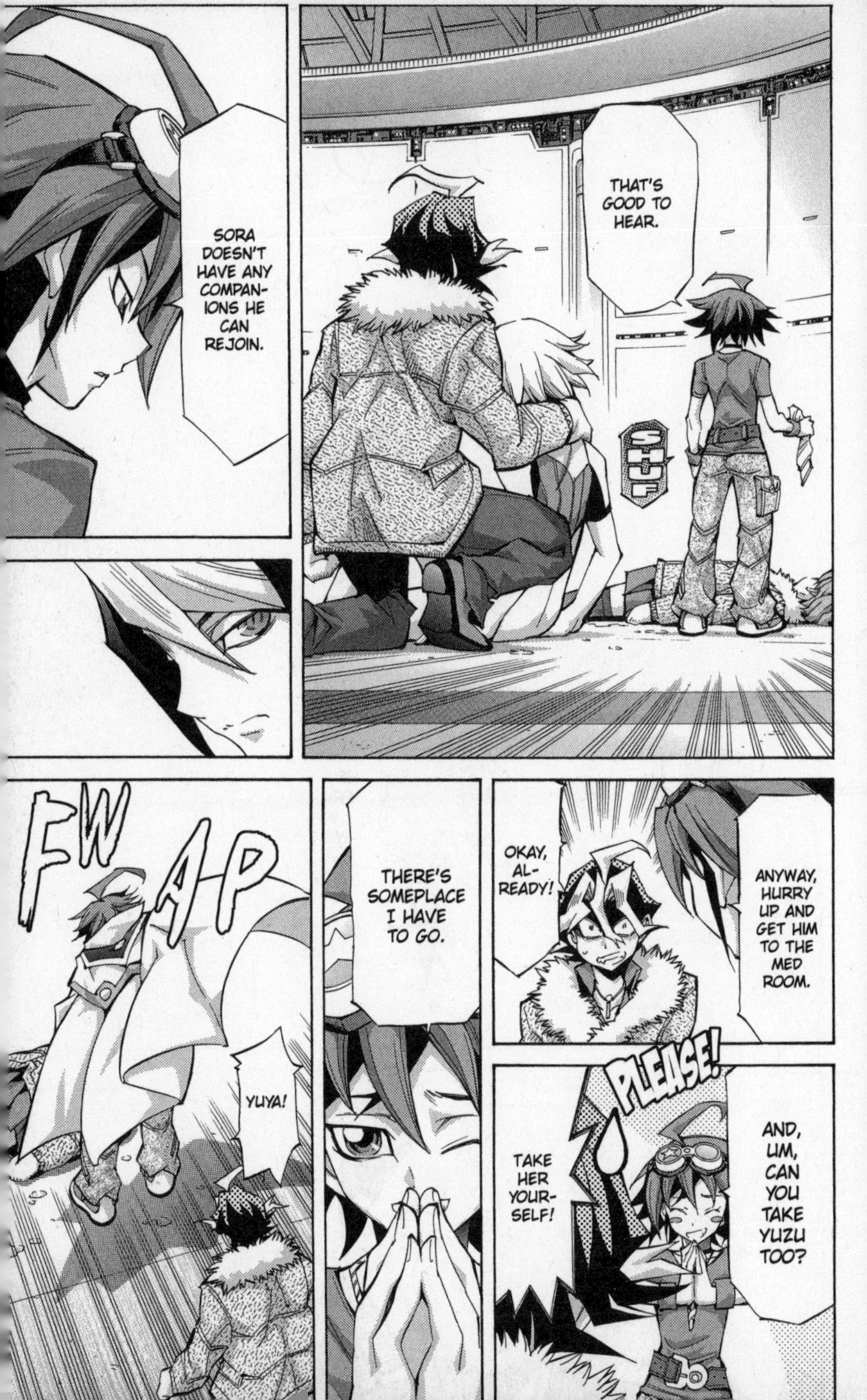
THAT'S GOOD TO HEAR.
SHUF
SORA DOESN'T HAVE ANY COMPANIONS HE CAN REJOIN.
ANYWAY, HURRY UP AND GET HIM TO THE MED ROOM.
OKAY, AL-READY!
AND, UM, CAN YOU TAKE YUZU TOO?
PLEASE!
TAKE HER YOURSELF!
THERE'S SOMEPLACE I HAVE TO GO.
FWAP
YUYA!

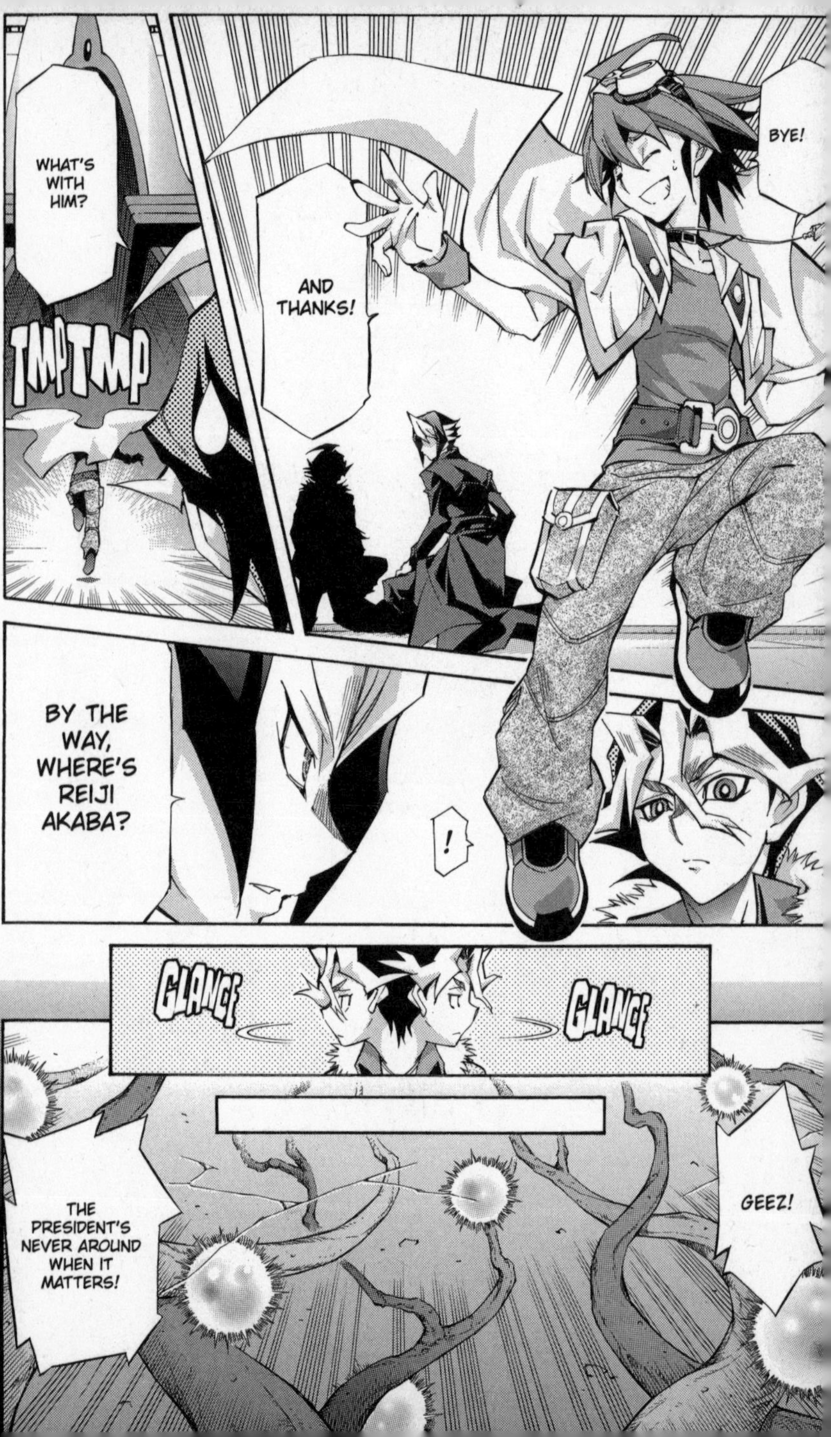
BYE!
AND THANKS!
WHAT'S WITH HIM?
TMPTMP
!
BY THE WAY, WHERE'S REIJI AKABA?
GLANCE
GLANCE
GEEZ!
THE PRESIDENT'S NEVER AROUND WHEN IT MATTERS!

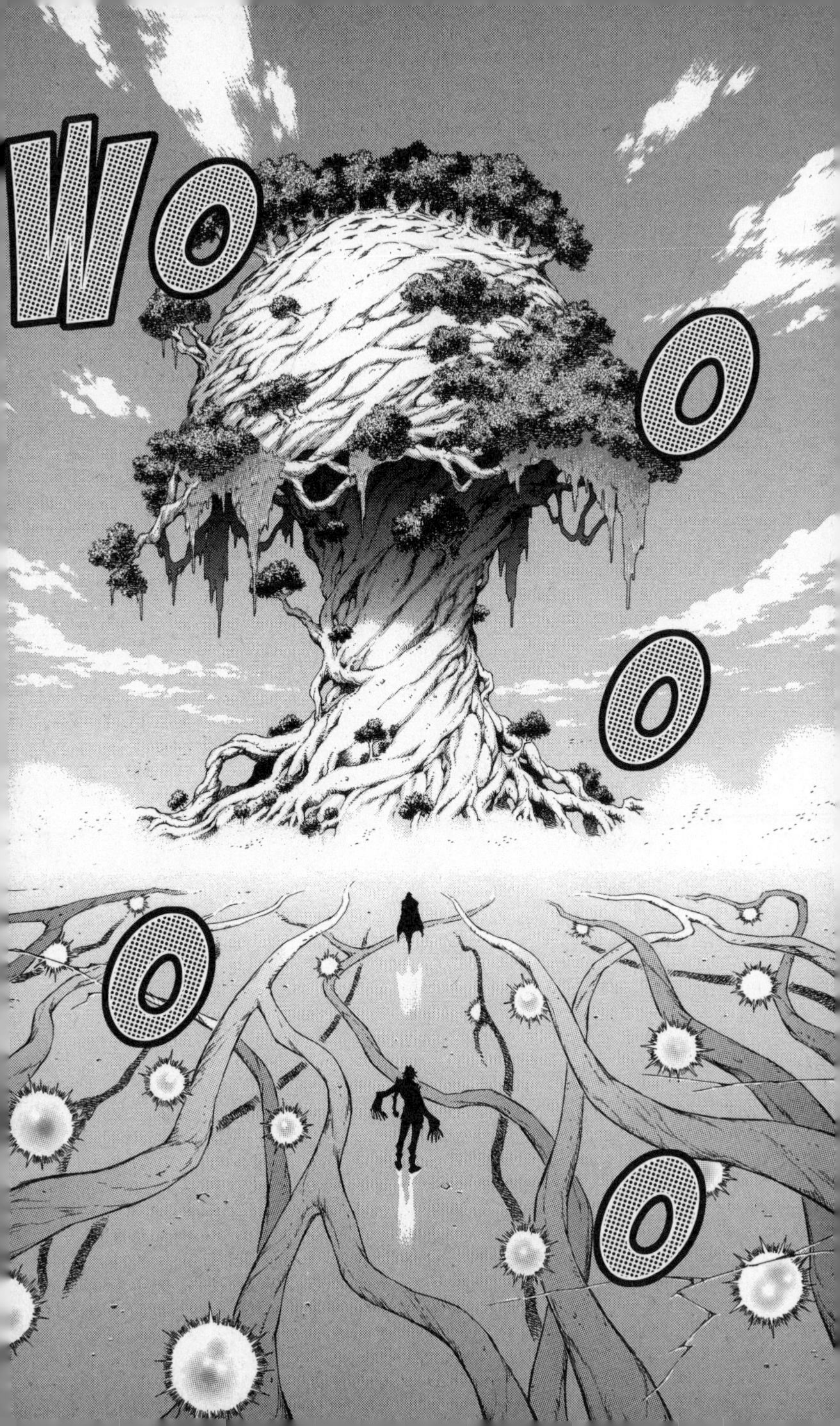
WOOOOO

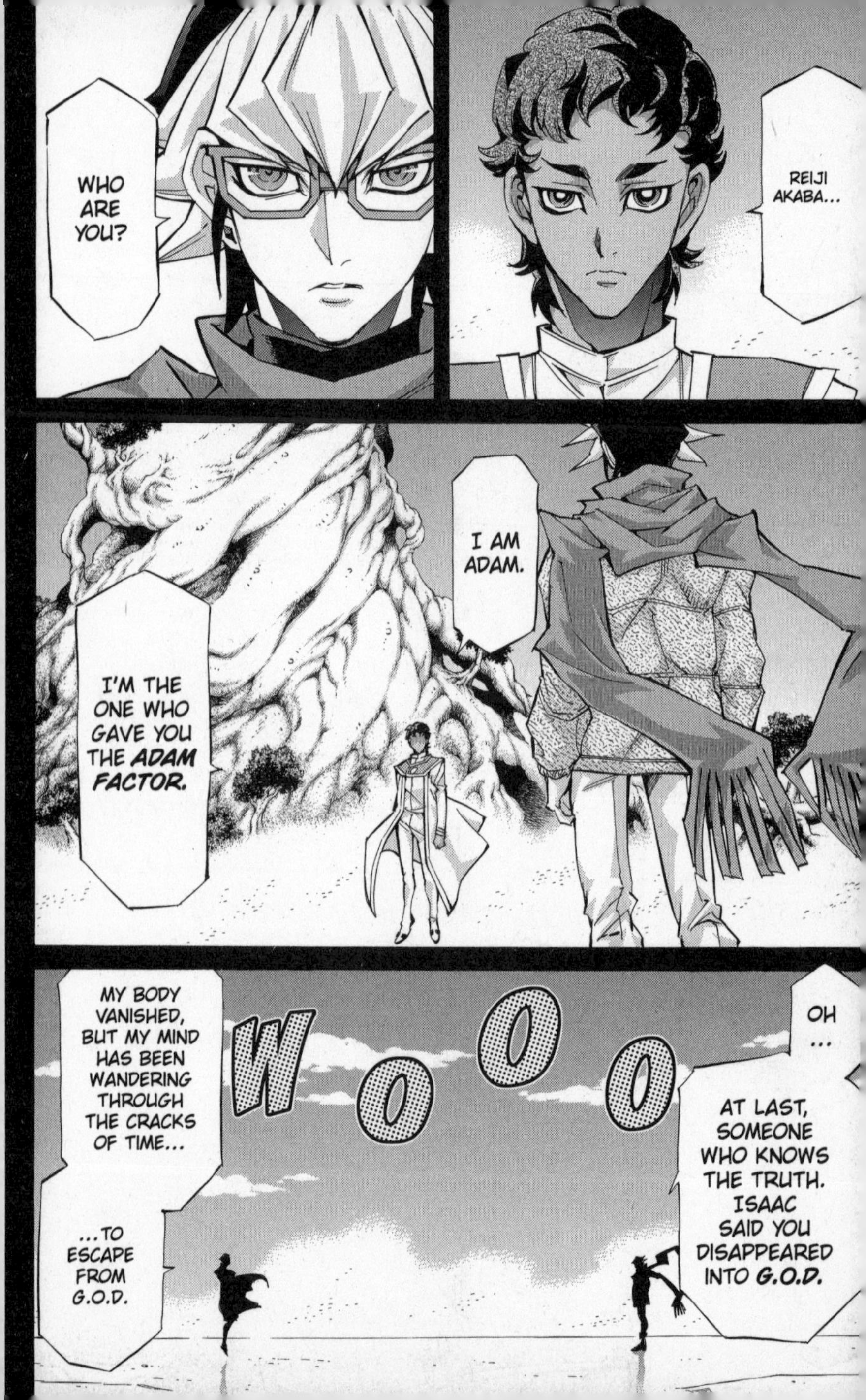
REIJI AKABA...
WHO ARE YOU?
I AM ADAM.
I'M THE ONE WHO GAVE YOU THE *ADAM FACTOR.*
OH ...
AT LAST, SOMEONE WHO KNOWS THE TRUTH. ISAAC SAID YOU DISAPPEARED INTO *G.O.D.*
WOOO
MY BODY VANISHED, BUT MY MIND HAS BEEN WANDERING THROUGH THE CRACKS OF TIME...
...TO ESCAPE FROM G.O.D.

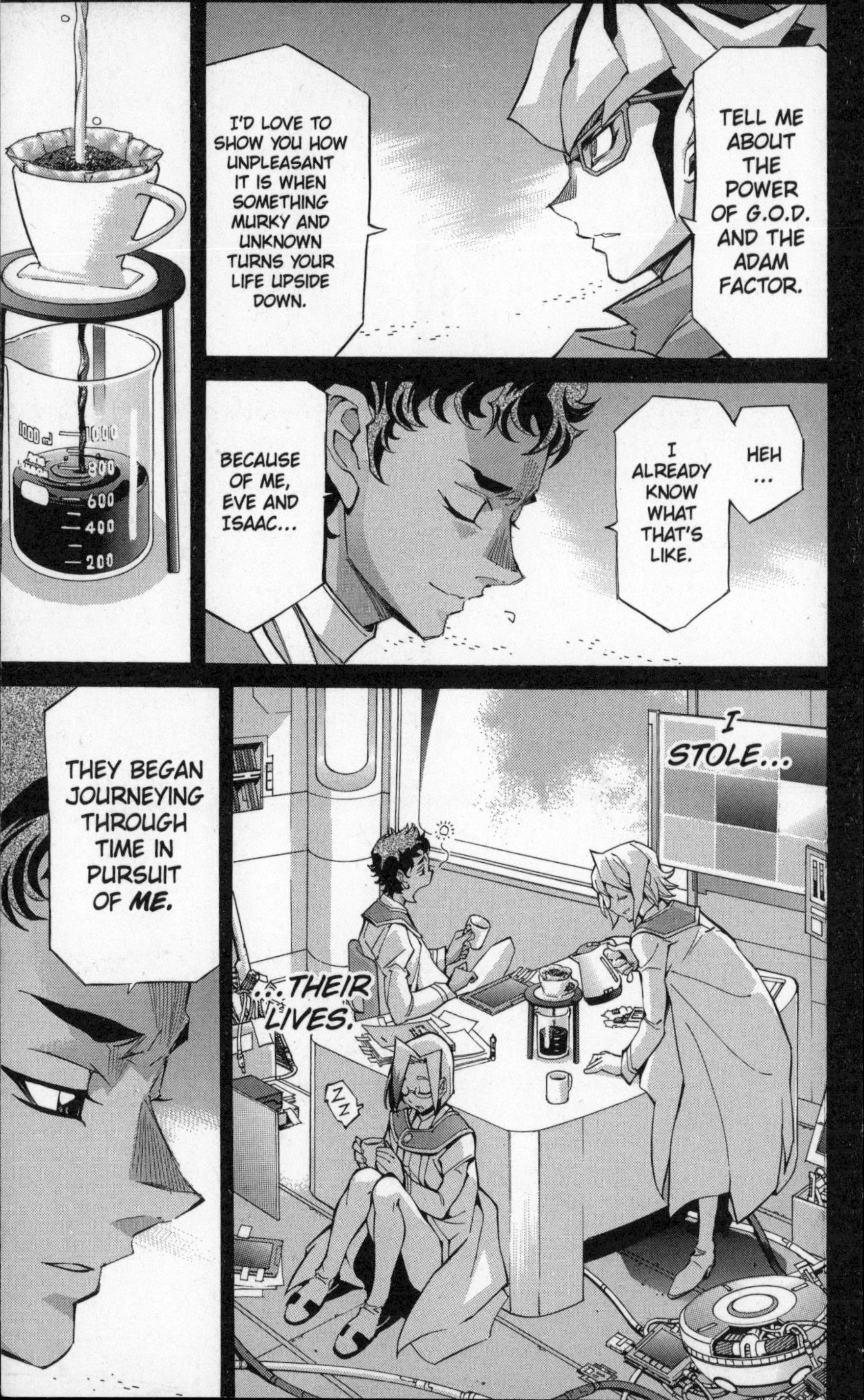
TELL ME ABOUT THE POWER OF G.O.D. AND THE ADAM FACTOR.
I'D LOVE TO SHOW YOU HOW UNPLEASANT IT IS WHEN SOMETHING MURKY AND UNKNOWN TURNS YOUR LIFE UPSIDE DOWN.
HEH...
I ALREADY KNOW WHAT THAT'S LIKE.
BECAUSE OF ME, EVE AND ISAAC...
I STOLE...
...THEIR LIVES.
ZZ
THEY BEGAN JOURNEYING THROUGH TIME IN PURSUIT OF *ME.*

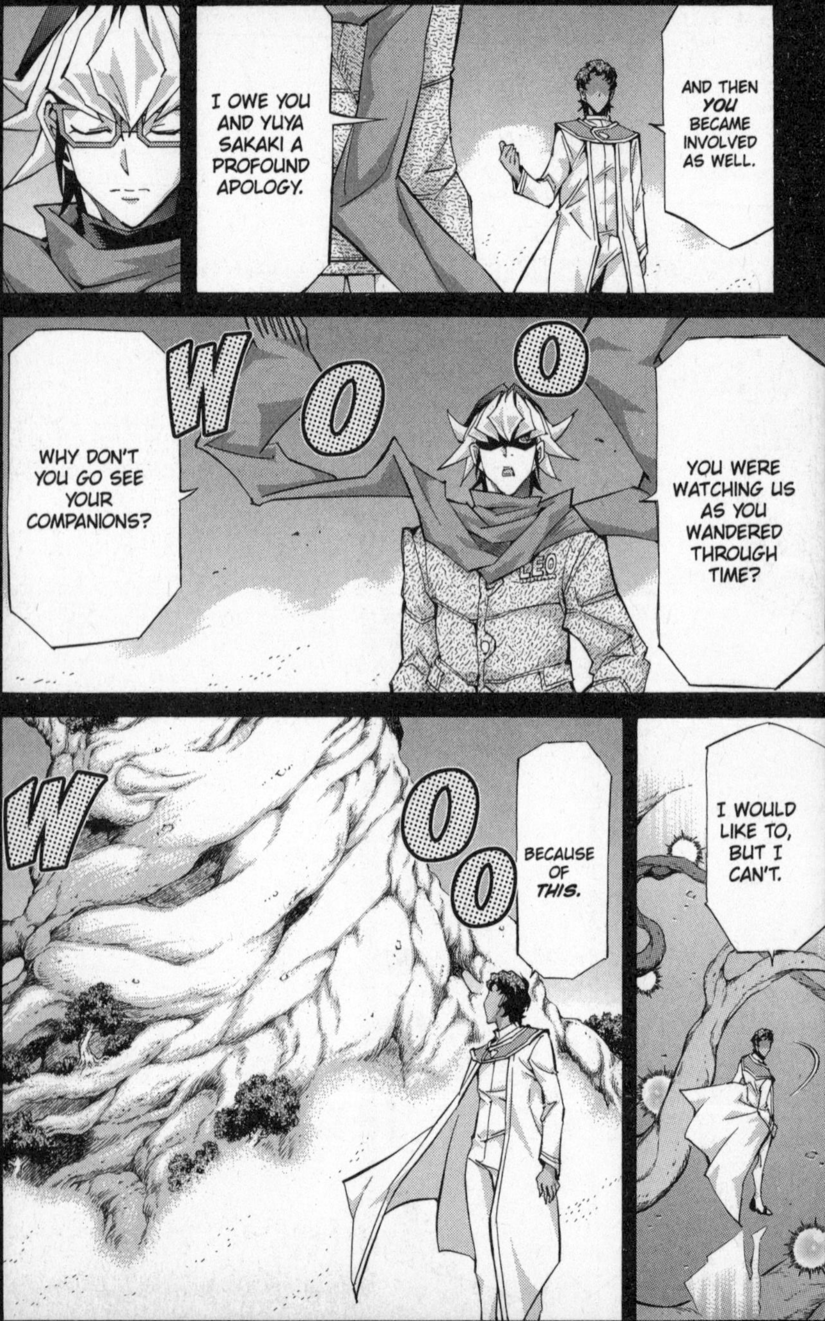
AND THEN *YOU* BECAME INVOLVED AS WELL.
I OWE YOU AND YUYA SAKAKI A PROFOUND APOLOGY.
YOU WERE WATCHING US AS YOU WANDERED THROUGH TIME?
WOOO
WHY DON'T YOU GO SEE YOUR COMPANIONS?
I WOULD LIKE TO, BUT I CAN'T.
BECAUSE OF *THIS.*
WOOO

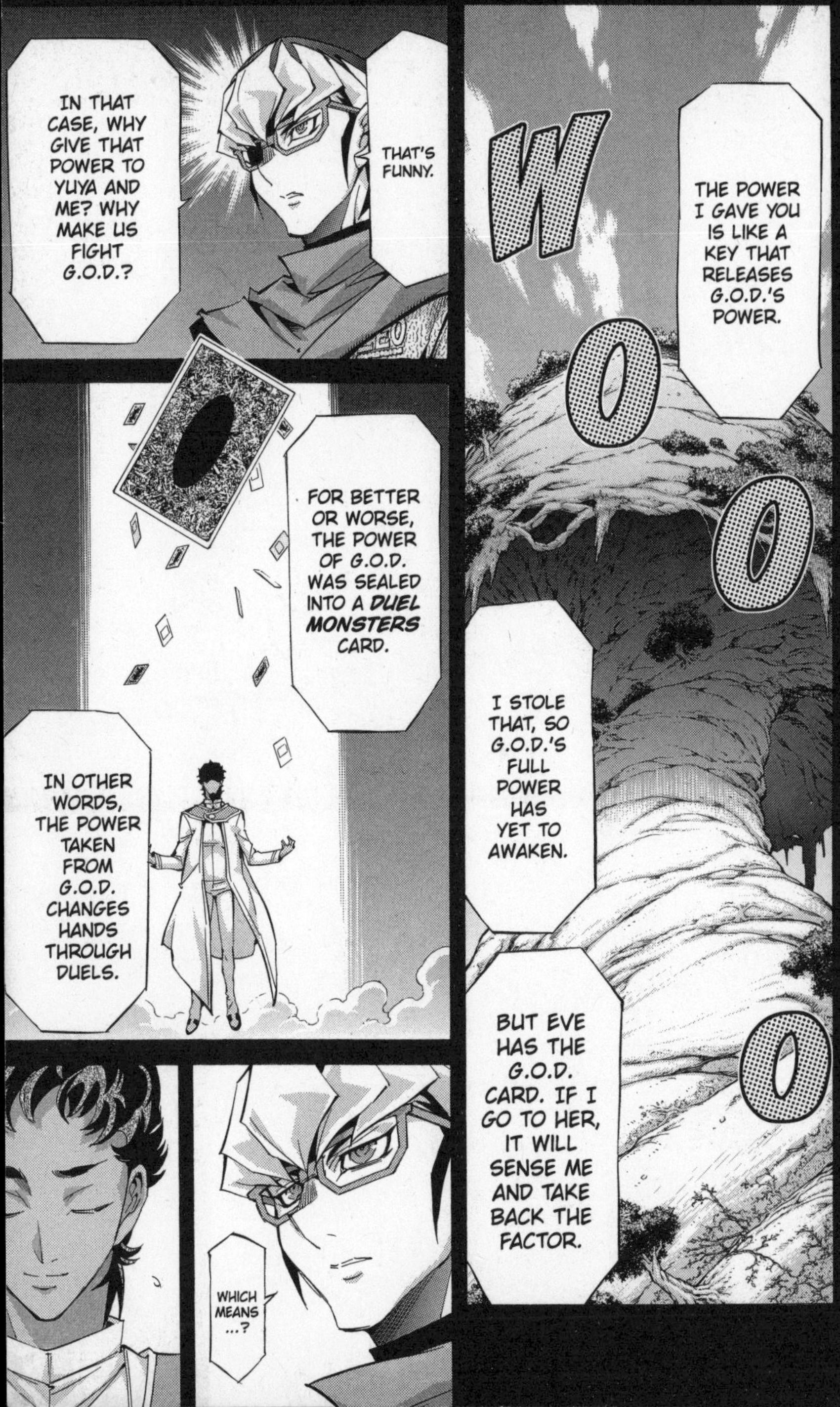
THE POWER I GAVE YOU IS LIKE A KEY THAT RELEASES G.O.D.'S POWER.
WOOOO
I STOLE THAT, SO G.O.D.'S FULL POWER HAS YET TO AWAKEN.
BUT EVE HAS THE G.O.D. CARD. IF I GO TO HER, IT WILL SENSE ME AND TAKE BACK THE FACTOR.
THAT'S FUNNY.
IN THAT CASE, WHY GIVE THAT POWER TO YUYA AND ME? WHY MAKE US FIGHT G.O.D.?
FOR BETTER OR WORSE, THE POWER OF G.O.D. WAS SEALED INTO A ***DUEL MONSTERS*** CARD.
IN OTHER WORDS, THE POWER TAKEN FROM G.O.D. CHANGES HANDS THROUGH DUELS.
WHICH MEANS ...?

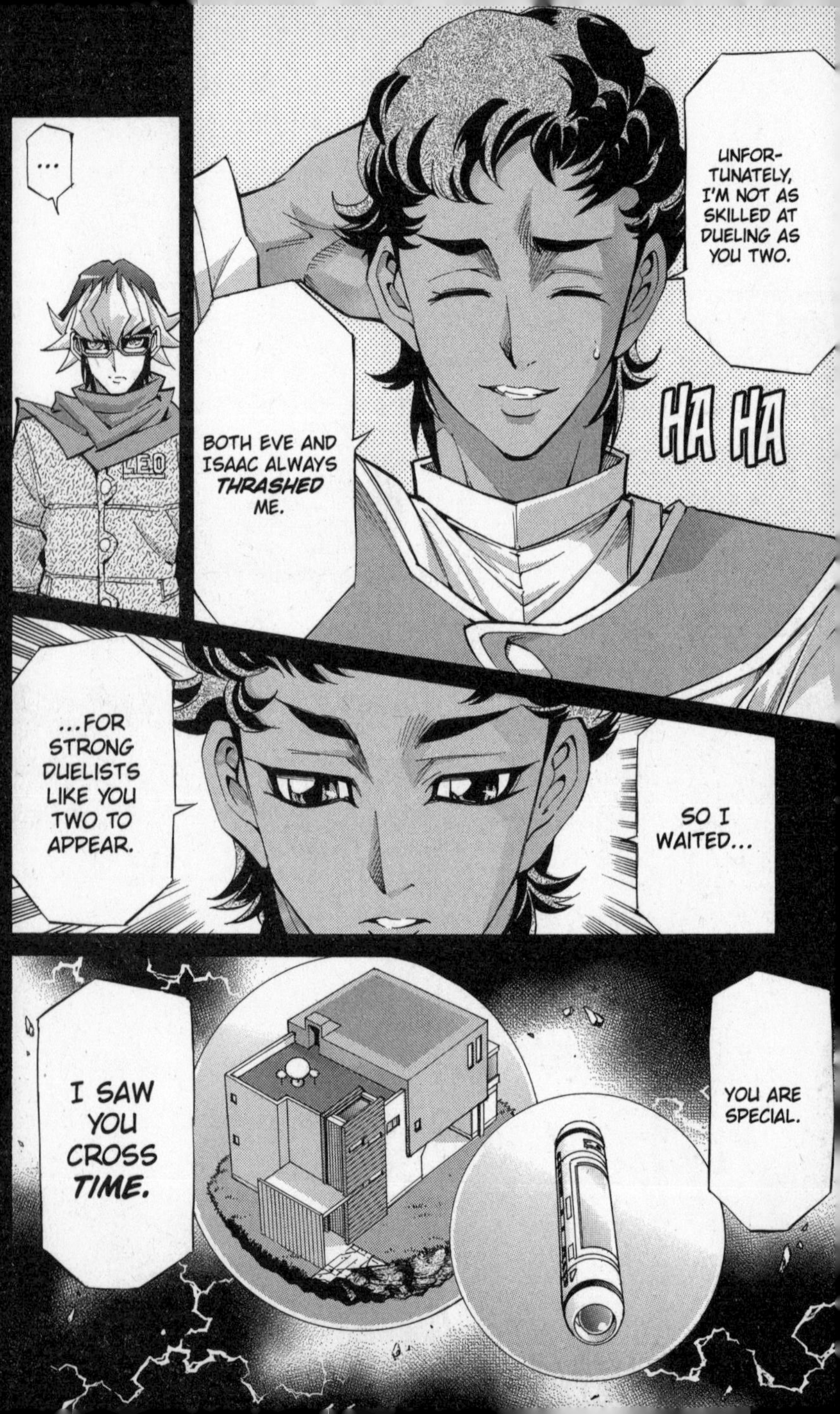
UNFORTUNATELY, I'M NOT AS SKILLED AT DUELING AS YOU TWO.
HA HA
BOTH EVE AND ISAAC ALWAYS *THRASHED* ME.
...
SO I WAITED...
...FOR STRONG DUELISTS LIKE YOU TWO TO APPEAR.
YOU ARE SPECIAL.
I SAW YOU CROSS *TIME.*

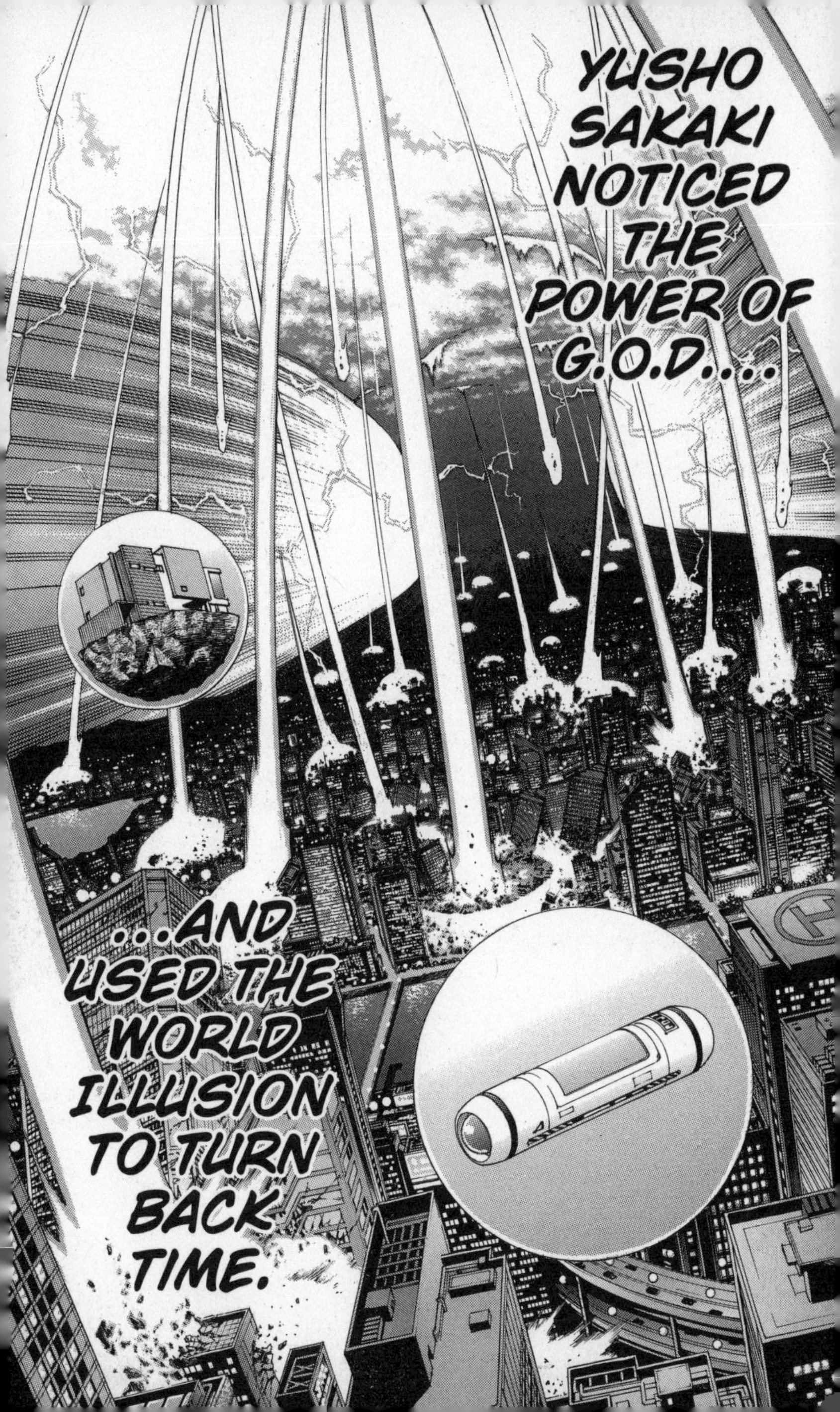
YUSHO SAKAKI NOTICED THE POWER OF G.O.D....
...AND USED THE WORLD ILLUSION TO TURN BACK TIME.

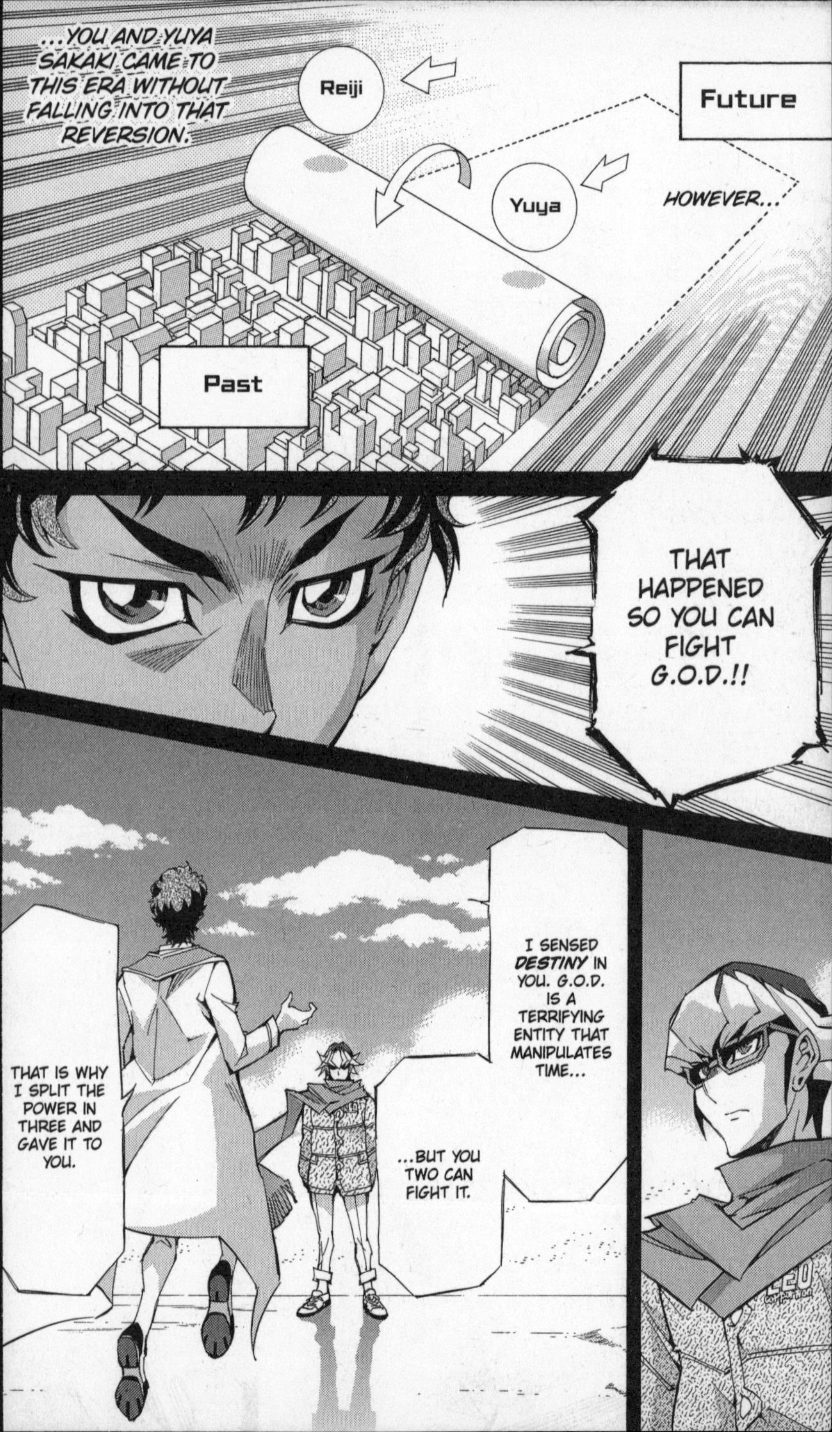

Future
Reiji
Yuya
HOWEVER...
...YOU AND YUYA SAKAKI CAME TO THIS ERA WITHOUT FALLING INTO THAT REVERSION.
Past
THAT HAPPENED SO YOU CAN FIGHT G.O.D.!!
I SENSED DESTINY IN YOU. G.O.D. IS A TERRIFYING ENTITY THAT MANIPULATES TIME...
...BUT YOU TWO CAN FIGHT IT.
THAT IS WHY I SPLIT THE POWER IN THREE AND GAVE IT TO YOU.

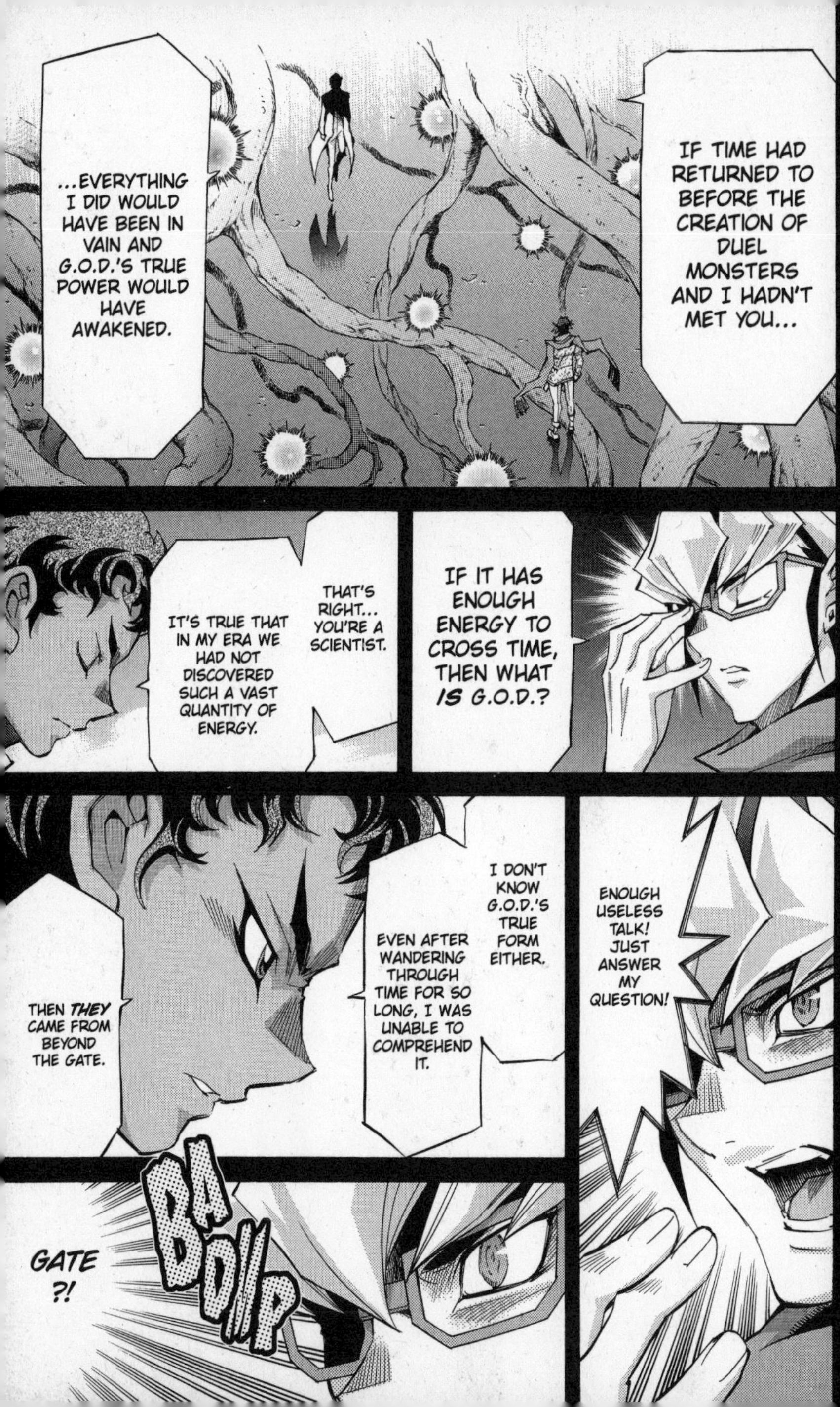
IF TIME HAD RETURNED TO BEFORE THE CREATION OF DUEL MONSTERS AND I HADN'T MET YOU...
...EVERYTHING I DID WOULD HAVE BEEN IN VAIN AND G.O.D.'S TRUE POWER WOULD HAVE AWAKENED.
IF IT HAS ENOUGH ENERGY TO CROSS TIME, THEN WHAT *IS* G.O.D.?
THAT'S RIGHT... YOU'RE A SCIENTIST.
IT'S TRUE THAT IN MY ERA WE HAD NOT DISCOVERED SUCH A VAST QUANTITY OF ENERGY.
ENOUGH USELESS TALK! JUST ANSWER MY QUESTION!
I DON'T KNOW G.O.D.'S TRUE FORM EITHER.
EVEN AFTER WANDERING THROUGH TIME FOR SO LONG, I WAS UNABLE TO COMPREHEND IT.
THEN *THEY* CAME FROM BEYOND THE GATE.
BADMP
GATE ?!

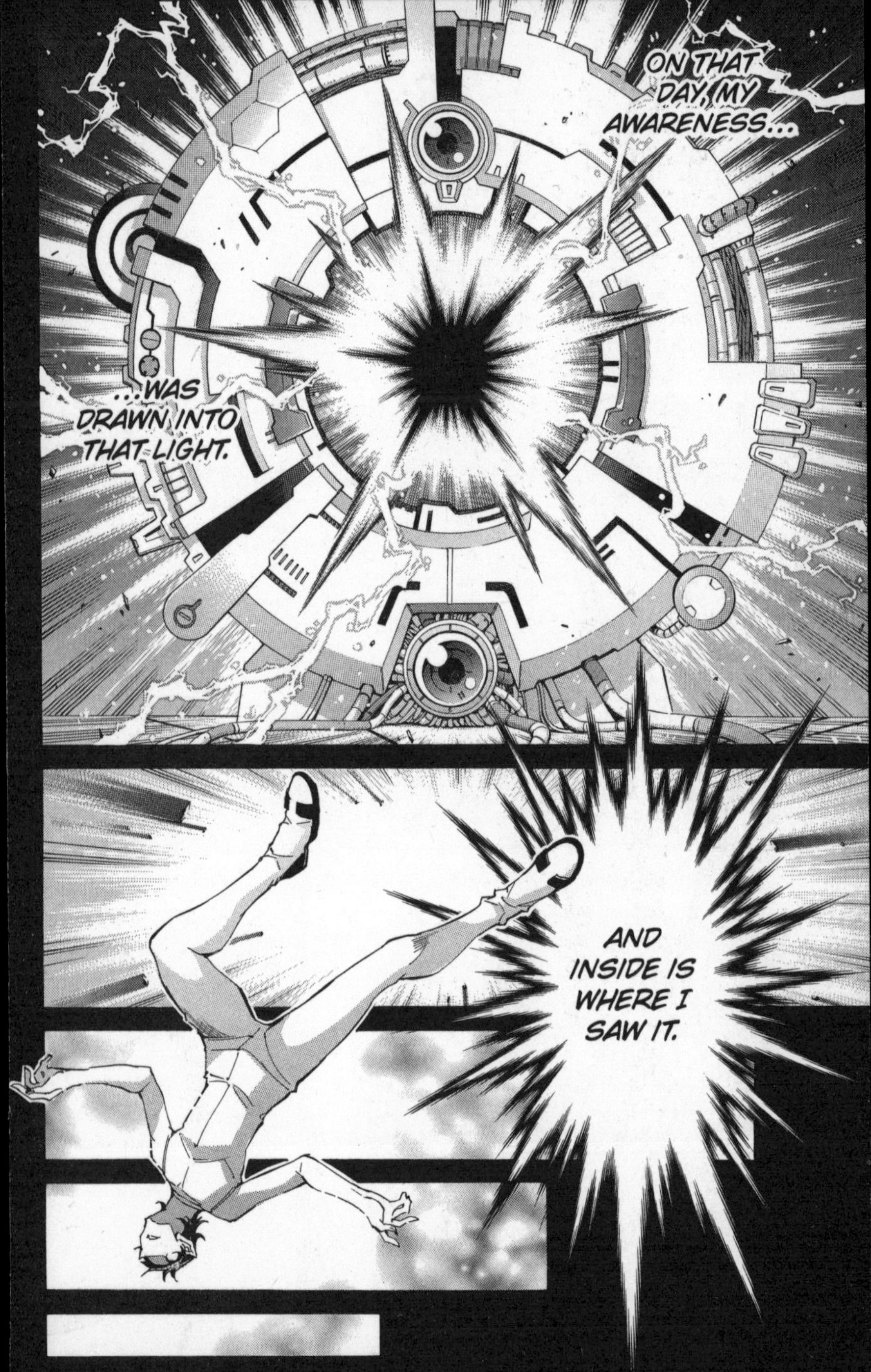
ON THAT DAY, MY AWARENESS...
...WAS DRAWN INTO THAT LIGHT.
AND INSIDE IS WHERE I SAW IT.

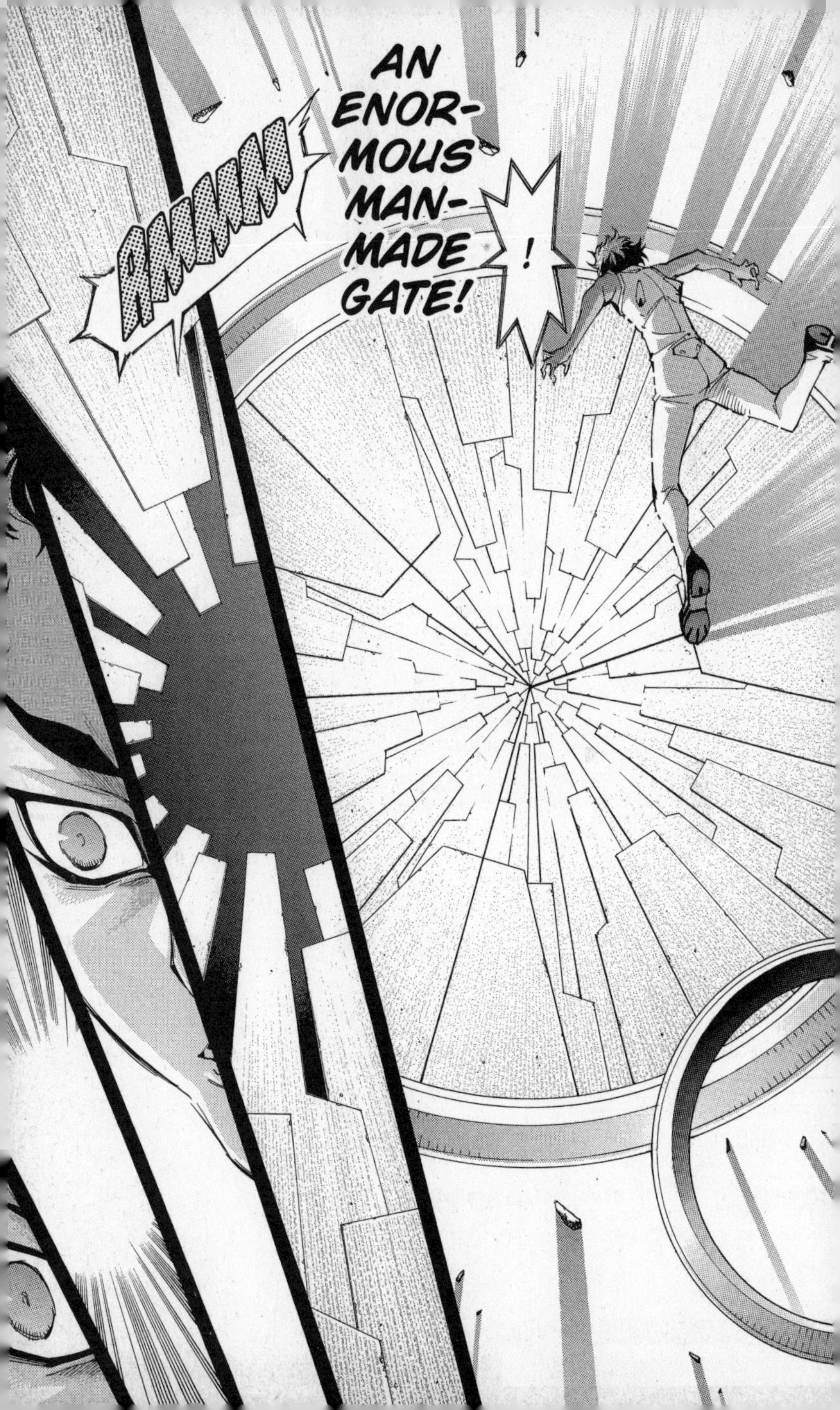
AN ENORMOUS MAN-MADE GATE!
!
RMMMM

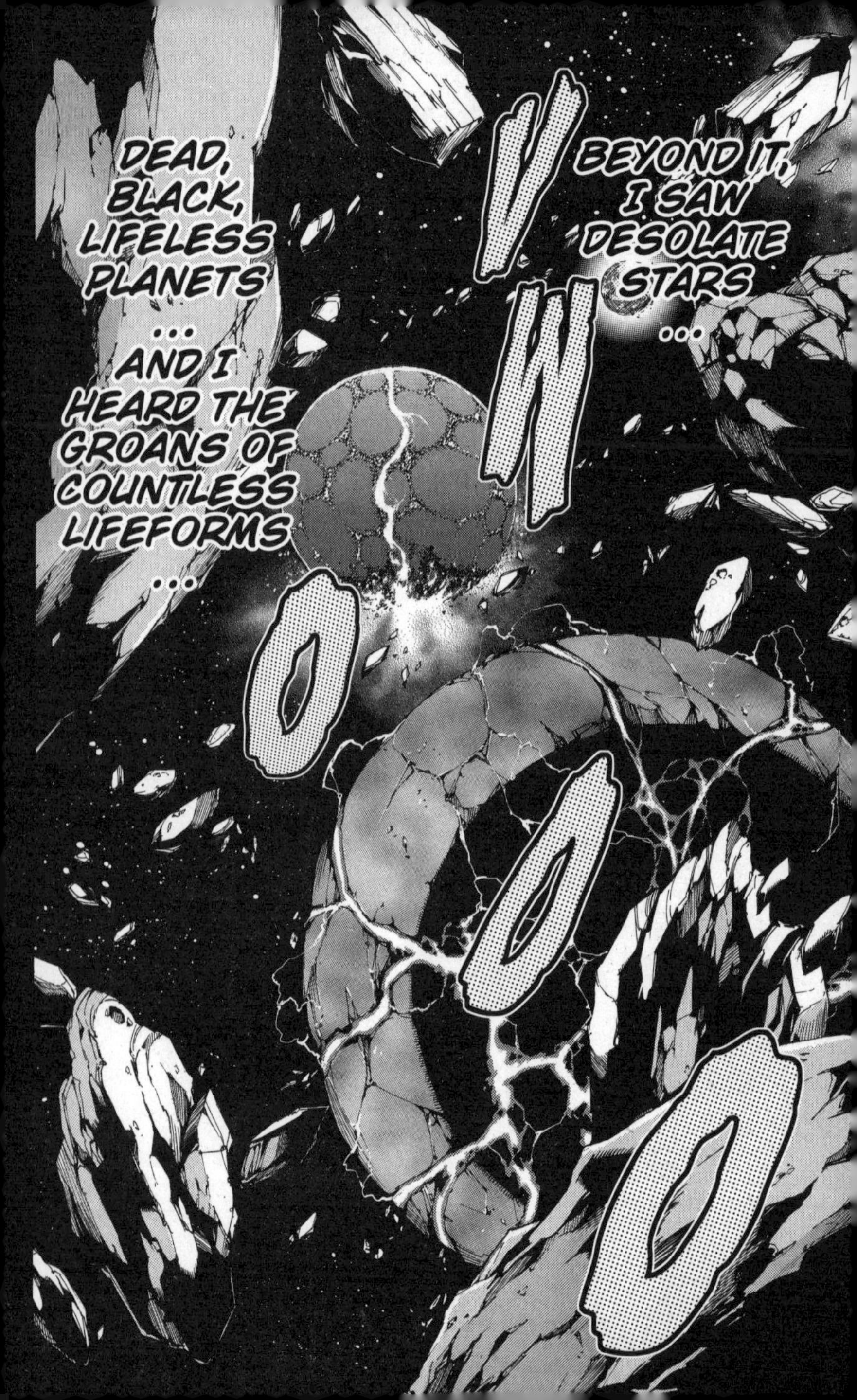
BEYOND IT, I SAW DESOLATE STARS...
VWOOO
DEAD, BLACK, LIFELESS PLANETS... AND I HEARD THE GROANS OF COUNTLESS LIFEFORMS...

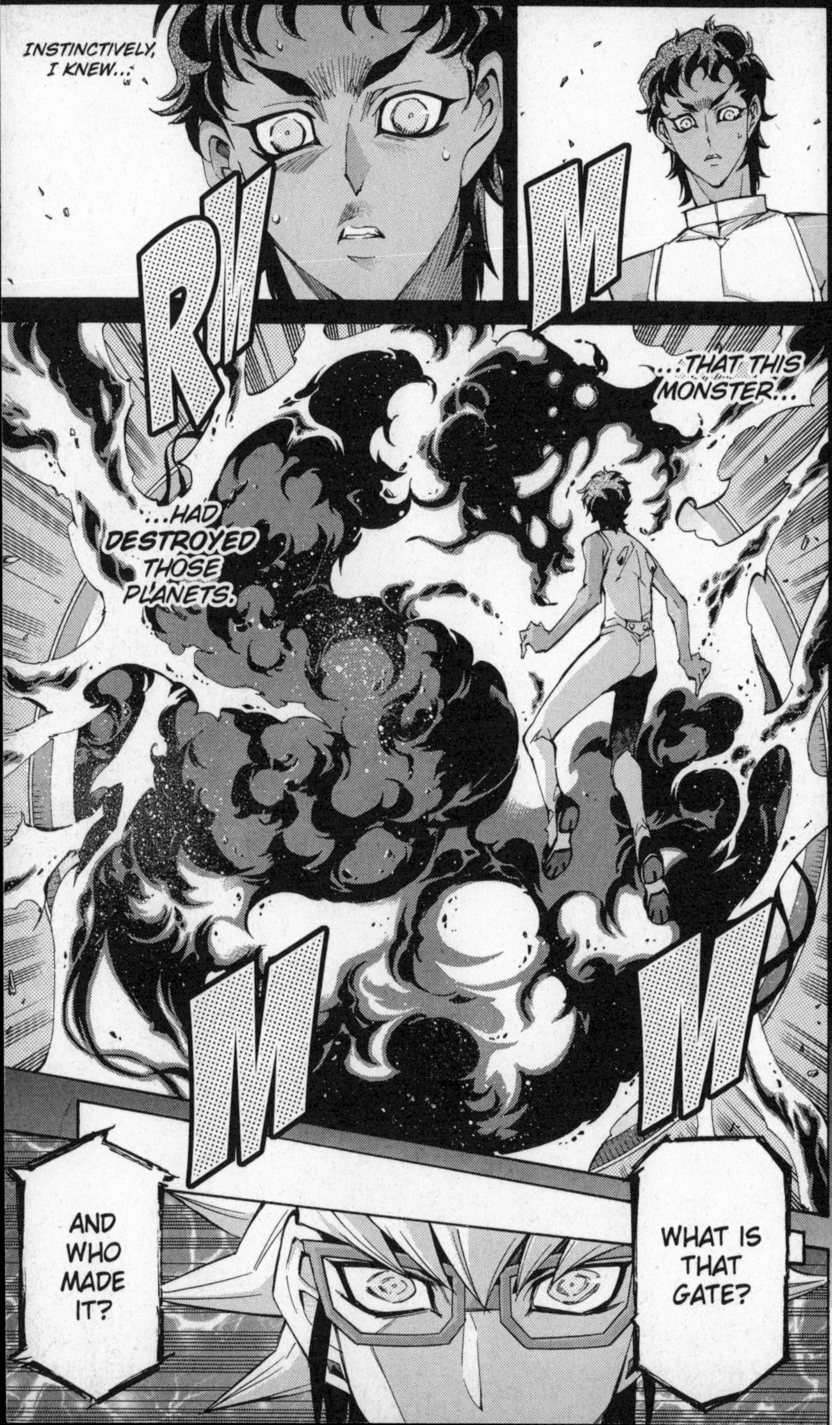
INSTINCTIVELY, I KNEW...
RMMM
...THAT THIS MONSTER...
...HAD DESTROYED THOSE PLANETS.
WHAT IS THAT GATE?
AND WHO MADE IT?

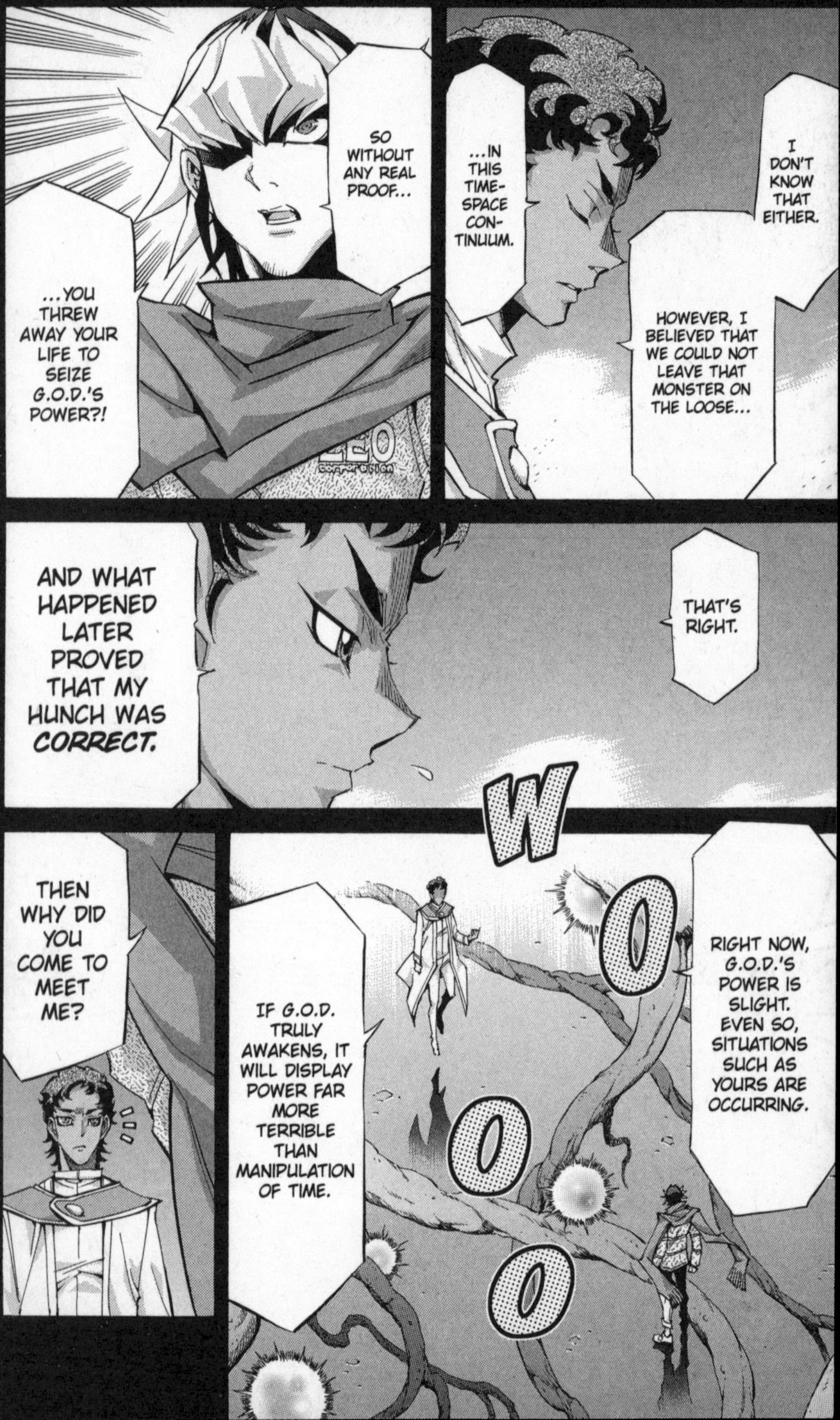

...IN THIS TIME-SPACE CONTINUUM.
I DON'T KNOW THAT EITHER.
HOWEVER, I BELIEVED THAT WE COULD NOT LEAVE THAT MONSTER ON THE LOOSE...
SO WITHOUT ANY REAL PROOF...
...YOU THREW AWAY YOUR LIFE TO SEIZE G.O.D.'S POWER?!
THAT'S RIGHT.
AND WHAT HAPPENED LATER PROVED THAT MY HUNCH WAS CORRECT.
WOOO
RIGHT NOW, G.O.D.'S POWER IS SLIGHT. EVEN SO, SITUATIONS SUCH AS YOURS ARE OCCURRING.
IF G.O.D. TRULY AWAKENS, IT WILL DISPLAY POWER FAR MORE TERRIBLE THAN MANIPULATION OF TIME.
THEN WHY DID YOU COME TO MEET ME?

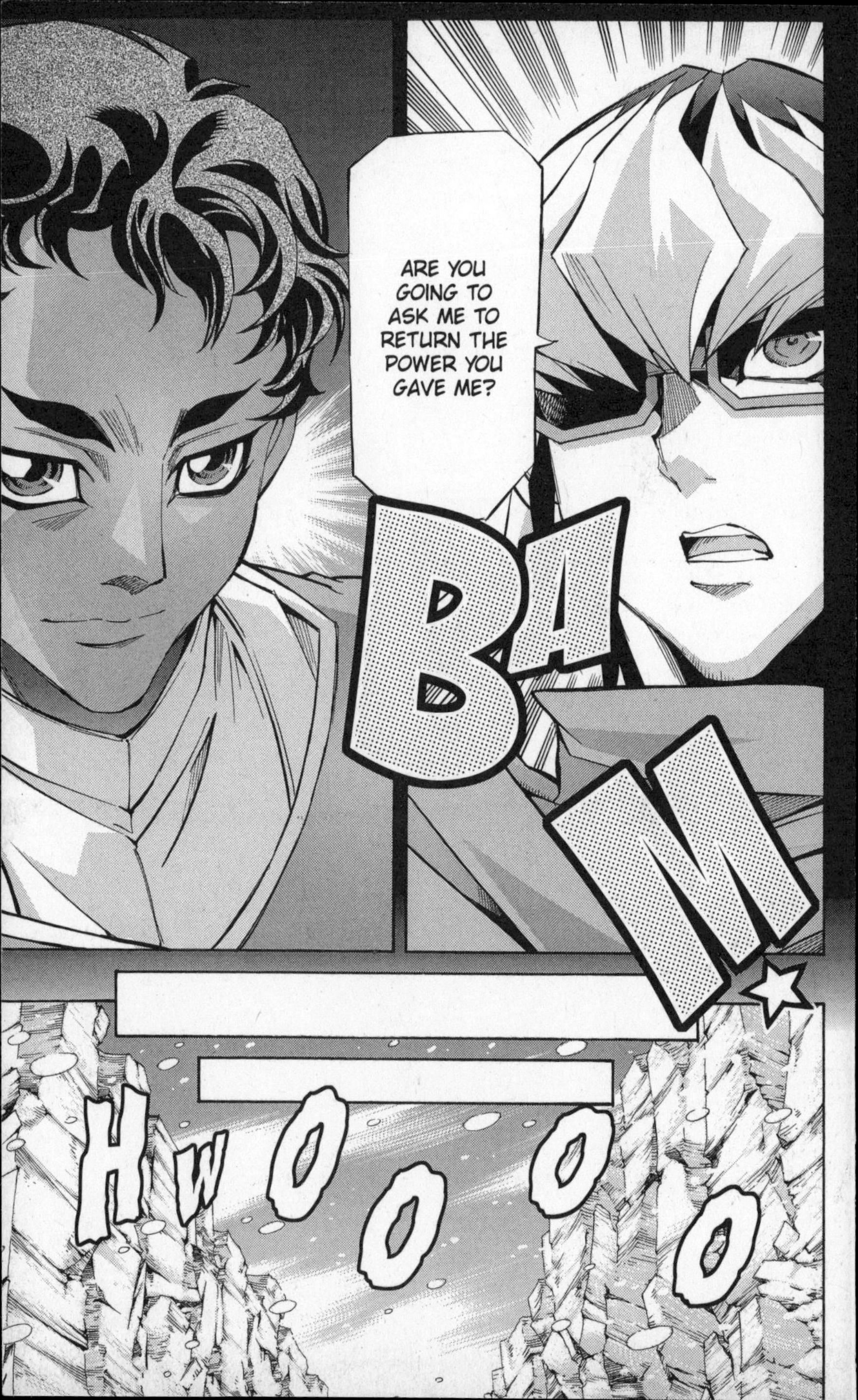
ARE YOU GOING TO ASK ME TO RETURN THE POWER YOU GAVE ME?
BAM
HWOOOO

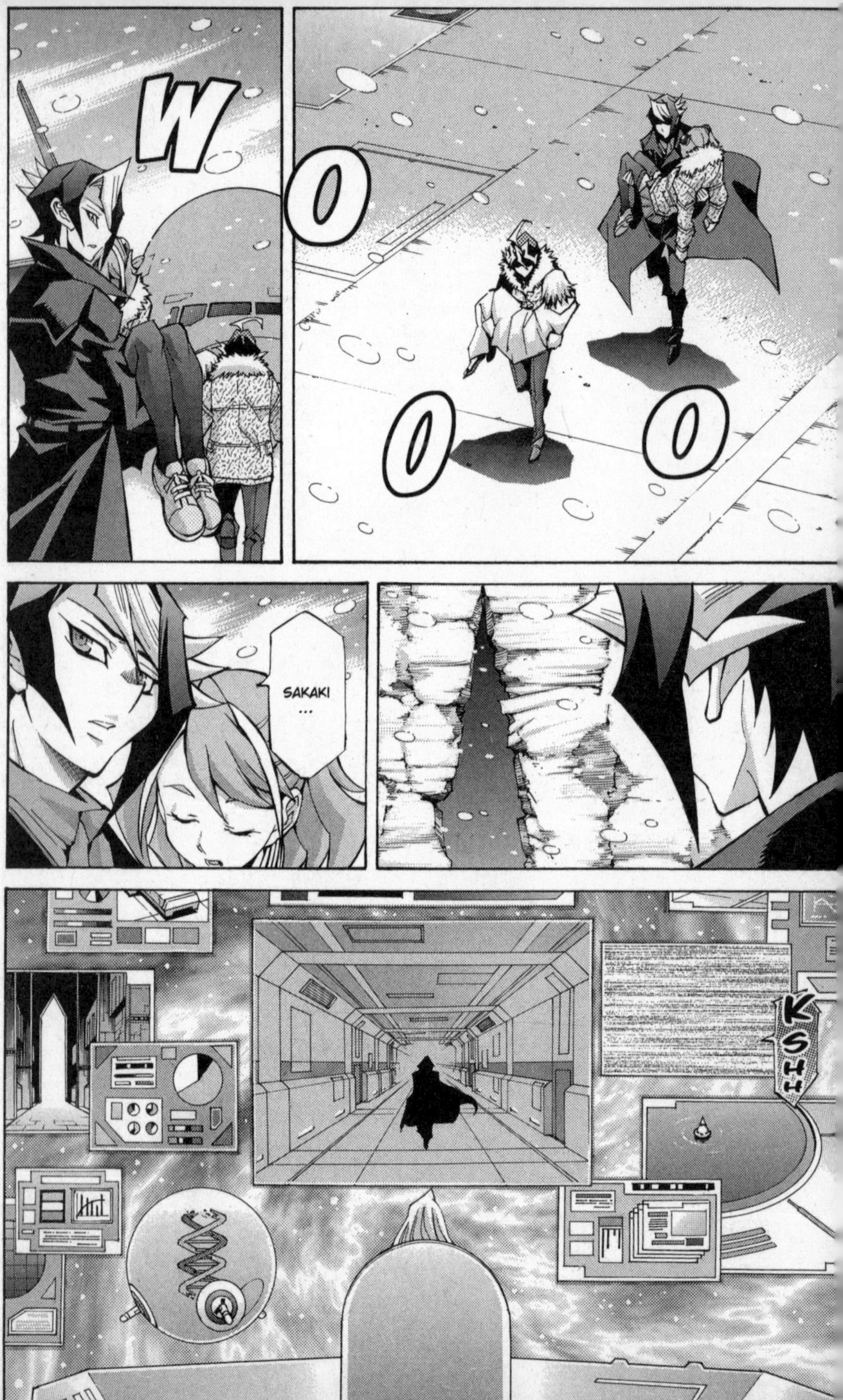
WOOO
SAKAKI ...
KSHH

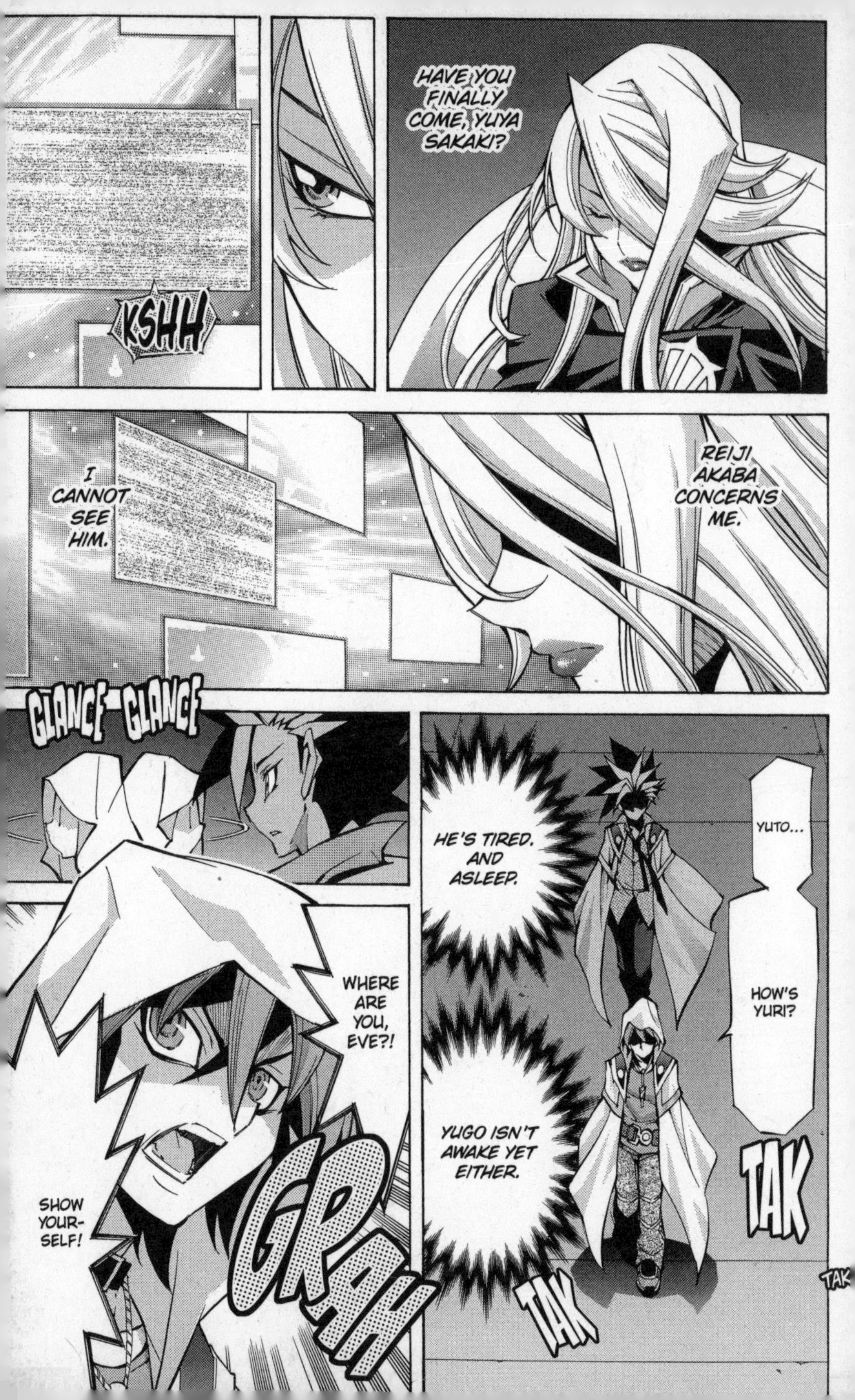
HAVE YOU FINALLY COME, YUYA SAKAKI?
KSHH
REIJI AKABA CONCERNS ME.
I CANNOT SEE HIM.
YUTO...
HOW'S YURI?
HE'S TIRED. AND ASLEEP.
YUGO ISN'T AWAKE YET EITHER.
TAK
TAK
TAK
GLANCE GLANCE
WHERE ARE YOU, EVE?!
SHOW YOUR-SELF!
GRAH

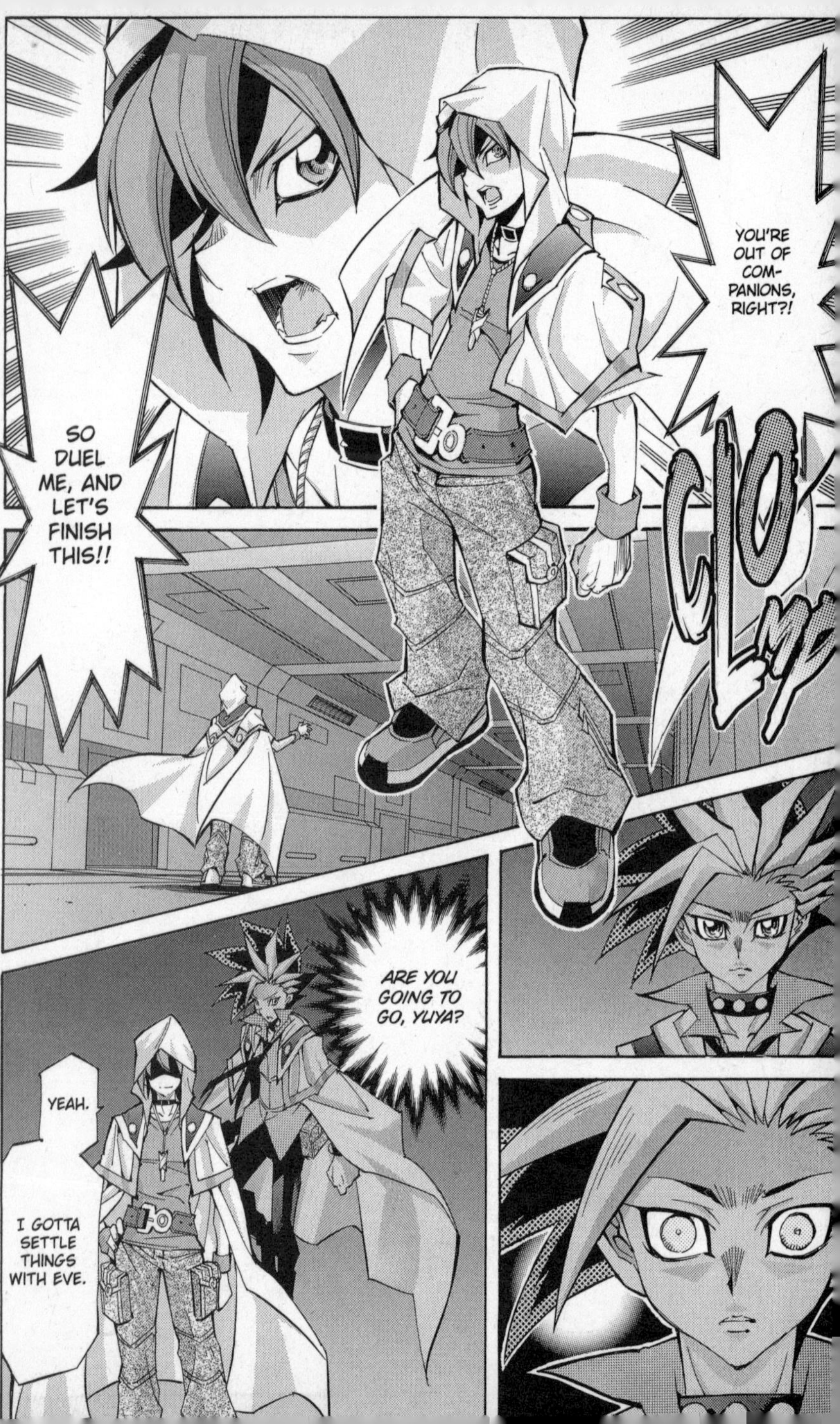
YOU'RE OUT OF COMPANIONS, RIGHT?!
SO DUEL ME, AND LET'S FINISH THIS!!
CLOMP
ARE YOU GOING TO GO, YUYA?
YEAH.
I GOTTA SETTLE THINGS WITH EVE.

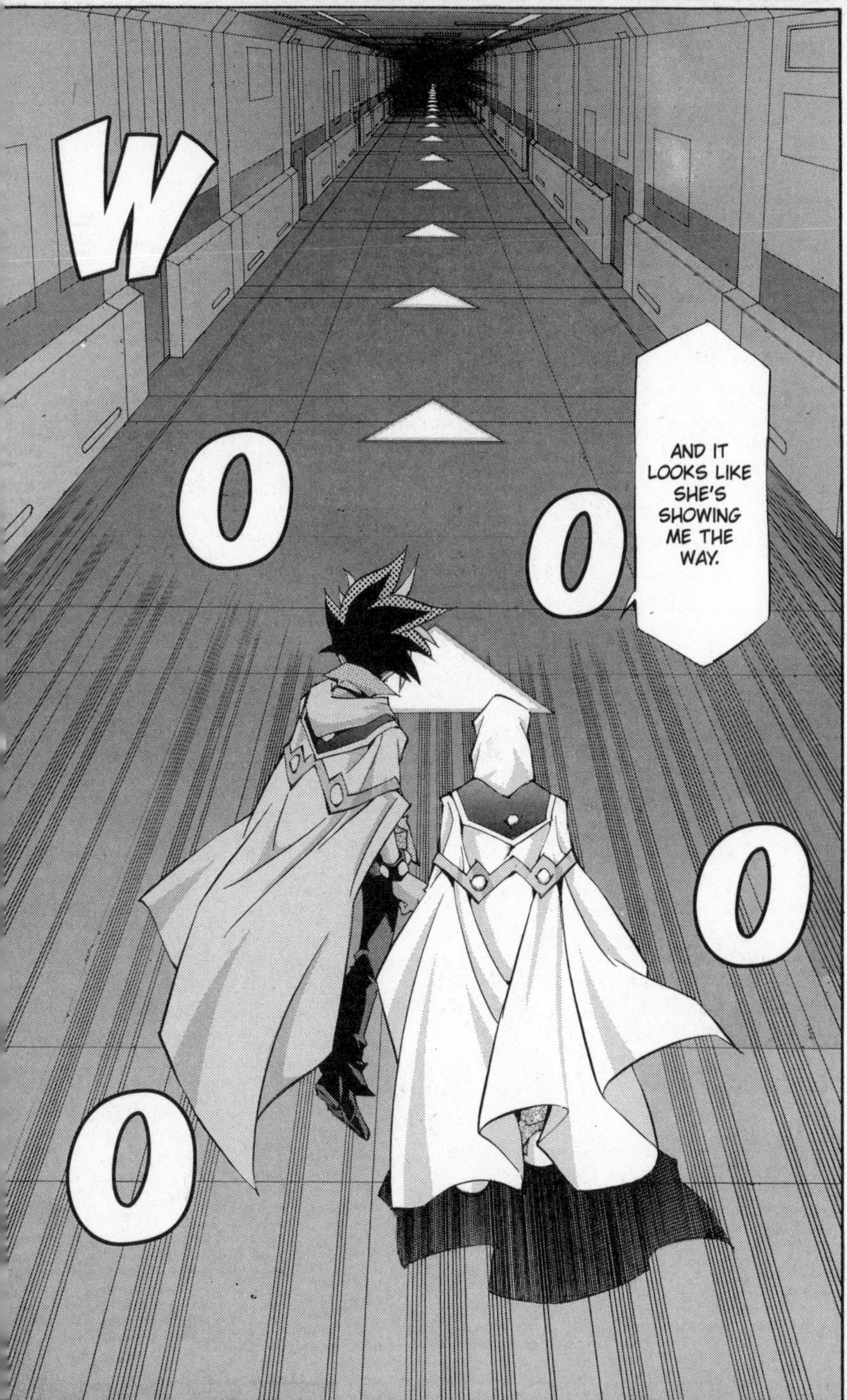
WOOOO
AND IT LOOKS LIKE SHE'S SHOWING ME THE WAY.

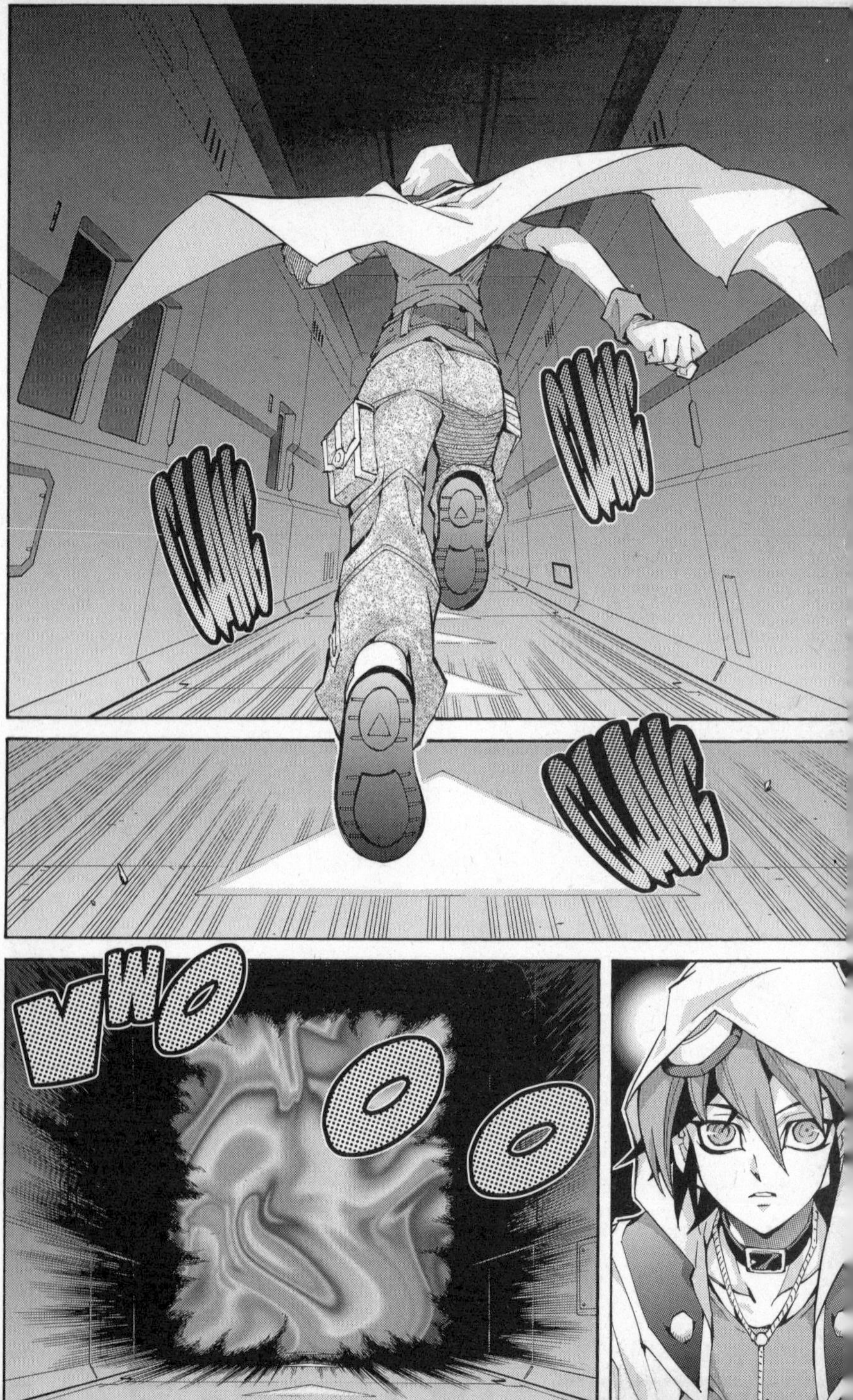
VWOOO

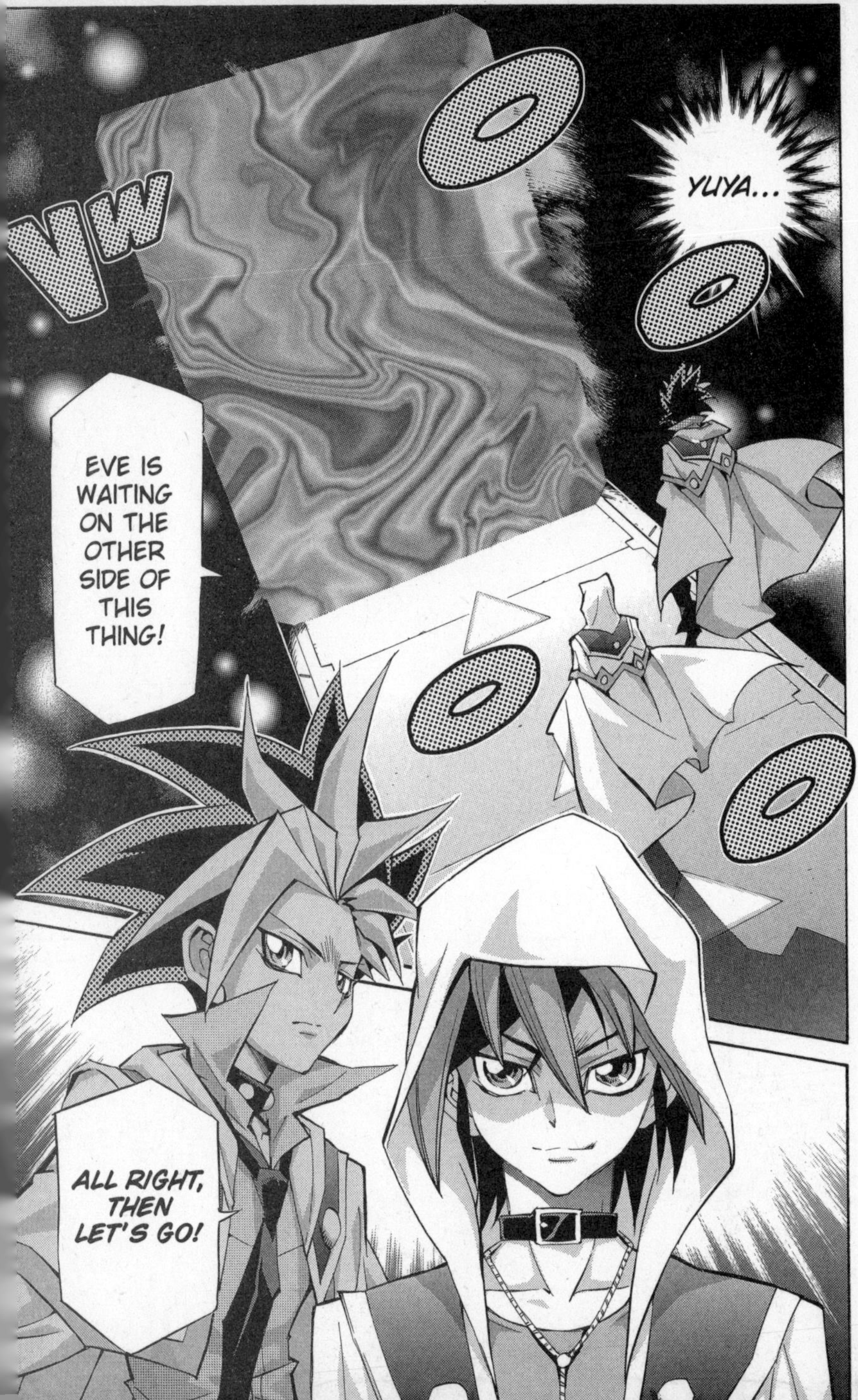
YUYA...
VWOOOO
EVE IS WAITING ON THE OTHER SIDE OF THIS THING!
ALL RIGHT, THEN LET'S GO!

PRESENTING MIYOSHI SENSEI'S EARLY DESIGNS!

ARC-V CHARACTER SKETCHES

D/D/D DESTINY KING ZERO LAPLACE

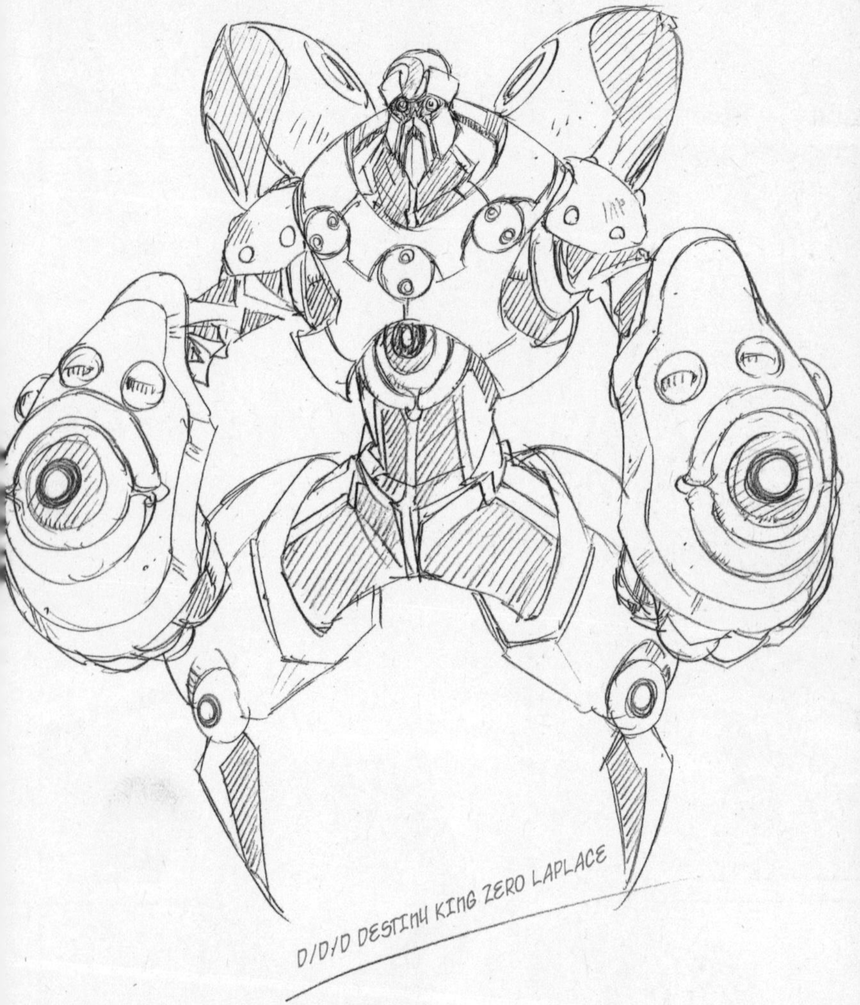
D/D/D DESTINY KING ZERO LAPLACE

D/D/D monsters are demons from another dimension that Reiji Akaba controls! This monster has a distinctive design featuring skull and goat elements emerging from a clock motif!

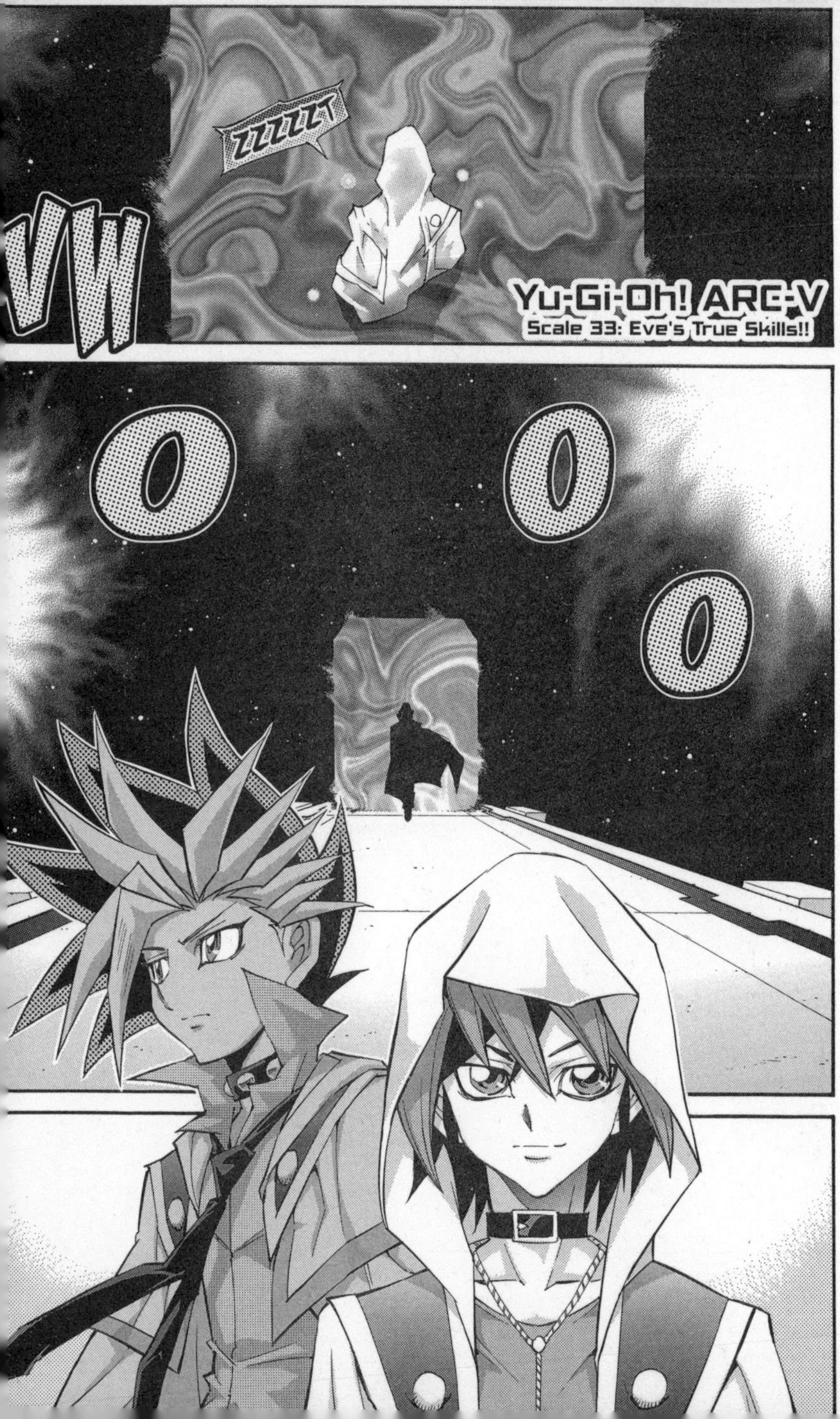
ZZZZZT
VW
Yu-Gi-Oh! ARC-V
Scale 33: Eve's True Skills!!
O
O
O

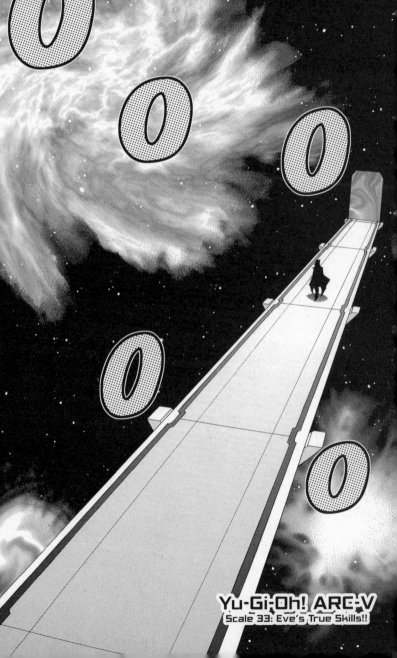

Yu-Gi-Oh! ARC-V
Scale 33: Eve's True Skills!!

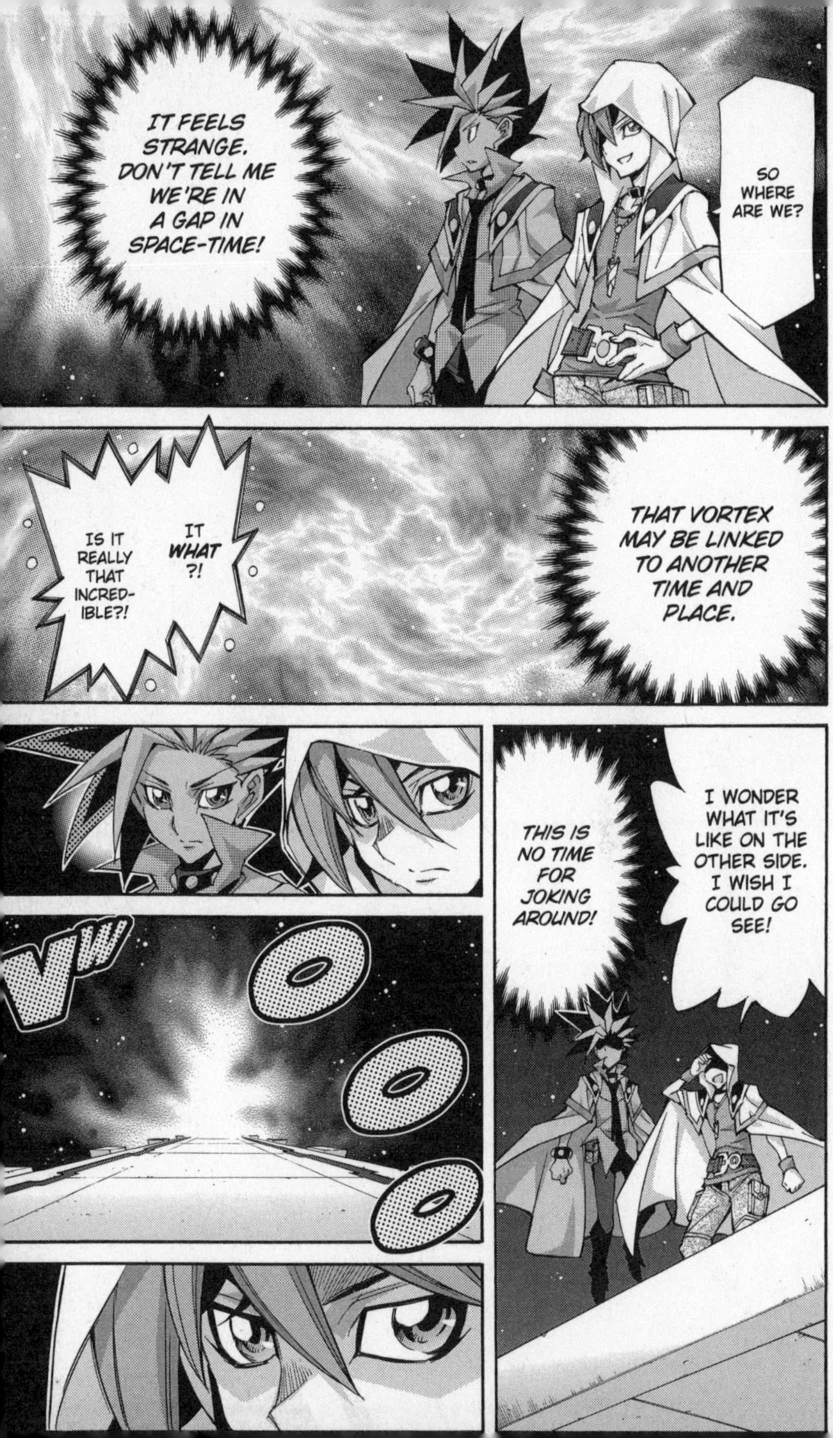
SO WHERE ARE WE?
IT FEELS STRANGE. DON'T TELL ME WE'RE IN A GAP IN SPACE-TIME!
THAT VORTEX MAY BE LINKED TO ANOTHER TIME AND PLACE.
IT *WHAT* ?!
IS IT REALLY THAT INCRED-IBLE?!
I WONDER WHAT IT'S LIKE ON THE OTHER SIDE. I WISH I COULD GO SEE!
THIS IS NO TIME FOR JOKING AROUND!

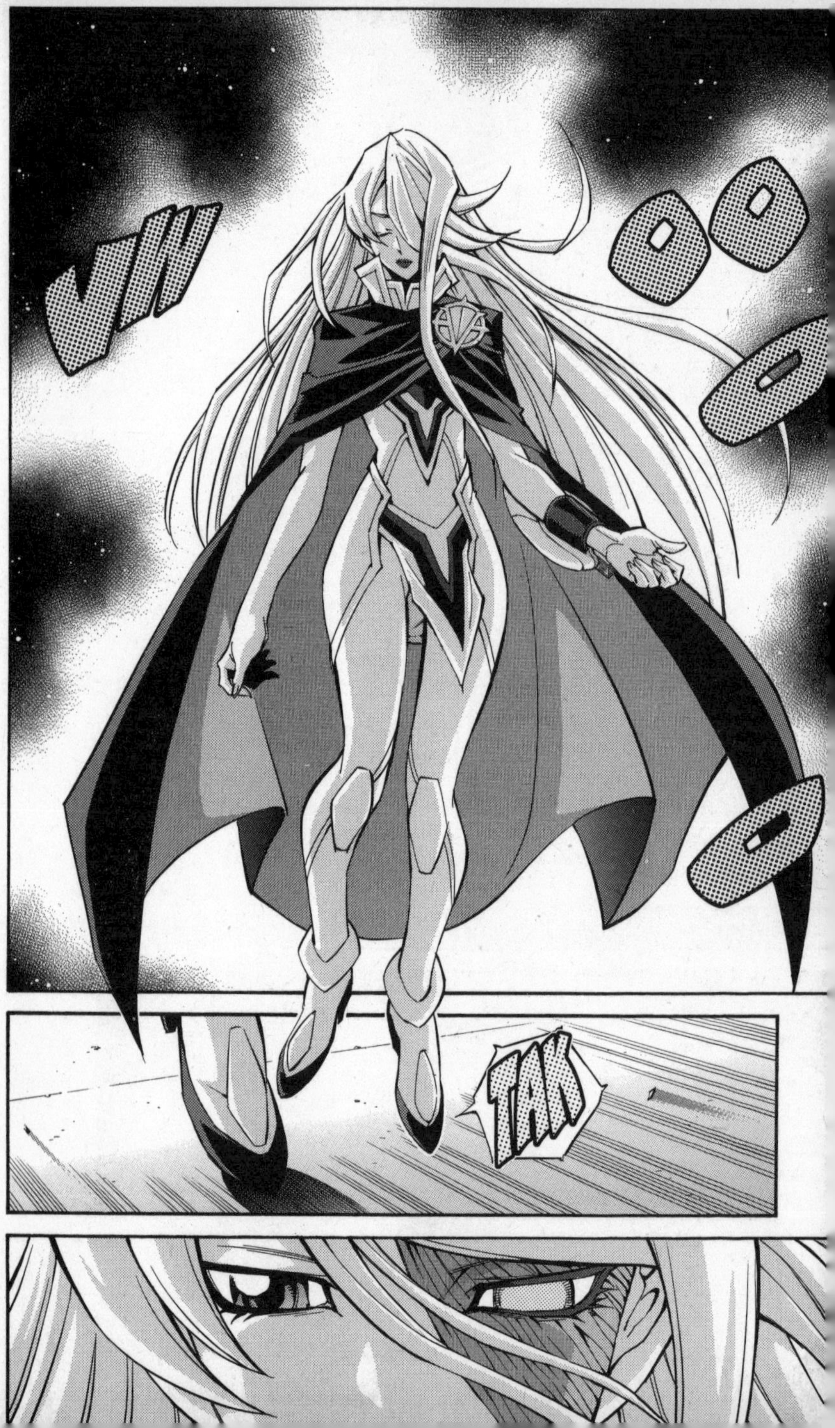
OOOO
TAK

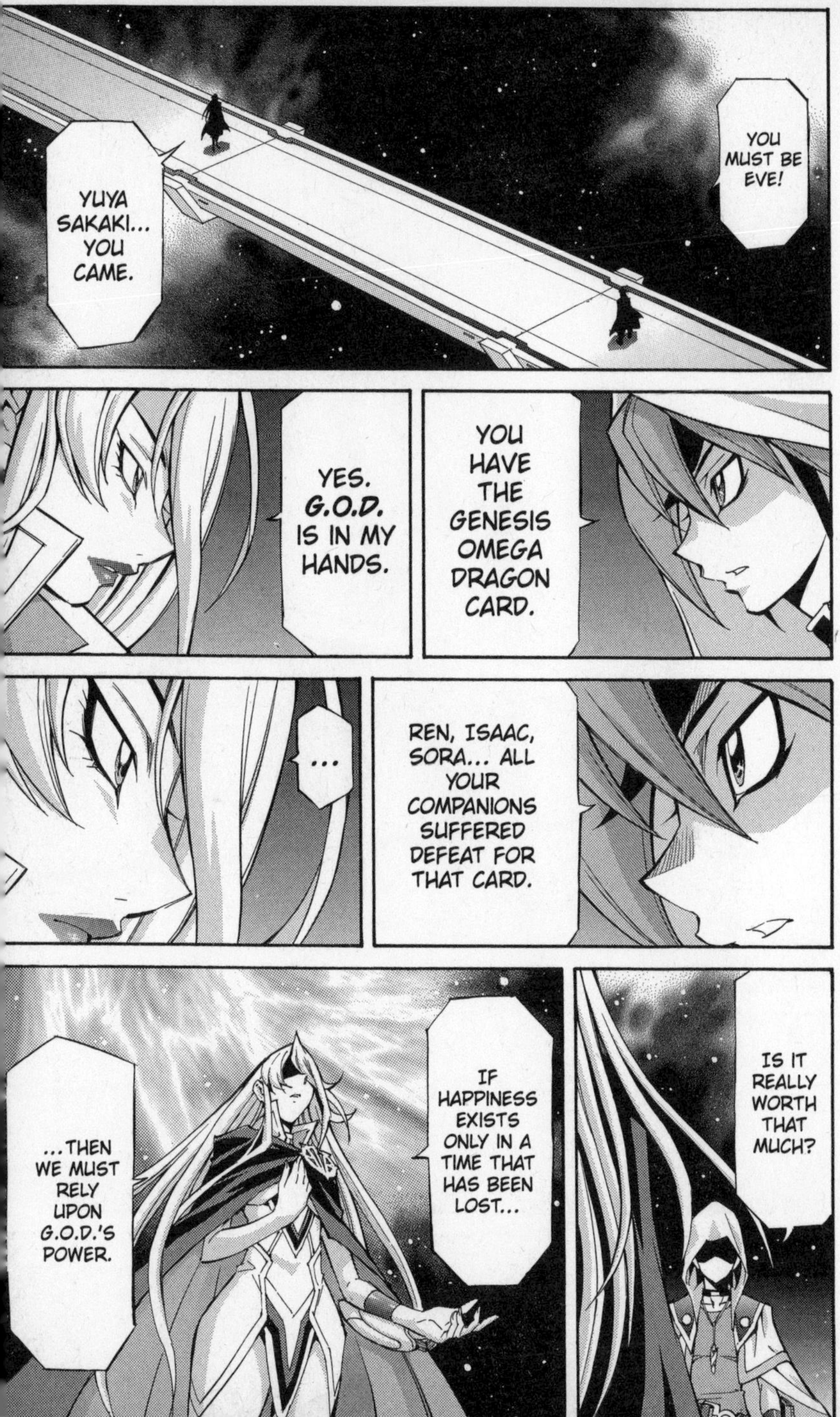
YOU MUST BE EVE!
YUYA SAKAKI... YOU CAME.
YOU HAVE THE GENESIS OMEGA DRAGON CARD.
YES. *G.O.D.* IS IN MY HANDS.
REN, ISAAC, SORA... ALL YOUR COMPANIONS SUFFERED DEFEAT FOR THAT CARD.
...
IS IT REALLY WORTH THAT MUCH?
IF HAPPINESS EXISTS ONLY IN A TIME THAT HAS BEEN LOST...
...THEN WE MUST RELY UPON G.O.D.'S POWER.

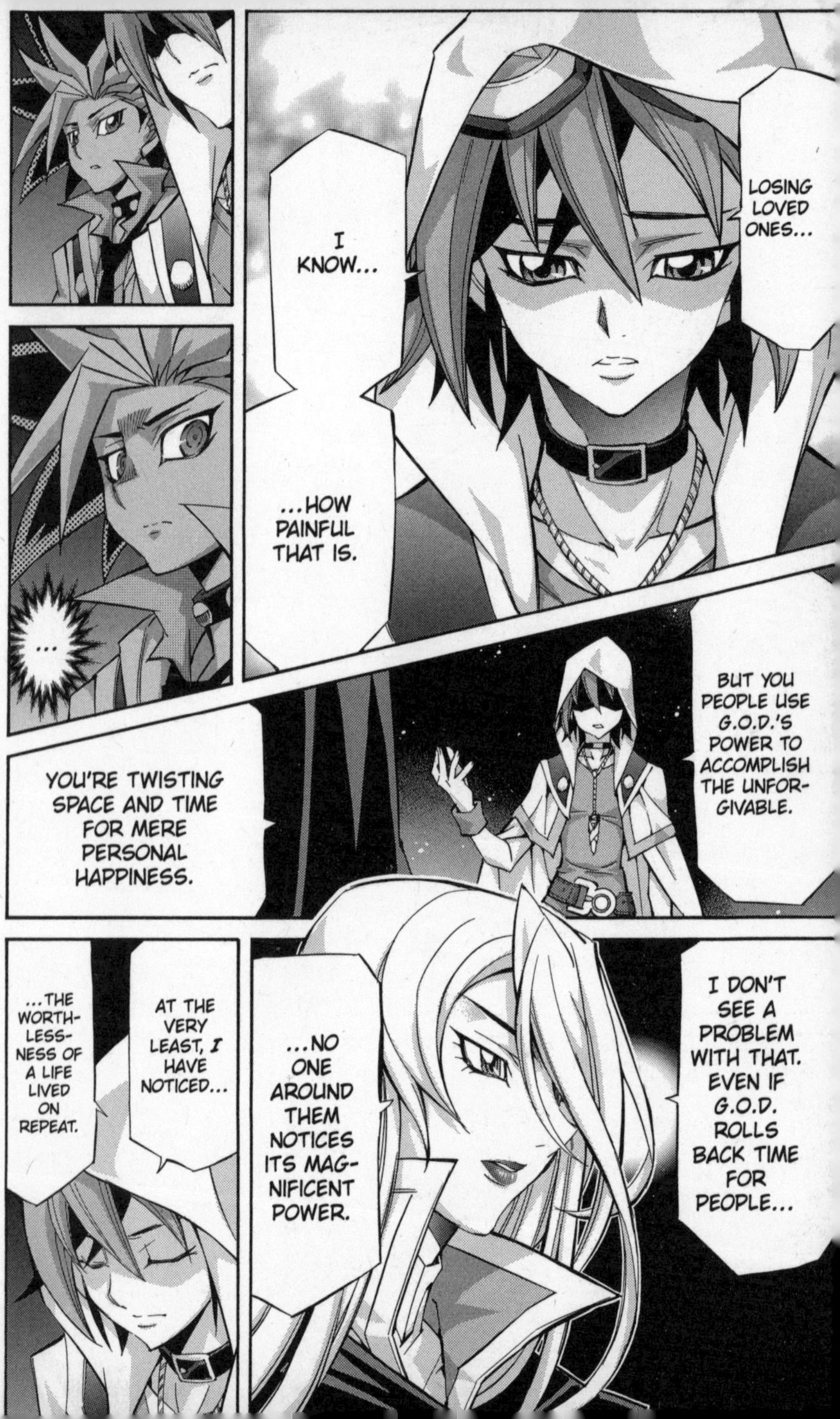
LOSING LOVED ONES...
I KNOW...
...HOW PAINFUL THAT IS.
...
BUT YOU PEOPLE USE G.O.D.'S POWER TO ACCOMPLISH THE UNFORGIVABLE.
YOU'RE TWISTING SPACE AND TIME FOR MERE PERSONAL HAPPINESS.
I DON'T SEE A PROBLEM WITH THAT. EVEN IF G.O.D. ROLLS BACK TIME FOR PEOPLE...
...NO ONE AROUND THEM NOTICES ITS MAGNIFICENT POWER.
AT THE VERY LEAST, *I* HAVE NOTICED...
...THE WORTHLESSNESS OF A LIFE LIVED ON REPEAT.

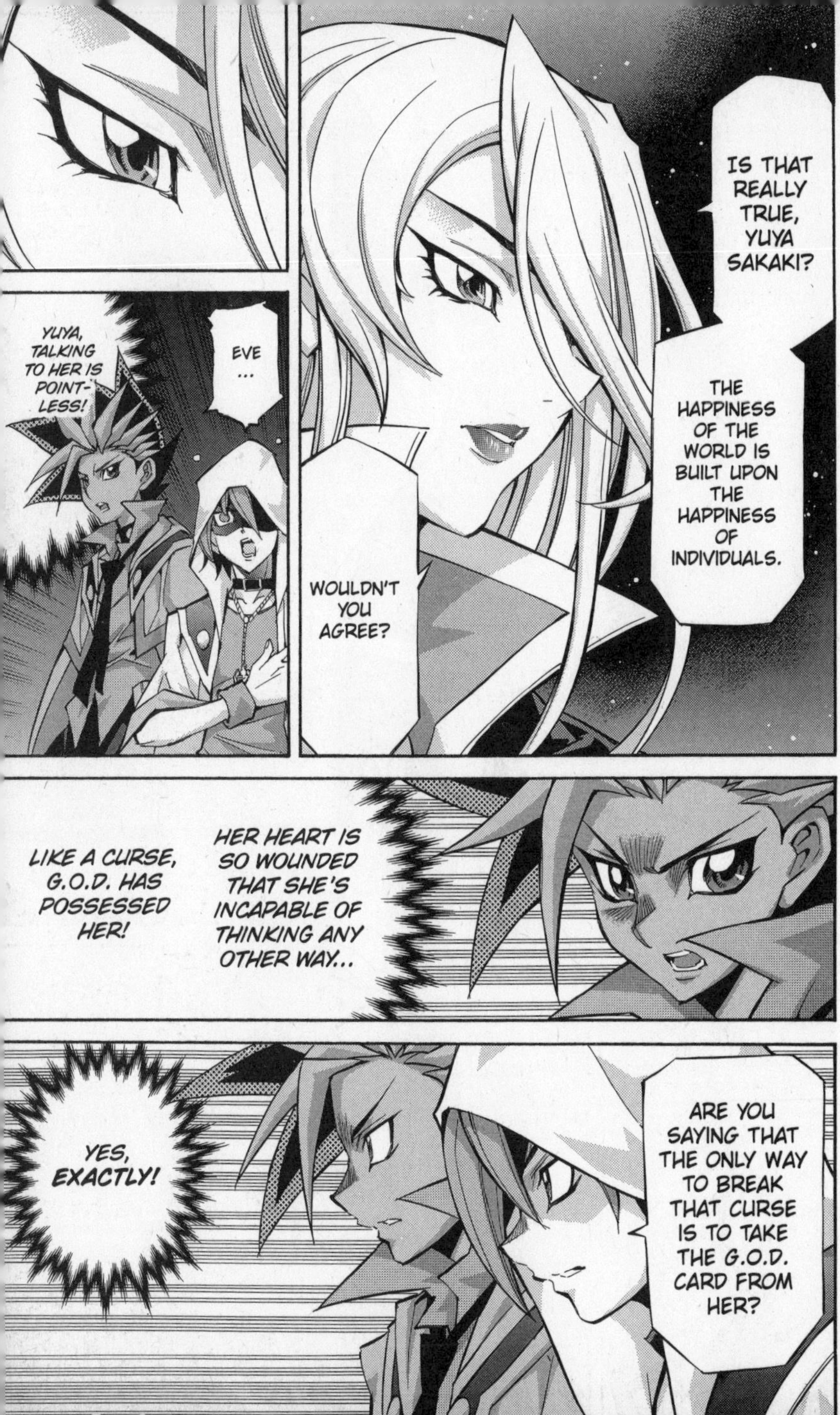
IS THAT REALLY TRUE, YUYA SAKAKI?
THE HAPPINESS OF THE WORLD IS BUILT UPON THE HAPPINESS OF INDIVIDUALS.
WOULDN'T YOU AGREE?
EVE ...
YUYA, TALKING TO HER IS POINT-LESS!
HER HEART IS SO WOUNDED THAT SHE'S INCAPABLE OF THINKING ANY OTHER WAY...
LIKE A CURSE, G.O.D. HAS POSSESSED HER!
ARE YOU SAYING THAT THE ONLY WAY TO BREAK THAT CURSE IS TO TAKE THE G.O.D. CARD FROM HER?
YES, EXACTLY!

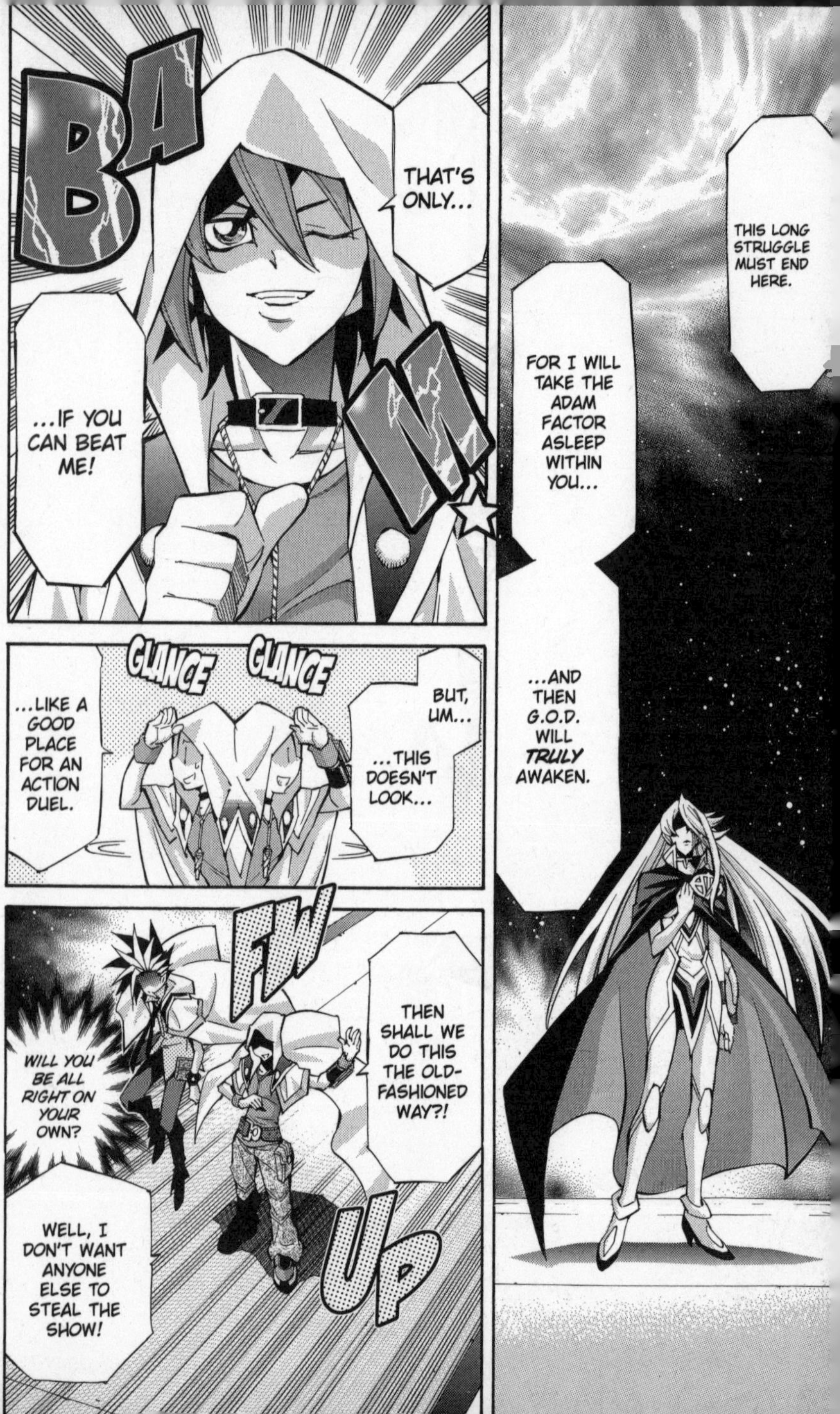
THIS LONG STRUGGLE MUST END HERE.
FOR I WILL TAKE THE ADAM FACTOR ASLEEP WITHIN YOU...
...AND THEN G.O.D. WILL *TRULY* AWAKEN.
BA
THAT'S ONLY...
M
...IF YOU CAN BEAT ME!
GLANCE
GLANCE
BUT, UM...
...THIS DOESN'T LOOK...
...LIKE A GOOD PLACE FOR AN ACTION DUEL.
FW
THEN SHALL WE DO THIS THE OLD-FASHIONED WAY?!
UP
WILL YOU BE ALL RIGHT ON YOUR OWN?
WELL, I DON'T WANT ANYONE ELSE TO STEAL THE SHOW!

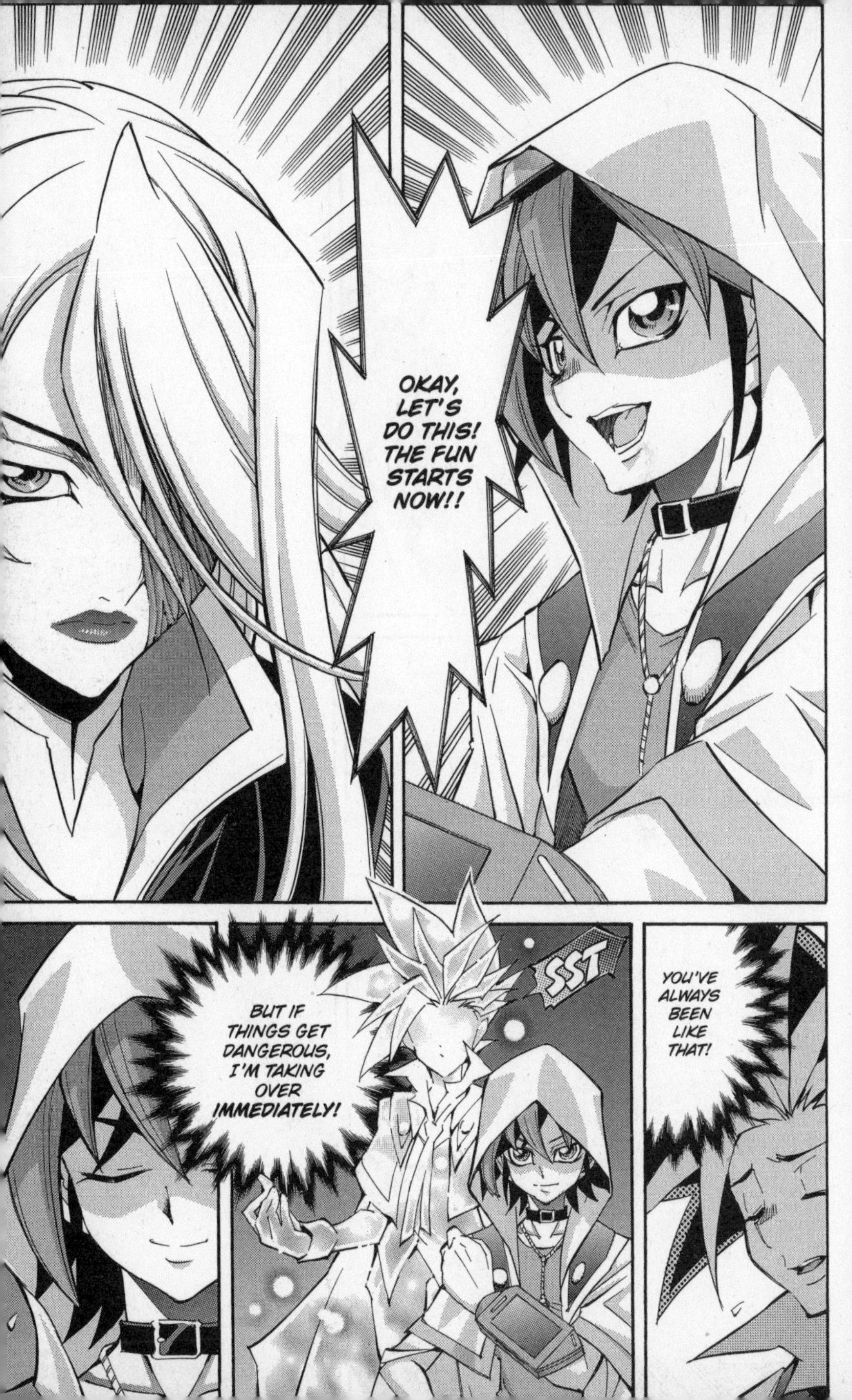
OKAY, LET'S DO THIS! THE FUN STARTS NOW!!
YOU'VE ALWAYS BEEN LIKE THAT!
SST
BUT IF THINGS GET DANGEROUS, I'M TAKING OVER IMMEDIATELY!

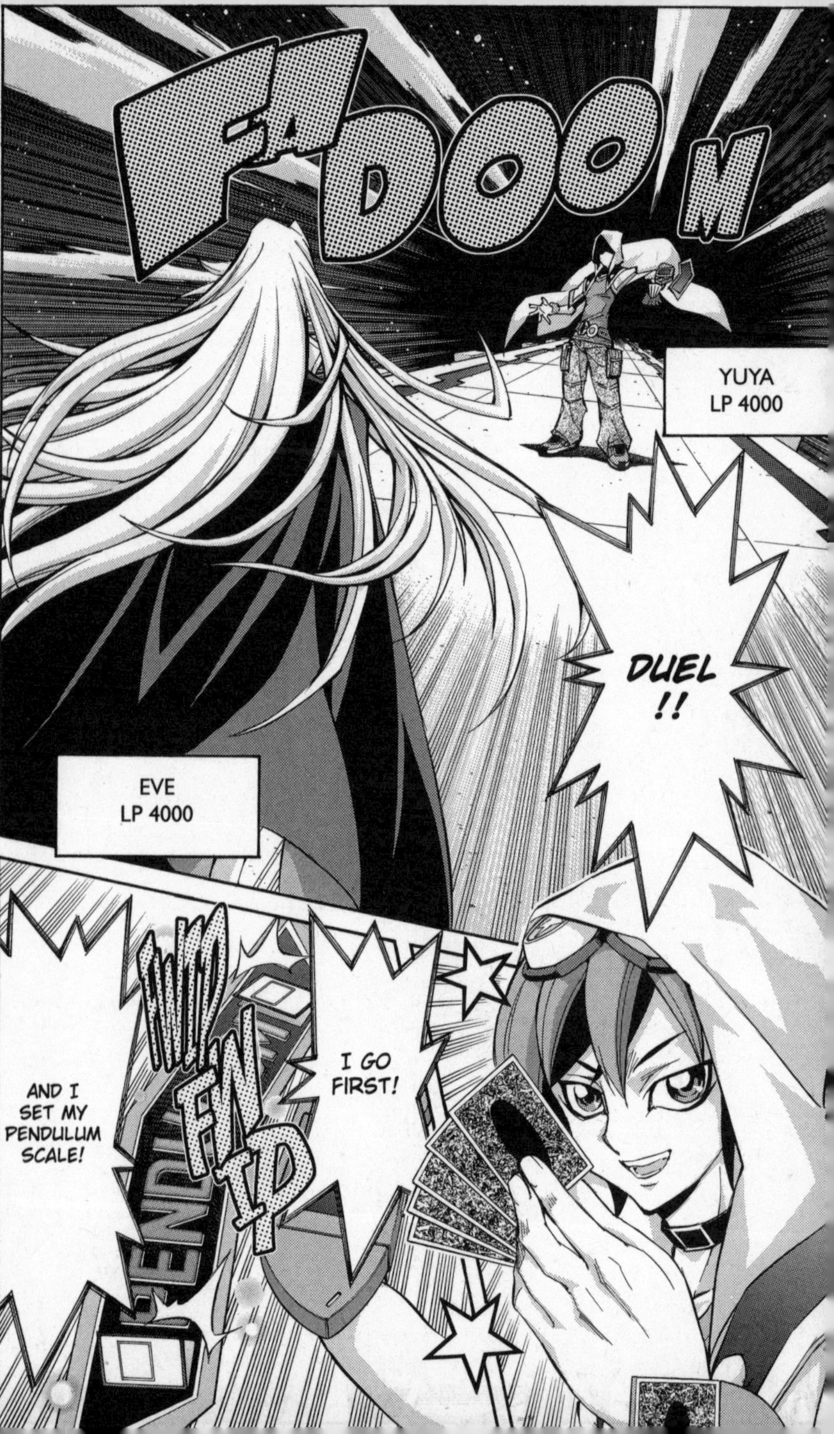
FA-DOOM
YUYA
LP 4000
DUEL!!
EVE
LP 4000
I GO FIRST!
AND I SET MY PENDULUM SCALE!

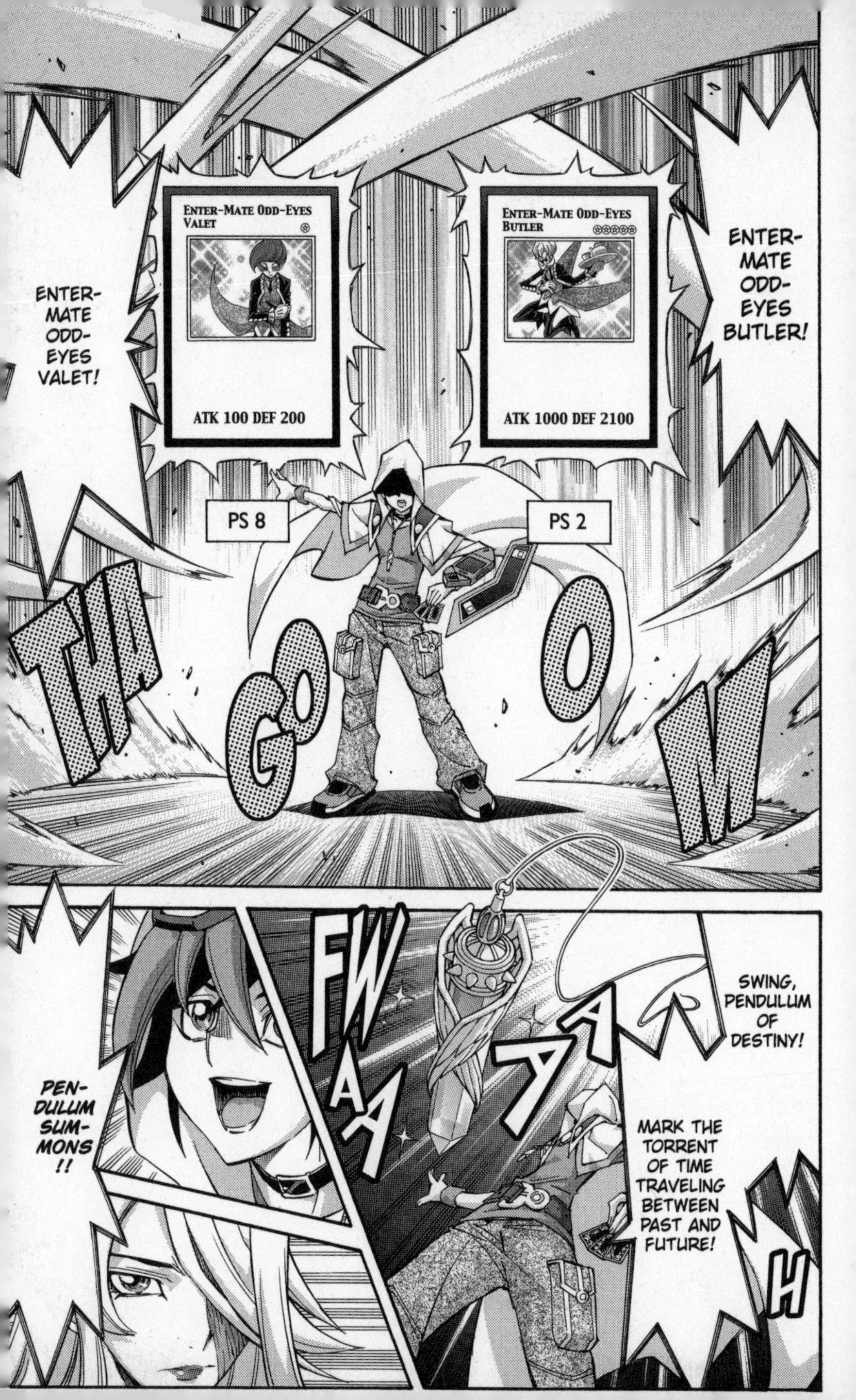
ENTER-MATE ODD-EYES BUTLER!
ENTER-MATE ODD-EYES BUTLER
ATK 1000 DEF 2100
ENTER-MATE ODD-EYES VALET
ATK 100 DEF 200
ENTER-MATE ODD-EYES VALET!
PS 2
PS 8
THA GO O OM
SWING, PENDULUM OF DESTINY!
MARK THE TORRENT OF TIME TRAVELING BETWEEN PAST AND FUTURE!
FWAAAAAH
PEN-DULUM SUM-MONS!!

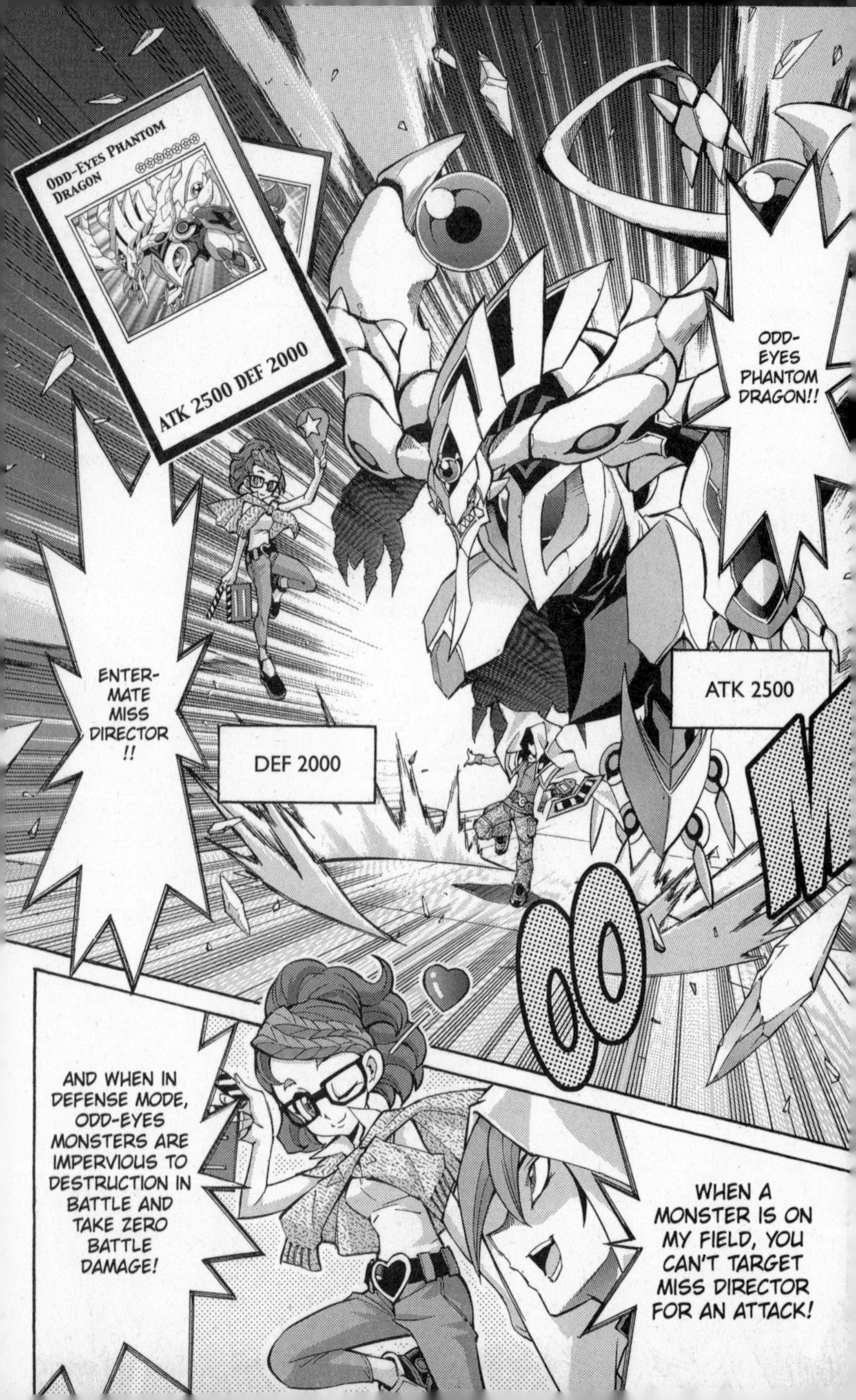

ODD-EYES PHANTOM DRAGON!!
ATK 2500
ODD-EYES PHANTOM DRAGON
ATK 2500 DEF 2000
ENTER-MATE MISS DIRECTOR!!
DEF 2000
WHEN A MONSTER IS ON MY FIELD, YOU CAN'T TARGET MISS DIRECTOR FOR AN ATTACK!
AND WHEN IN DEFENSE MODE, ODD-EYES MONSTERS ARE IMPERVIOUS TO DESTRUCTION IN BATTLE AND TAKE ZERO BATTLE DAMAGE!

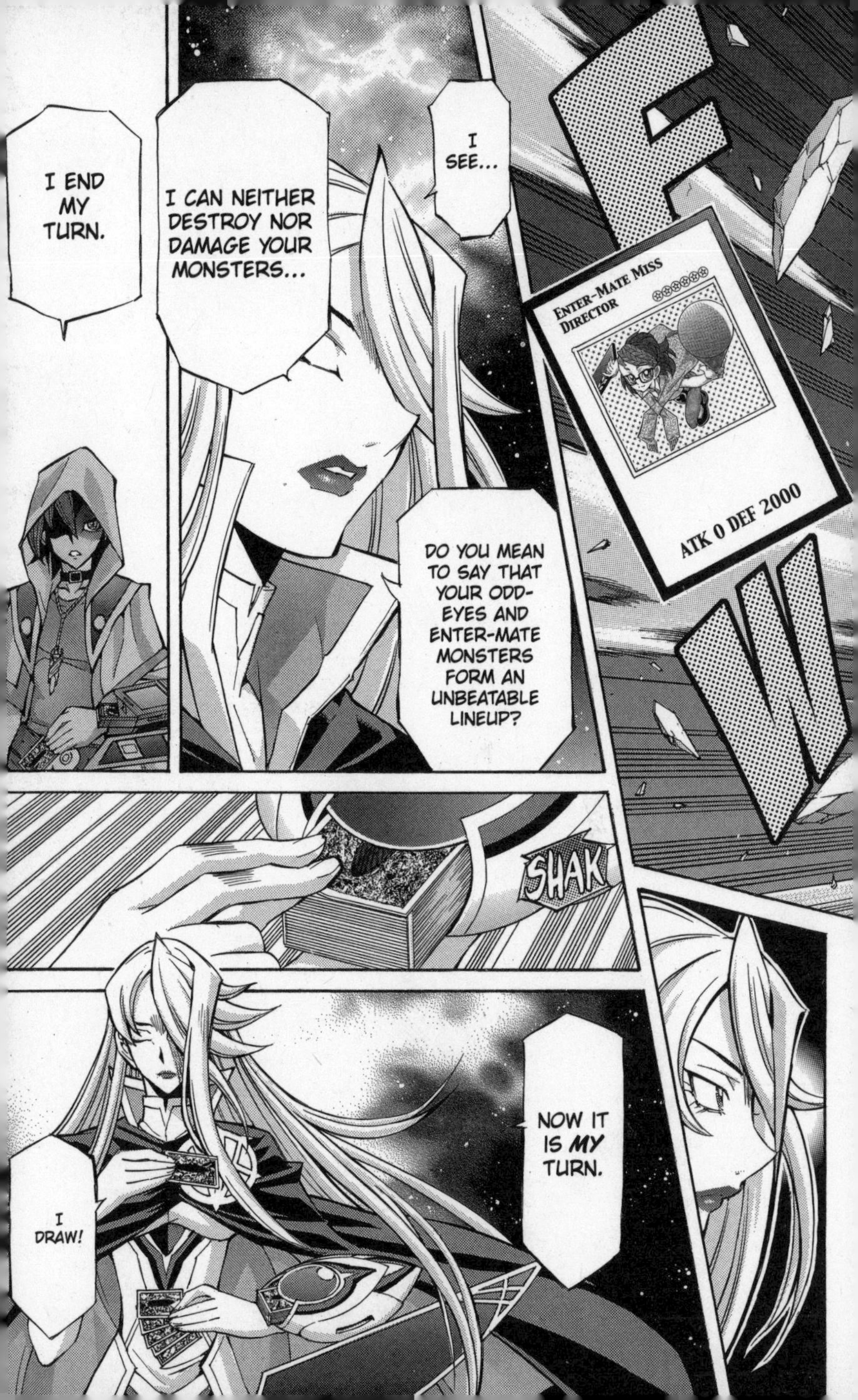

ENTER-MATE MISS DIRECTOR
ATK 0 DEF 2000
I SEE...
I CAN NEITHER DESTROY NOR DAMAGE YOUR MONSTERS...
DO YOU MEAN TO SAY THAT YOUR ODD-EYES AND ENTER-MATE MONSTERS FORM AN UNBEATABLE LINEUP?
I END MY TURN.
SHAK
NOW IT IS *MY* TURN.
I DRAW!

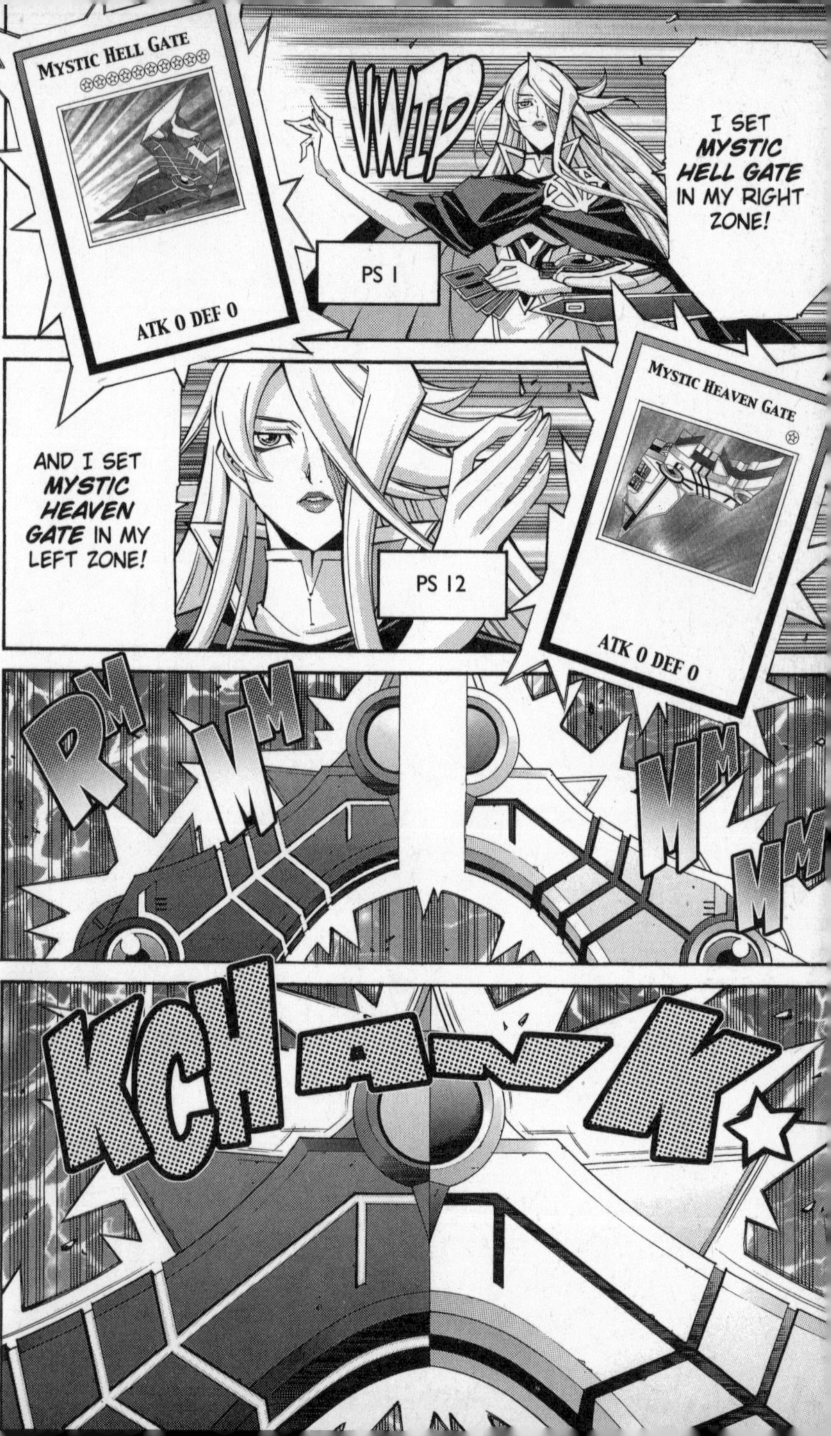
I SET MYSTIC HELL GATE IN MY RIGHT ZONE!
VWIP
PS 1
MYSTIC HELL GATE
ATK 0 DEF 0
MYSTIC HEAVEN GATE
ATK 0 DEF 0
PS 12
AND I SET MYSTIC HEAVEN GATE IN MY LEFT ZONE!
MMMM
RMMM
KCHANK

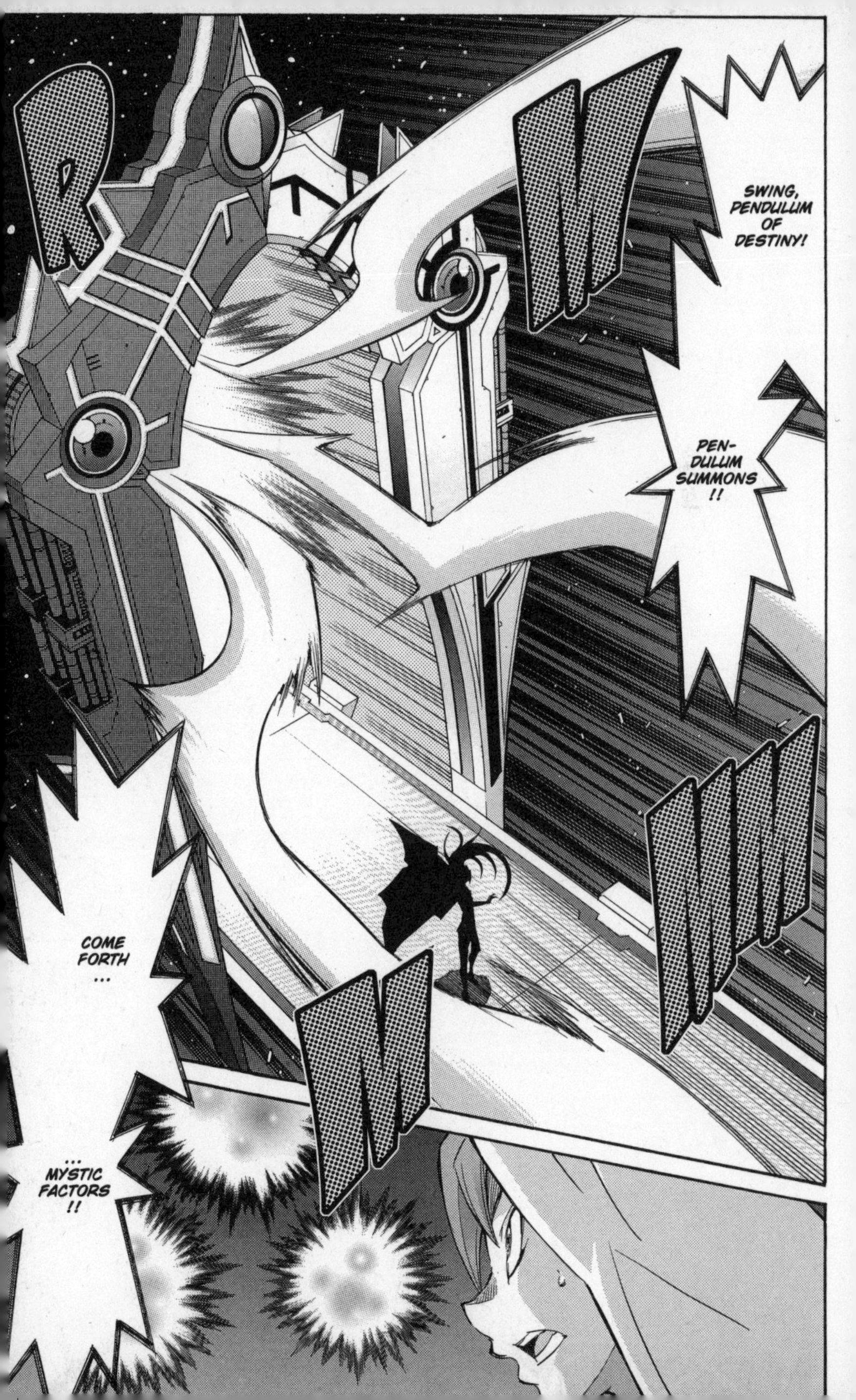
SWING, PENDULUM OF DESTINY!
PEN-DULUM SUMMONS !!
COME FORTH ...
... MYSTIC FACTORS !!

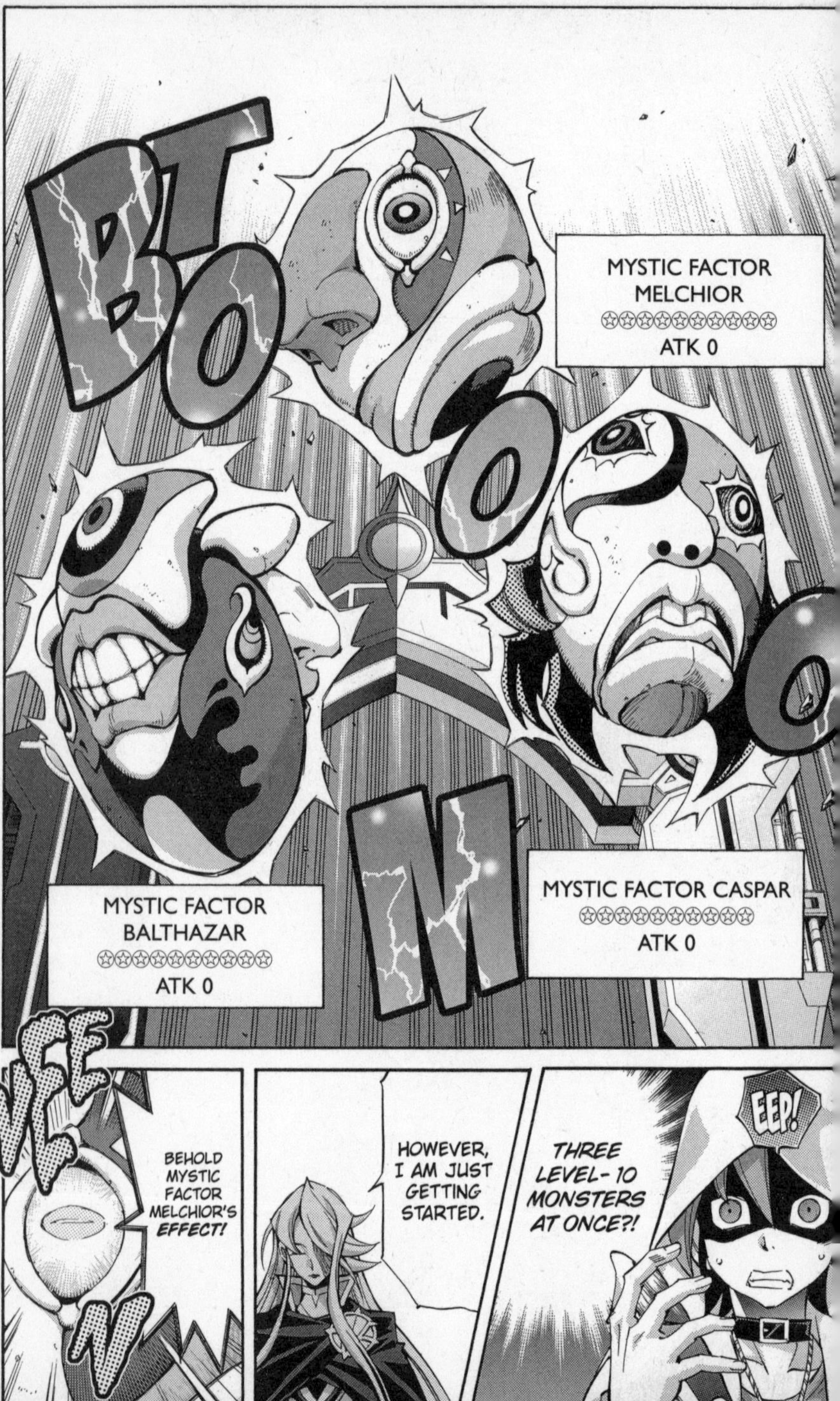
MYSTIC FACTOR MELCHIOR
☆☆☆☆☆☆☆☆☆☆
ATK 0
BOOOOM
MYSTIC FACTOR CASPAR
☆☆☆☆☆☆☆☆☆☆
ATK 0
MYSTIC FACTOR BALTHAZAR
☆☆☆☆☆☆☆☆☆☆
ATK 0
EEP!
THREE LEVEL-10 MONSTERS AT ONCE?!
HOWEVER, I AM JUST GETTING STARTED.
BEHOLD MYSTIC FACTOR MELCHIOR'S *EFFECT!*

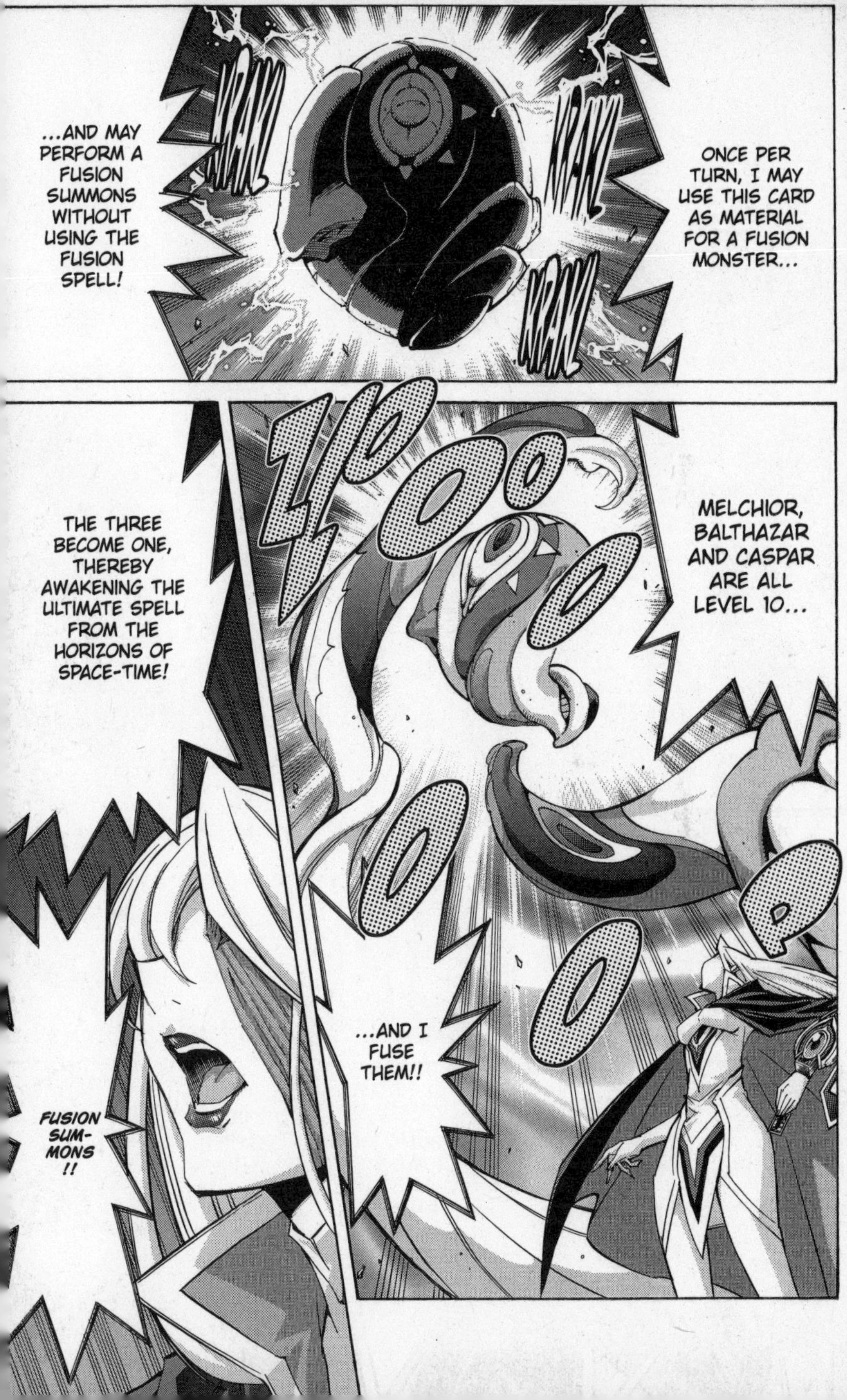
ONCE PER TURN, I MAY USE THIS CARD AS MATERIAL FOR A FUSION MONSTER...
...AND MAY PERFORM A FUSION SUMMONS WITHOUT USING THE FUSION SPELL!
MELCHIOR, BALTHAZAR AND CASPAR ARE ALL LEVEL 10...
THE THREE BECOME ONE, THEREBY AWAKENING THE ULTIMATE SPELL FROM THE HORIZONS OF SPACE-TIME!
...AND I FUSE THEM!!
FUSION SUM-MONS !!

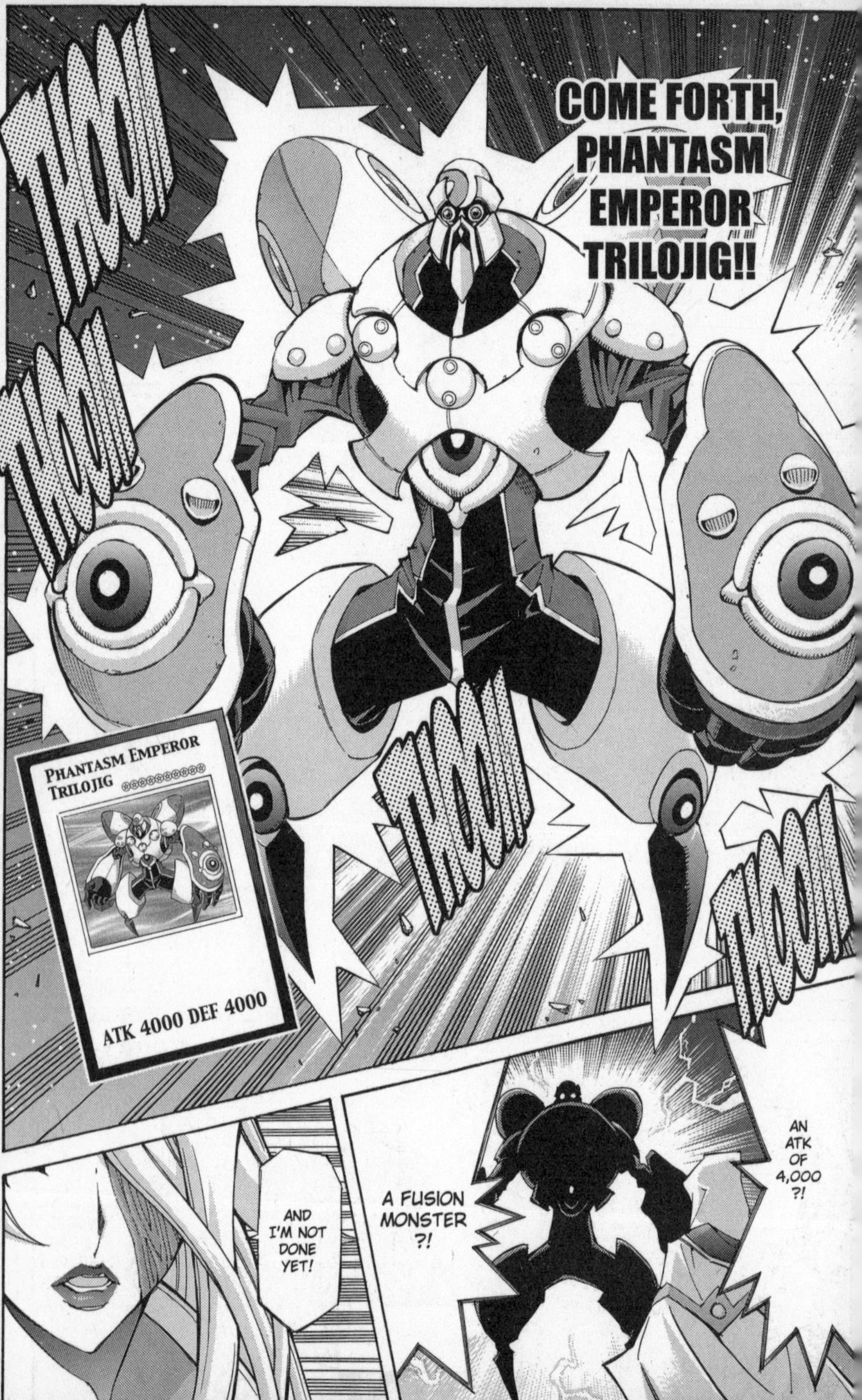
COME FORTH, PHANTASM EMPEROR TRILOJIG!!
THOOM
THOOM
THOOM
THOOM
THOOM
PHANTASM EMPEROR TRILOJIG
ATK 4000 DEF 4000
AN ATK OF 4,000 ?!
A FUSION MONSTER ?!
AND I'M NOT DONE YET!

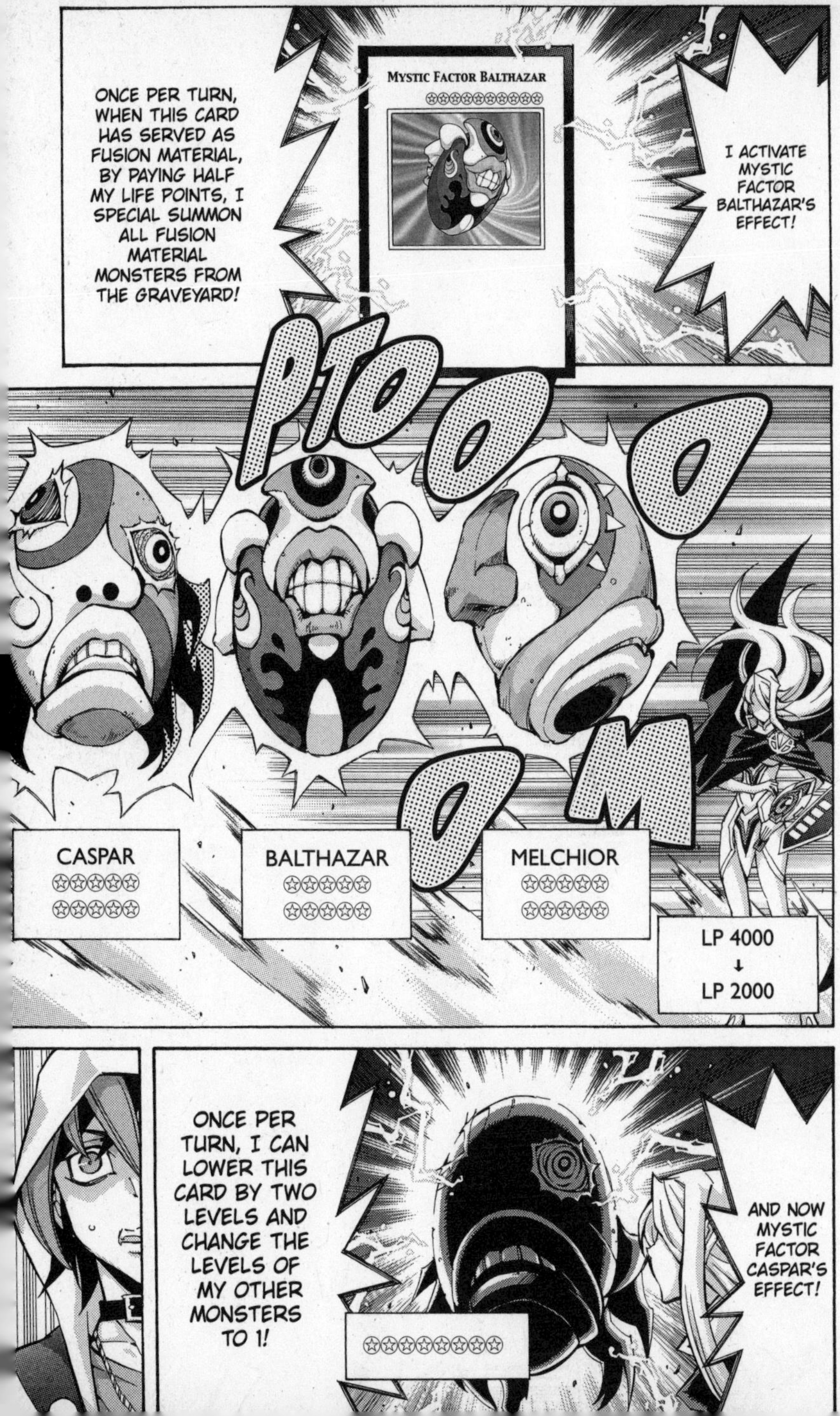
I ACTIVATE MYSTIC FACTOR BALTHAZAR'S EFFECT!
MYSTIC FACTOR BALTHAZAR
ONCE PER TURN, WHEN THIS CARD HAS SERVED AS FUSION MATERIAL, BY PAYING HALF MY LIFE POINTS, I SPECIAL SUMMON ALL FUSION MATERIAL MONSTERS FROM THE GRAVEYARD!
PTOOOOOM
LP 4000 ↓ LP 2000
MELCHIOR
BALTHAZAR
CASPAR
AND NOW MYSTIC FACTOR CASPAR'S EFFECT!
ONCE PER TURN, I CAN LOWER THIS CARD BY TWO LEVELS AND CHANGE THE LEVELS OF MY OTHER MONSTERS TO 1!

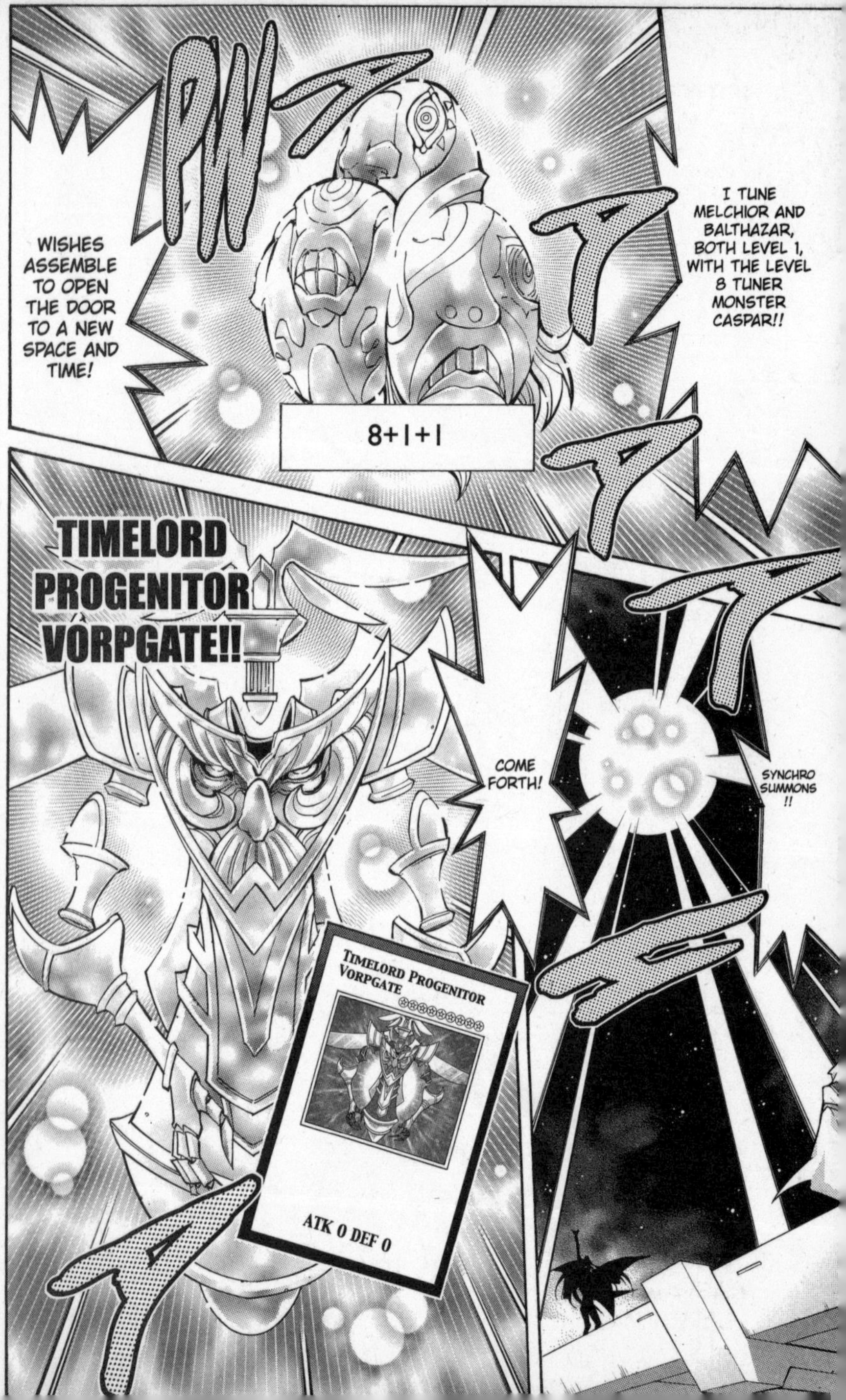
I TUNE MELCHIOR AND BALTHAZAR, BOTH LEVEL 1, WITH THE LEVEL 8 TUNER MONSTER CASPAR!!
WISHES ASSEMBLE TO OPEN THE DOOR TO A NEW SPACE AND TIME!
8+1+1
SYNCHRO SUMMONS!!
COME FORTH!
TIMELORD PROGENITOR VORPGATE!!
TIMELORD PROGENITOR VORPGATE
ATK 0 DEF 0

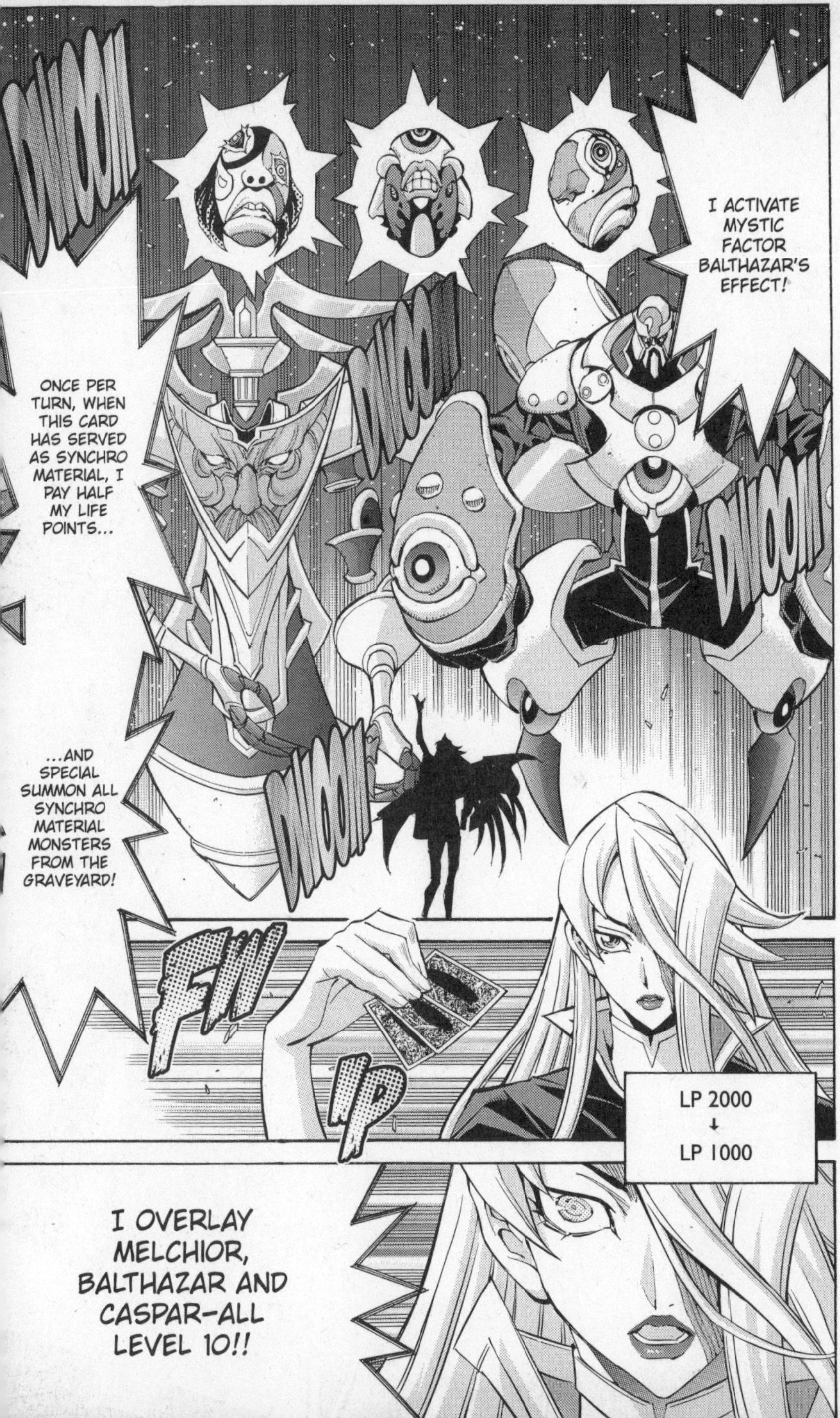

DWOOM
I ACTIVATE MYSTIC FACTOR BALTHAZAR'S EFFECT!
DWOOM
DWOOM
ONCE PER TURN, WHEN THIS CARD HAS SERVED AS SYNCHRO MATERIAL, I PAY HALF MY LIFE POINTS...
DWOOM
...AND SPECIAL SUMMON ALL SYNCHRO MATERIAL MONSTERS FROM THE GRAVEYARD!
LP 2000 ↓ LP 1000
FWIP
I OVERLAY MELCHIOR, BALTHAZAR AND CASPAR—ALL LEVEL 10!!

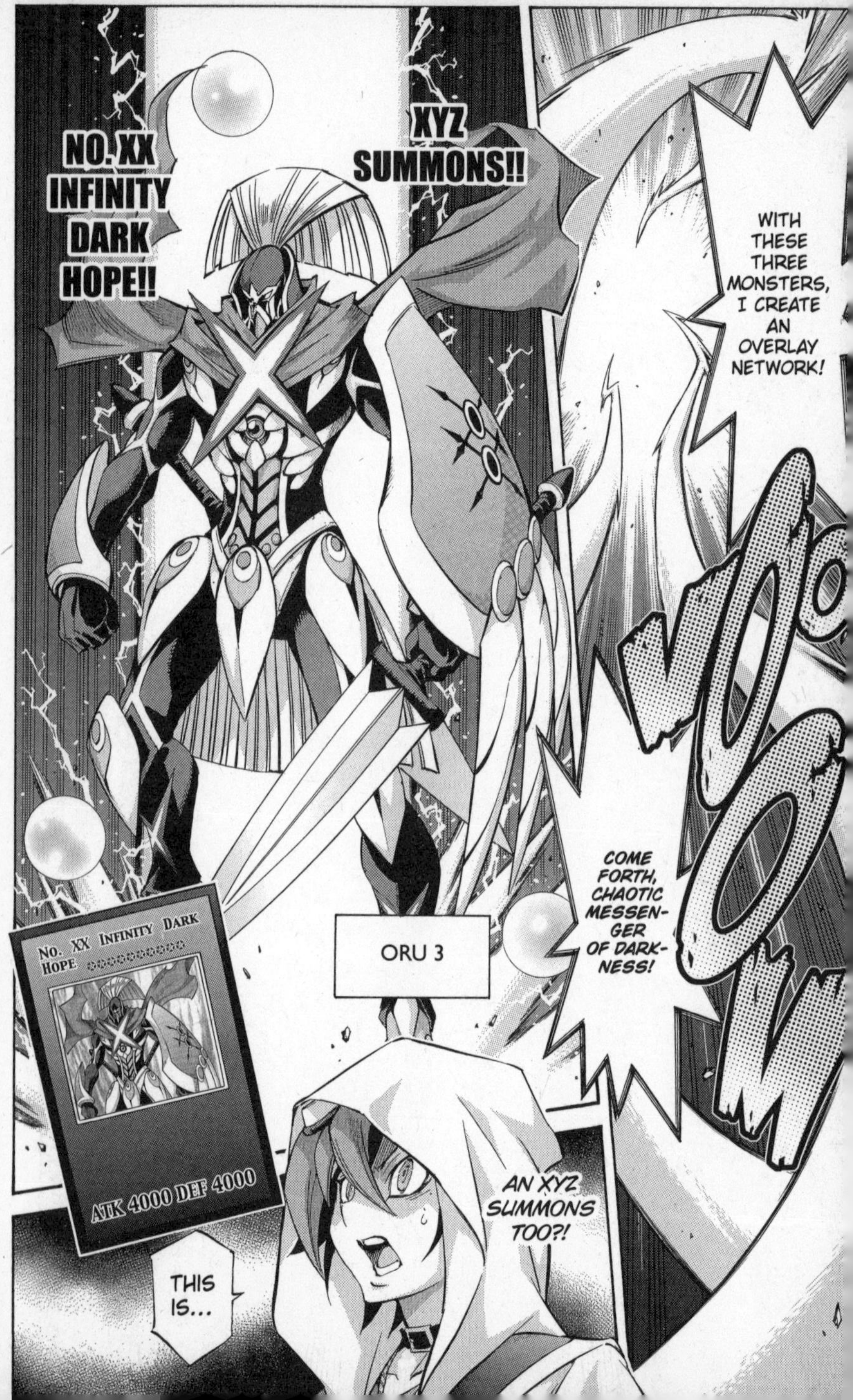

WITH THESE THREE MONSTERS, I CREATE AN OVERLAY NETWORK!
COME FORTH, CHAOTIC MESSENGER OF DARKNESS!
VOOOM
XYZ SUMMONS!!
NO. XX INFINITY DARK HOPE!!
ORU 3
No. XX Infinity Dark Hope
ATK 4000 DEF 4000
AN XYZ SUMMONS TOO?!
THIS IS...

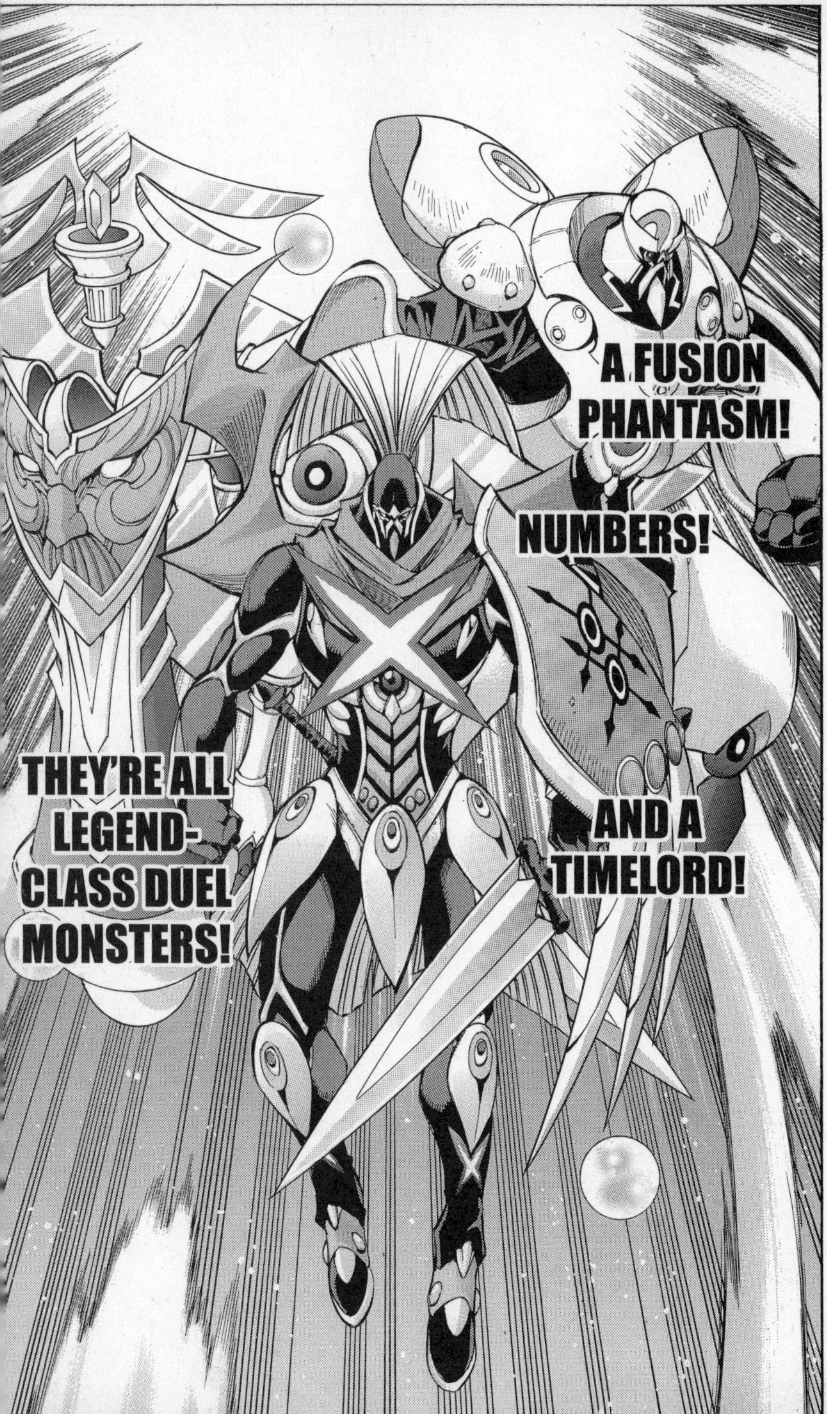
A FUSION PHANTASM!
NUMBERS!
AND A TIMELORD!
THEY'RE ALL LEGEND-CLASS DUEL MONSTERS!

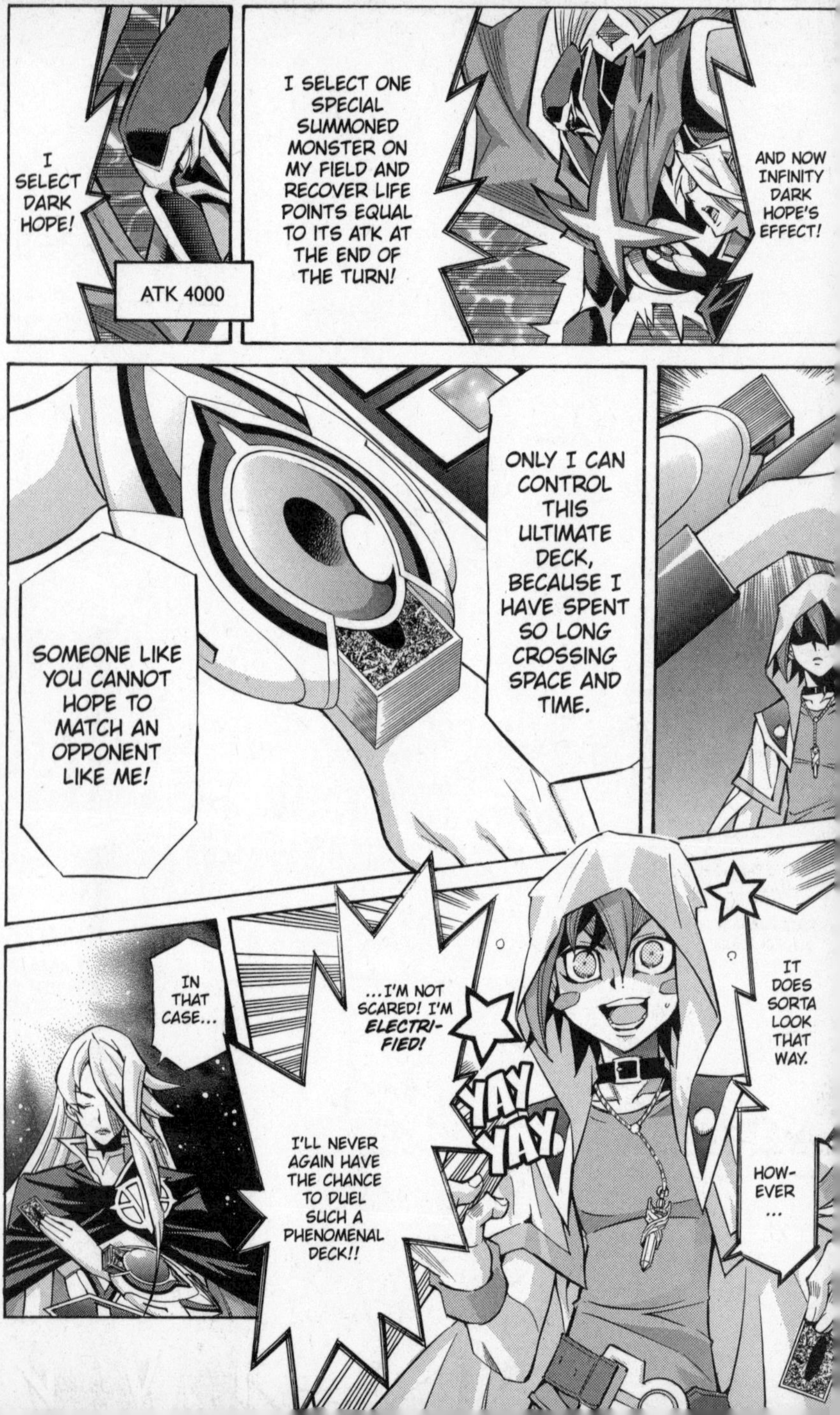
AND NOW INFINITY DARK HOPE'S EFFECT!
I SELECT ONE SPECIAL SUMMONED MONSTER ON MY FIELD AND RECOVER LIFE POINTS EQUAL TO ITS ATK AT THE END OF THE TURN!
I SELECT DARK HOPE!
ATK 4000
ONLY I CAN CONTROL THIS ULTIMATE DECK, BECAUSE I HAVE SPENT SO LONG CROSSING SPACE AND TIME.
SOMEONE LIKE YOU CANNOT HOPE TO MATCH AN OPPONENT LIKE ME!
IT DOES SORTA LOOK THAT WAY.
...I'M NOT SCARED! I'M *ELECTRIFIED!*
YAY YAY
HOW-EVER...
I'LL NEVER AGAIN HAVE THE CHANCE TO DUEL SUCH A PHENOMENAL DECK!!
IN THAT CASE...

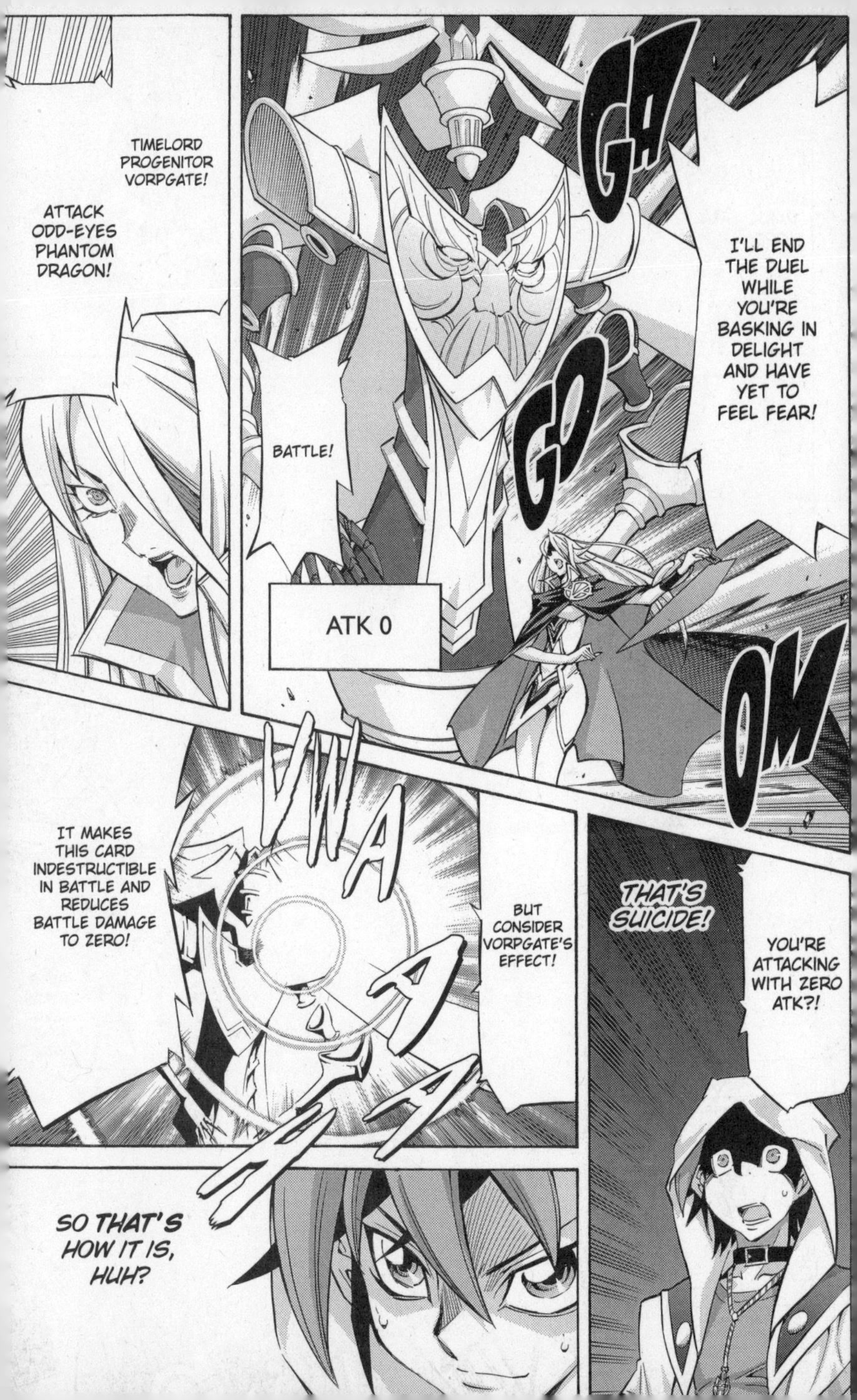
I'LL END THE DUEL WHILE YOU'RE BASKING IN DELIGHT AND HAVE YET TO FEEL FEAR!
BATTLE!
GA
GO
OM
ATK 0
TIMELORD PROGENITOR VORPGATE!
ATTACK ODD-EYES PHANTOM DRAGON!
THAT'S SUICIDE!
YOU'RE ATTACKING WITH ZERO ATK?!
BUT CONSIDER VORPGATE'S EFFECT!
VWAAAA
IT MAKES THIS CARD INDESTRUCTIBLE IN BATTLE AND REDUCES BATTLE DAMAGE TO ZERO!
SO THAT'S HOW IT IS, HUH?

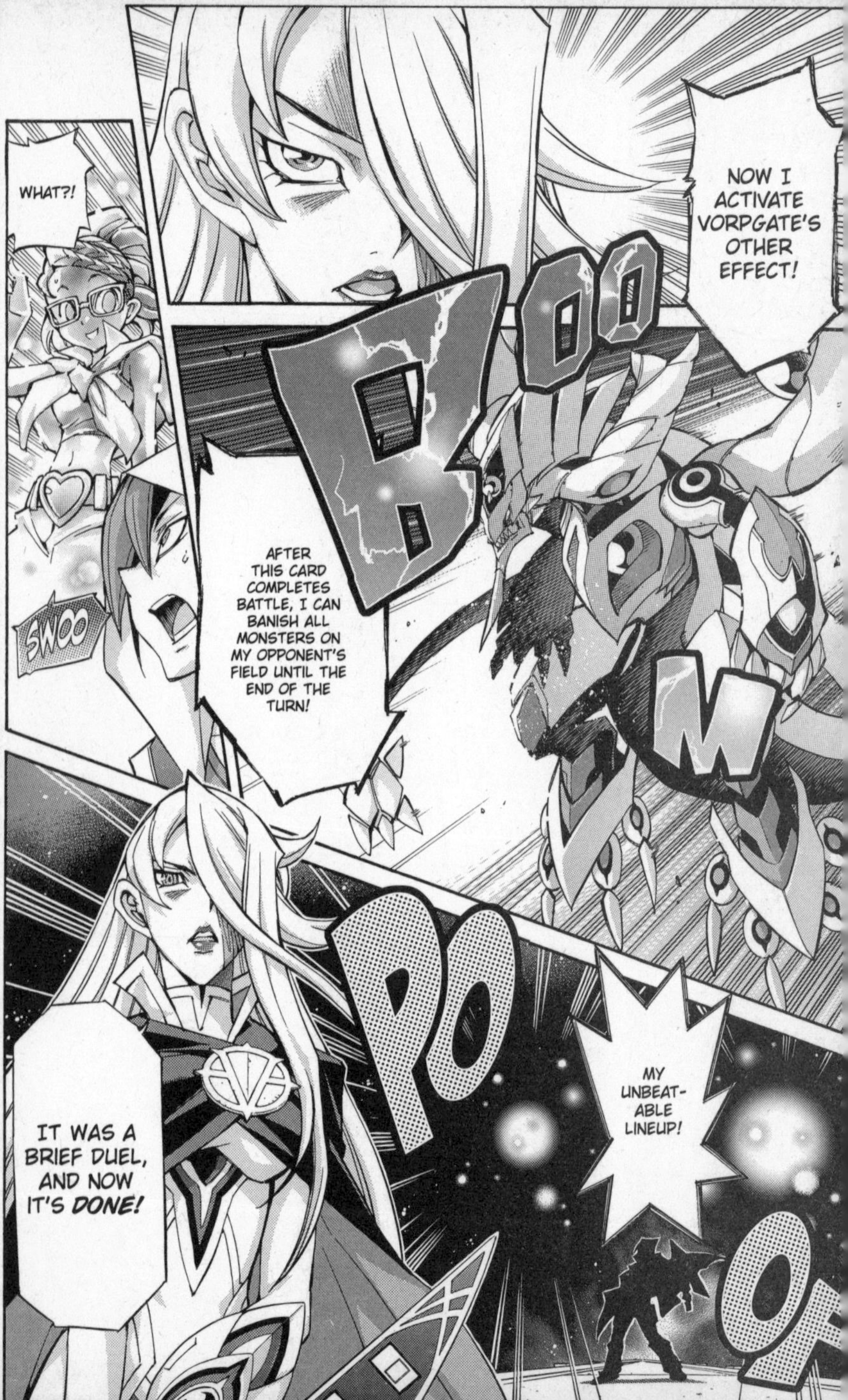

NOW I ACTIVATE VORPGATE'S OTHER EFFECT!
BOOOM
AFTER THIS CARD COMPLETES BATTLE, I CAN BANISH ALL MONSTERS ON MY OPPONENT'S FIELD UNTIL THE END OF THE TURN!
WHAT?!
SWOO
MY UNBEAT-ABLE LINEUP!
POOF
IT WAS A BRIEF DUEL, AND NOW IT'S *DONE!*

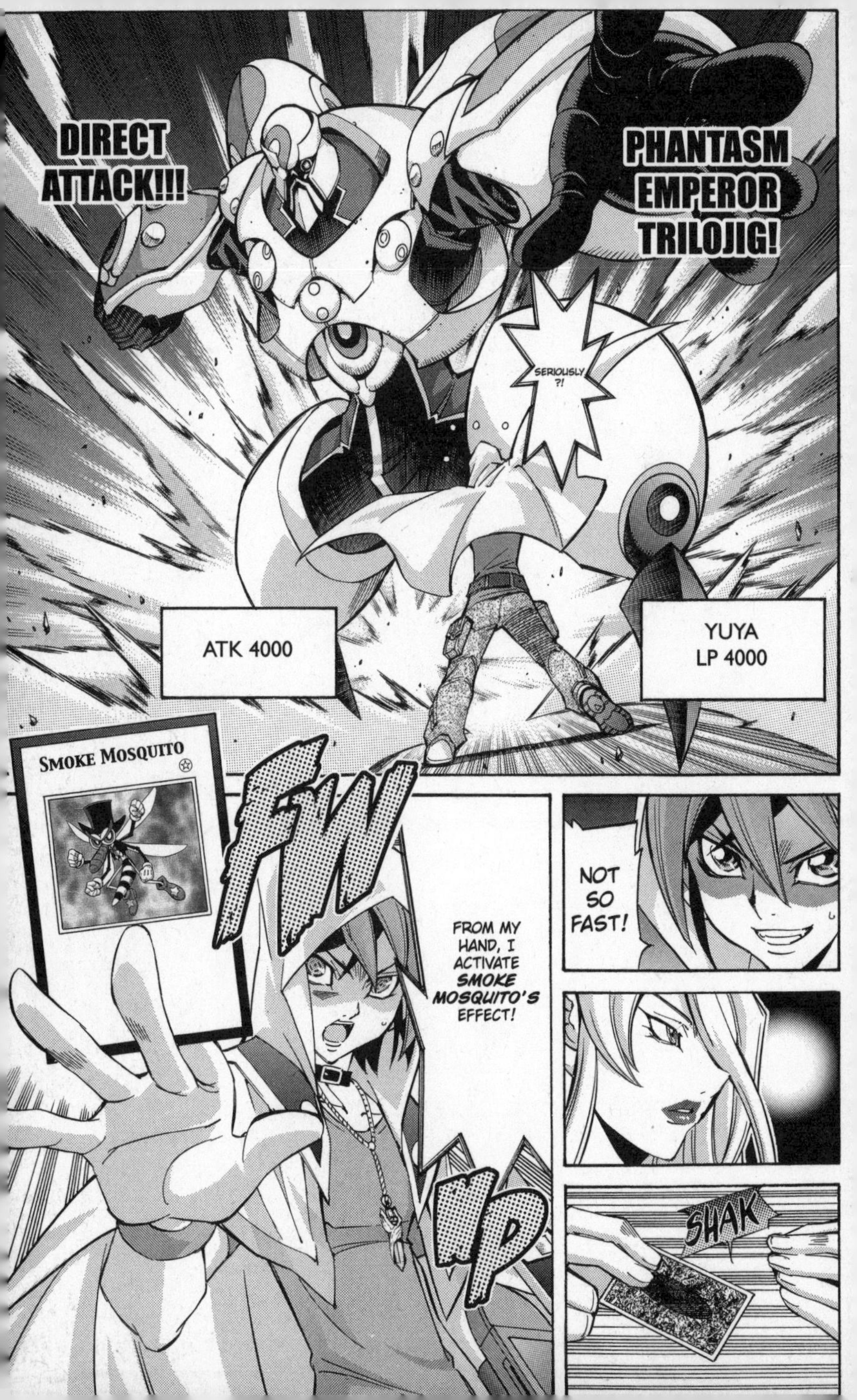
PHANTASM EMPEROR TRILOJIG!
DIRECT ATTACK!!!
SERIOUSLY ?!
YUYA LP 4000
ATK 4000
NOT SO FAST!
SHAK
FW
FROM MY HAND, I ACTIVATE **SMOKE MOSQUITO'S** EFFECT!
Smoke Mosquito
IP

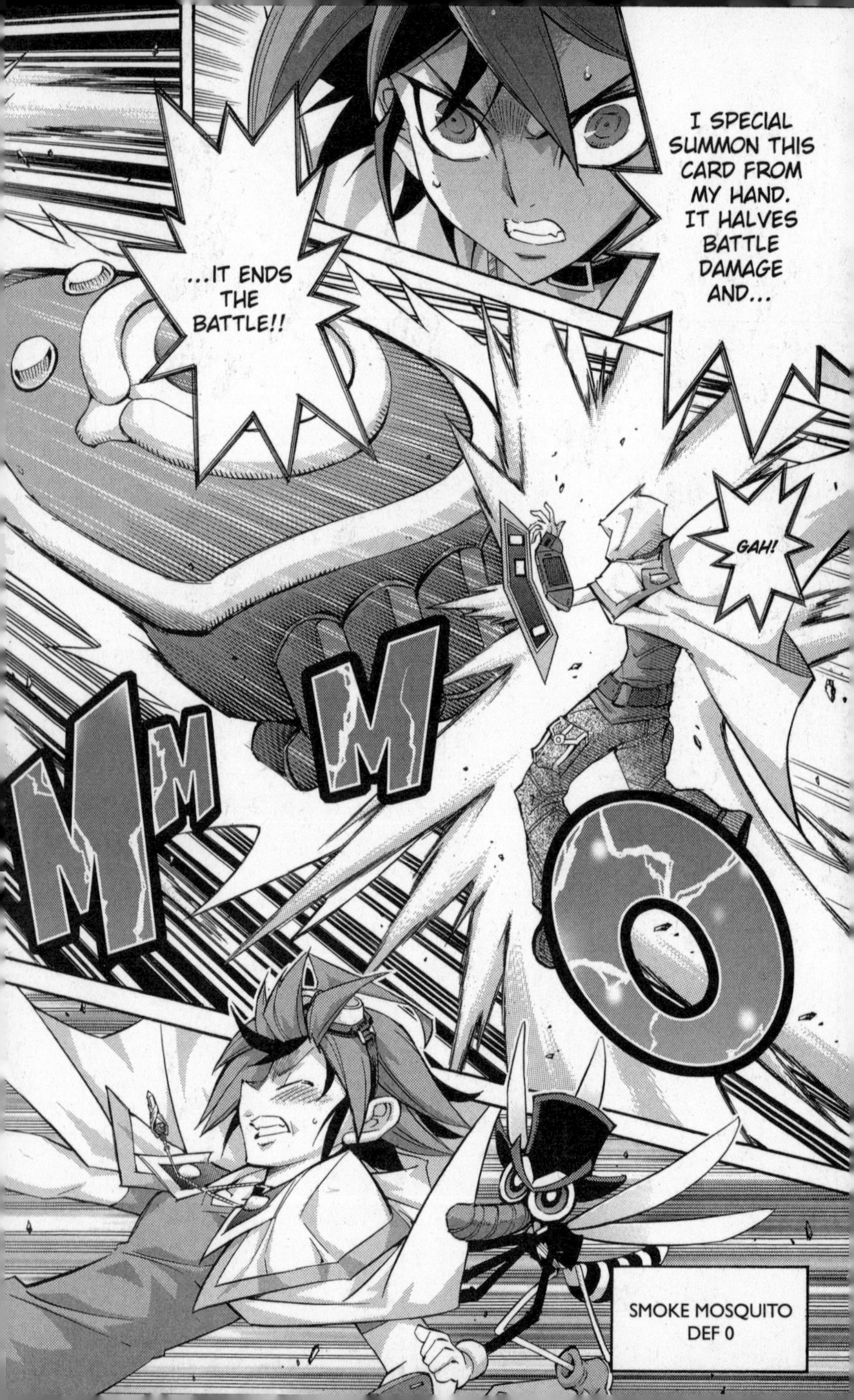
I SPECIAL SUMMON THIS CARD FROM MY HAND. IT HALVES BATTLE DAMAGE AND...
...IT ENDS THE BATTLE!!
GAH!
MMMO
SMOKE MOSQUITO
DEF 0

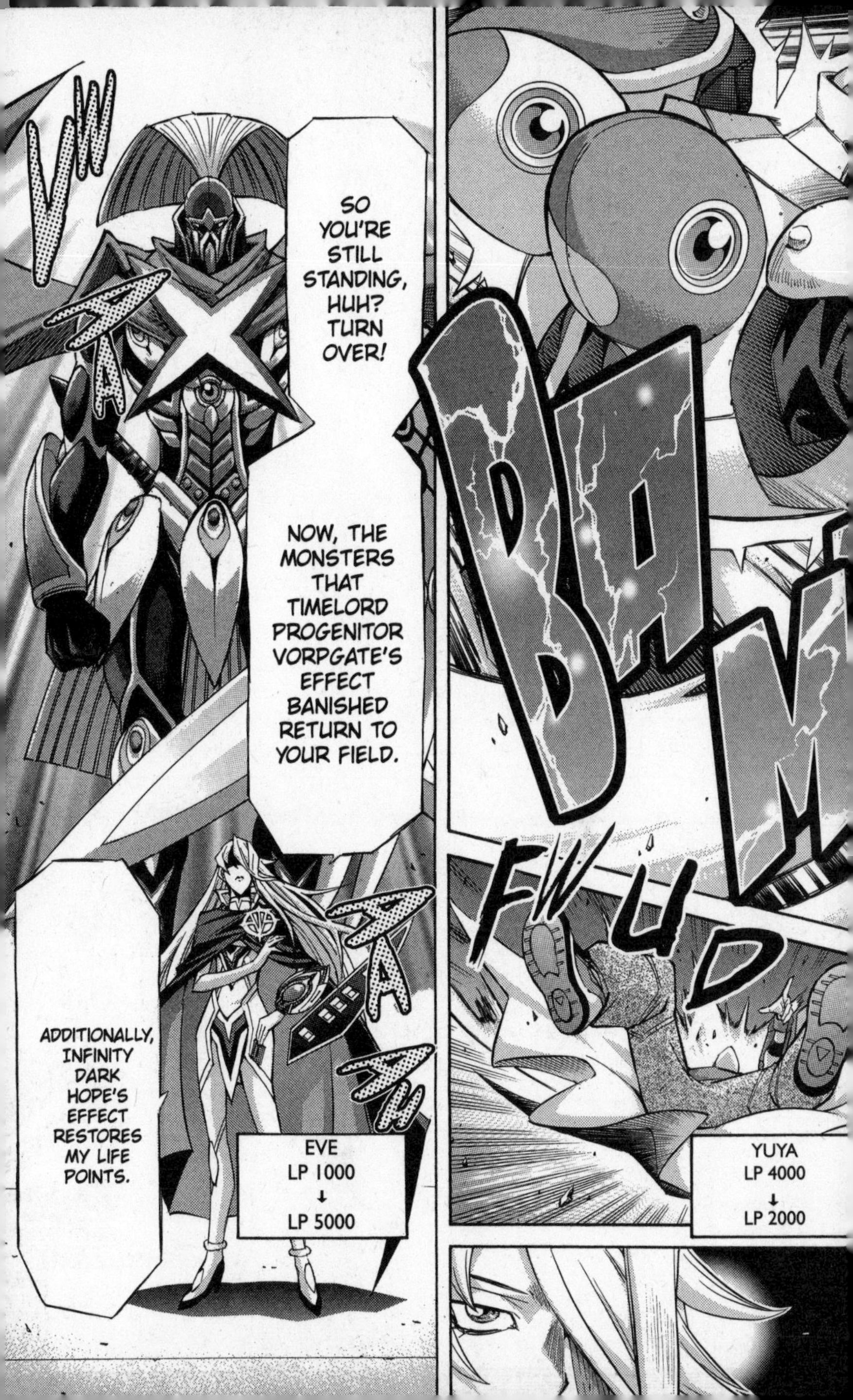
BAM
FWUD
YUYA LP 4000 ↓ LP 2000
SO YOU'RE STILL STANDING, HUH? TURN OVER!
NOW, THE MONSTERS THAT TIMELORD PROGENITOR VORPGATE'S EFFECT BANISHED RETURN TO YOUR FIELD.
ADDITIONALLY, INFINITY DARK HOPE'S EFFECT RESTORES MY LIFE POINTS.
EVE LP 1000 ↓ LP 5000

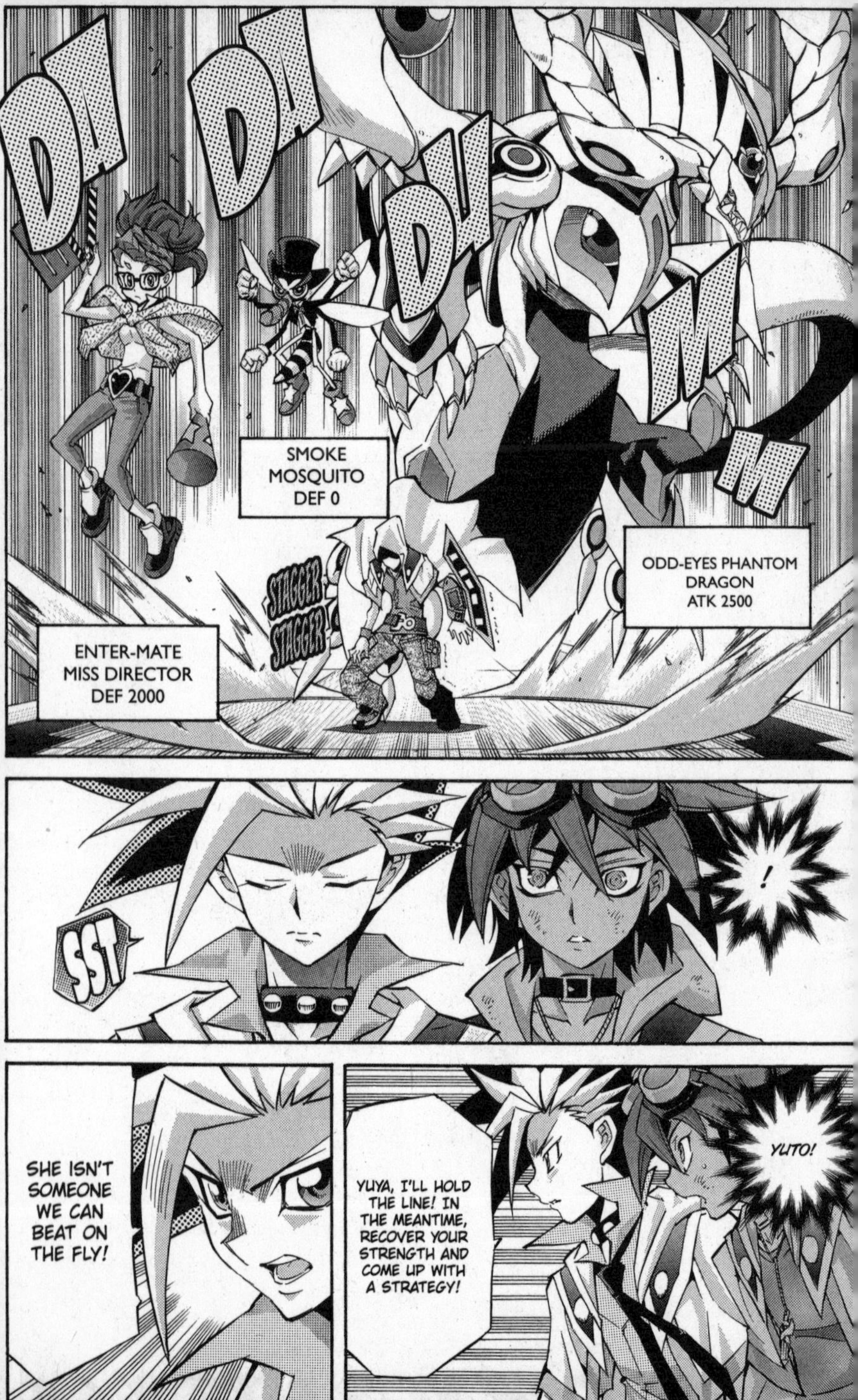
DA DA DA
M M
ODD-EYES PHANTOM DRAGON ATK 2500
SMOKE MOSQUITO DEF 0
STAGGER STAGGER
ENTER-MATE MISS DIRECTOR DEF 2000
!
SST
YUTO!
YUYA, I'LL HOLD THE LINE! IN THE MEANTIME, RECOVER YOUR STRENGTH AND COME UP WITH A STRATEGY!
SHE ISN'T SOMEONE WE CAN BEAT ON THE FLY!

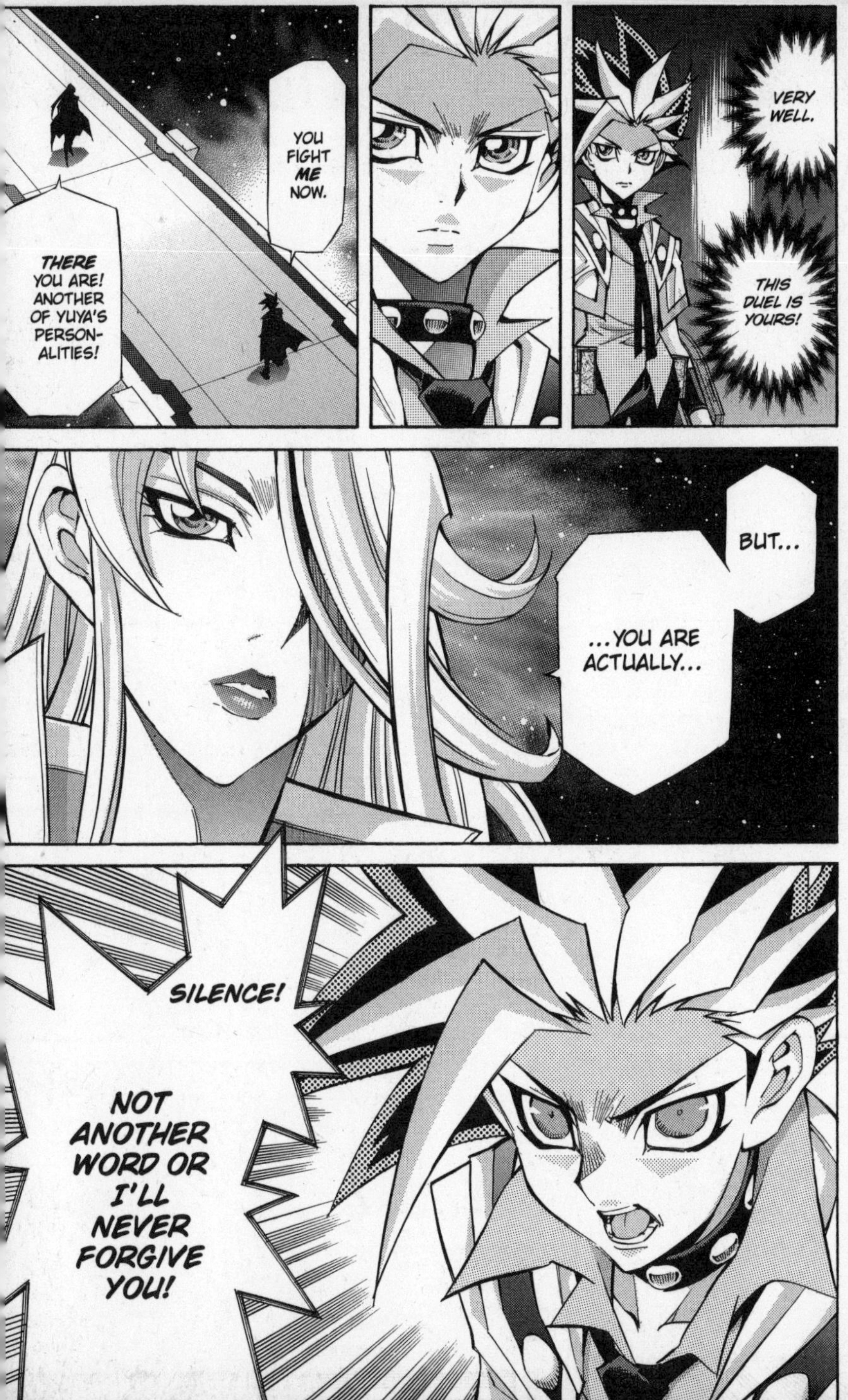
VERY WELL.
THIS DUEL IS YOURS!
YOU FIGHT ME NOW.
THERE YOU ARE! ANOTHER OF YUYA'S PERSONALITIES!
BUT...
...YOU ARE ACTUALLY...
SILENCE!
NOT ANOTHER WORD OR I'LL NEVER FORGIVE YOU!

scale 24 ARC-V CHARACTER SKETCHES

TIMELORD PROGENITOR VORPGATE

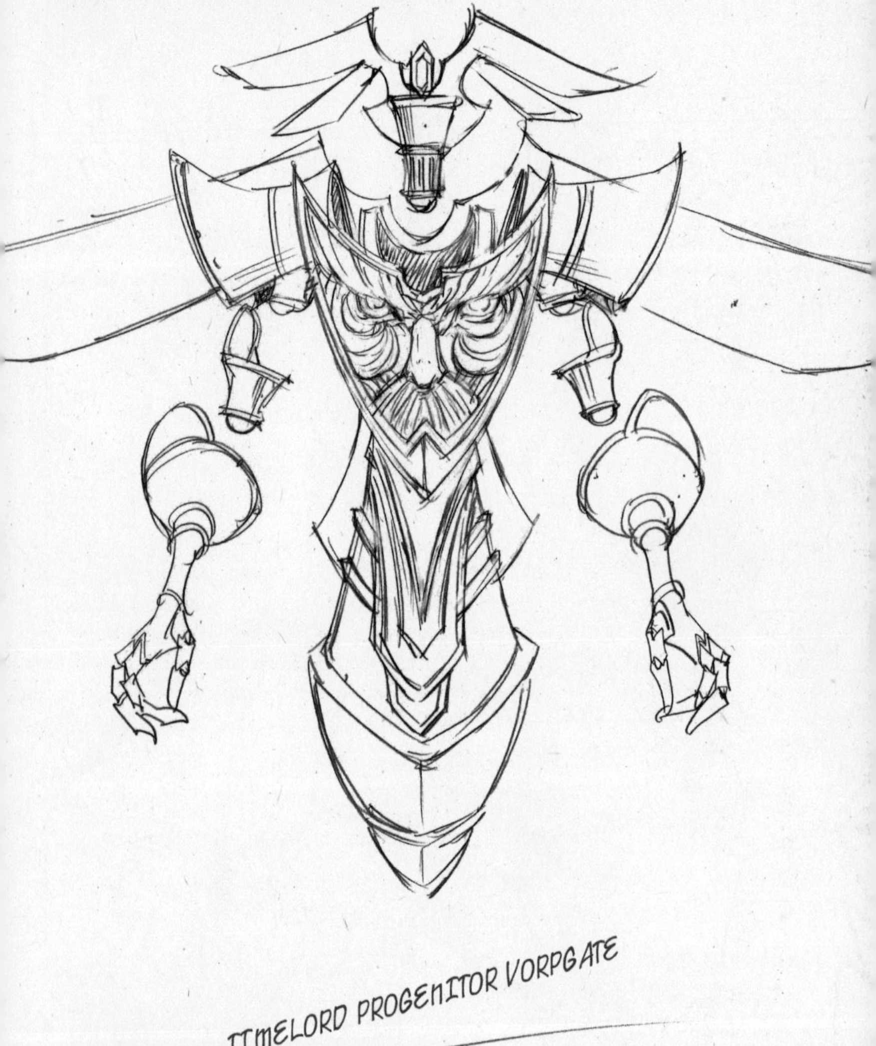
TIMELORD PROGENITOR VORPGATE

The Timelords were created from void, infinity and endless light. Even these omnipotent gods had a progenitor. Timelord Progenitor Vorpgate descends to the battlefield and blows all enemies away!

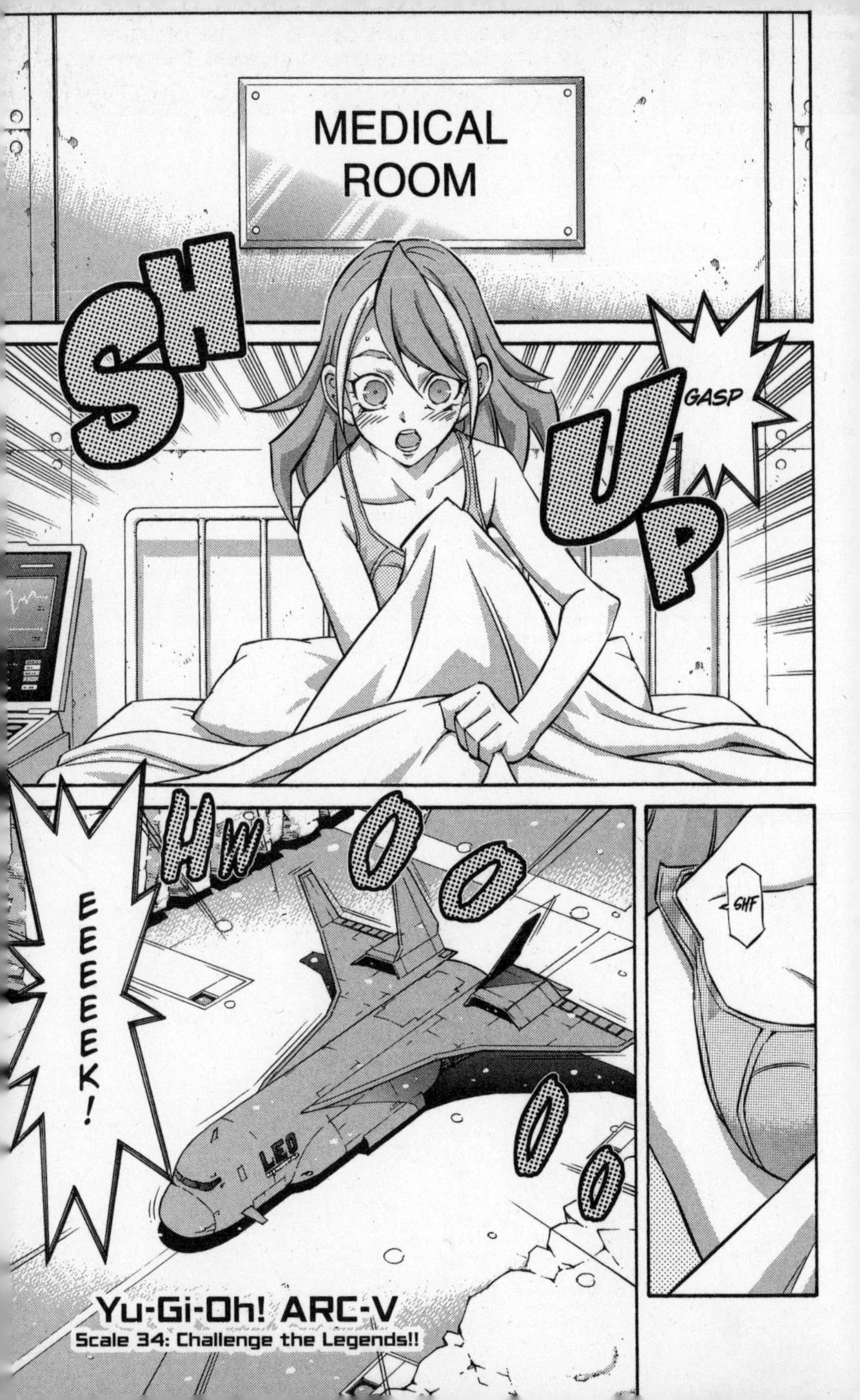
MEDICAL ROOM
GASP
SH UP
SHF
HWOOOO
EEEEEEK!
Yu-Gi-Oh! ARC-V
Scale 34: Challenge the Legends!!

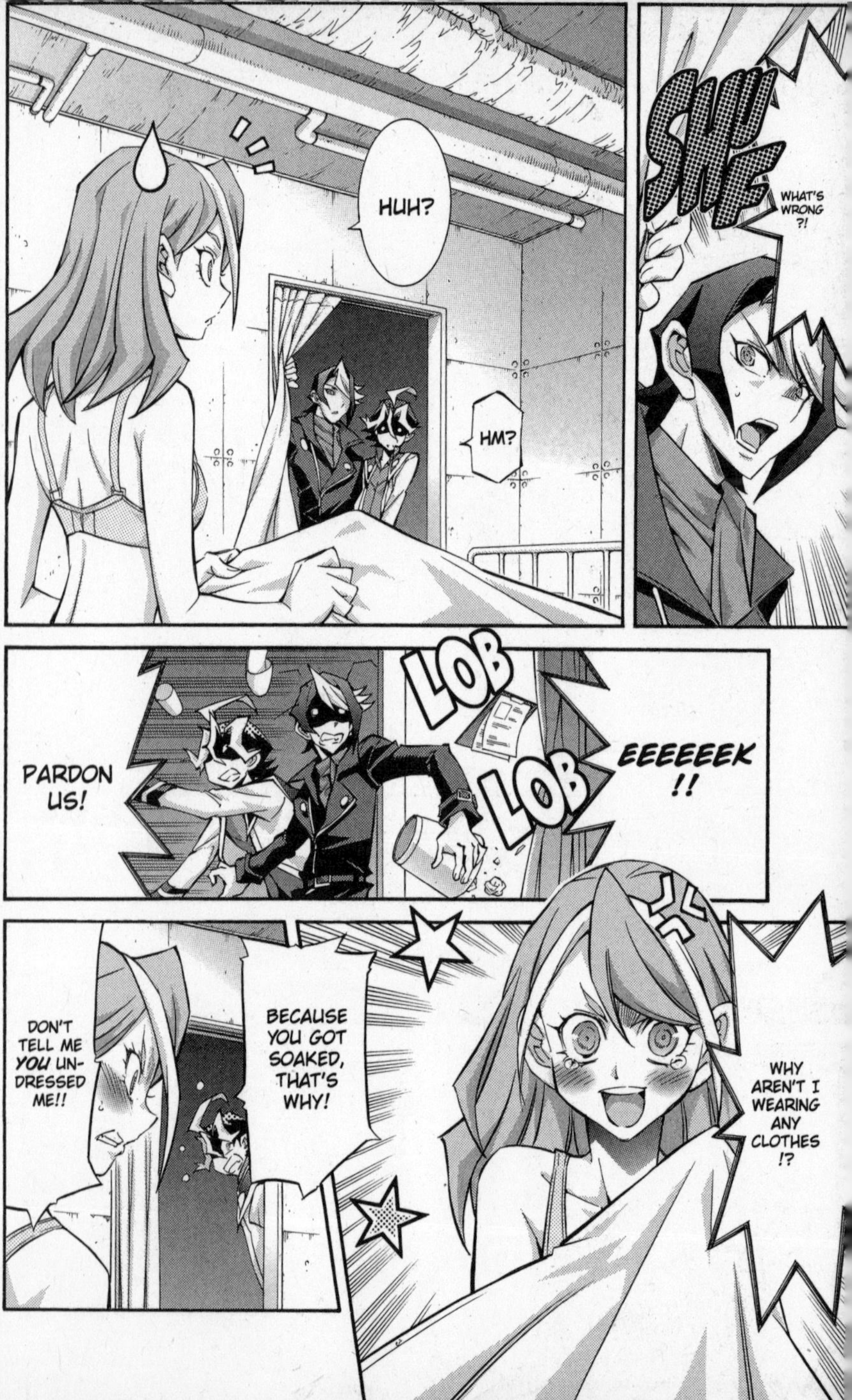
SHU SHF
WHAT'S WRONG ?!
HUH?
HM?
EEEEEEK !!
LOB
LOB
PARDON US!
WHY AREN'T I WEARING ANY CLOTHES !?
BECAUSE YOU GOT SOAKED, THAT'S WHY!
DON'T TELL ME *YOU* UNDRESSED ME!!

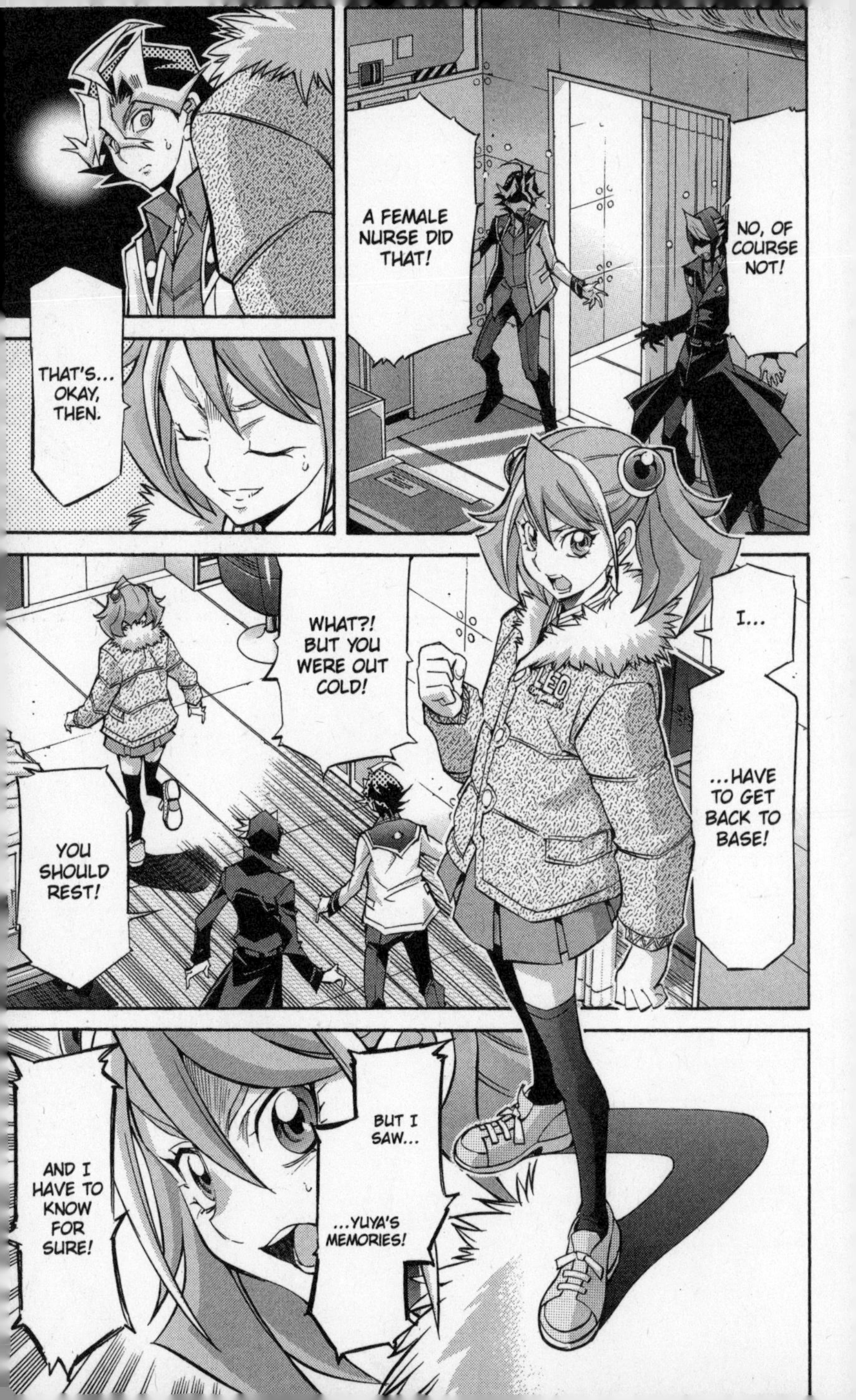
NO, OF COURSE NOT!
A FEMALE NURSE DID THAT!
THAT'S... OKAY, THEN.
I...
...HAVE TO GET BACK TO BASE!
WHAT?! BUT YOU WERE OUT COLD!
YOU SHOULD REST!
BUT I SAW...
...YUYA'S MEMORIES!
AND I HAVE TO KNOW FOR SURE!

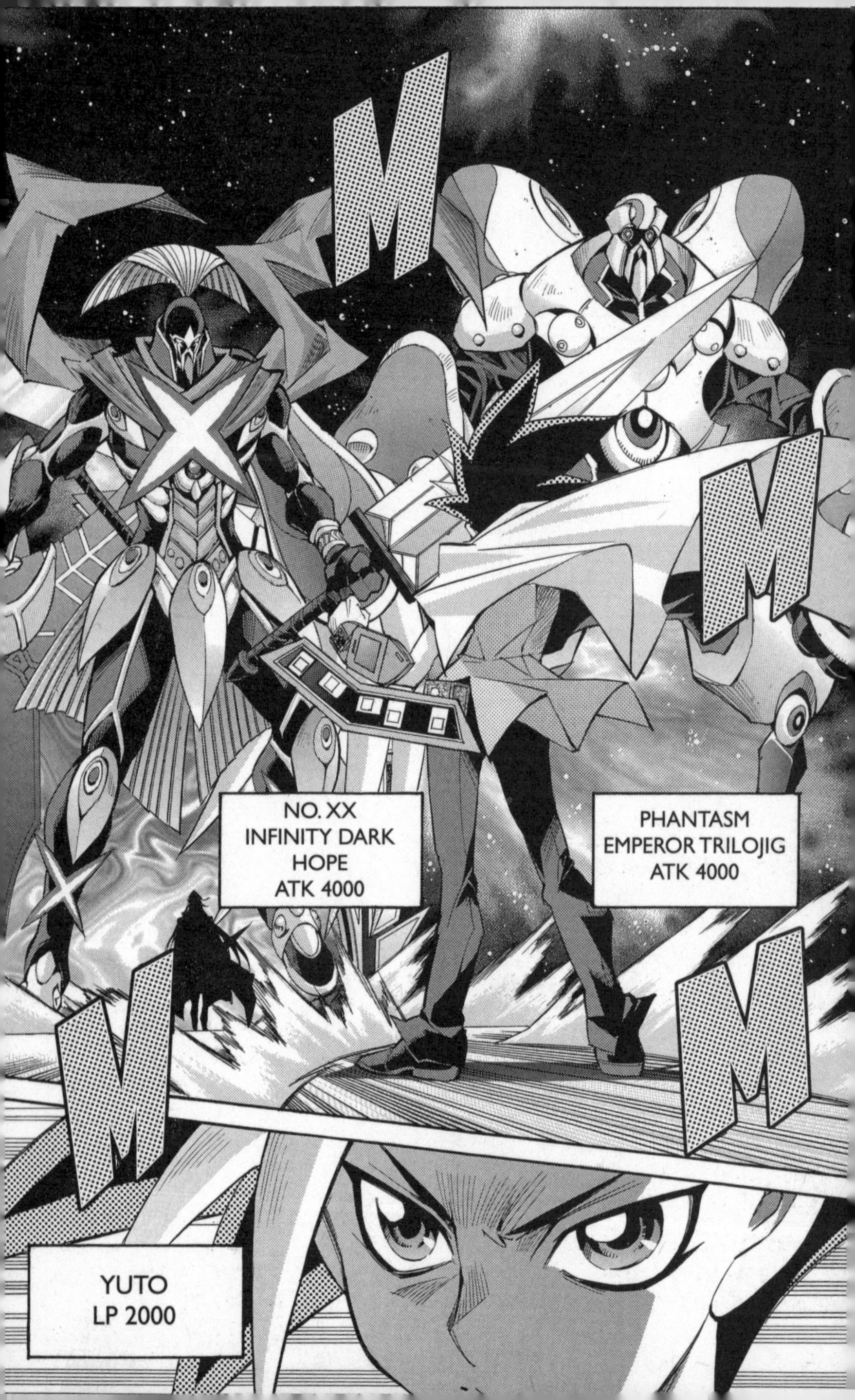
M
M
PHANTASM EMPEROR TRILOJIG ATK 4000
NO. XX INFINITY DARK HOPE ATK 4000
M
M
YUTO LP 2000

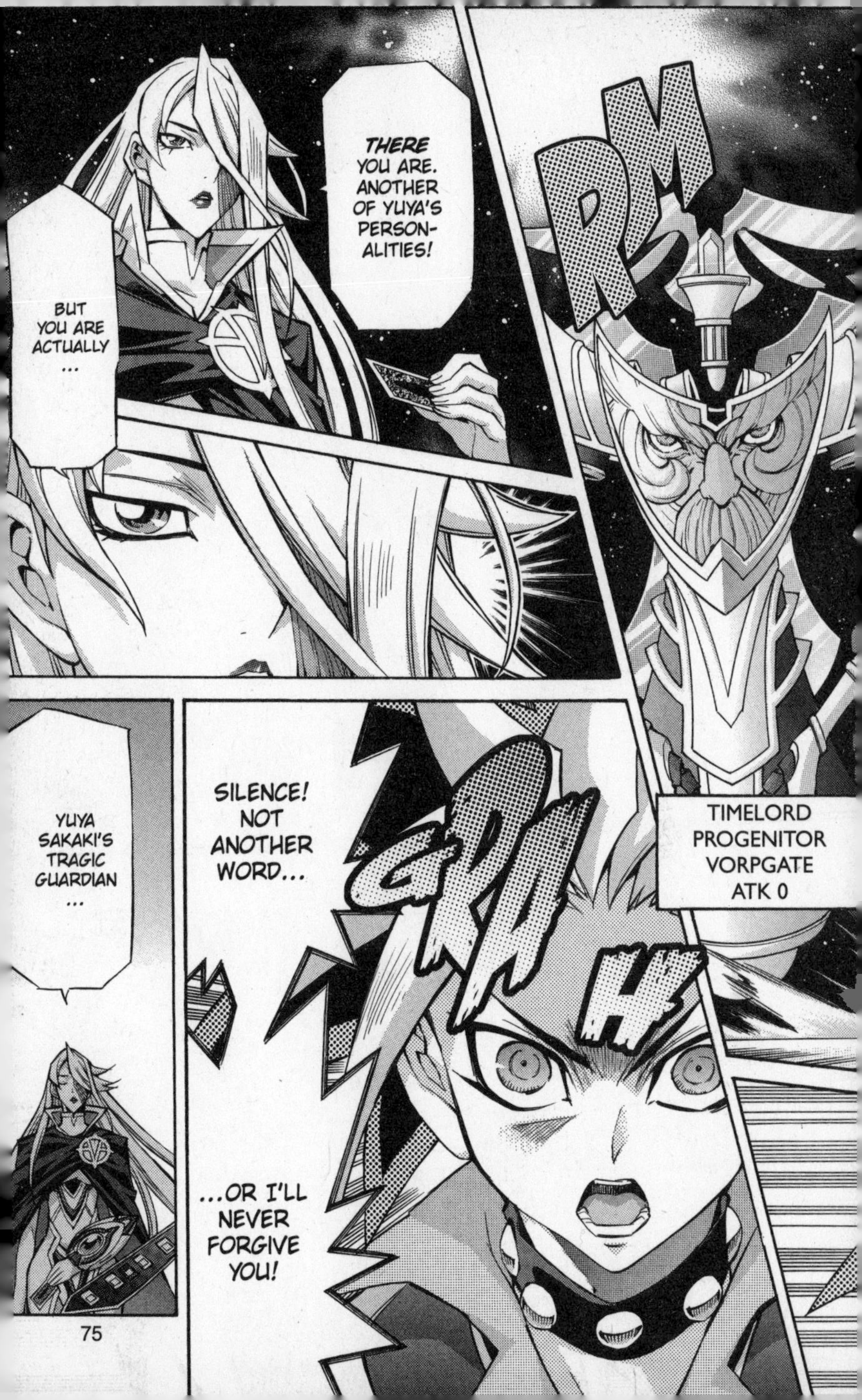

RM
TIMELORD PROGENITOR VORPGATE ATK 0
THERE YOU ARE. ANOTHER OF YUYA'S PERSON-ALITIES!
BUT YOU ARE ACTUALLY ...
SILENCE! NOT ANOTHER WORD...
GRAH
...OR I'LL NEVER FORGIVE YOU!
YUYA SAKAKI'S TRAGIC GUARDIAN ...

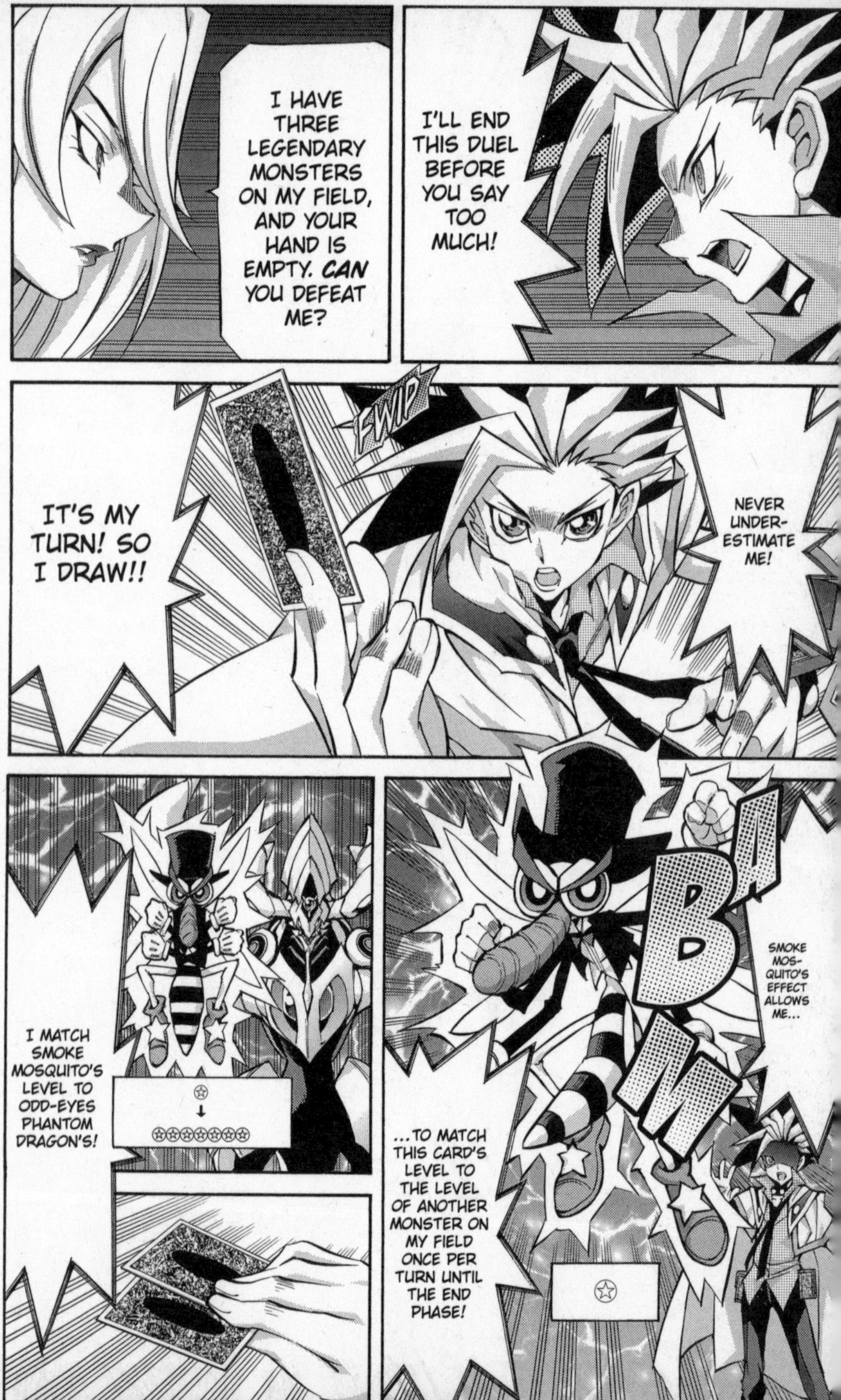
I'LL END THIS DUEL BEFORE YOU SAY TOO MUCH!
I HAVE THREE LEGENDARY MONSTERS ON MY FIELD, AND YOUR HAND IS EMPTY. CAN YOU DEFEAT ME?
FWIP
NEVER UNDER-ESTIMATE ME!
IT'S MY TURN! SO I DRAW!!
BAM
SMOKE MOS-QUITO'S EFFECT ALLOWS ME...
...TO MATCH THIS CARD'S LEVEL TO THE LEVEL OF ANOTHER MONSTER ON MY FIELD ONCE PER TURN UNTIL THE END PHASE!
I MATCH SMOKE MOSQUITO'S LEVEL TO ODD-EYES PHANTOM DRAGON'S!

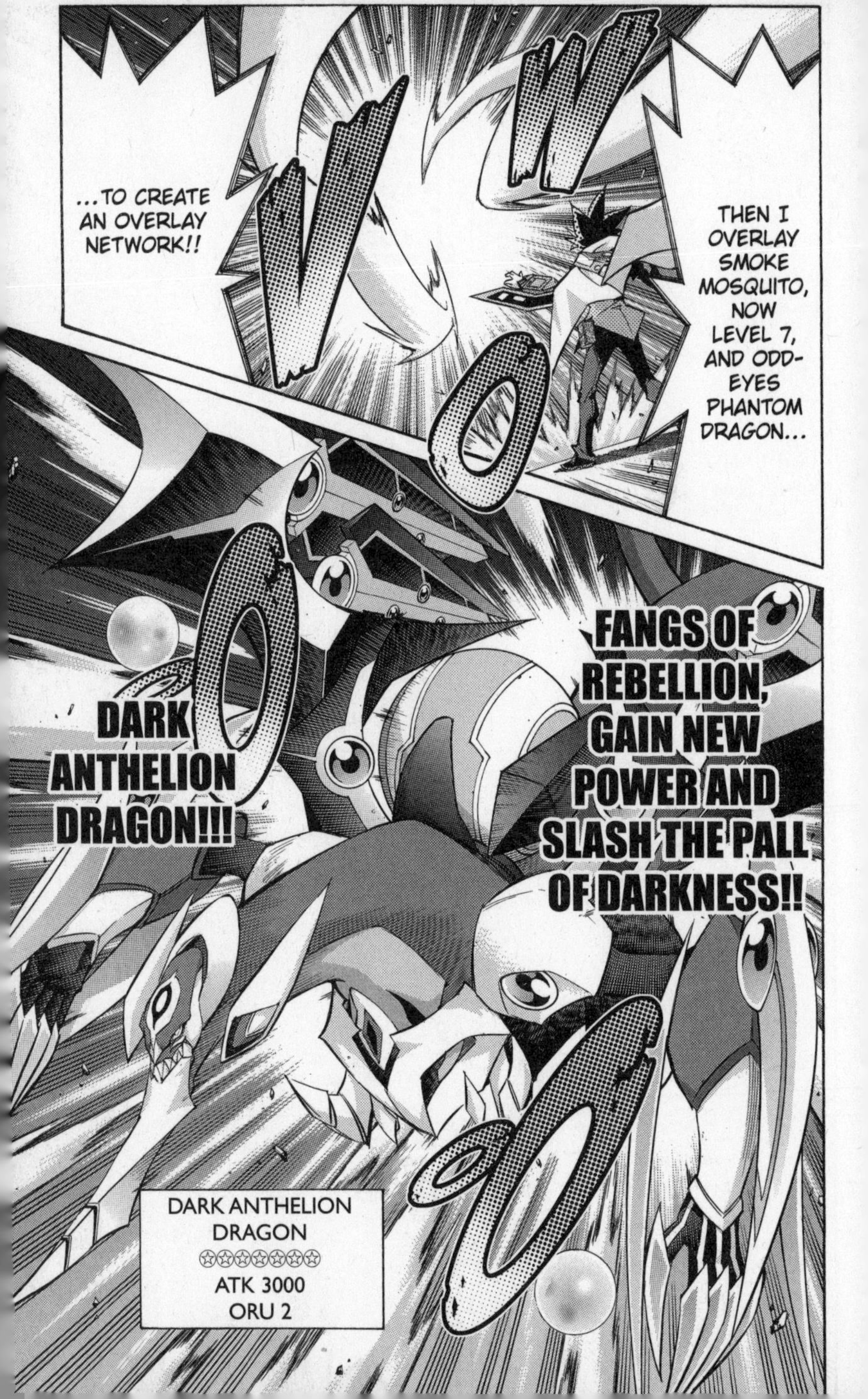
THEN I OVERLAY SMOKE MOSQUITO, NOW LEVEL 7, AND ODD-EYES PHANTOM DRAGON...
...TO CREATE AN OVERLAY NETWORK!!
FANGS OF REBELLION, GAIN NEW POWER AND SLASH THE PALL OF DARKNESS!!
DARK ANTHELION DRAGON!!!
DARK ANTHELION DRAGON
☆☆☆☆☆☆☆
ATK 3000
ORU 2

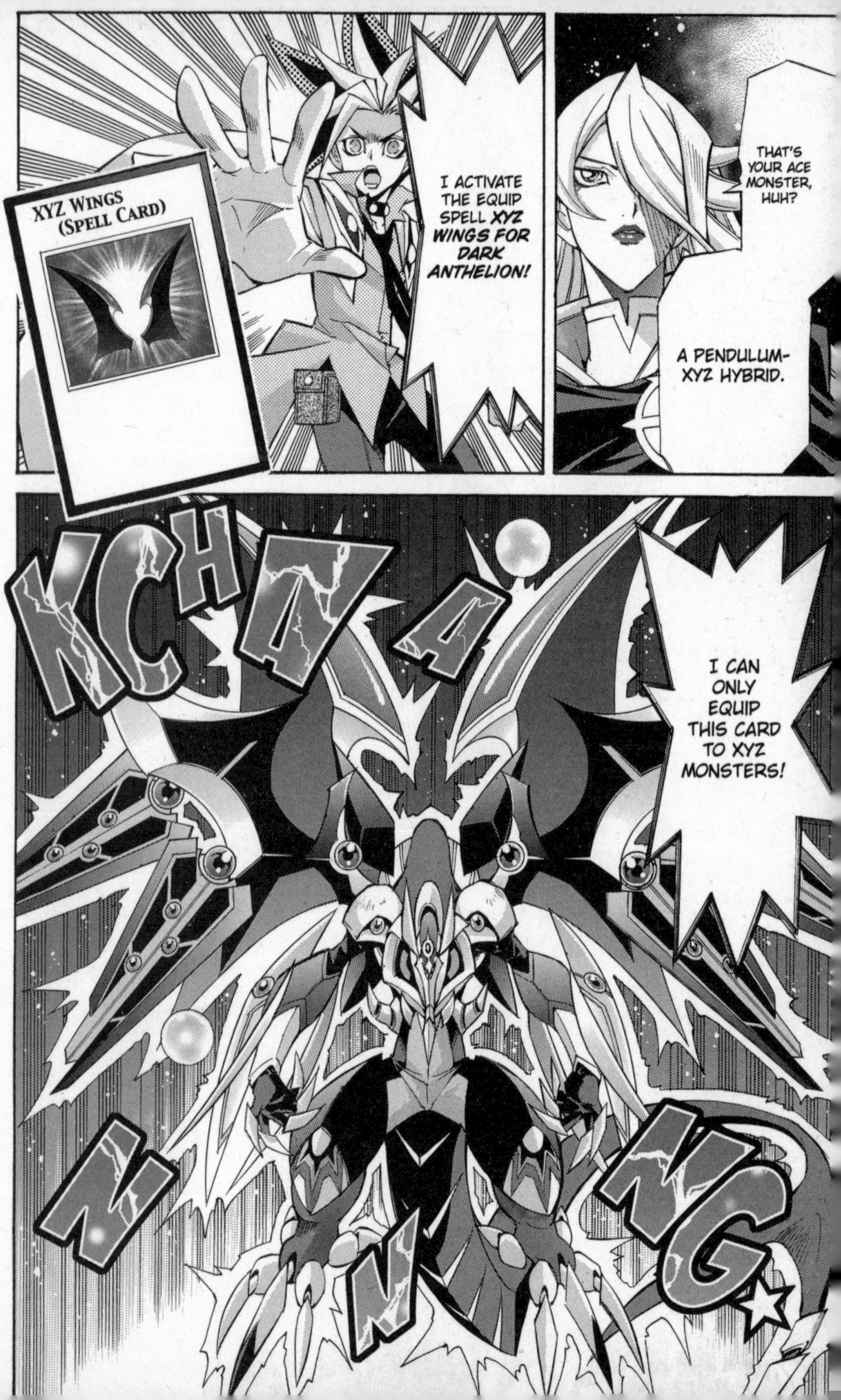
THAT'S YOUR ACE MONSTER, HUH?
A PENDULUM-XYZ HYBRID.
I ACTIVATE THE EQUIP SPELL XYZ WINGS FOR DARK ANTHELION!
XYZ Wings (Spell Card)
I CAN ONLY EQUIP THIS CARD TO XYZ MONSTERS!
KCHAA
NNNG

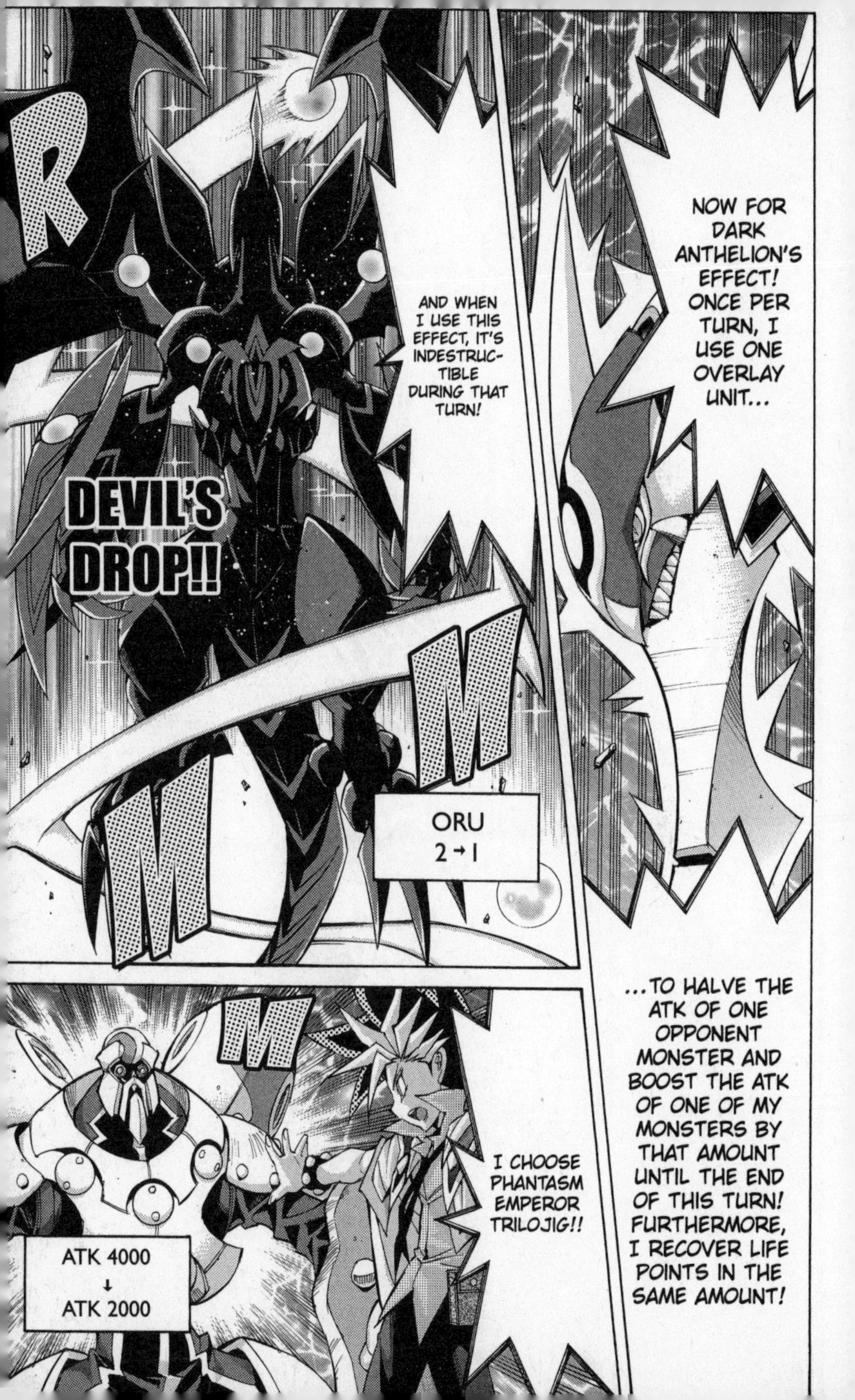
NOW FOR DARK ANTHELION'S EFFECT! ONCE PER TURN, I USE ONE OVERLAY UNIT...
...TO HALVE THE ATK OF ONE OPPONENT MONSTER AND BOOST THE ATK OF ONE OF MY MONSTERS BY THAT AMOUNT UNTIL THE END OF THIS TURN! FURTHERMORE, I RECOVER LIFE POINTS IN THE SAME AMOUNT!
AND WHEN I USE THIS EFFECT, IT'S INDESTRUC-TIBLE DURING THAT TURN!
DEVIL'S DROP!!
R
M
M
M
ORU 2→1
I CHOOSE PHANTASM EMPEROR TRILOJIG!!
M
ATK 4000 ↓ ATK 2000

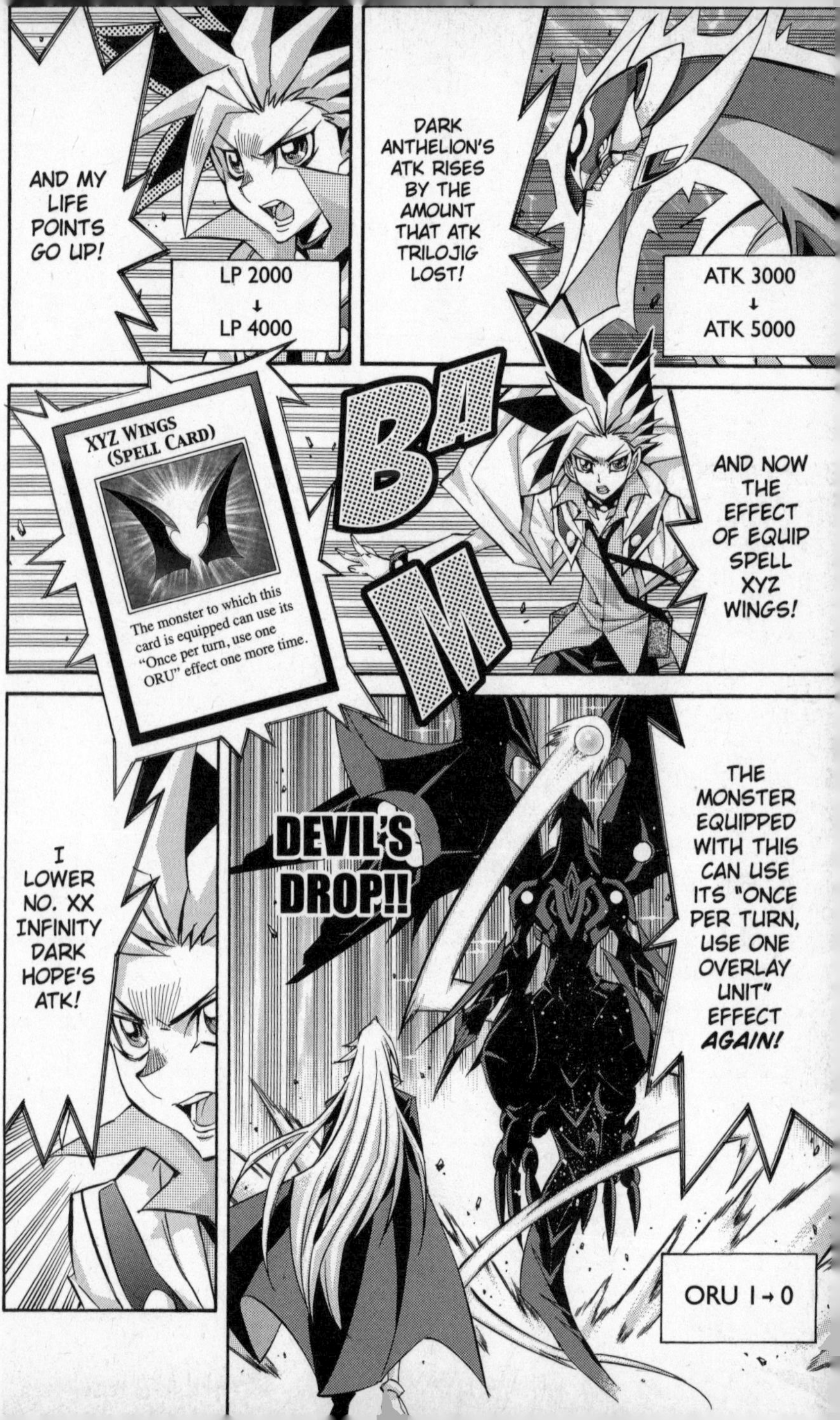
DARK ANTHELION'S ATK RISES BY THE AMOUNT THAT ATK TRILOJIG LOST!
ATK 3000 ↓ ATK 5000
AND MY LIFE POINTS GO UP!
LP 2000 ↓ LP 4000
AND NOW THE EFFECT OF EQUIP SPELL XYZ WINGS!
BAM
XYZ WINGS (SPELL CARD)
The monster to which this card is equipped can use its "Once per turn, use one ORU" effect one more time.
THE MONSTER EQUIPPED WITH THIS CAN USE ITS "ONCE PER TURN, USE ONE OVERLAY UNIT" EFFECT AGAIN!
DEVIL'S DROP!!
ORU 1→0
I LOWER NO. XX INFINITY DARK HOPE'S ATK!

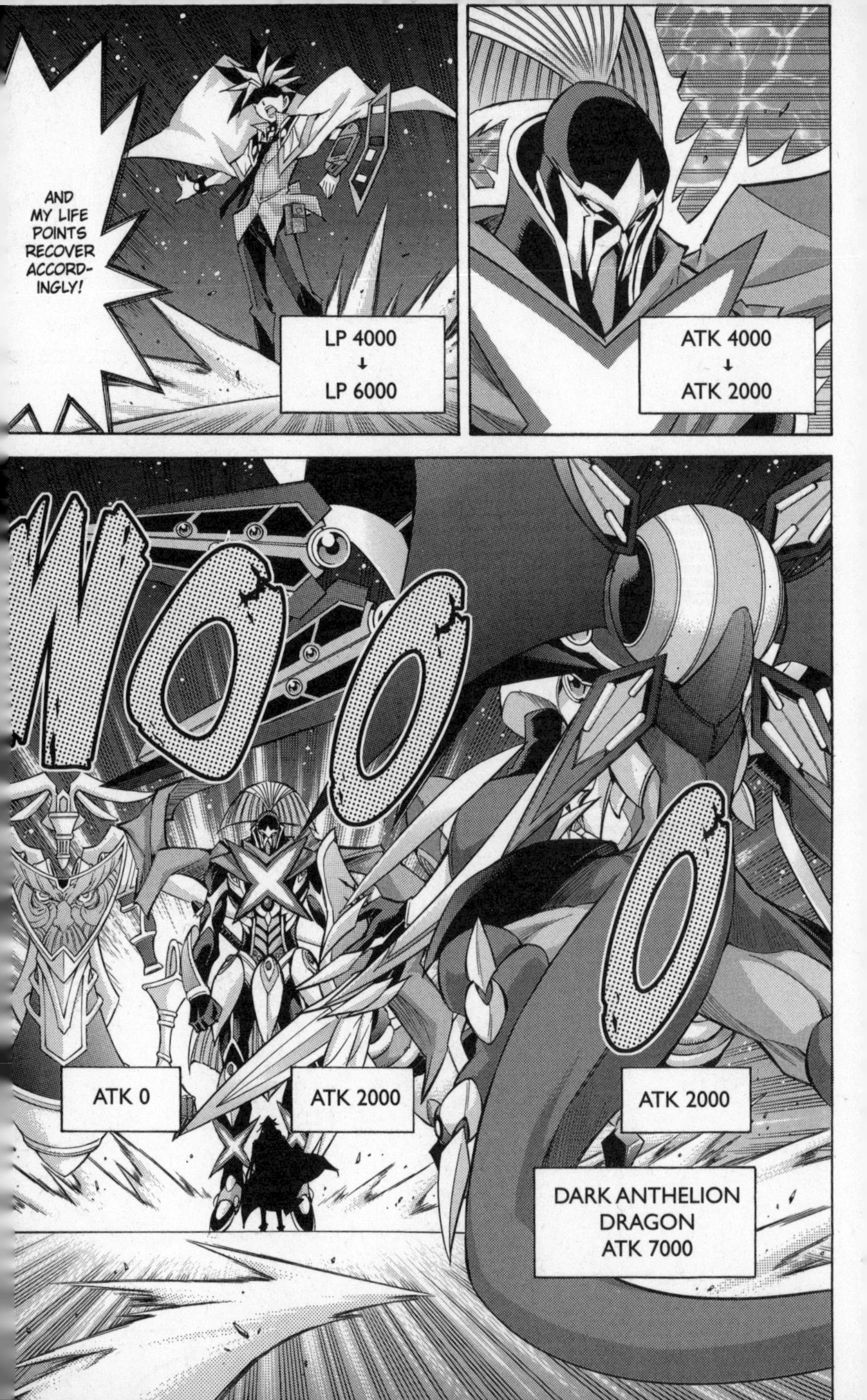
ATK 4000
↓
ATK 2000
AND MY LIFE POINTS RECOVER ACCORD-INGLY!
LP 4000
↓
LP 6000
WOOO
ATK 2000
DARK ANTHELION DRAGON ATK 7000
ATK 2000
ATK 0

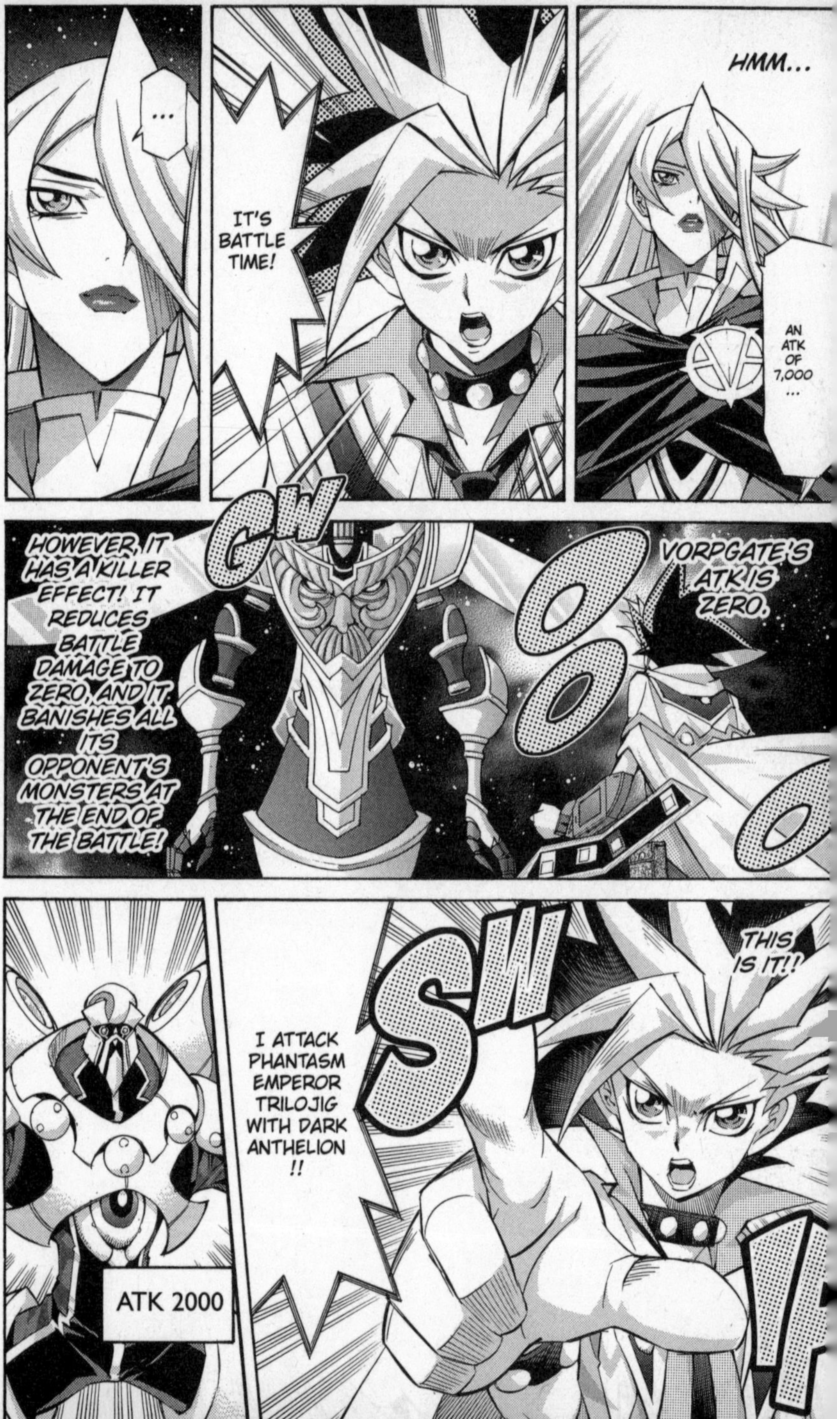
HMM...
AN ATK OF 7,000 ...
IT'S BATTLE TIME!
...
GW
VORPGATE'S ATK IS ZERO.
HOWEVER, IT HAS A KILLER EFFECT! IT REDUCES BATTLE DAMAGE TO ZERO, AND IT BANISHES ALL ITS OPPONENT'S MONSTERS AT THE END OF THE BATTLE!
THIS IS IT!!
SW
I ATTACK PHANTASM EMPEROR TRILOJIG WITH DARK ANTHELION !!
ATK 2000

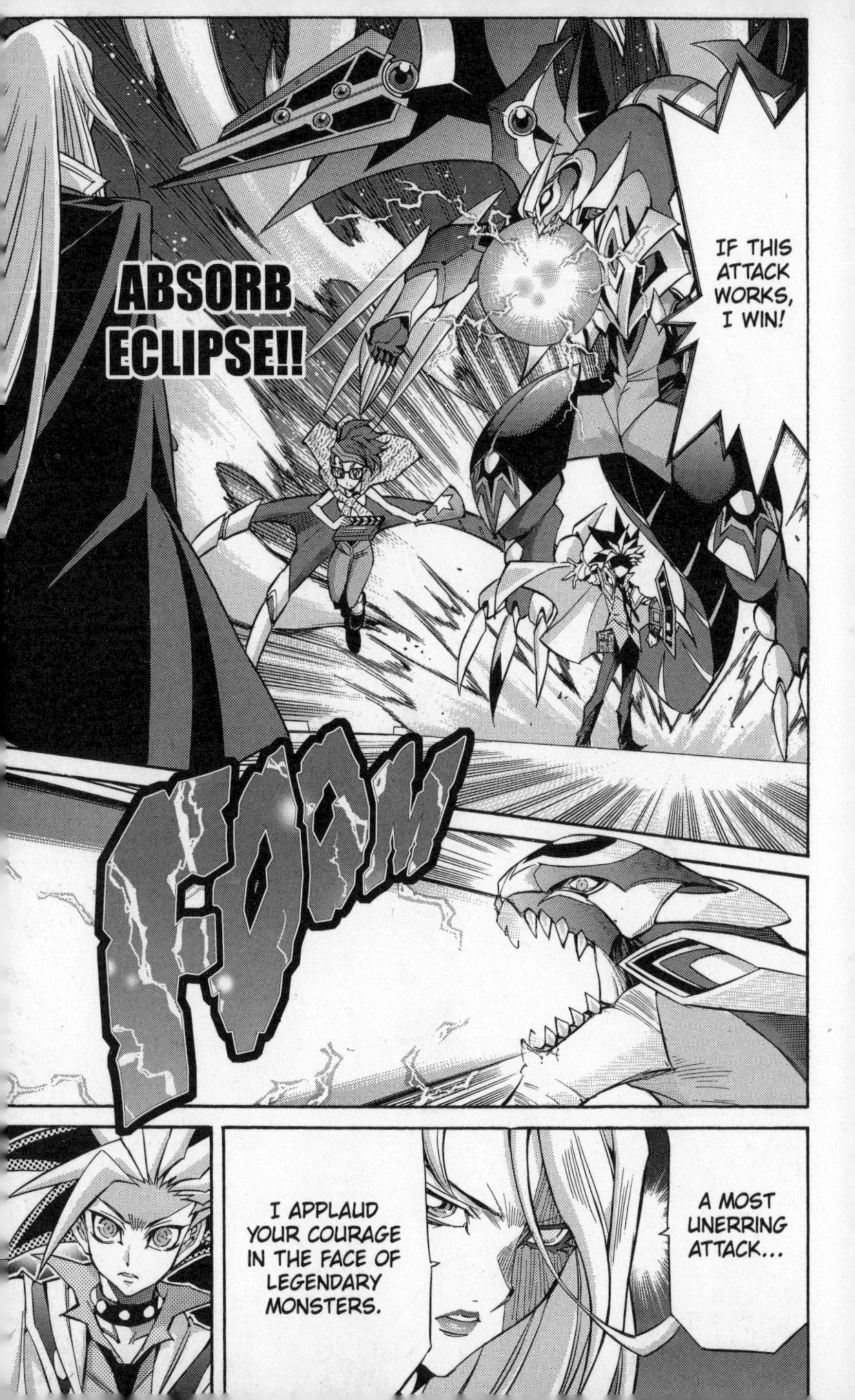
IF THIS ATTACK WORKS, I WIN!
ABSORB ECLIPSE!!
FOOM
A MOST UNERRING ATTACK...
I APPLAUD YOUR COURAGE IN THE FACE OF LEGENDARY MONSTERS.

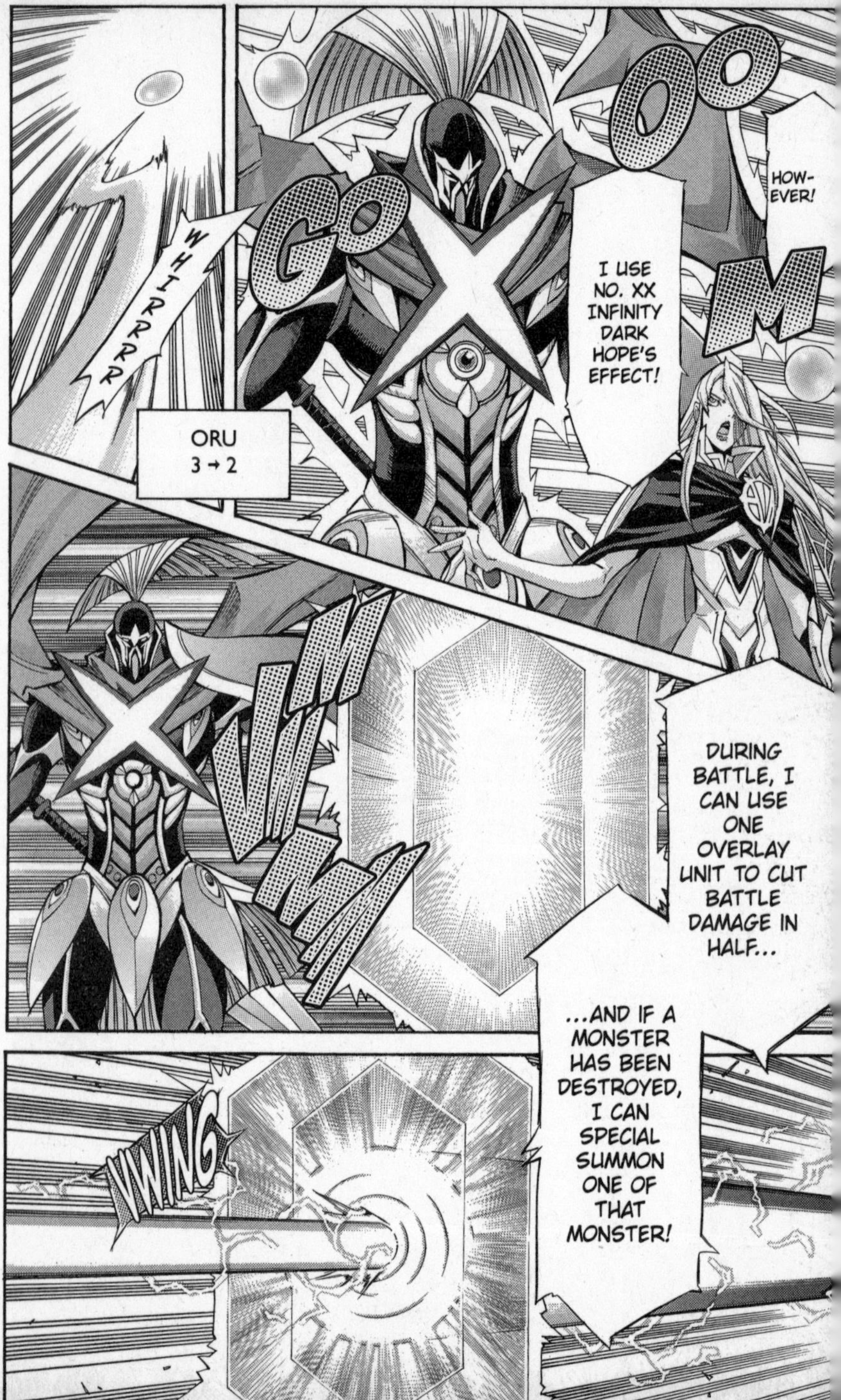
HOW-EVER!
GOOOM
I USE NO. XX INFINITY DARK HOPE'S EFFECT!
WHIRRRR
ORU 3→2
DURING BATTLE, I CAN USE ONE OVERLAY UNIT TO CUT BATTLE DAMAGE IN HALF...
VMM
VMM
...AND IF A MONSTER HAS BEEN DESTROYED, I CAN SPECIAL SUMMON ONE OF THAT MONSTER!
VWING

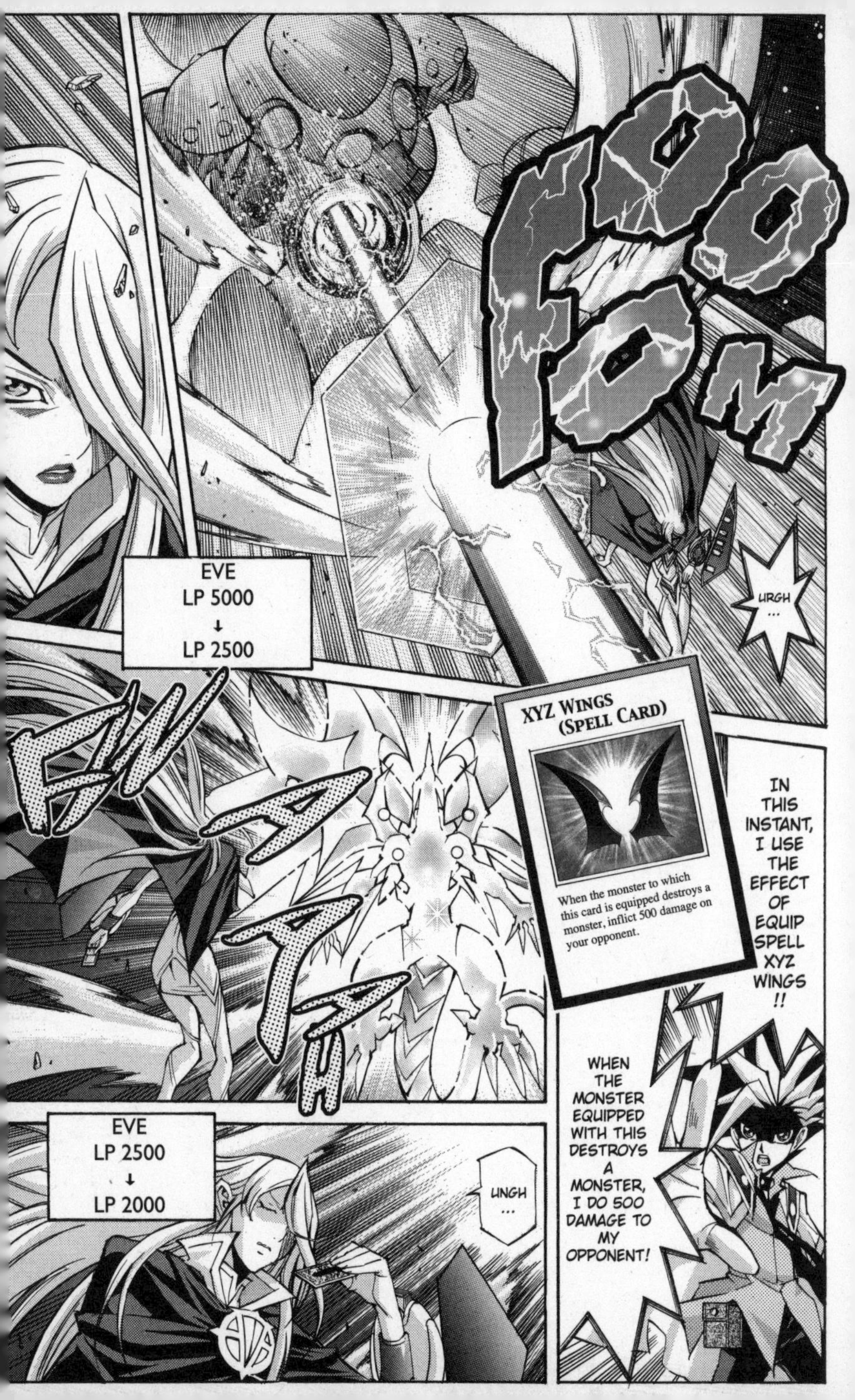
KOOOM
URGH ...
EVE
LP 5000
↓
LP 2500
IN THIS INSTANT, I USE THE EFFECT OF EQUIP SPELL XYZ WINGS!!
XYZ WINGS (SPELL CARD)
When the monster to which this card is equipped destroys a monster, inflict 500 damage on your opponent.
FWAAAAH
WHEN THE MONSTER EQUIPPED WITH THIS DESTROYS A MONSTER, I DO 500 DAMAGE TO MY OPPONENT!
UNGH ...
EVE
LP 2500
↓
LP 2000

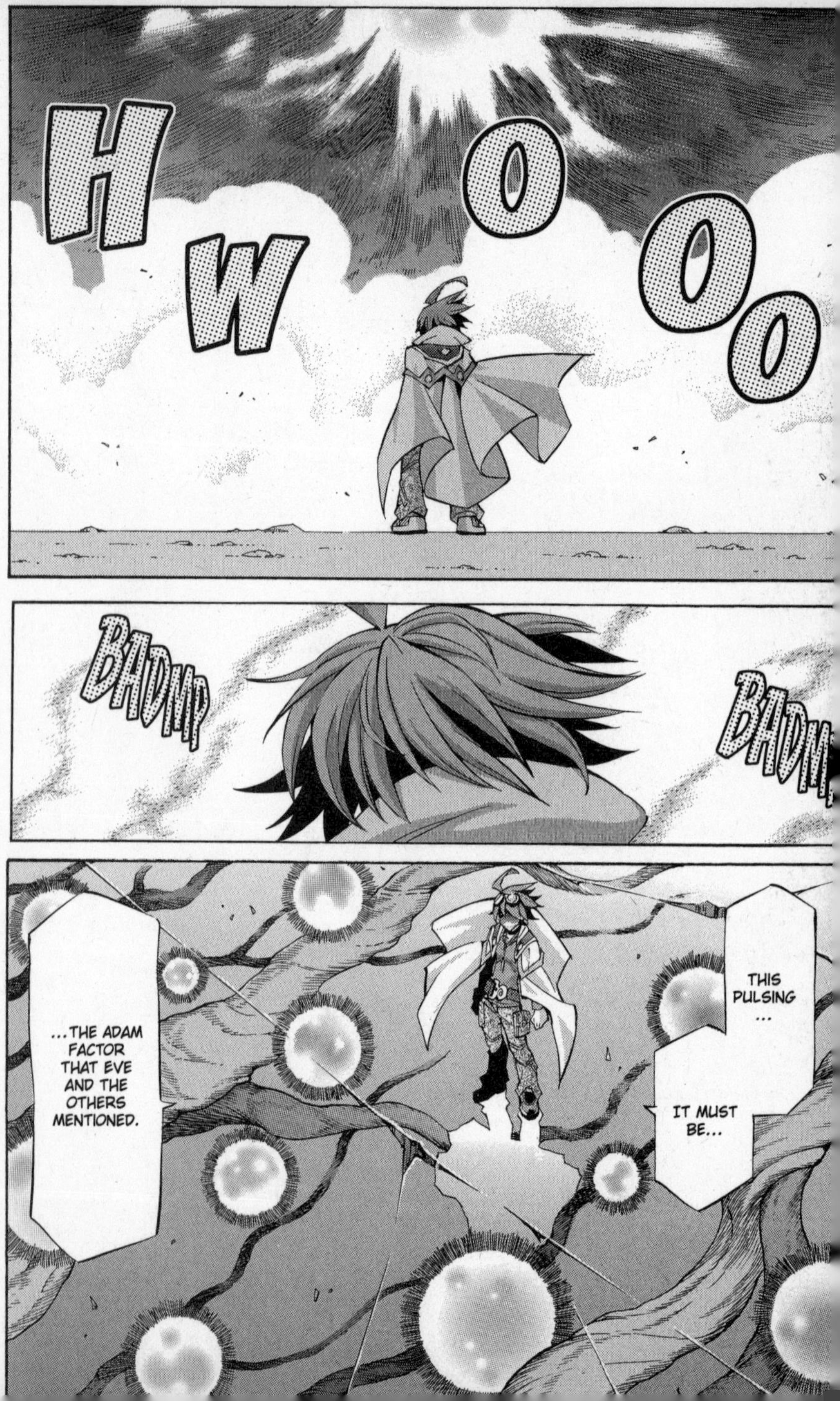
HWOOOO
BADM
BADMP
THIS PULSING ...
IT MUST BE...
...THE ADAM FACTOR THAT EVE AND THE OTHERS MENTIONED.

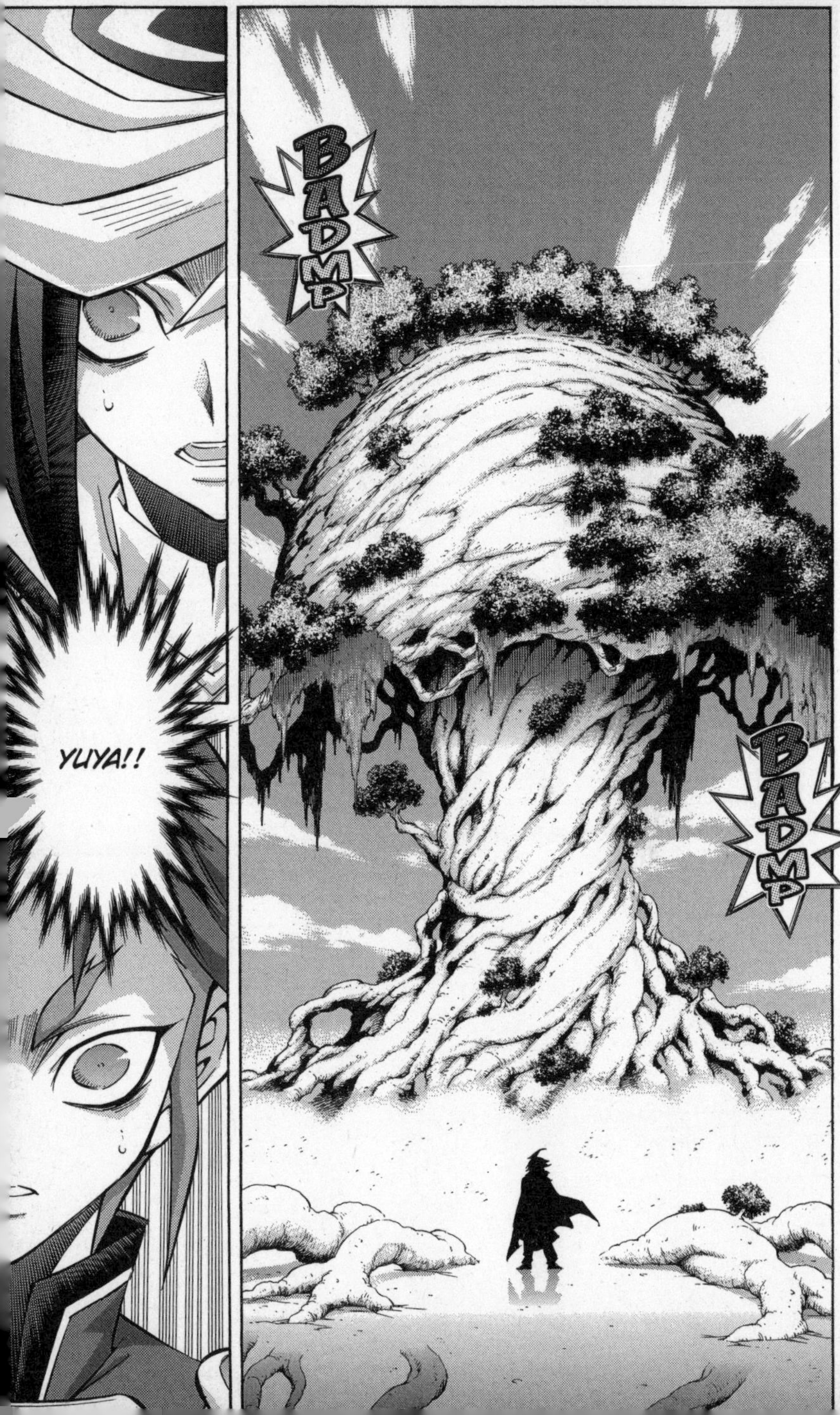
BADMP
BADMP
YUYA!!

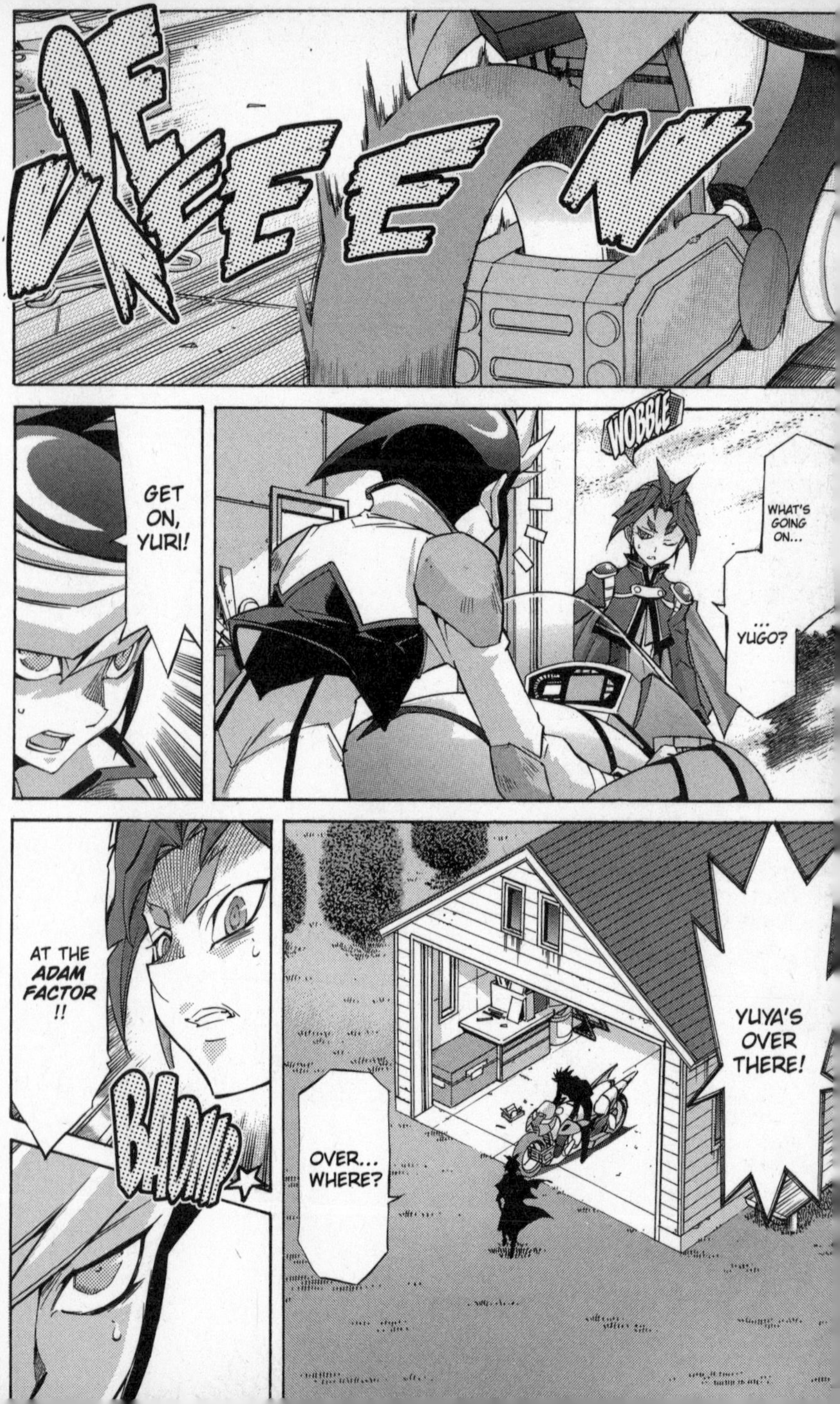
VREEEN
WOBBLE
WHAT'S GOING ON...
... YUGO?
GET ON, YURI!
YUYA'S OVER THERE!
OVER... WHERE?
AT THE ADAM FACTOR!!
BADMP

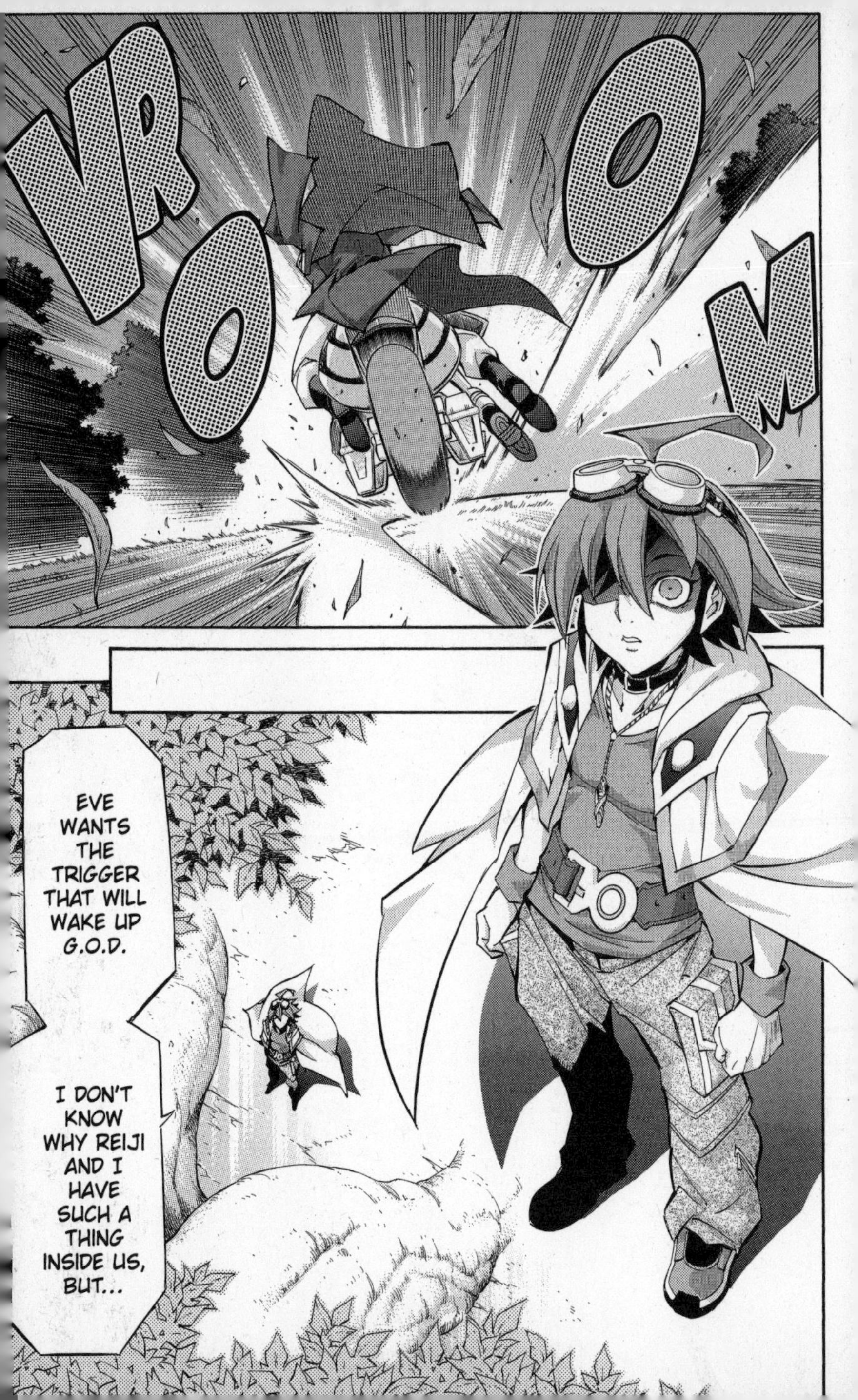
VROOOM
EVE WANTS THE TRIGGER THAT WILL WAKE UP G.O.D.
I DON'T KNOW WHY REIJI AND I HAVE SUCH A THING INSIDE US, BUT...

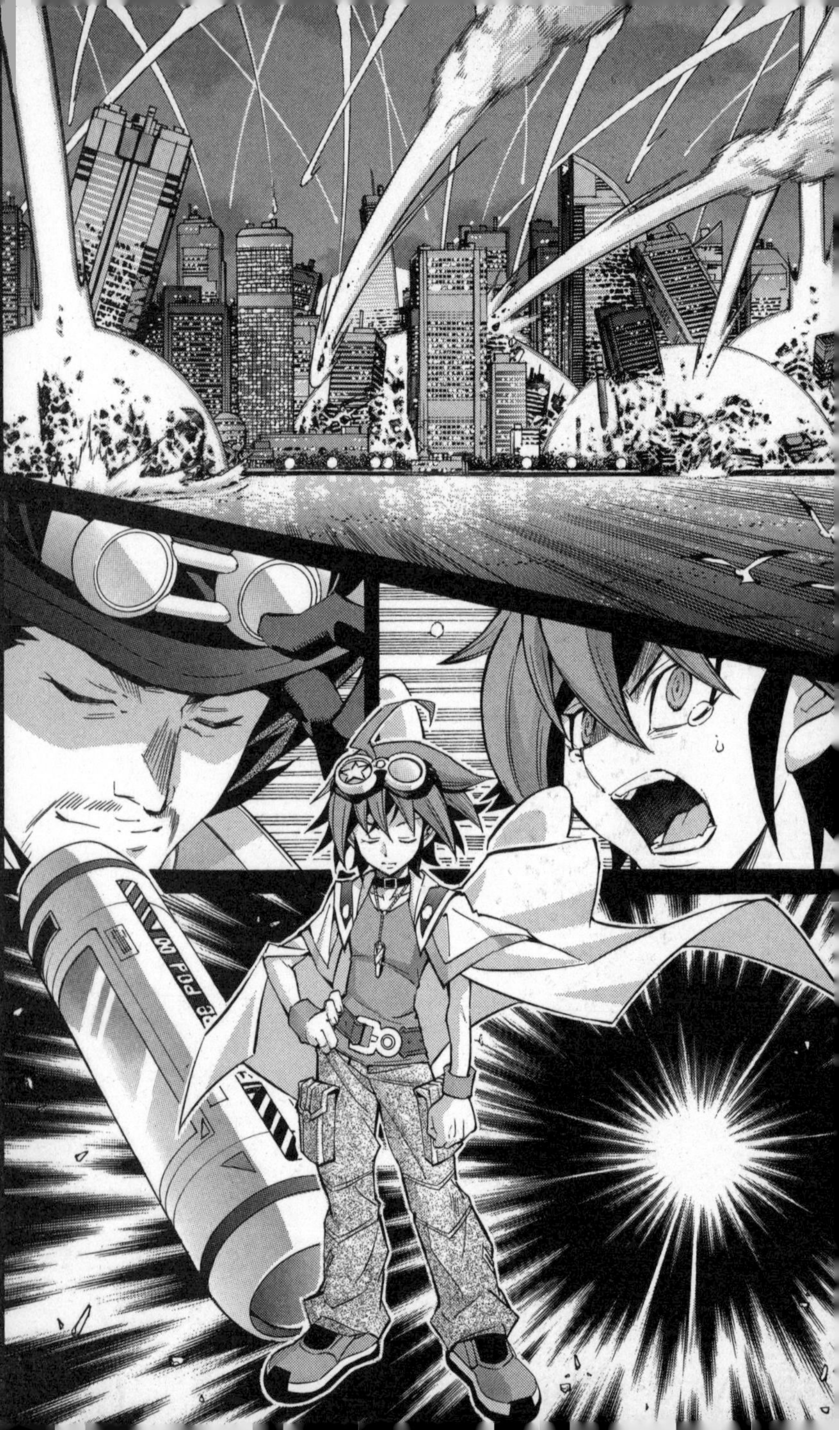

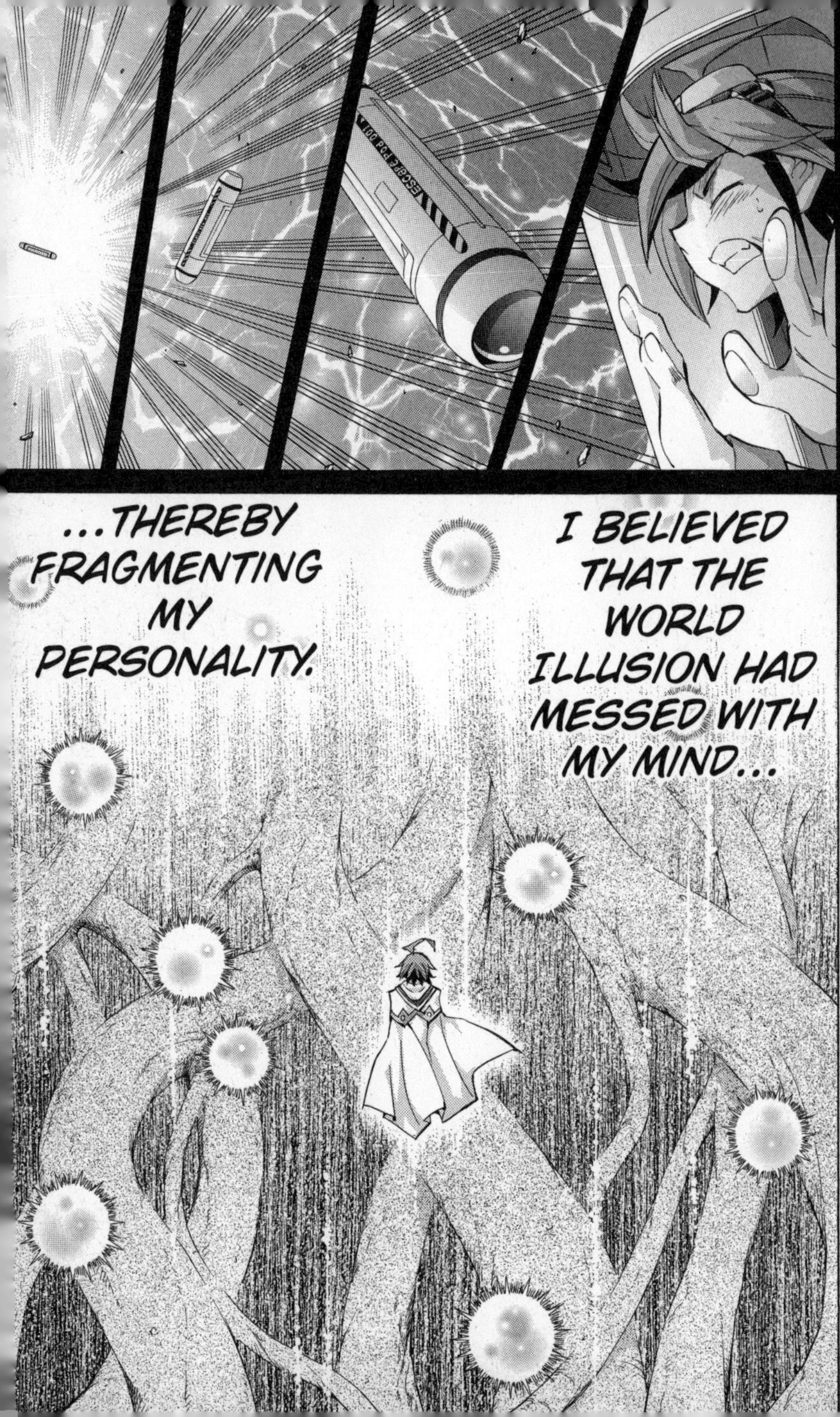
I BELIEVED THAT THE WORLD ILLUSION HAD MESSED WITH MY MIND...
...THEREBY FRAGMENTING MY PERSONALITY.

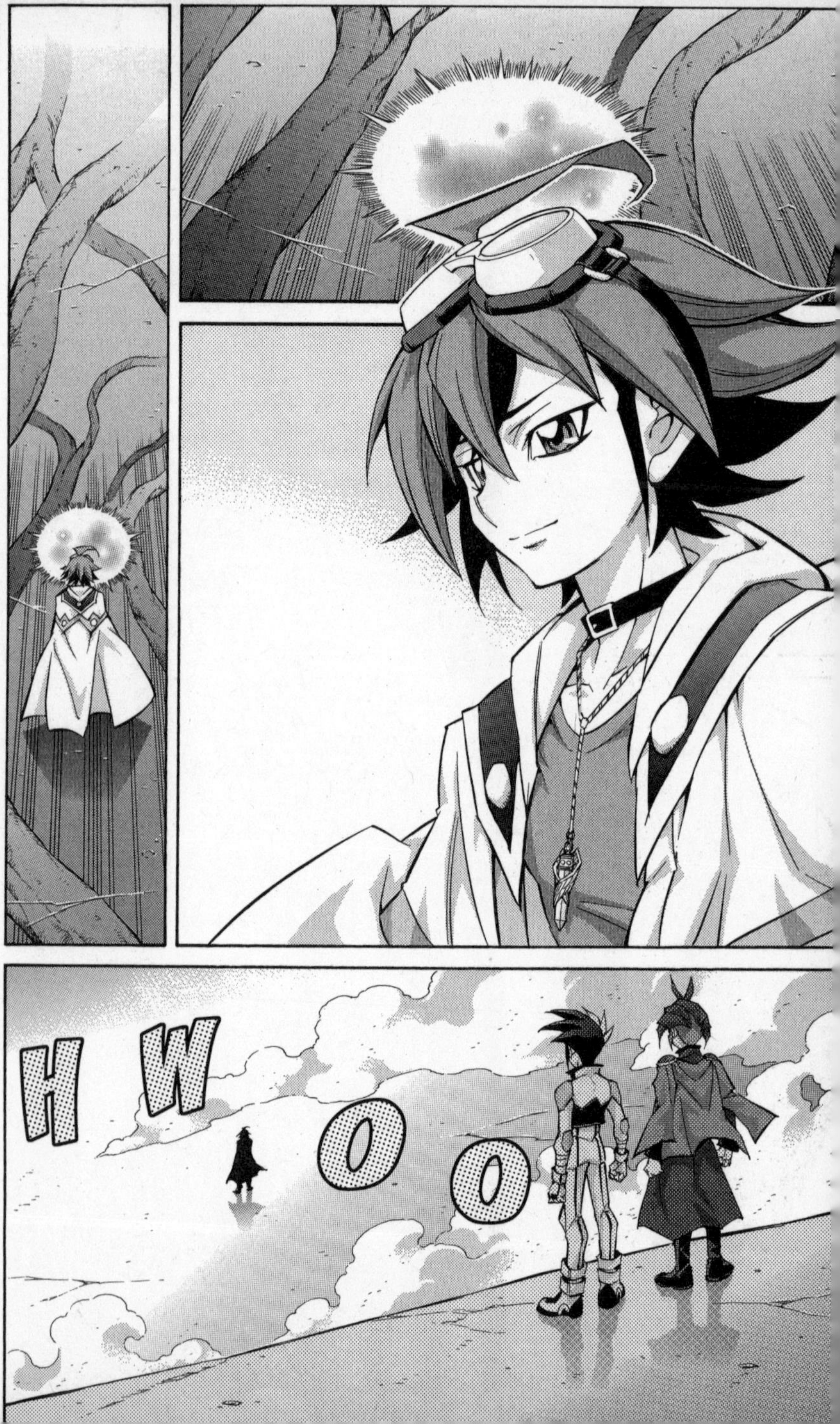
HWOO

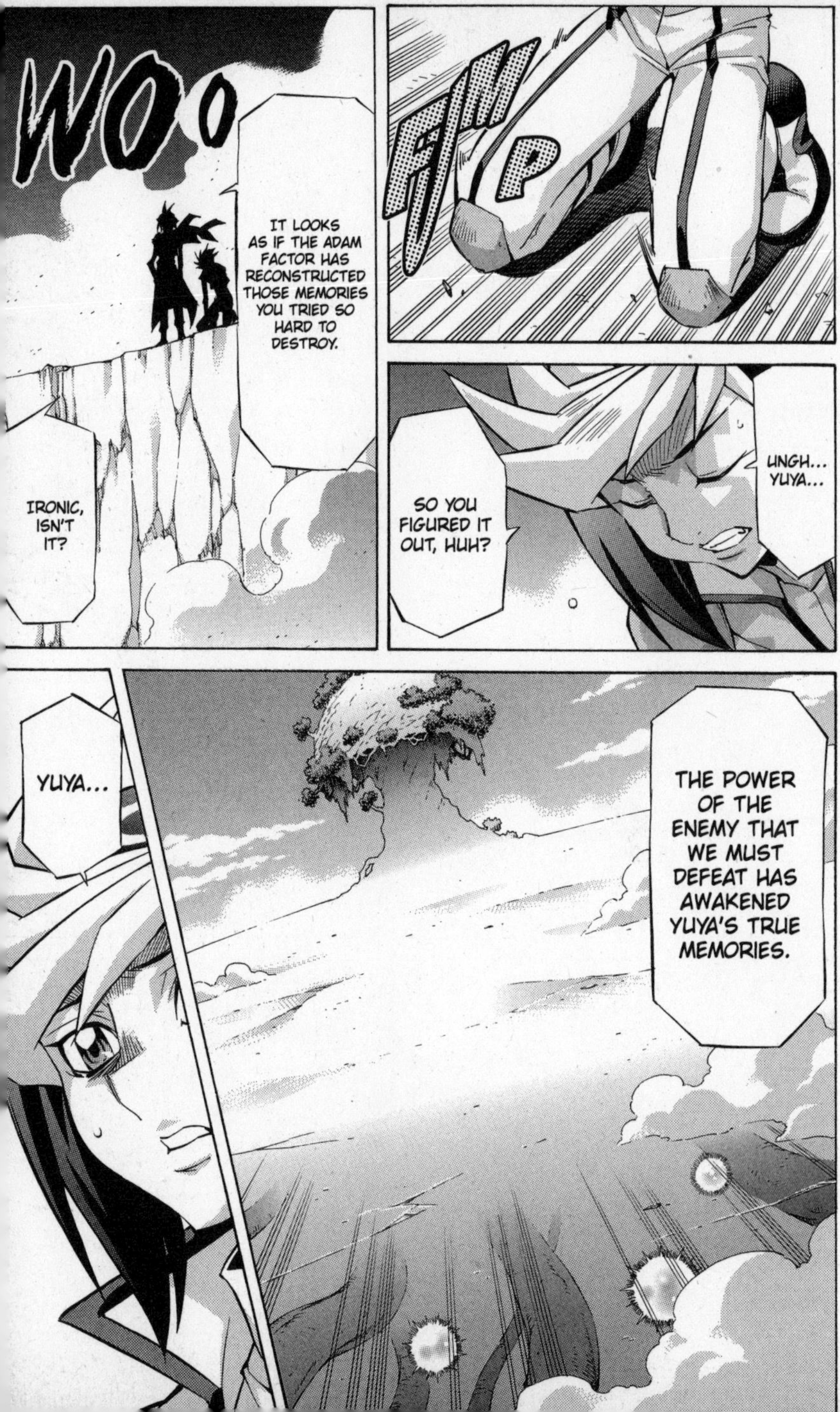
FMP
UNGH... YUYA...
SO YOU FIGURED IT OUT, HUH?
WOO
IT LOOKS AS IF THE ADAM FACTOR HAS RECONSTRUCTED THOSE MEMORIES YOU TRIED SO HARD TO DESTROY.
IRONIC, ISN'T IT?
THE POWER OF THE ENEMY THAT WE MUST DEFEAT HAS AWAKENED YUYA'S TRUE MEMORIES.
YUYA...

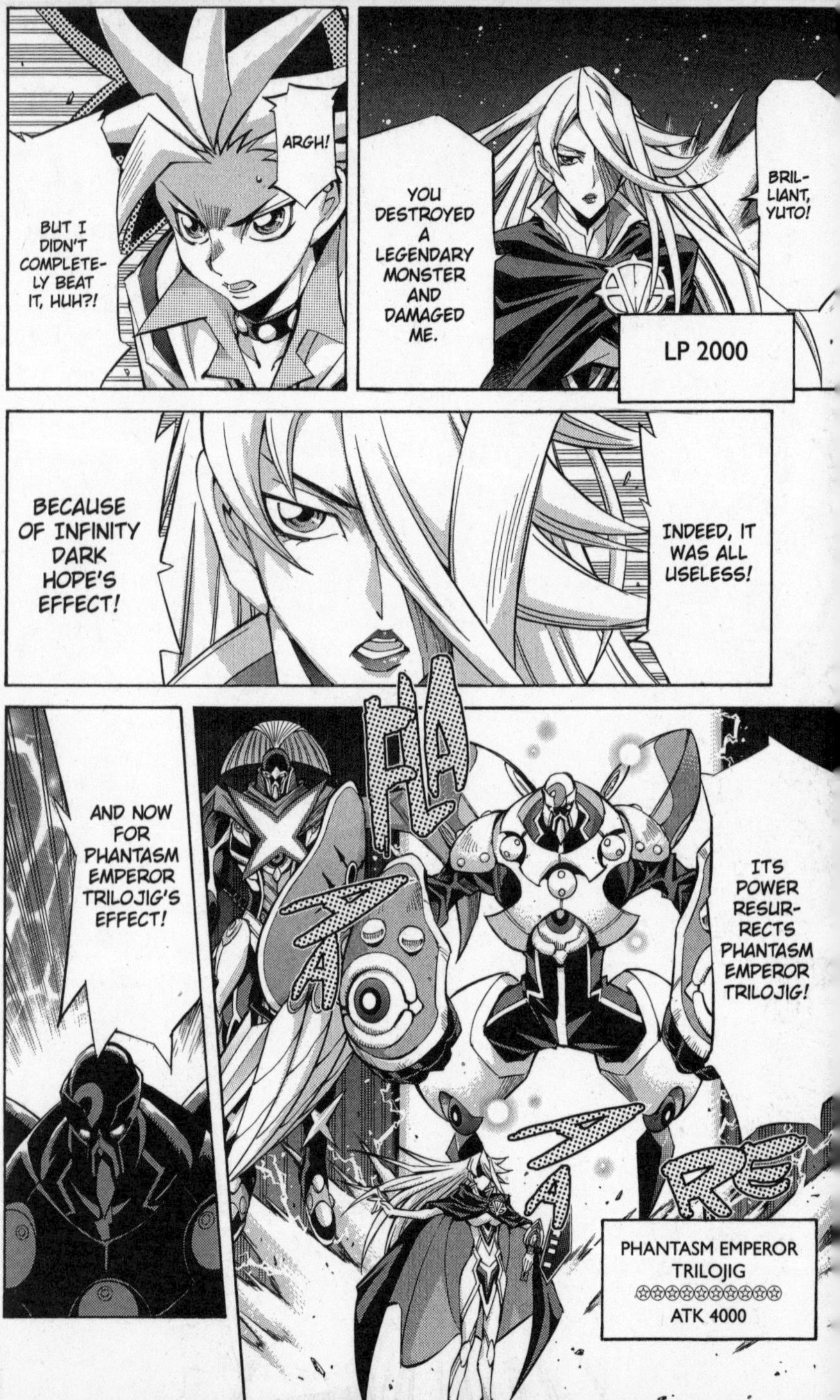
BRIL-LIANT, YUTO!
YOU DESTROYED A LEGENDARY MONSTER AND DAMAGED ME.
LP 2000
ARGH!
BUT I DIDN'T COMPLETE-LY BEAT IT, HUH?!
INDEED, IT WAS ALL USELESS!
BECAUSE OF INFINITY DARK HOPE'S EFFECT!
ITS POWER RESUR-RECTS PHANTASM EMPEROR TRILOJIG!
PHANTASM EMPEROR TRILOJIG
ATK 4000
AND NOW FOR PHANTASM EMPEROR TRILOJIG'S EFFECT!

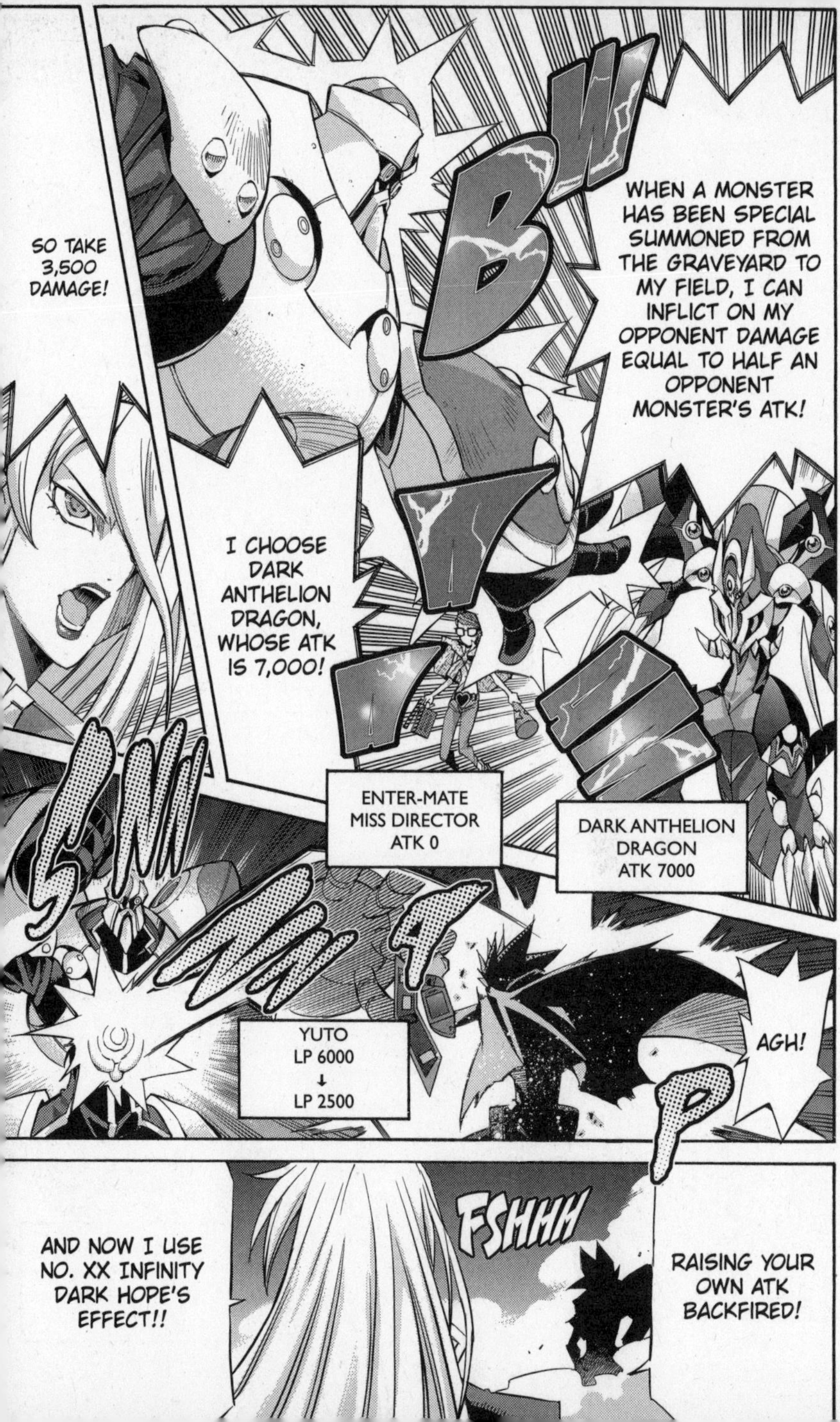
WHEN A MONSTER HAS BEEN SPECIAL SUMMONED FROM THE GRAVEYARD TO MY FIELD, I CAN INFLICT ON MY OPPONENT DAMAGE EQUAL TO HALF AN OPPONENT MONSTER'S ATK!
I CHOOSE DARK ANTHELION DRAGON, WHOSE ATK IS 7,000!
SO TAKE 3,500 DAMAGE!
DARK ANTHELION DRAGON ATK 7000
ENTER-MATE MISS DIRECTOR ATK 0
AGH!
YUTO LP 6000 ↓ LP 2500
RAISING YOUR OWN ATK BACKFIRED!
FSHHH
AND NOW I USE NO. XX INFINITY DARK HOPE'S EFFECT!!

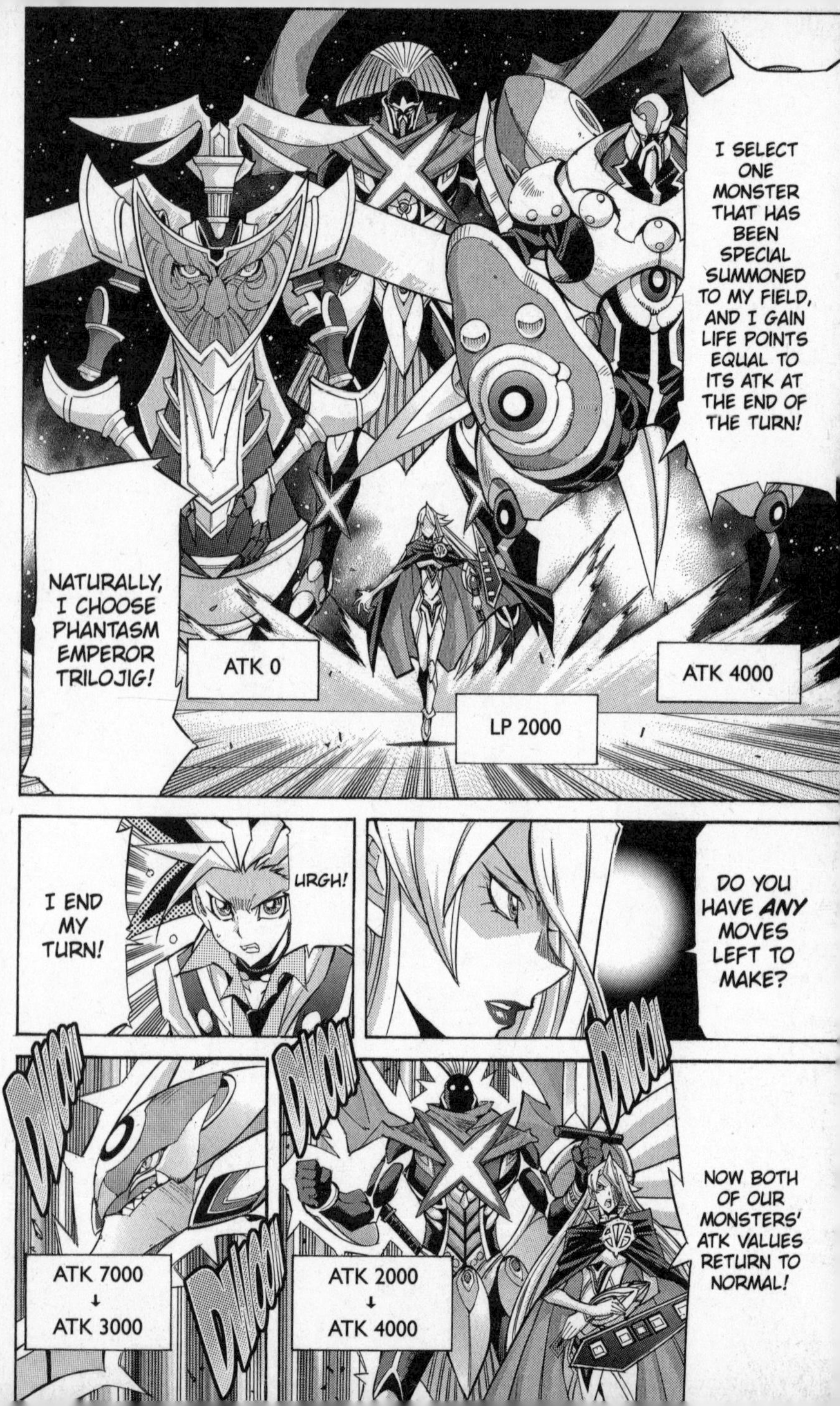
I SELECT ONE MONSTER THAT HAS BEEN SPECIAL SUMMONED TO MY FIELD, AND I GAIN LIFE POINTS EQUAL TO ITS ATK AT THE END OF THE TURN!
ATK 4000
NATURALLY, I CHOOSE PHANTASM EMPEROR TRILOJIG!
ATK 0
LP 2000
DO YOU HAVE ANY MOVES LEFT TO MAKE?
URGH!
I END MY TURN!
NOW BOTH OF OUR MONSTERS' ATK VALUES RETURN TO NORMAL!
ATK 2000 ↓ ATK 4000
ATK 7000 ↓ ATK 3000

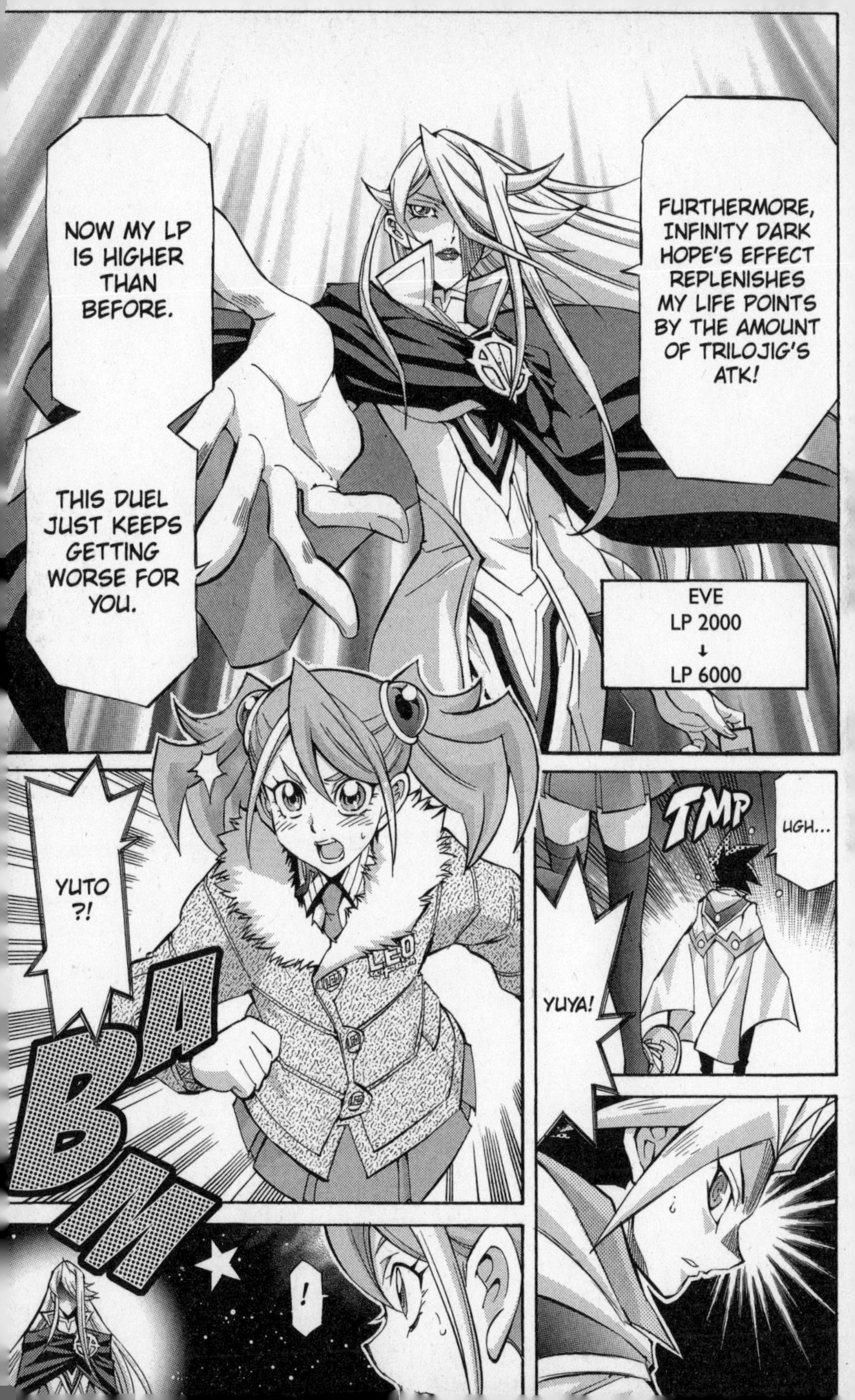
FURTHERMORE, INFINITY DARK HOPE'S EFFECT REPLENISHES MY LIFE POINTS BY THE AMOUNT OF TRILOJIG'S ATK!
NOW MY LP IS HIGHER THAN BEFORE.
THIS DUEL JUST KEEPS GETTING WORSE FOR YOU.
EVE LP 2000 ↓ LP 6000
TMP
UGH...
YUYA!
YUTO ?!
BAM
!

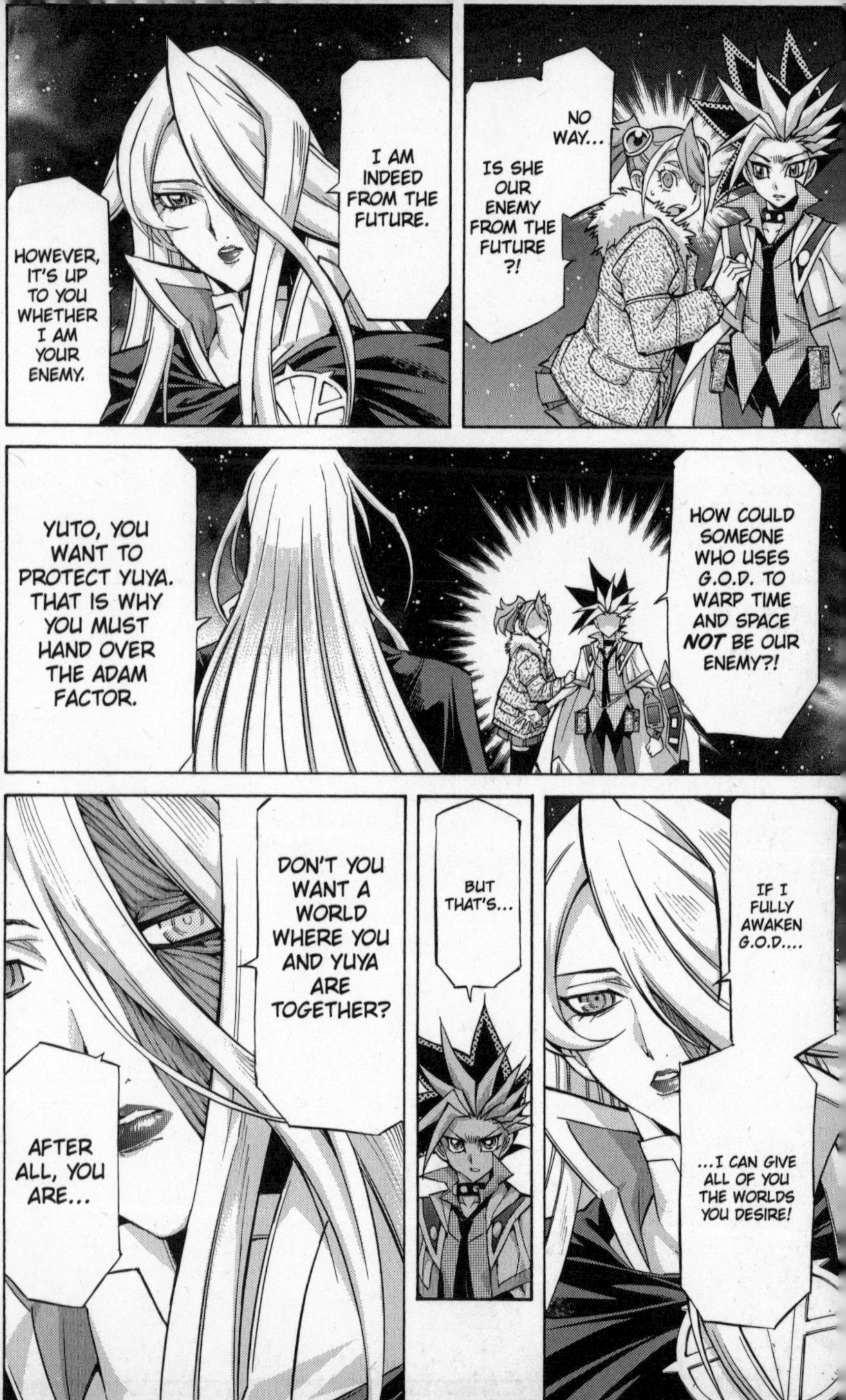
NO WAY...
IS SHE OUR ENEMY FROM THE FUTURE?!
I AM INDEED FROM THE FUTURE.
HOWEVER, IT'S UP TO YOU WHETHER I AM YOUR ENEMY.
HOW COULD SOMEONE WHO USES G.O.D. TO WARP TIME AND SPACE ***NOT*** BE OUR ENEMY?!
YUTO, YOU WANT TO PROTECT YUYA. THAT IS WHY YOU MUST HAND OVER THE ADAM FACTOR.
IF I FULLY AWAKEN G.O.D....
...I CAN GIVE ALL OF YOU THE WORLDS YOU DESIRE!
BUT THAT'S...
DON'T YOU WANT A WORLD WHERE YOU AND YUYA ARE TOGETHER?
AFTER ALL, YOU ARE...

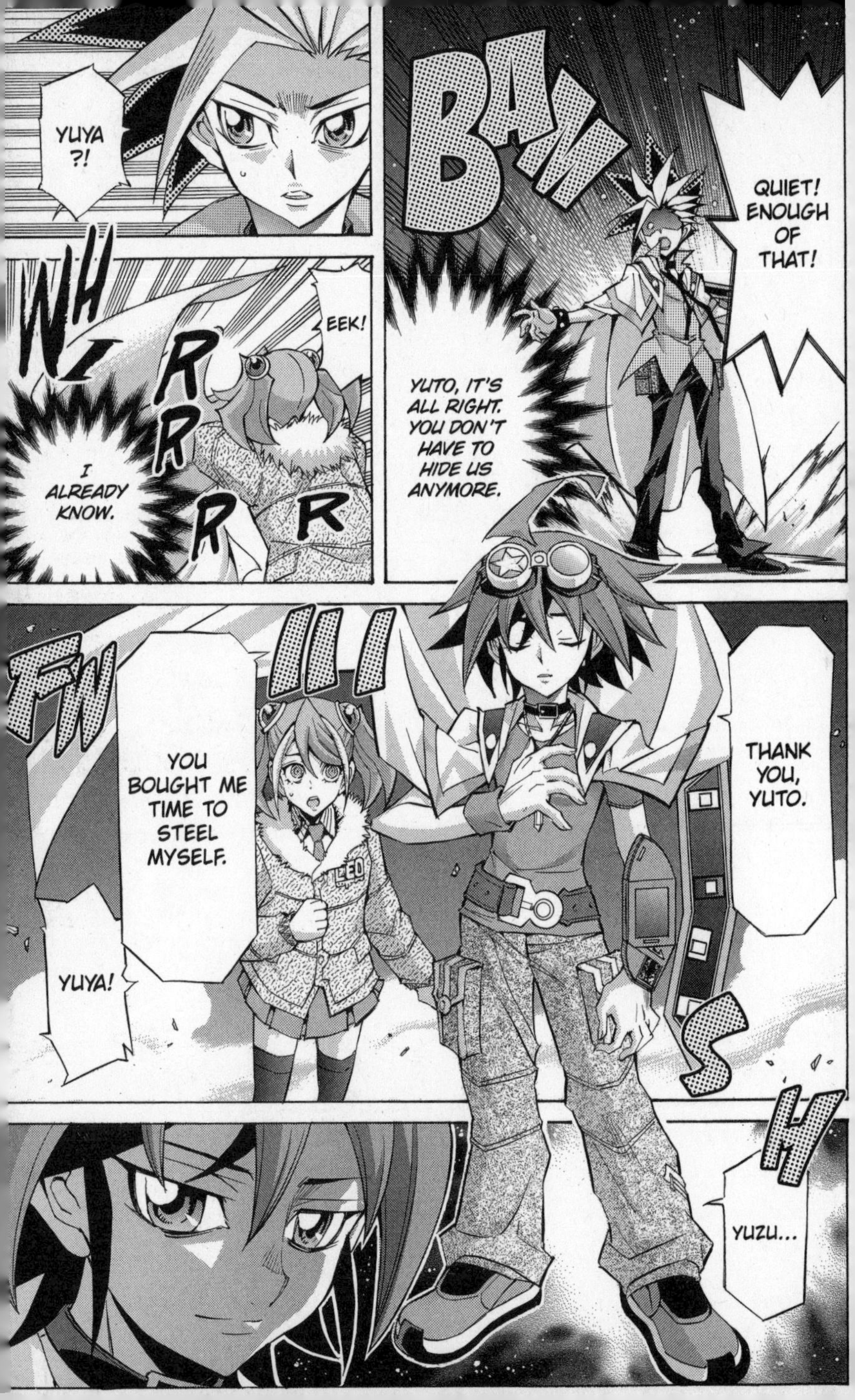
BAM
QUIET! ENOUGH OF THAT!
YUTO, IT'S ALL RIGHT. YOU DON'T HAVE TO HIDE US ANYMORE.
YUYA ?!
WHIRRRR
EEK!
I ALREADY KNOW.
THANK YOU, YUTO.
YOU BOUGHT ME TIME TO STEEL MYSELF.
YUYA!
YUZU...

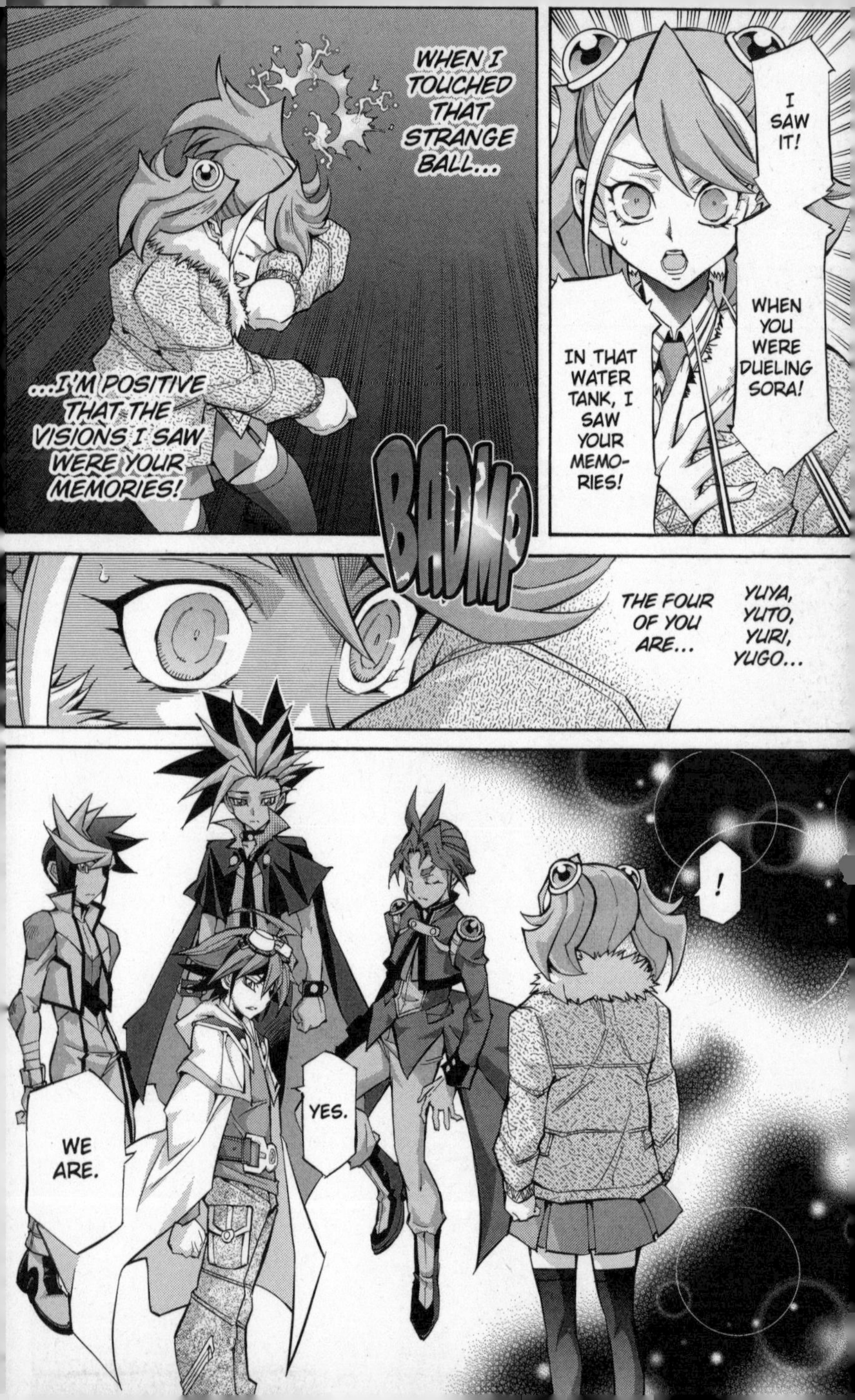
I SAW IT!
WHEN YOU WERE DUELING SORA!
IN THAT WATER TANK, I SAW YOUR MEMORIES!
WHEN I TOUCHED THAT STRANGE BALL...
...I'M POSITIVE THAT THE VISIONS I SAW WERE YOUR MEMORIES!
BADMP
YUYA, YUTO, YURI, YUGO...
THE FOUR OF YOU ARE...
!
YES.
WE ARE.

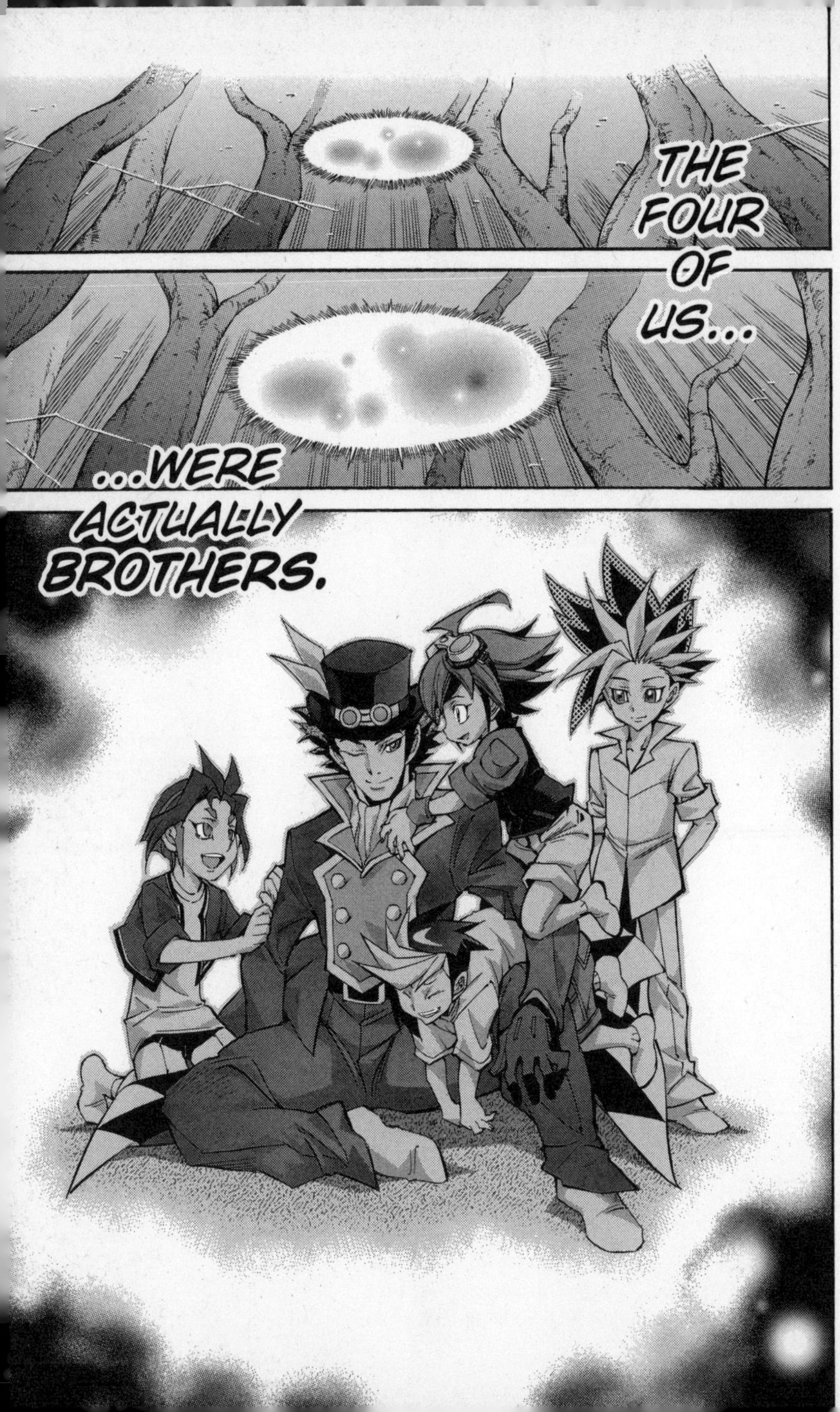
THE FOUR OF US...
...WERE ACTUALLY BROTHERS.

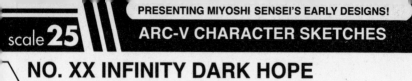

NO. XX INFINITY DARK HOPE

no. XX INfINITY DARK HOPE

Among the Numbers scattered across the dimensions, this one is spoken of as legend. Its stalwart shield and revival effect render its user immortal!

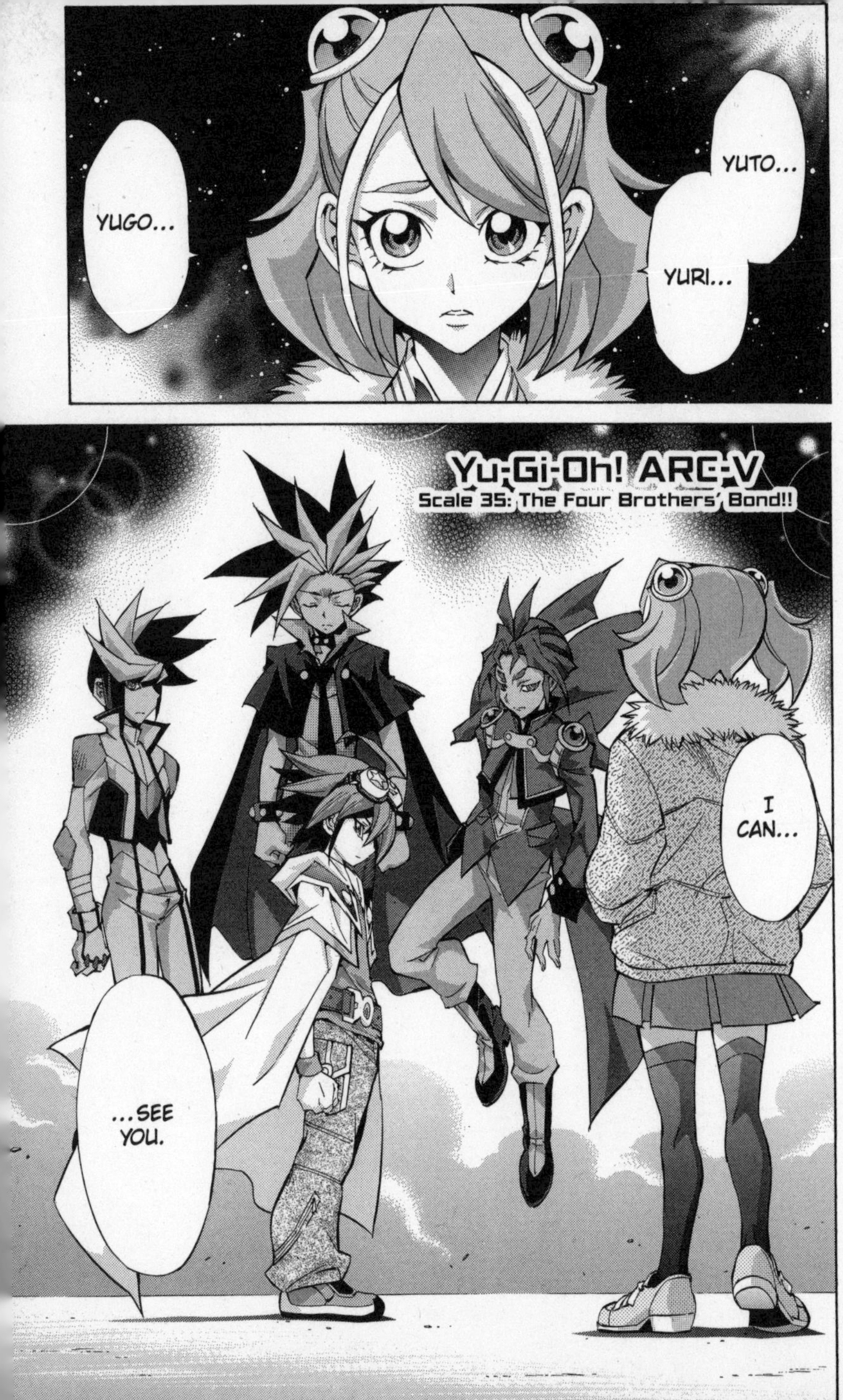
YUTO...
YURI...
YUGO...
Yu-Gi-Oh! ARC-V
Scale 35: The Four Brothers' Bond!!
I CAN...
...SEE YOU.

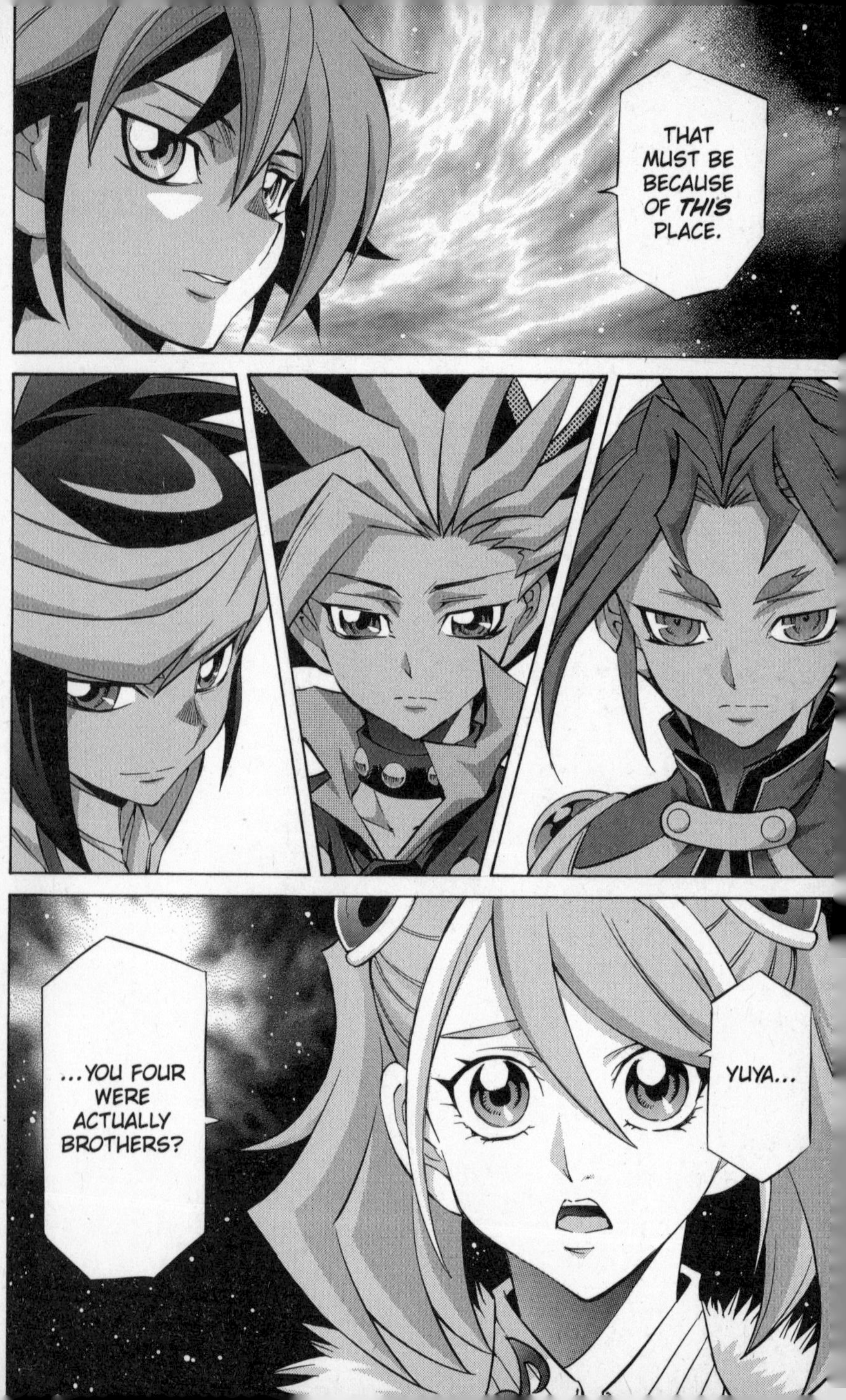
THAT MUST BE BECAUSE OF *THIS* PLACE.
YUYA...
...YOU FOUR WERE ACTUALLY BROTHERS?

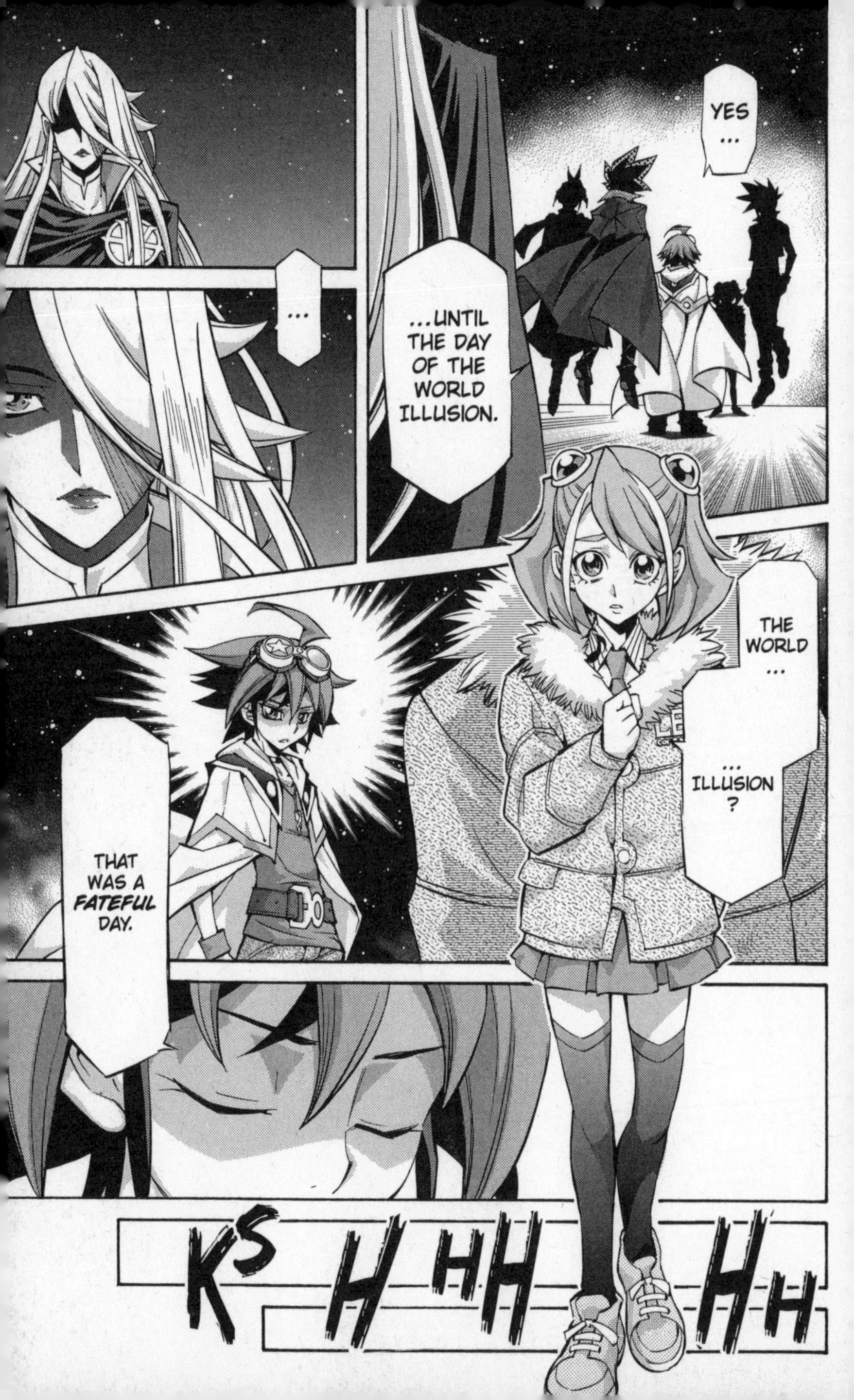
YES ...
...UNTIL THE DAY OF THE WORLD ILLUSION.
...
THE WORLD ...
... ILLUSION ?
THAT WAS A FATEFUL DAY.
KSHHHHHH

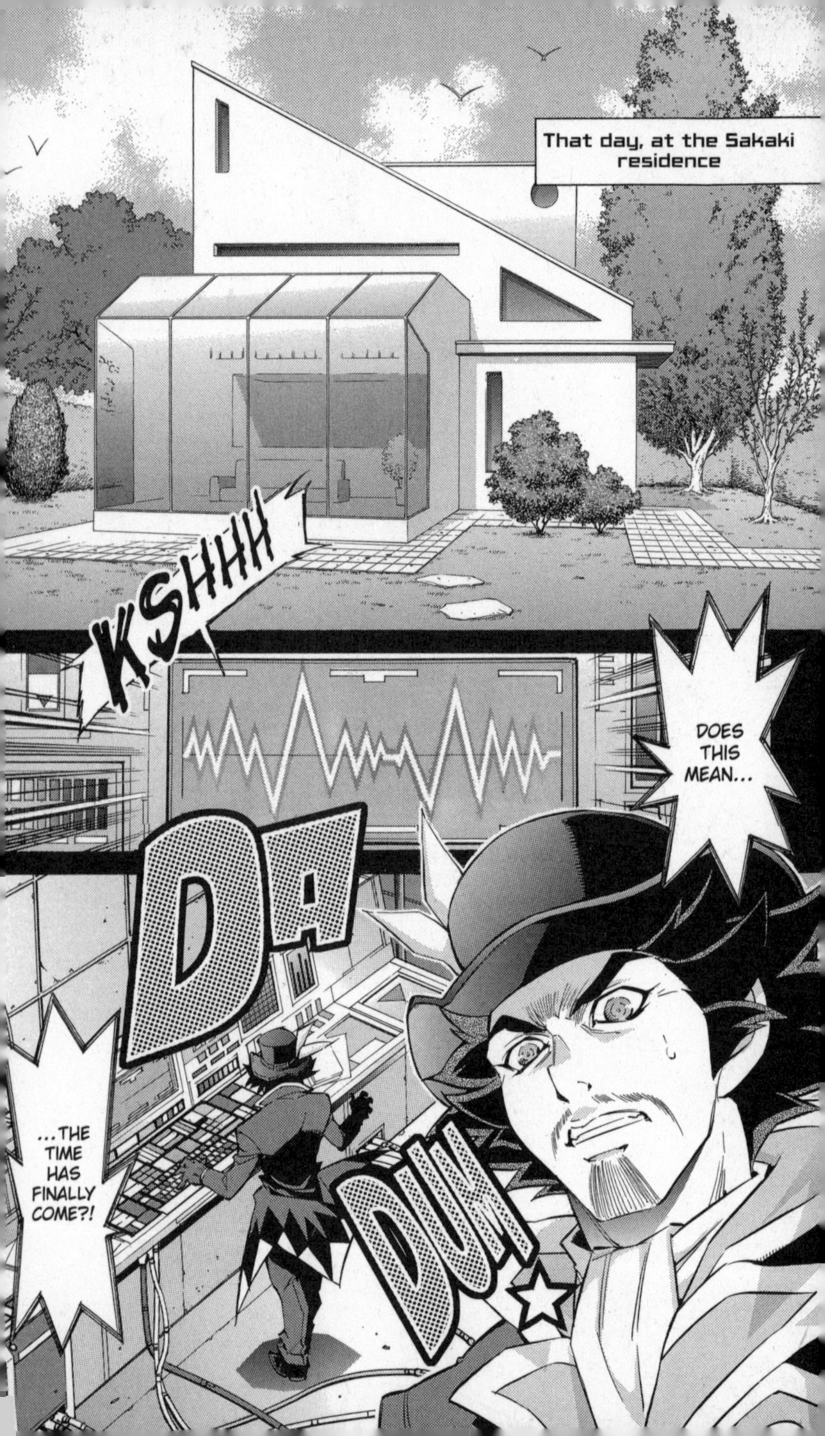
That day, at the Sakaki residence
KSHHH
DOES THIS MEAN...
...THE TIME HAS FINALLY COME?!
DA
DUM

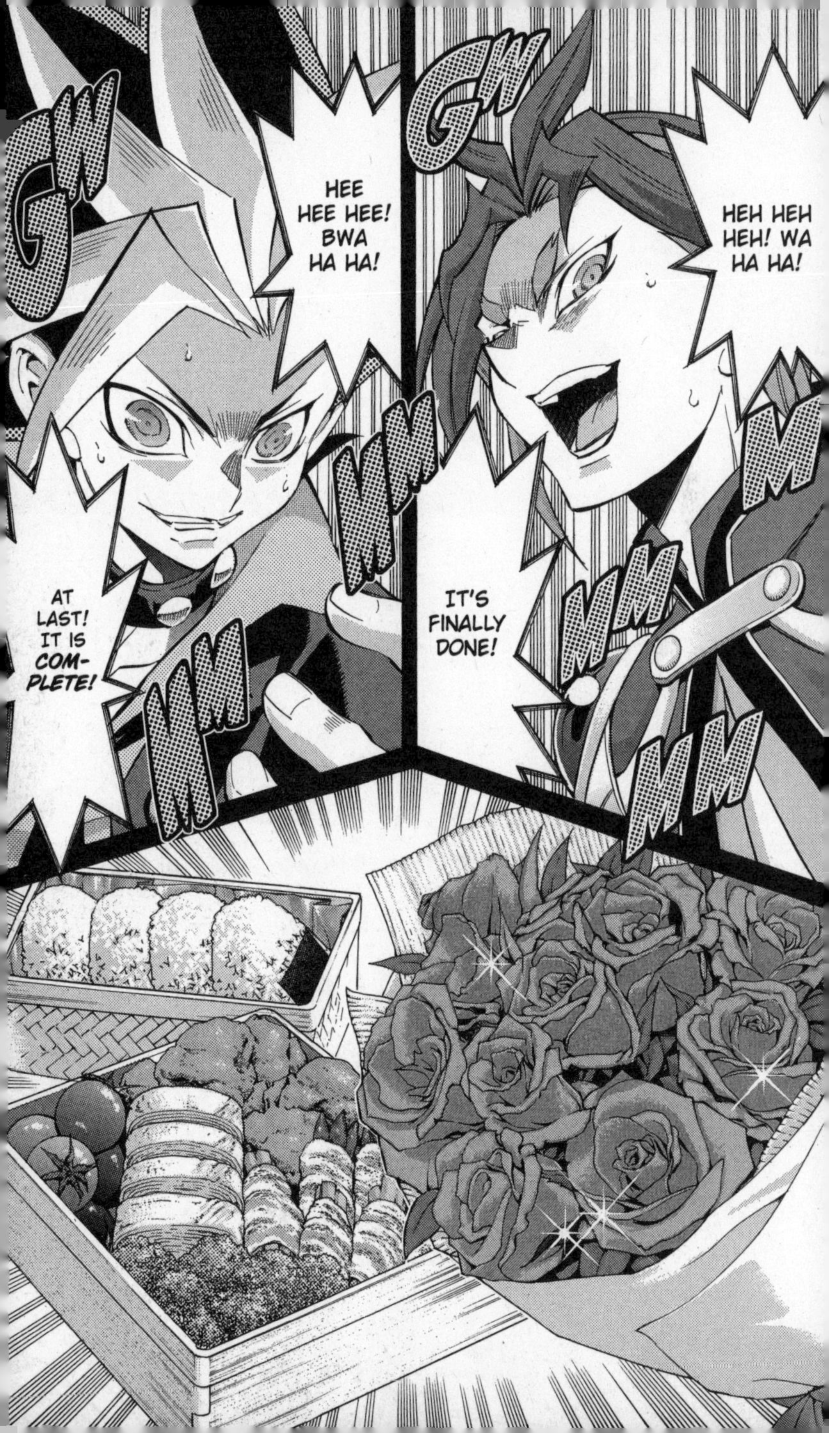
GW
HEH HEH HEH! WA HA HA!
M
MMM
MMM
IT'S FINALLY DONE!
GW
HEE HEE HEE! BWA HA HA!
MMM
MMM
AT LAST! IT IS COM-PLETE!

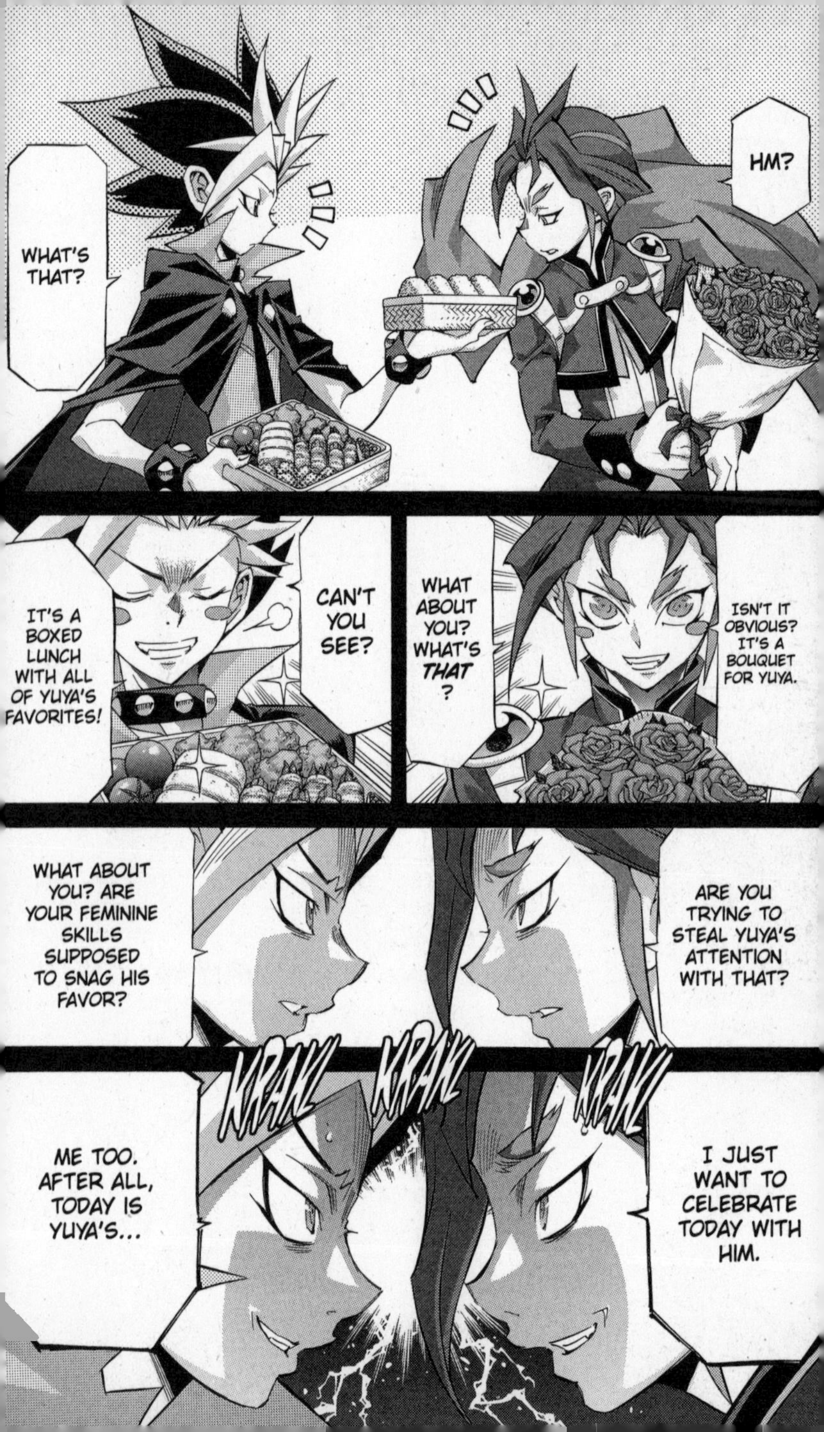
HM?
WHAT'S THAT?
ISN'T IT OBVIOUS? IT'S A BOUQUET FOR YUYA.
WHAT ABOUT YOU? WHAT'S *THAT*?
CAN'T YOU SEE?
IT'S A BOXED LUNCH WITH ALL OF YUYA'S FAVORITES!
ARE YOU TRYING TO STEAL YUYA'S ATTENTION WITH THAT?
WHAT ABOUT YOU? ARE YOUR FEMININE SKILLS SUPPOSED TO SNAG HIS FAVOR?
KRAK!
KRAK!
KRAK!
I JUST WANT TO CELEBRATE TODAY WITH HIM.
ME TOO. AFTER ALL, TODAY IS YUYA'S...

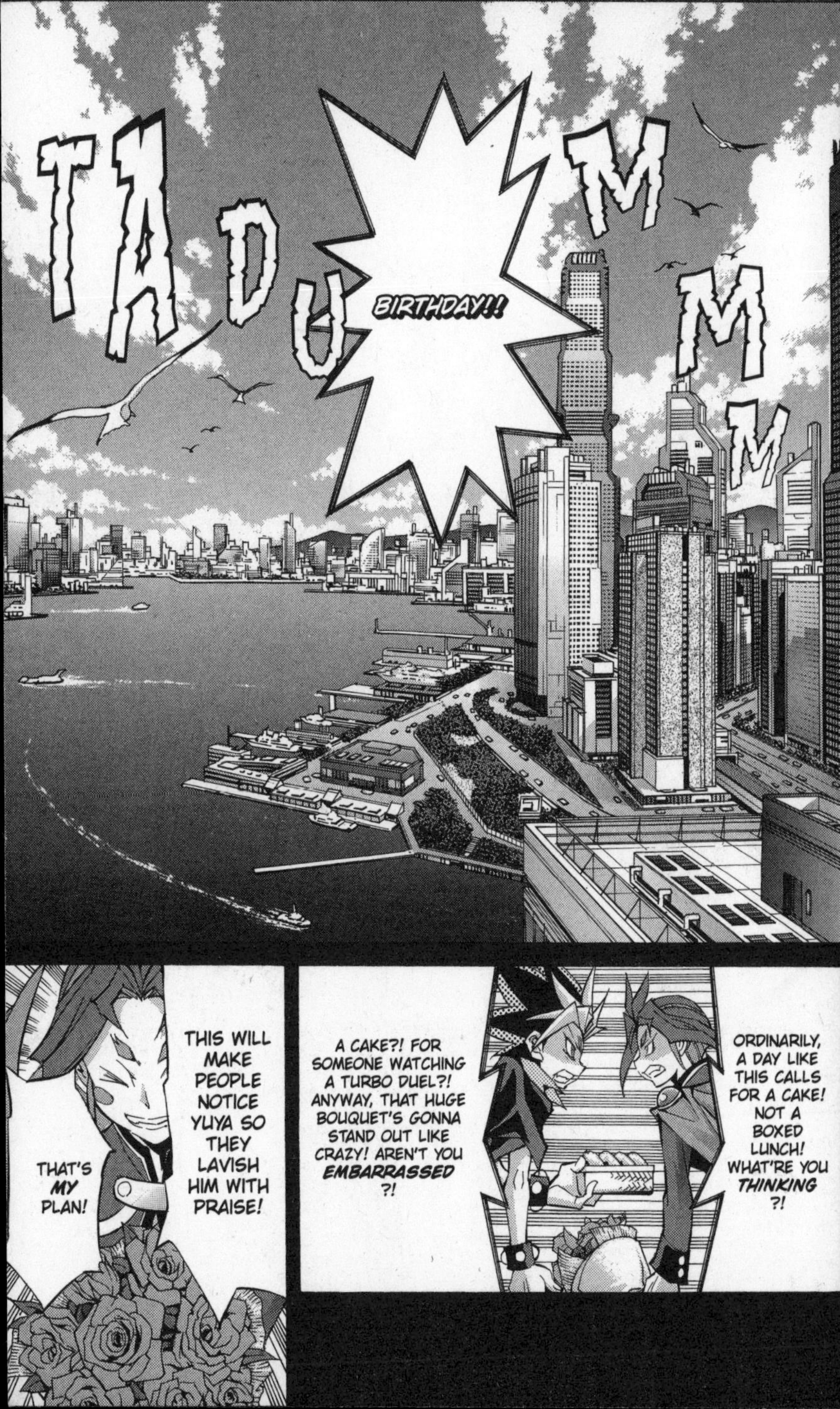
TADUMMM
BIRTHDAY!!
ORDINARILY, A DAY LIKE THIS CALLS FOR A CAKE! NOT A BOXED LUNCH! WHAT'RE YOU *THINKING*?!
A CAKE?! FOR SOMEONE WATCHING A TURBO DUEL?! ANYWAY, THAT HUGE BOUQUET'S GONNA STAND OUT LIKE CRAZY! AREN'T YOU *EMBARRASSED*?!
THIS WILL MAKE PEOPLE NOTICE YUYA SO THEY LAVISH HIM WITH PRAISE!
THAT'S *MY* PLAN!

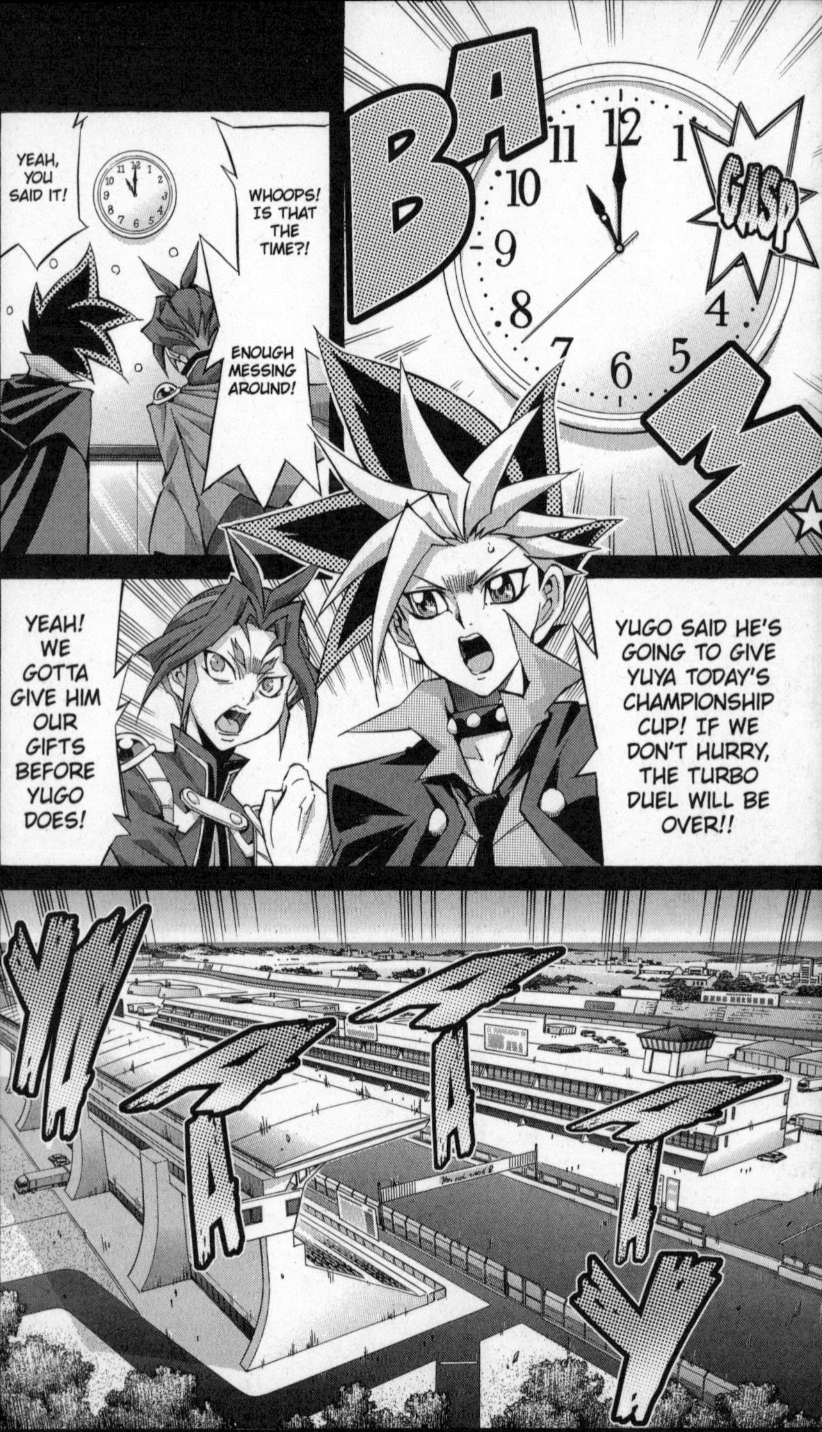
BAM
GASP
WHOOPS! IS THAT THE TIME?!
YEAH, YOU SAID IT!
ENOUGH MESSING AROUND!
YUGO SAID HE'S GOING TO GIVE YUYA TODAY'S CHAMPIONSHIP CUP! IF WE DON'T HURRY, THE TURBO DUEL WILL BE OVER!!
YEAH! WE GOTTA GIVE HIM OUR GIFTS BEFORE YUGO DOES!

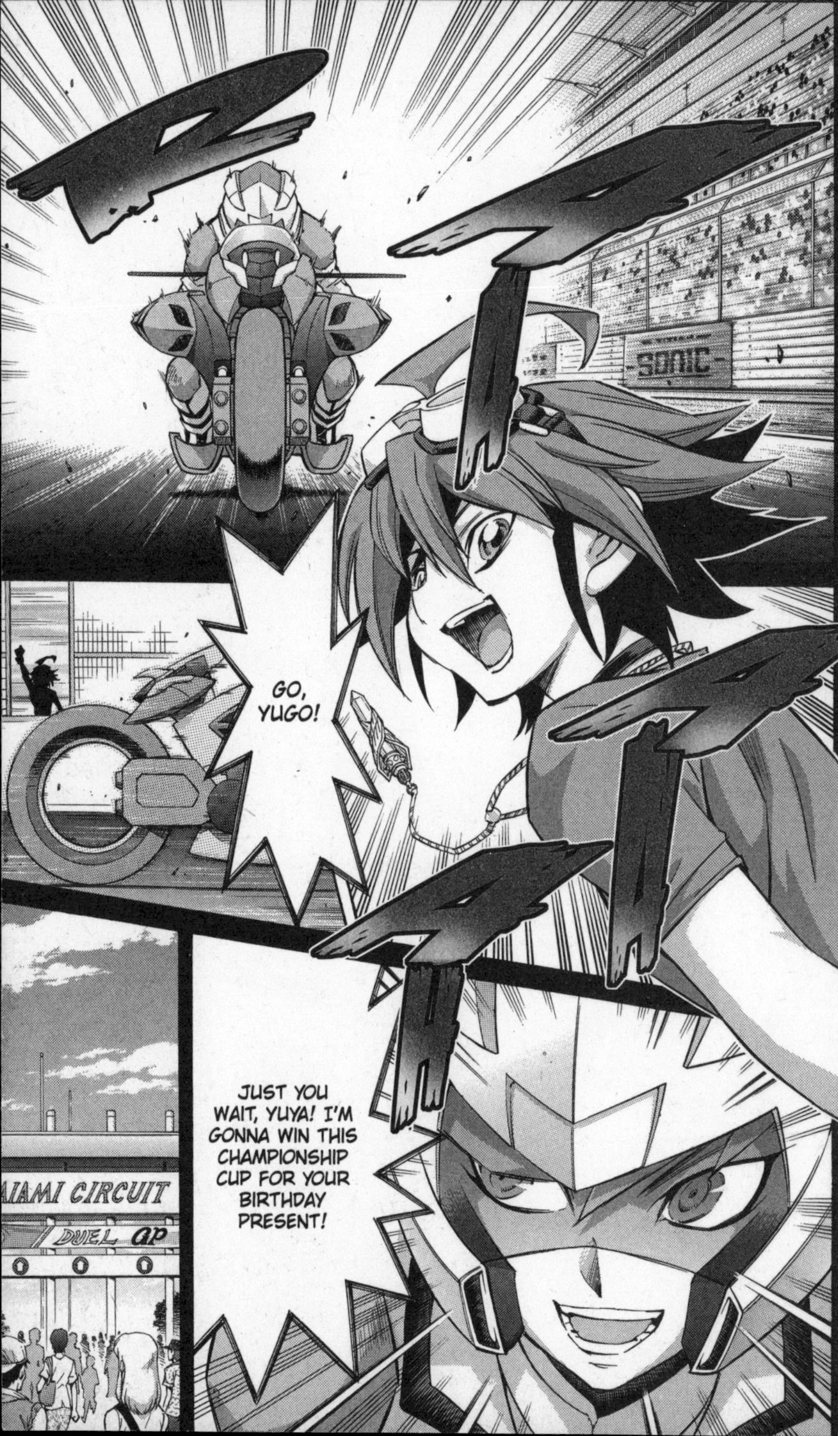
SONIC
GO, YUGO!
JUST YOU WAIT, YUYA! I'M GONNA WIN THIS CHAMPIONSHIP CUP FOR YOUR BIRTHDAY PRESENT!
AIAMI CIRCUIT
DUEL GP

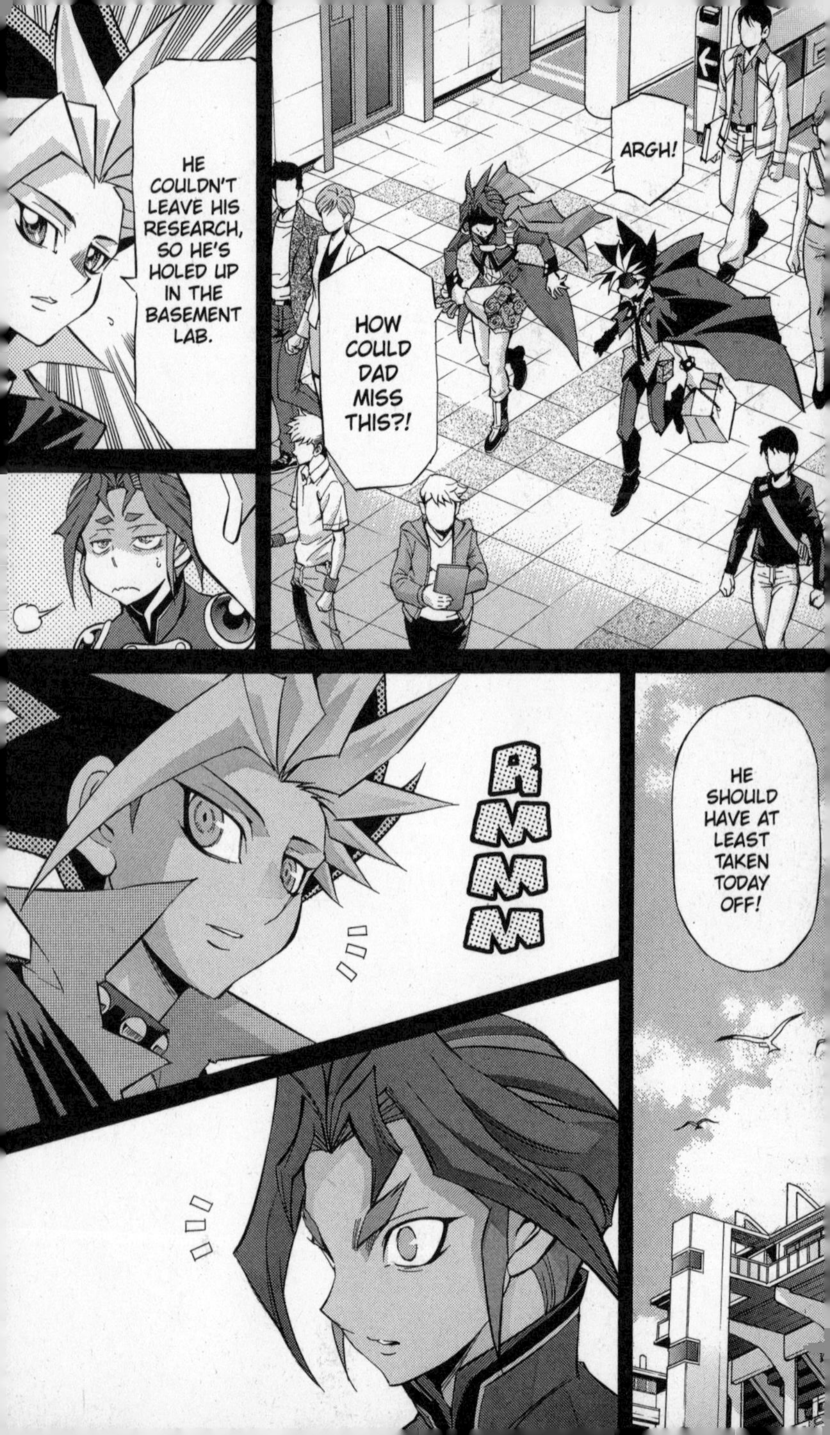
ARGH!
HOW COULD DAD MISS THIS?!
HE COULDN'T LEAVE HIS RESEARCH, SO HE'S HOLED UP IN THE BASEMENT LAB.
HE SHOULD HAVE AT LEAST TAKEN TODAY OFF!
RMMM

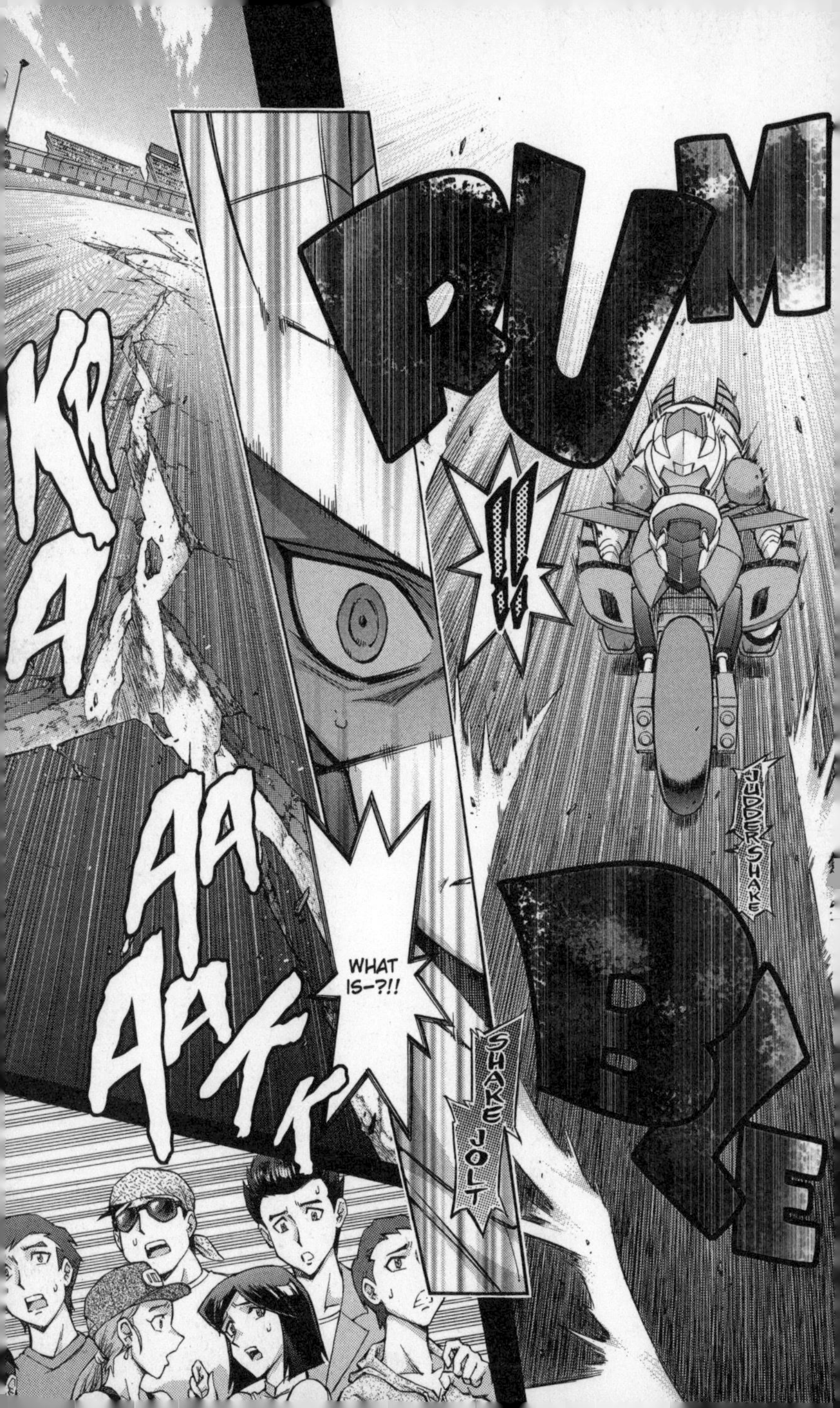
JUDDER SHAKE
!!
SHAKE JOLT
WHAT IS–?!!

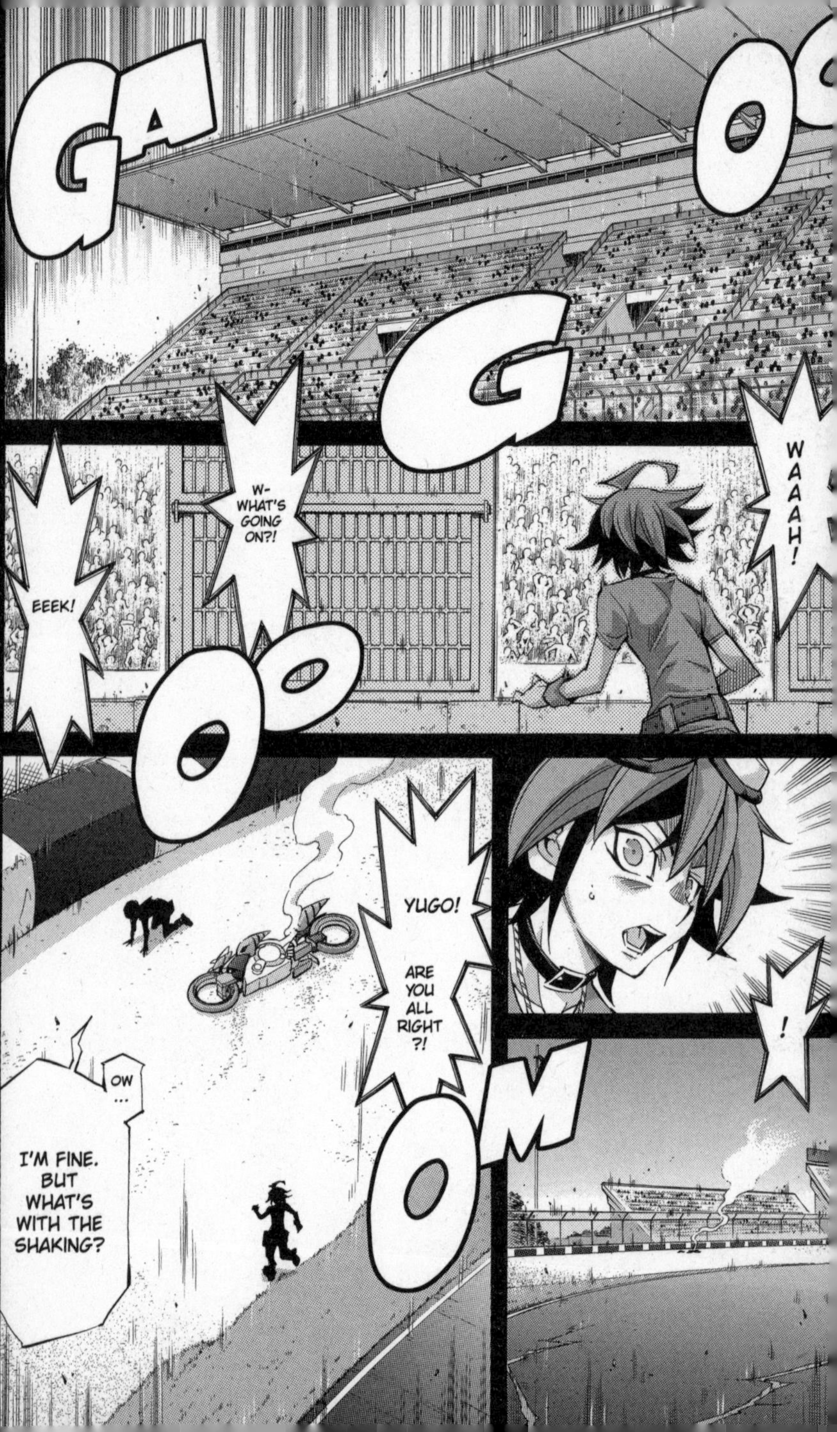
GAGOOOOOM
WAAAH!
W-WHAT'S GOING ON?!
EEEK!
!
YUGO! ARE YOU ALL RIGHT?!
OW...
I'M FINE. BUT WHAT'S WITH THE SHAKING?

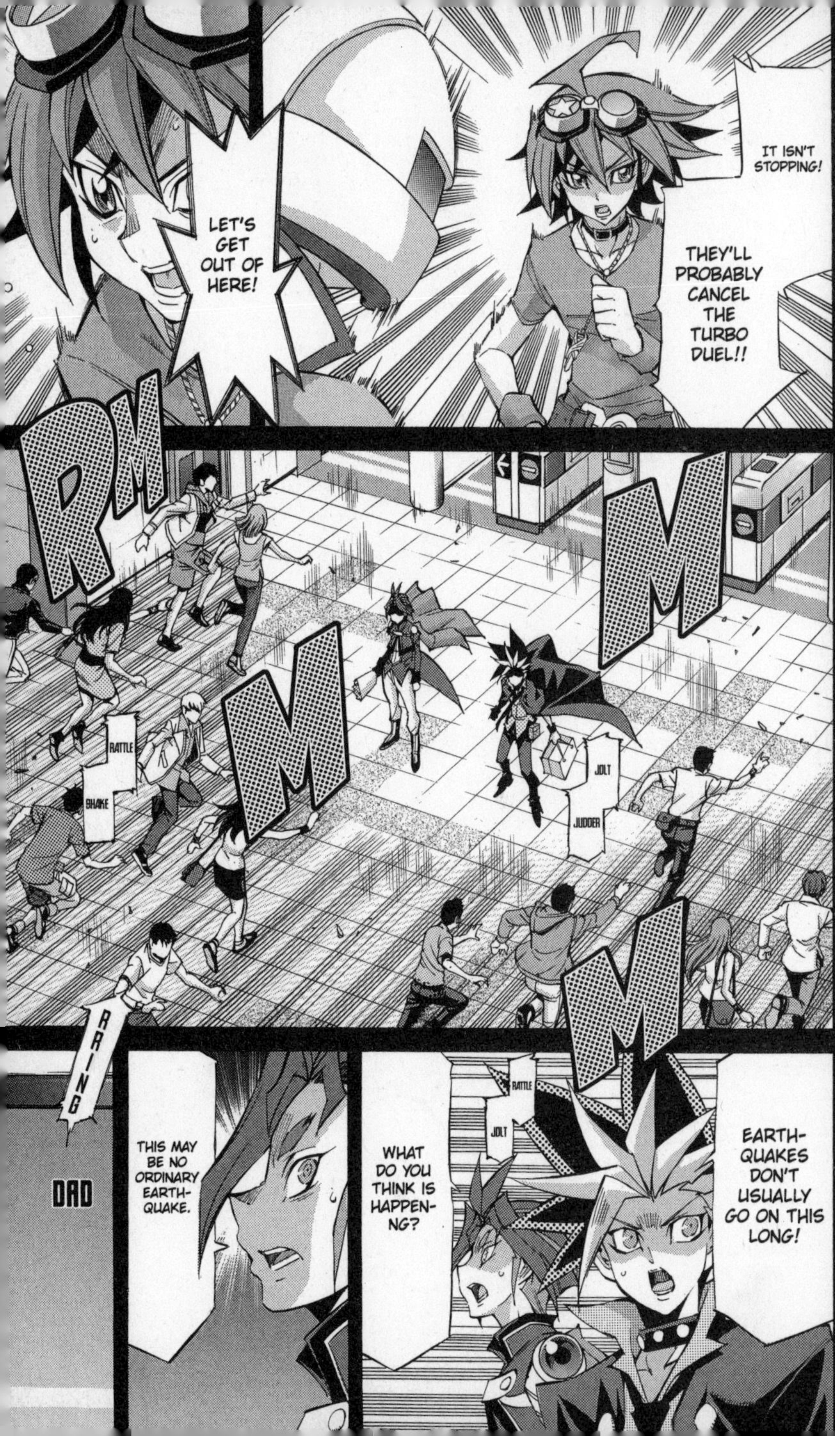
IT ISN'T STOPPING!
THEY'LL PROBABLY CANCEL THE TURBO DUEL!!
LET'S GET OUT OF HERE!
RMMMM
JOLT
JUDDER
RATTLE
SHAKE
RATTLE
JOLT
EARTH-QUAKES DON'T USUALLY GO ON THIS LONG!
WHAT DO YOU THINK IS HAPPEN-NG?
THIS MAY BE NO ORDINARY EARTH-QUAKE.
RRING
DAD

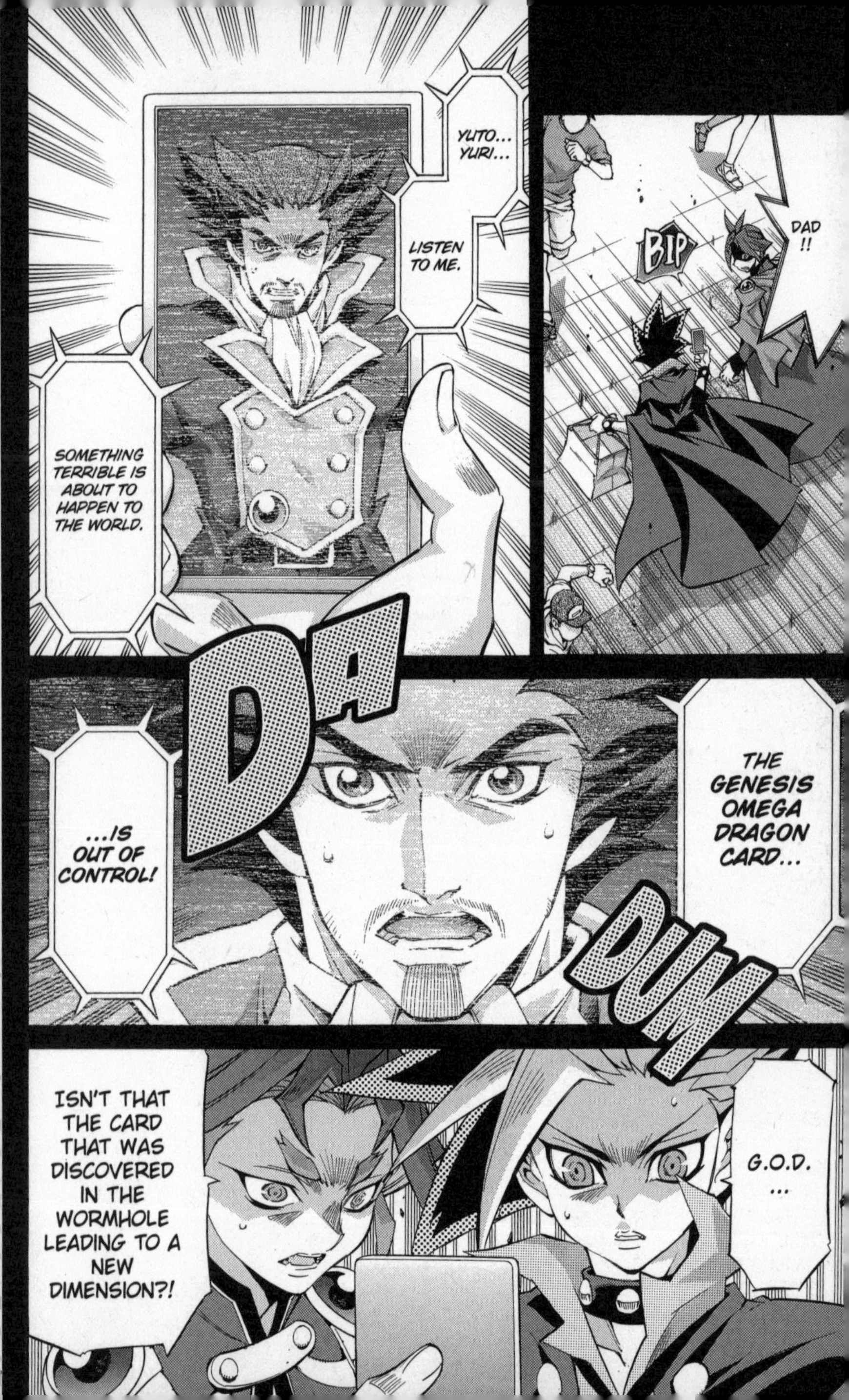
DAD !!
BIP
YUTO... YURI...
LISTEN TO ME.
SOMETHING TERRIBLE IS ABOUT TO HAPPEN TO THE WORLD.
THE GENESIS OMEGA DRAGON CARD...
DA
DUM
...IS OUT OF CONTROL!
G.O.D. ...
ISN'T THAT THE CARD THAT WAS DISCOVERED IN THE WORMHOLE LEADING TO A NEW DIMENSION?!

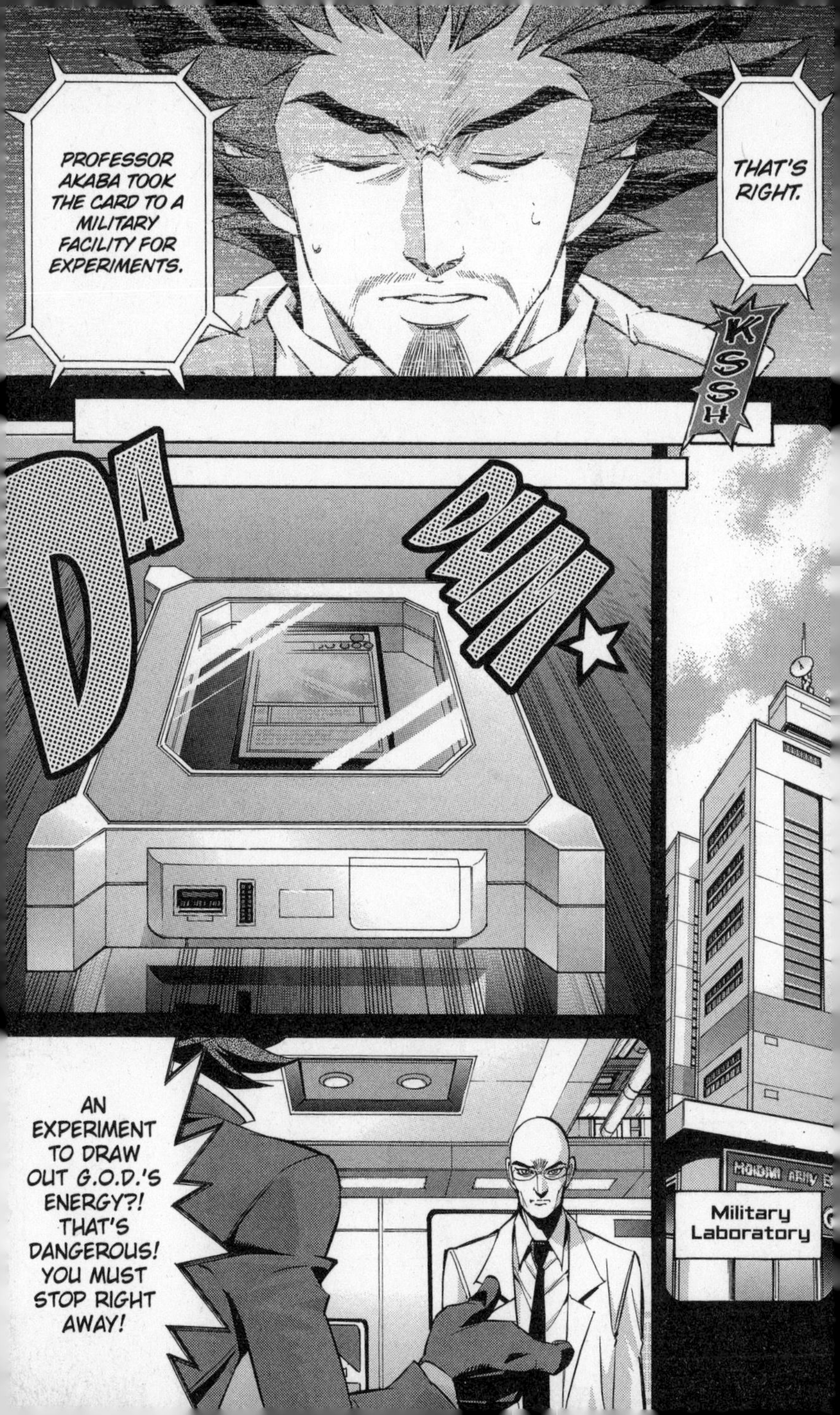
PROFESSOR AKABA TOOK THE CARD TO A MILITARY FACILITY FOR EXPERIMENTS.
THAT'S RIGHT.
KSSH
Military Laboratory
AN EXPERIMENT TO DRAW OUT G.O.D.'S ENERGY?! THAT'S DANGEROUS! YOU MUST STOP RIGHT AWAY!

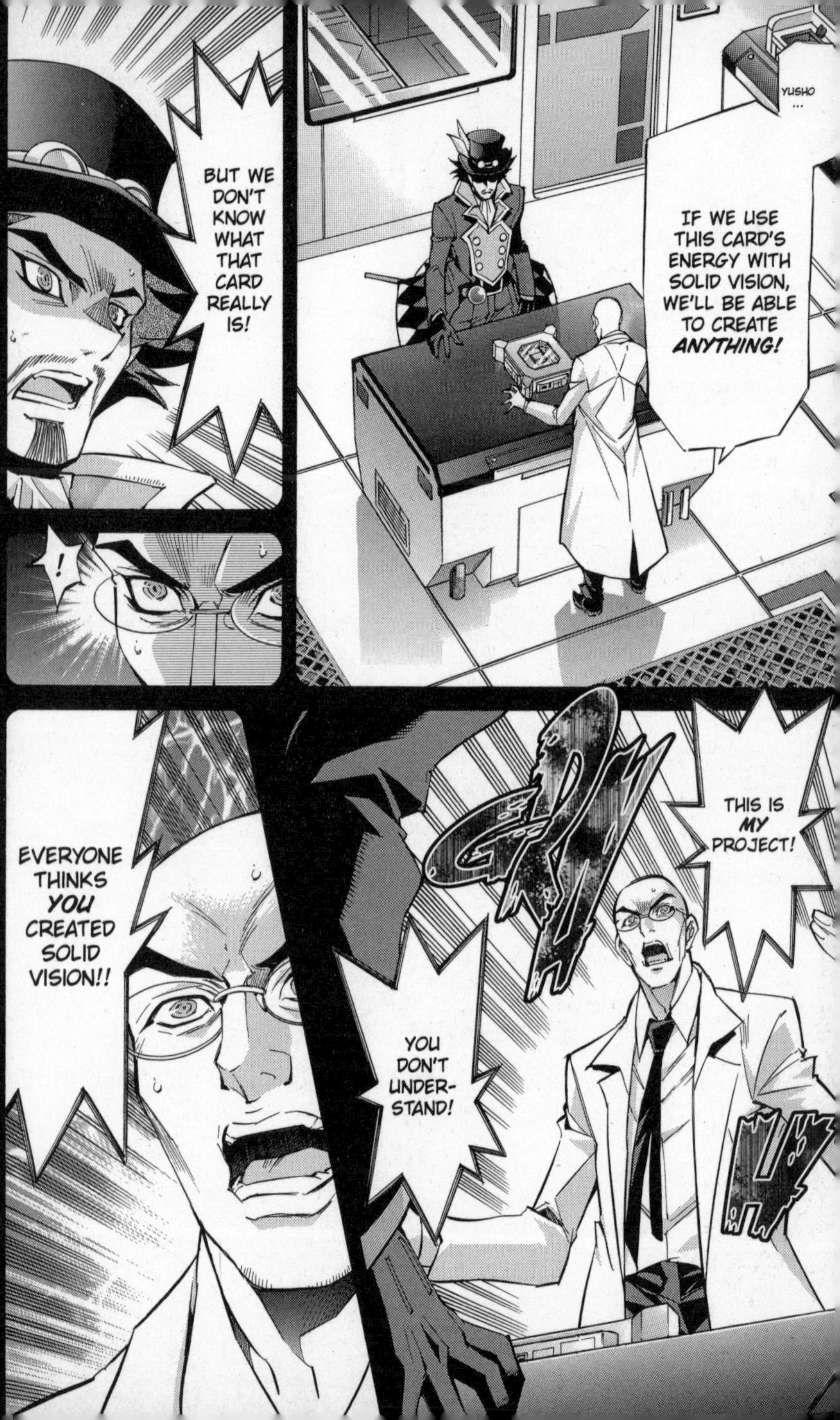
YUSHO ...
IF WE USE THIS CARD'S ENERGY WITH SOLID VISION, WE'LL BE ABLE TO CREATE ANYTHING!
BUT WE DON'T KNOW WHAT THAT CARD REALLY IS!
!
THIS IS MY PROJECT!
YOU DON'T UNDER-STAND!
EVERYONE THINKS YOU CREATED SOLID VISION!!

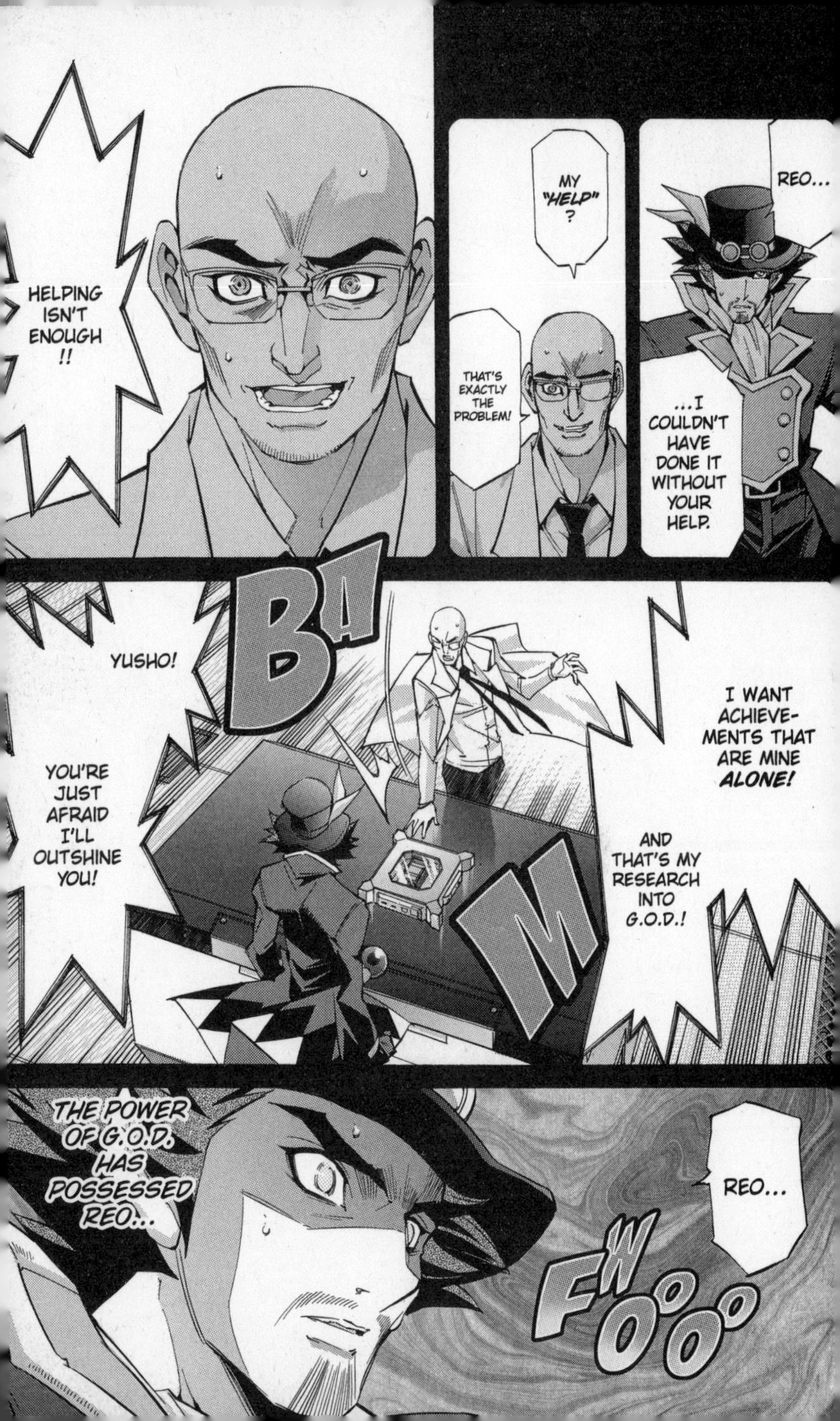
REO...
...I COULDN'T HAVE DONE IT WITHOUT YOUR HELP.
MY "HELP"?
THAT'S EXACTLY THE PROBLEM!
HELPING ISN'T ENOUGH!!
BAM
I WANT ACHIEVEMENTS THAT ARE MINE ALONE!
AND THAT'S MY RESEARCH INTO G.O.D.!
YUSHO!
YOU'RE JUST AFRAID I'LL OUTSHINE YOU!
REO...
FWOOO
THE POWER OF G.O.D. HAS POSSESSED REO...

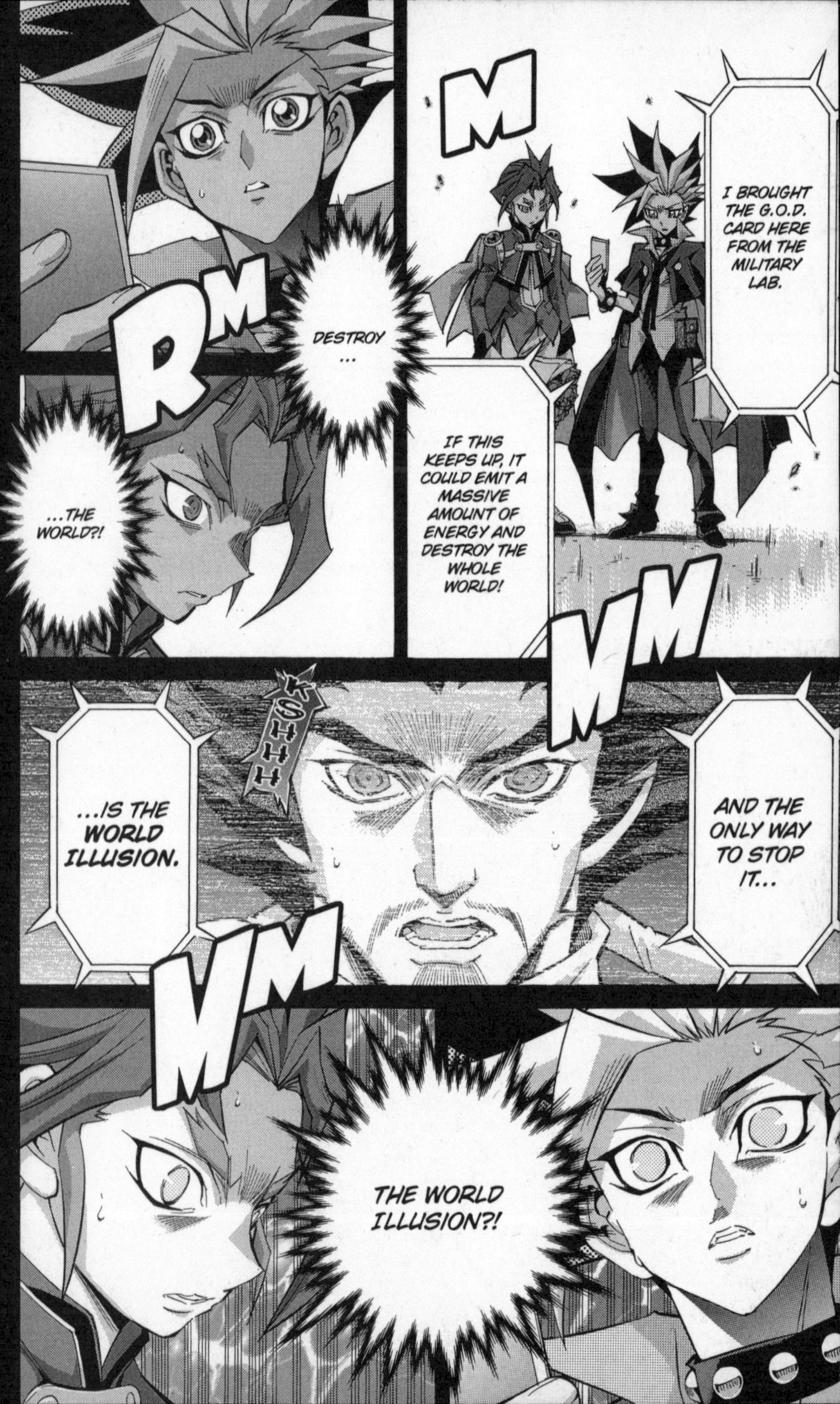
M
I BROUGHT THE G.O.D. CARD HERE FROM THE MILITARY LAB.
IF THIS KEEPS UP, IT COULD EMIT A MASSIVE AMOUNT OF ENERGY AND DESTROY THE WHOLE WORLD!
RM
DESTROY ...
...THE WORLD?!
MM
AND THE ONLY WAY TO STOP IT...
KSHHH
...IS THE WORLD ILLUSION.
MM
THE WORLD ILLUSION?!

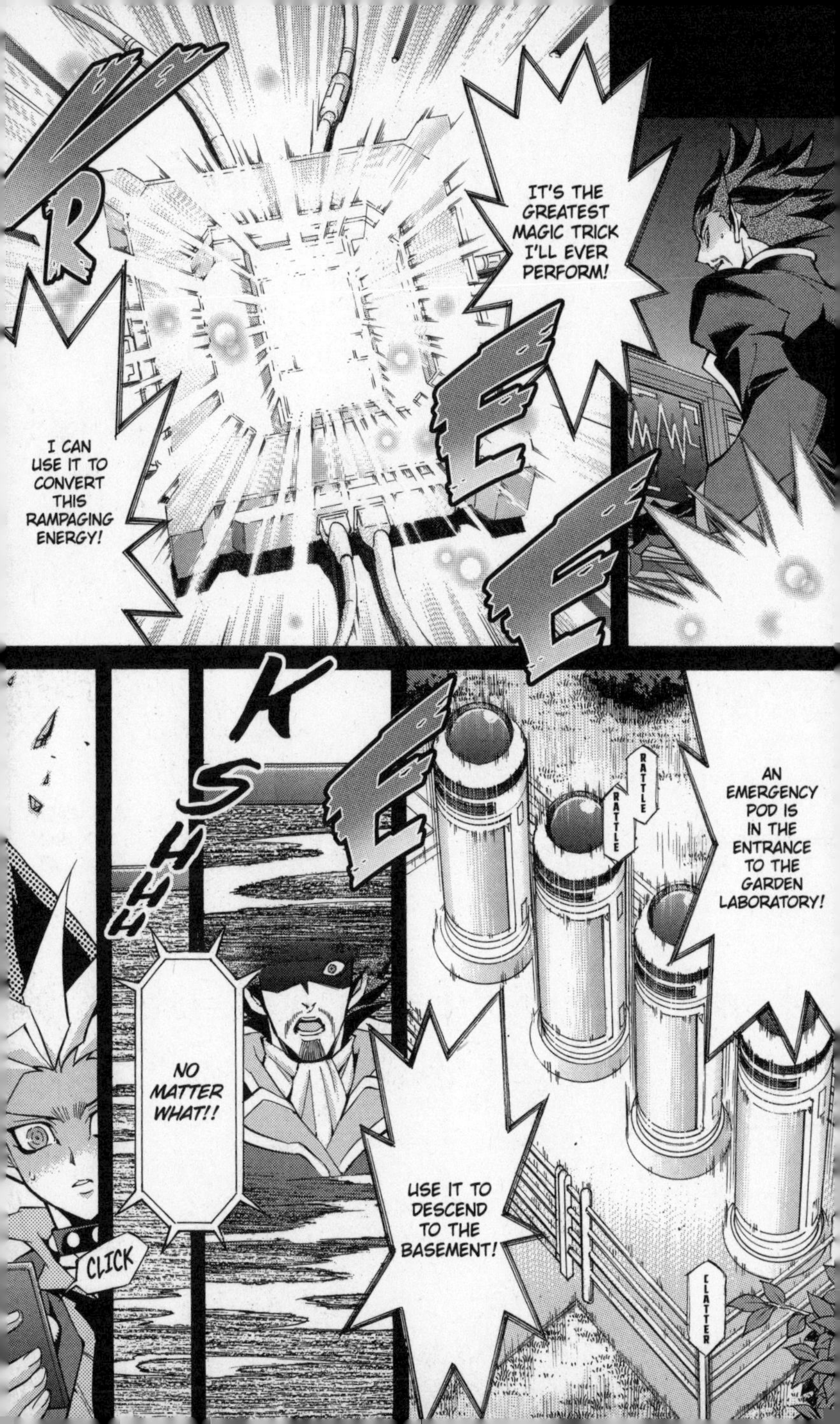

IT'S THE GREATEST MAGIC TRICK I'LL EVER PERFORM!
I CAN USE IT TO CONVERT THIS RAMPAGING ENERGY!
AN EMERGENCY POD IS IN THE ENTRANCE TO THE GARDEN LABORATORY!
RATTLE
RATTLE
USE IT TO DESCEND TO THE BASEMENT!
CLATTER
KSHHHH
NO MATTER WHAT!!
CLICK

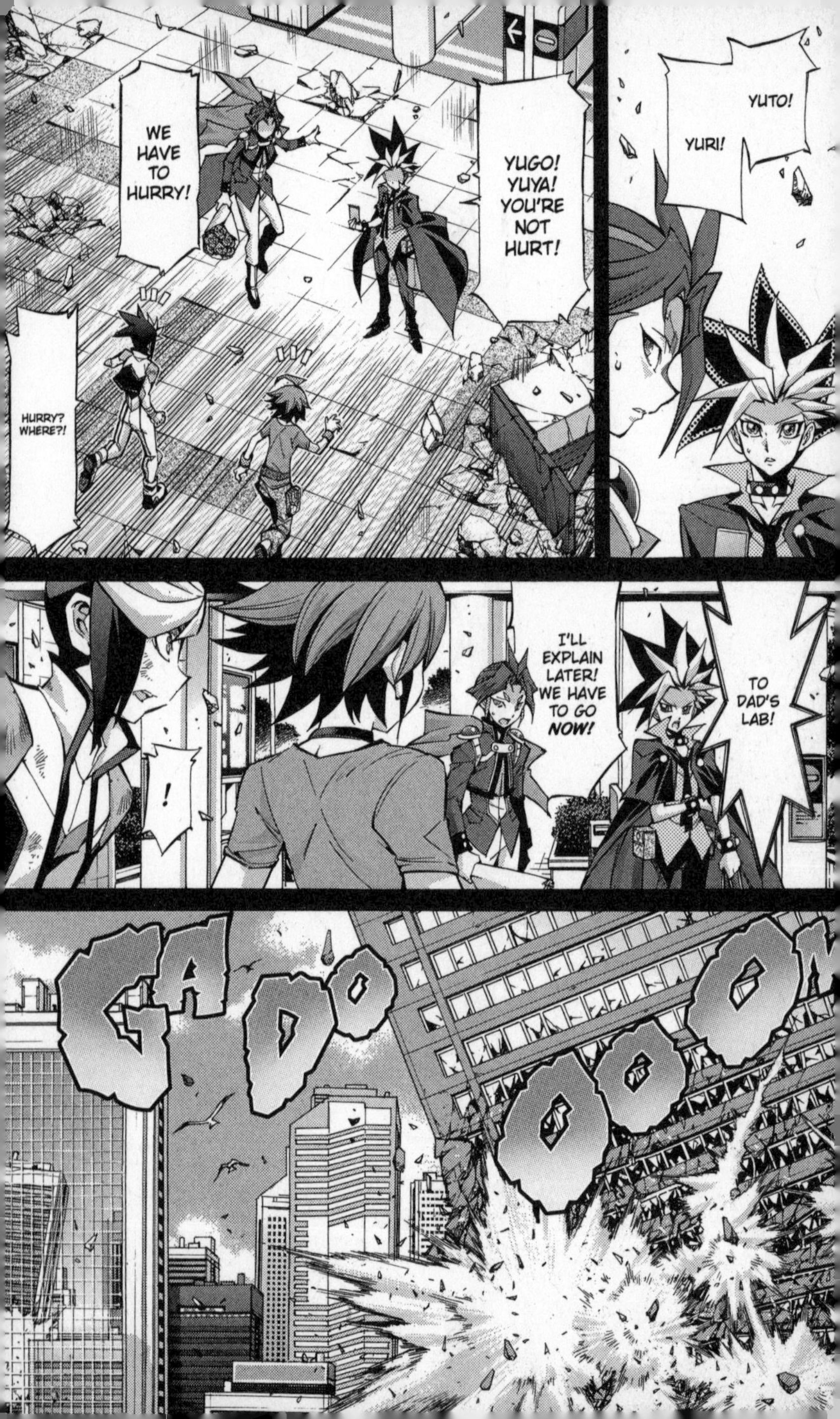
YUTO!
YURI!
YUGO! YUYA! YOU'RE NOT HURT!
WE HAVE TO HURRY!
HURRY? WHERE?!
TO DAD'S LAB!
I'LL EXPLAIN LATER! WE HAVE TO GO *NOW!*
!
GADOOOO

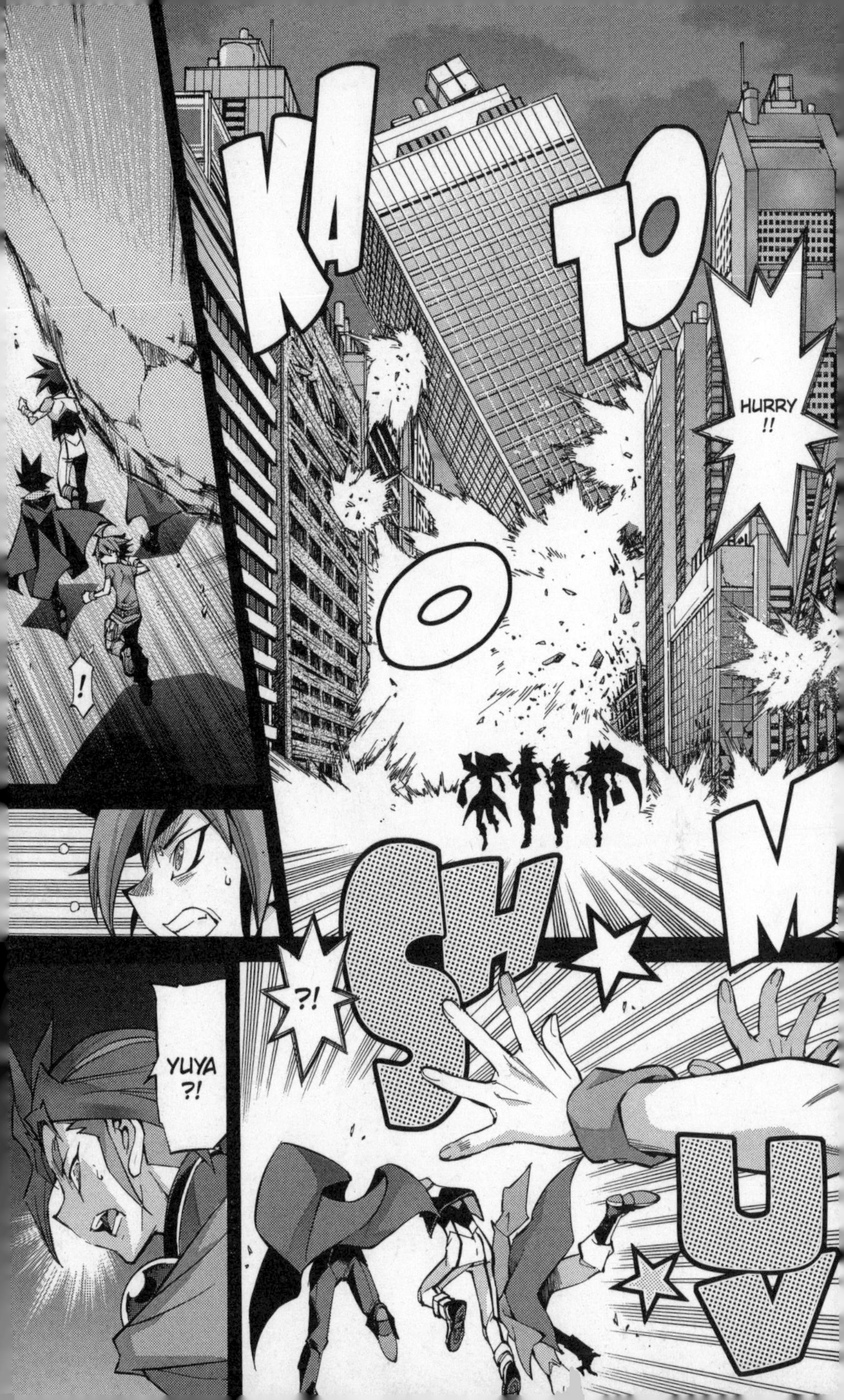
KA
TO
O
M
HURRY!!
!
SH
U
V
?!
YUYA ?!

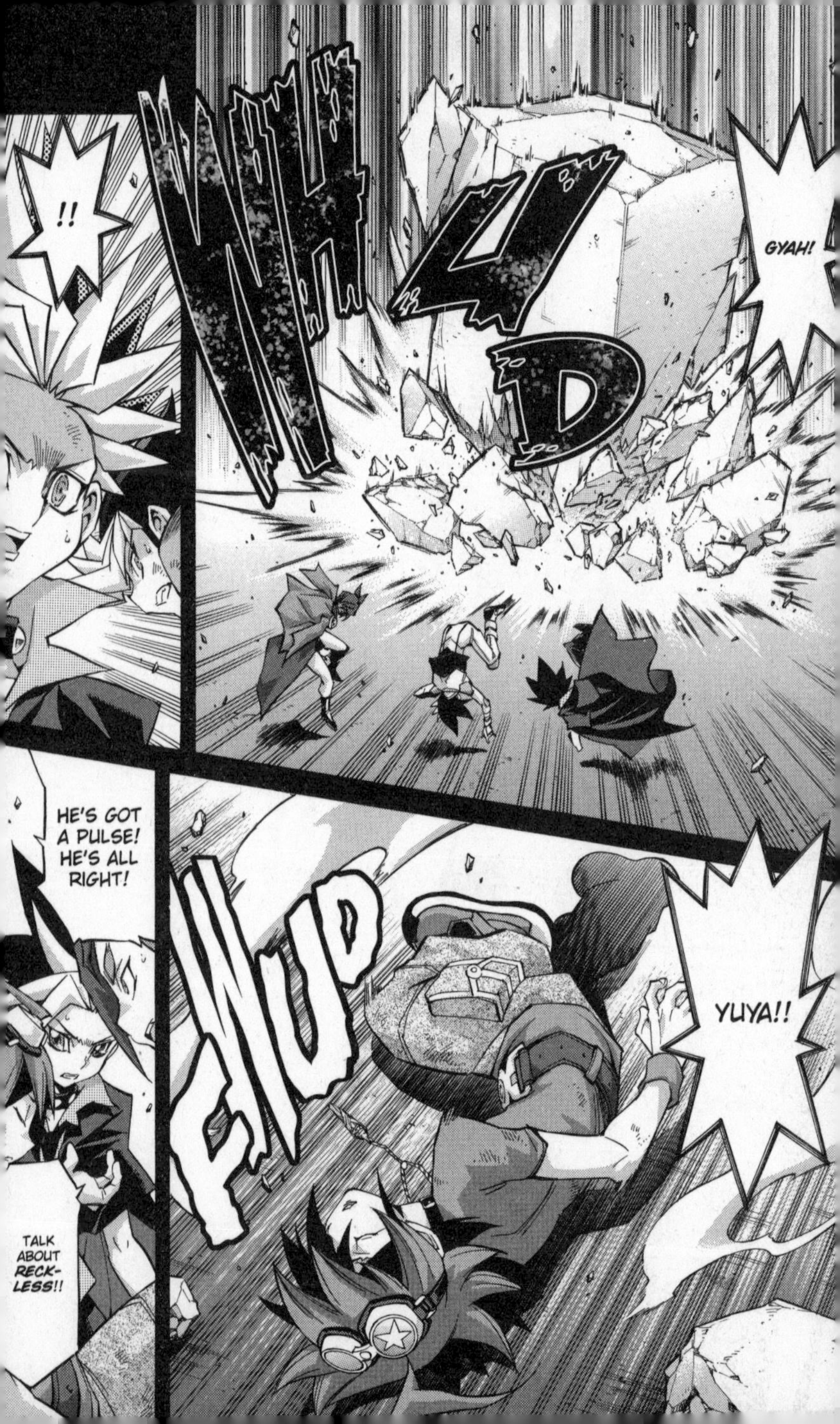
GYAH!
WHUD
!!
YUYA!!
CHUP
HE'S GOT A PULSE! HE'S ALL RIGHT!
TALK ABOUT RECKLESS!!

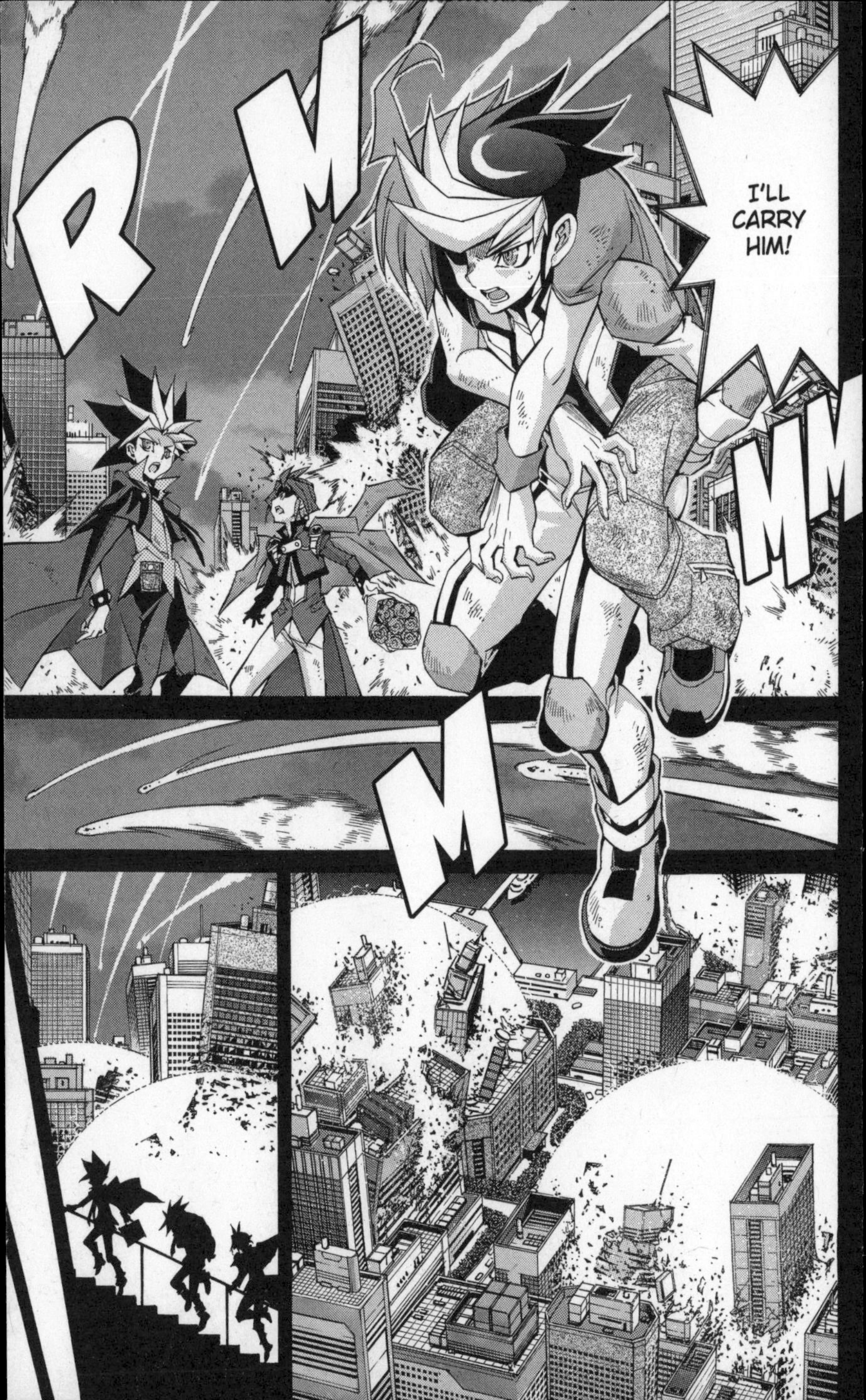
I'LL CARRY HIM!

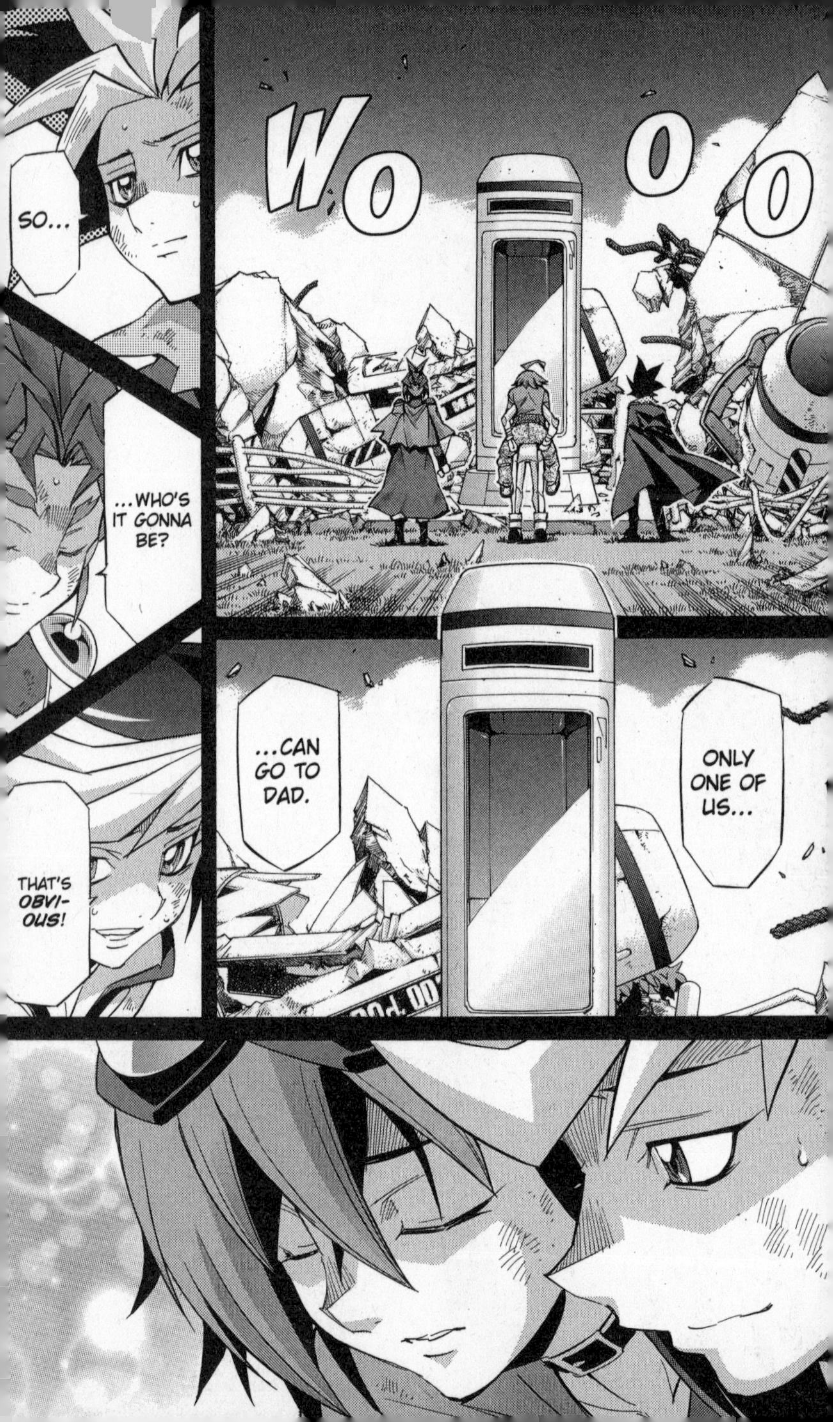
WOOOO
ONLY ONE OF US...
...CAN GO TO DAD.
SO...
...WHO'S IT GONNA BE?
THAT'S OBVIOUS!

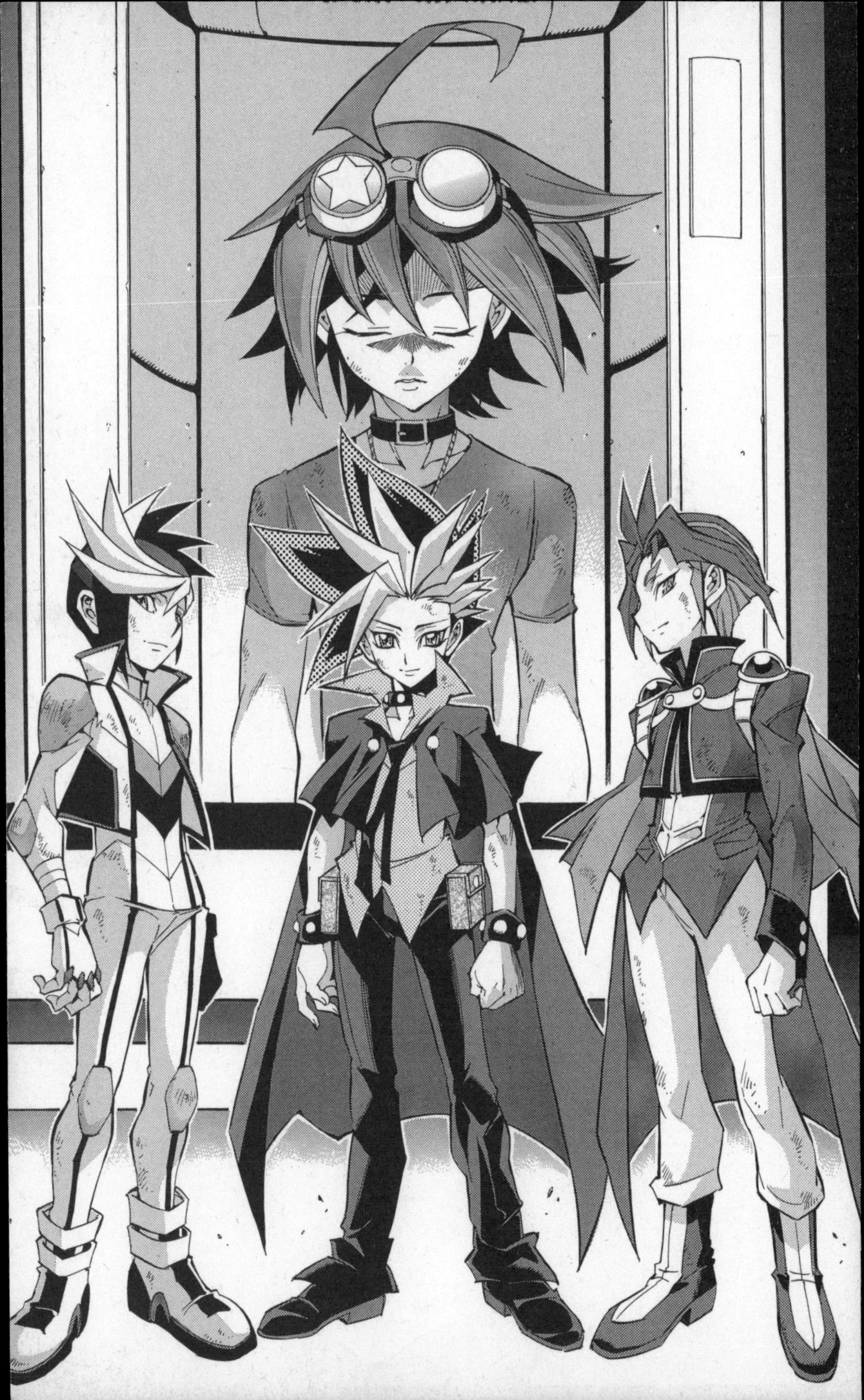

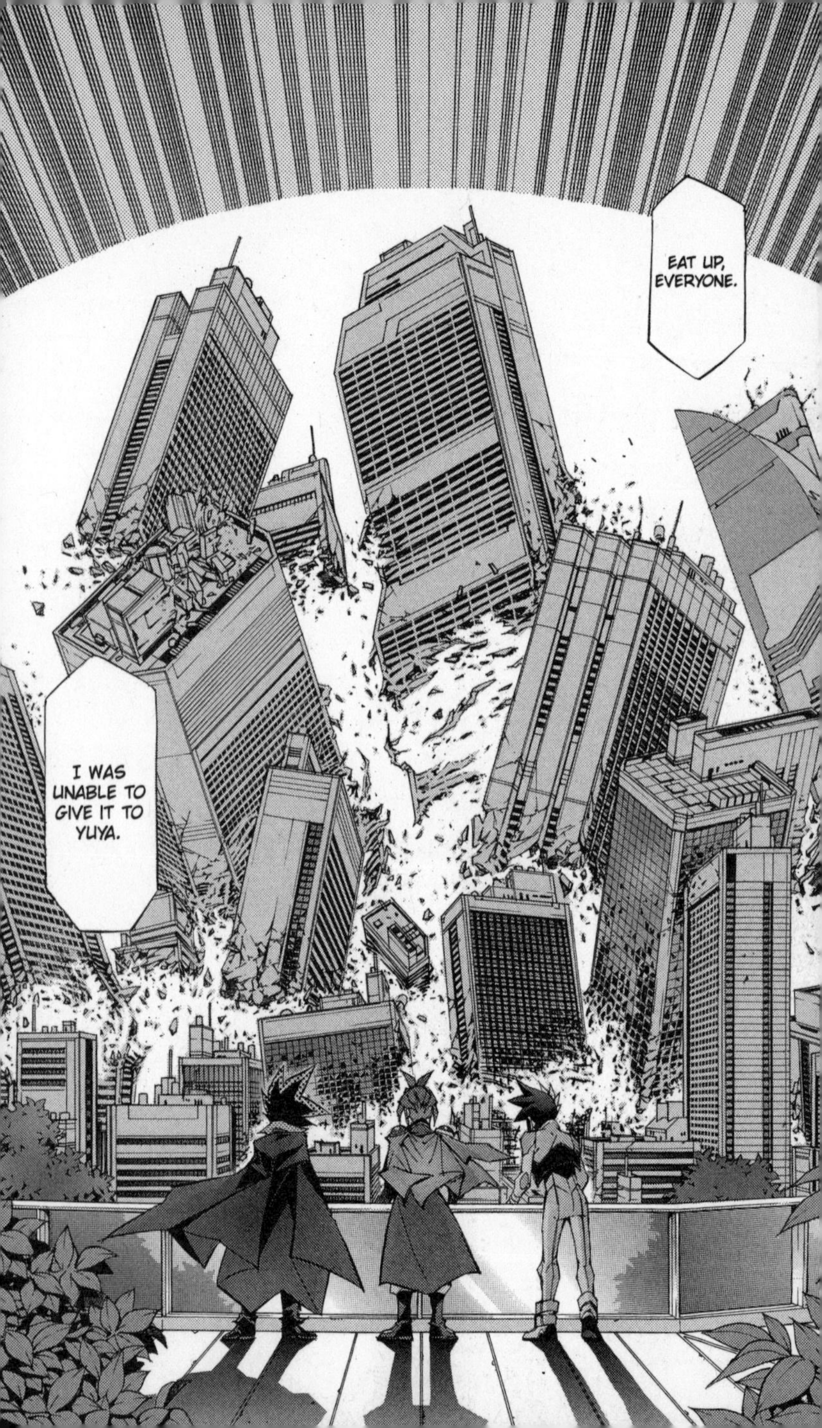
EAT UP, EVERYONE.
I WAS UNABLE TO GIVE IT TO YUYA.

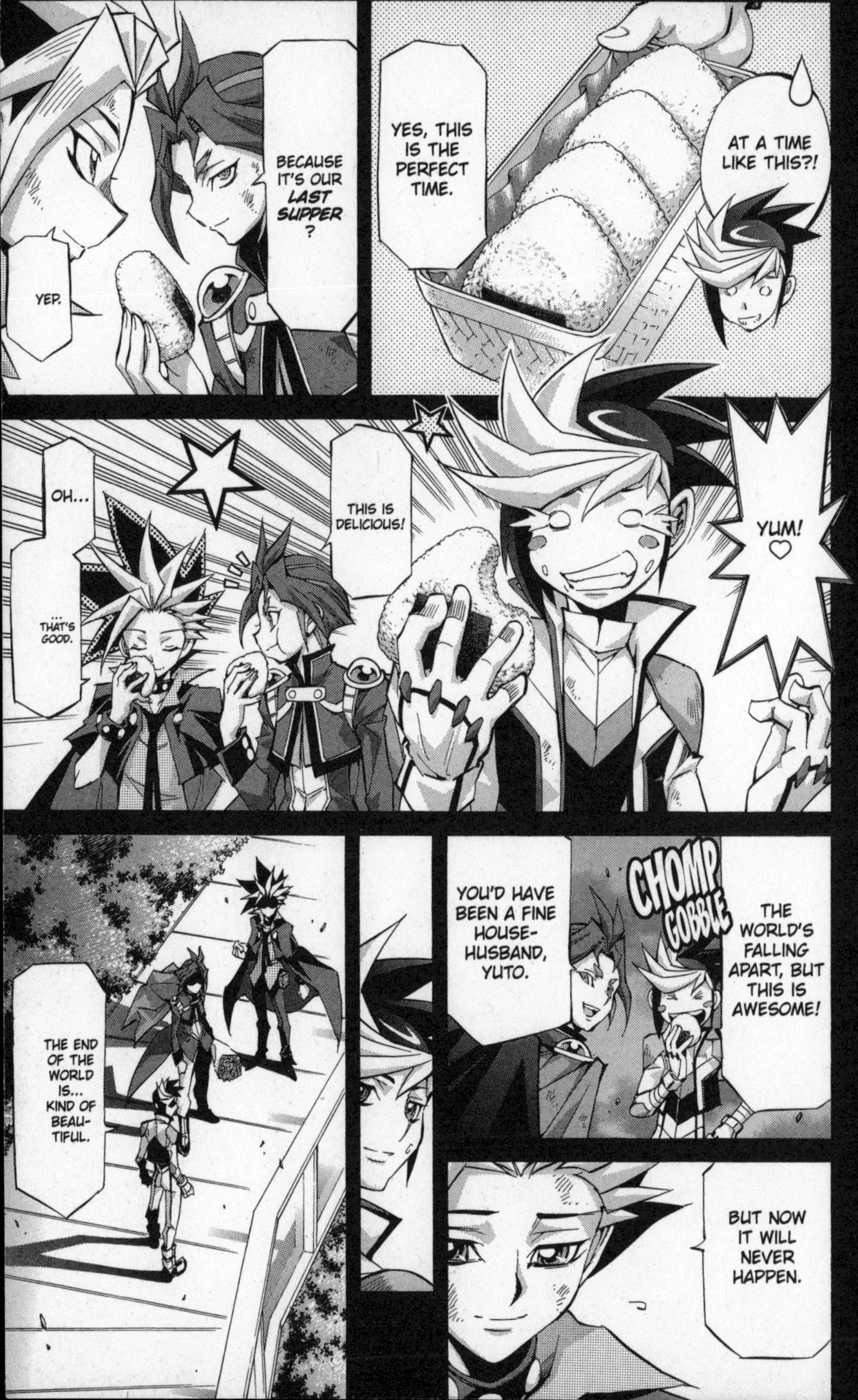
AT A TIME LIKE THIS?!
YES, THIS IS THE PERFECT TIME.
BECAUSE IT'S OUR *LAST SUPPER* ?
YEP.
YUM! ♡
THIS IS DELICIOUS!
OH...
...THAT'S GOOD.
CHOMP
GOBBLE
THE WORLD'S FALLING APART, BUT THIS IS AWESOME!
YOU'D HAVE BEEN A FINE HOUSE-HUSBAND, YUTO.
BUT NOW IT WILL NEVER HAPPEN.
THE END OF THE WORLD IS... KIND OF BEAU-TIFUL.

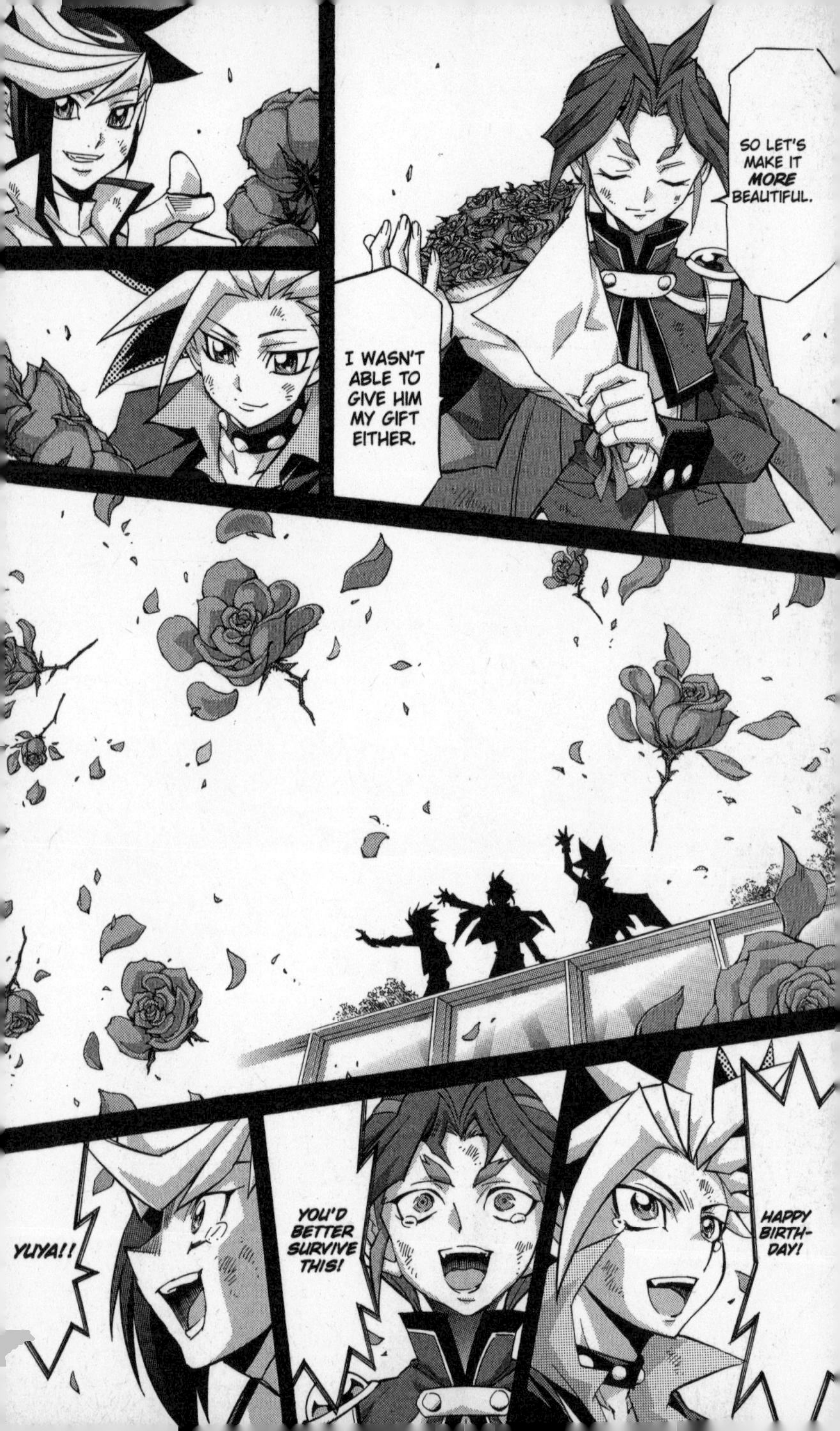
SO LET'S MAKE IT ***MORE*** BEAUTIFUL.
I WASN'T ABLE TO GIVE HIM MY GIFT EITHER.
HAPPY BIRTH-DAY!
YOU'D BETTER SURVIVE THIS!
YUYA!!

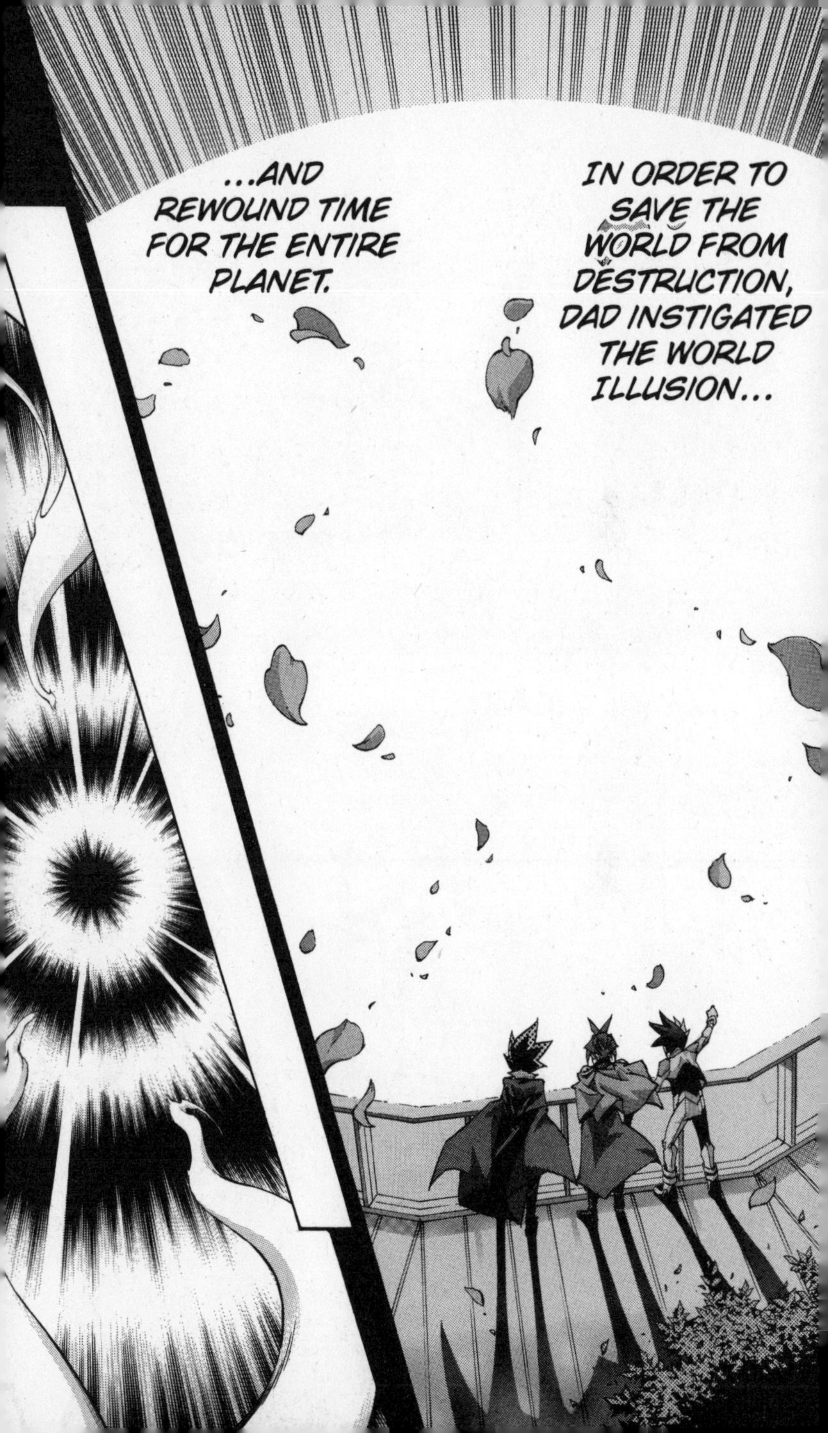
IN ORDER TO SAVE THE WORLD FROM DESTRUCTION, DAD INSTIGATED THE WORLD ILLUSION...
...AND REWOUND TIME FOR THE ENTIRE PLANET.

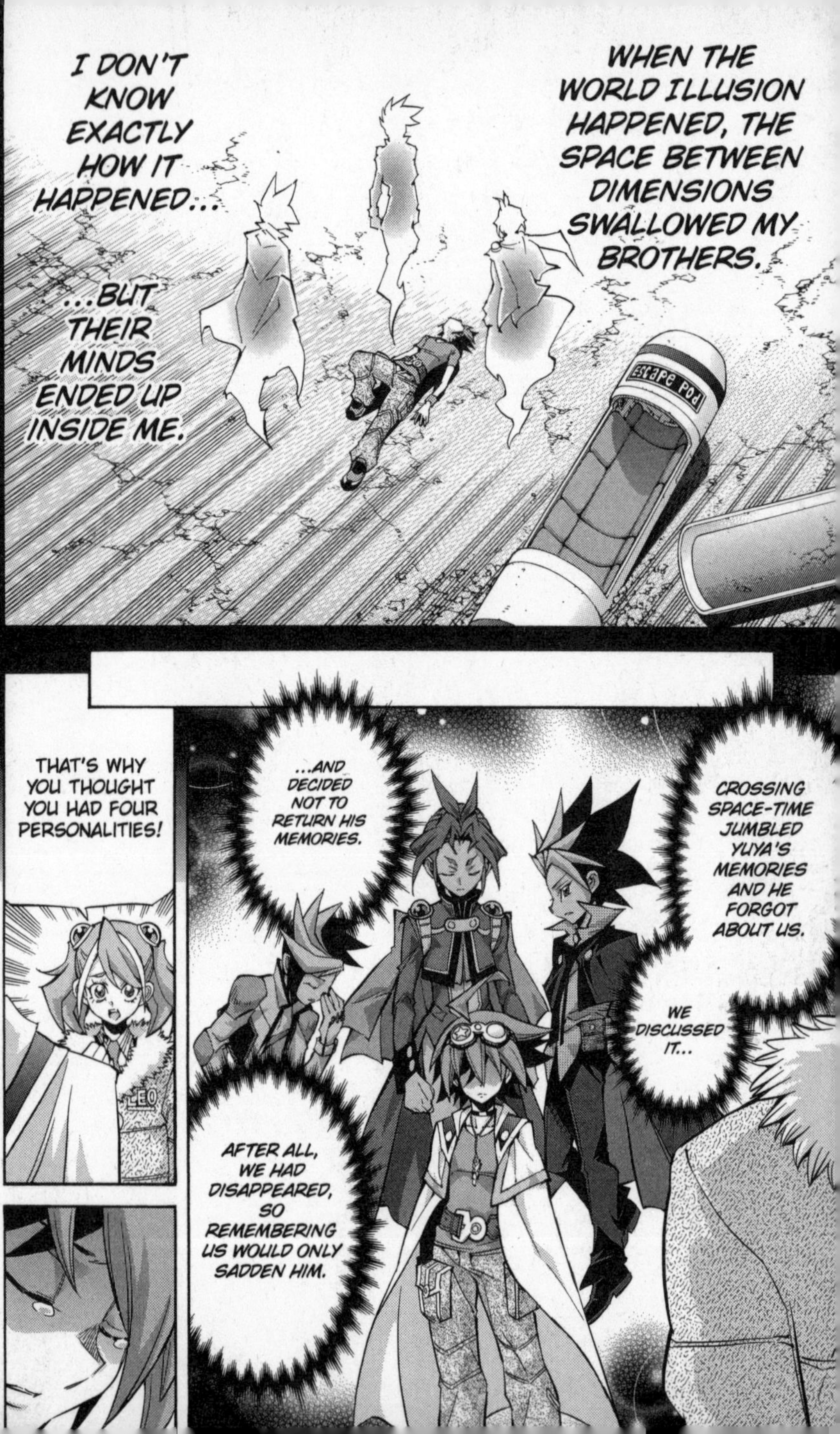
WHEN THE WORLD ILLUSION HAPPENED, THE SPACE BETWEEN DIMENSIONS SWALLOWED MY BROTHERS.
I DON'T KNOW EXACTLY HOW IT HAPPENED...
...BUT THEIR MINDS ENDED UP INSIDE ME.
ESCAPE POD
CROSSING SPACE-TIME JUMBLED YUYA'S MEMORIES AND HE FORGOT ABOUT US.
WE DISCUSSED IT...
...AND DECIDED NOT TO RETURN HIS MEMORIES.
AFTER ALL, WE HAD DISAPPEARED, SO REMEMBERING US WOULD ONLY SADDEN HIM.
THAT'S WHY YOU THOUGHT YOU HAD FOUR PERSONALITIES!
LEO

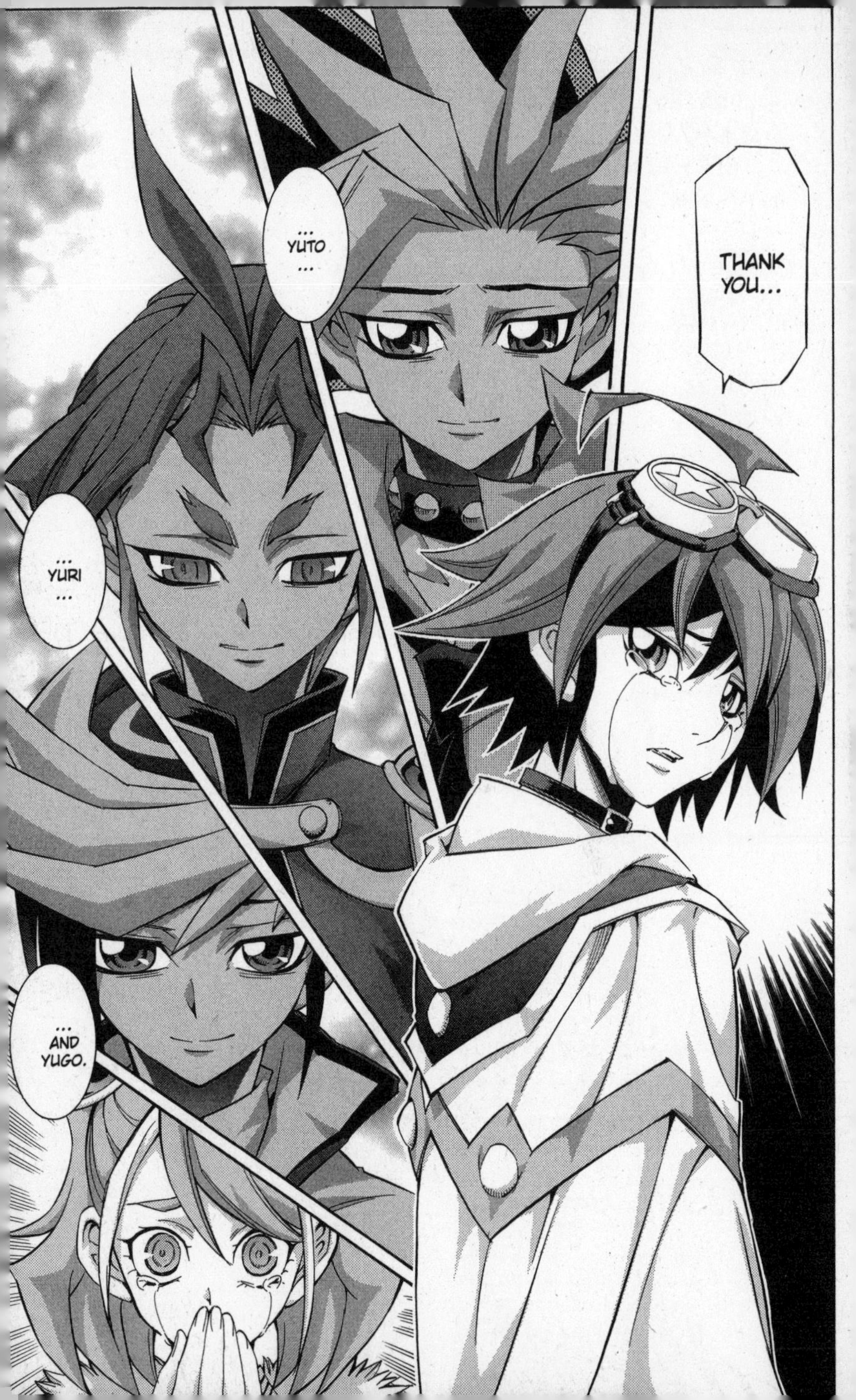
THANK YOU...
...YUTO...
...YURI...
...AND YUGO.

GENESIS OMEGA DRAGON

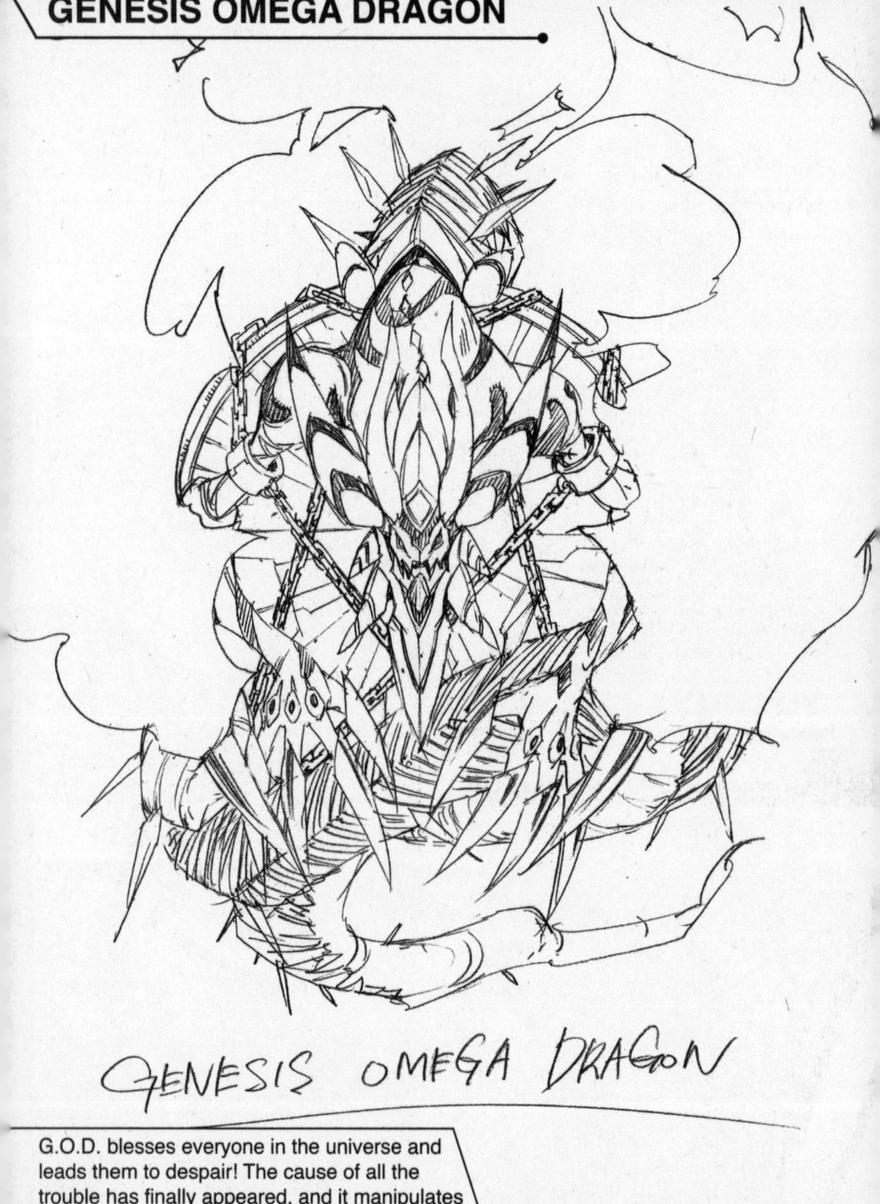
GENESIS OMEGA DRAGON

G.O.D. blesses everyone in the universe and leads them to despair! The cause of all the trouble has finally appeared, and it manipulates time and space! How will this Duel end?!

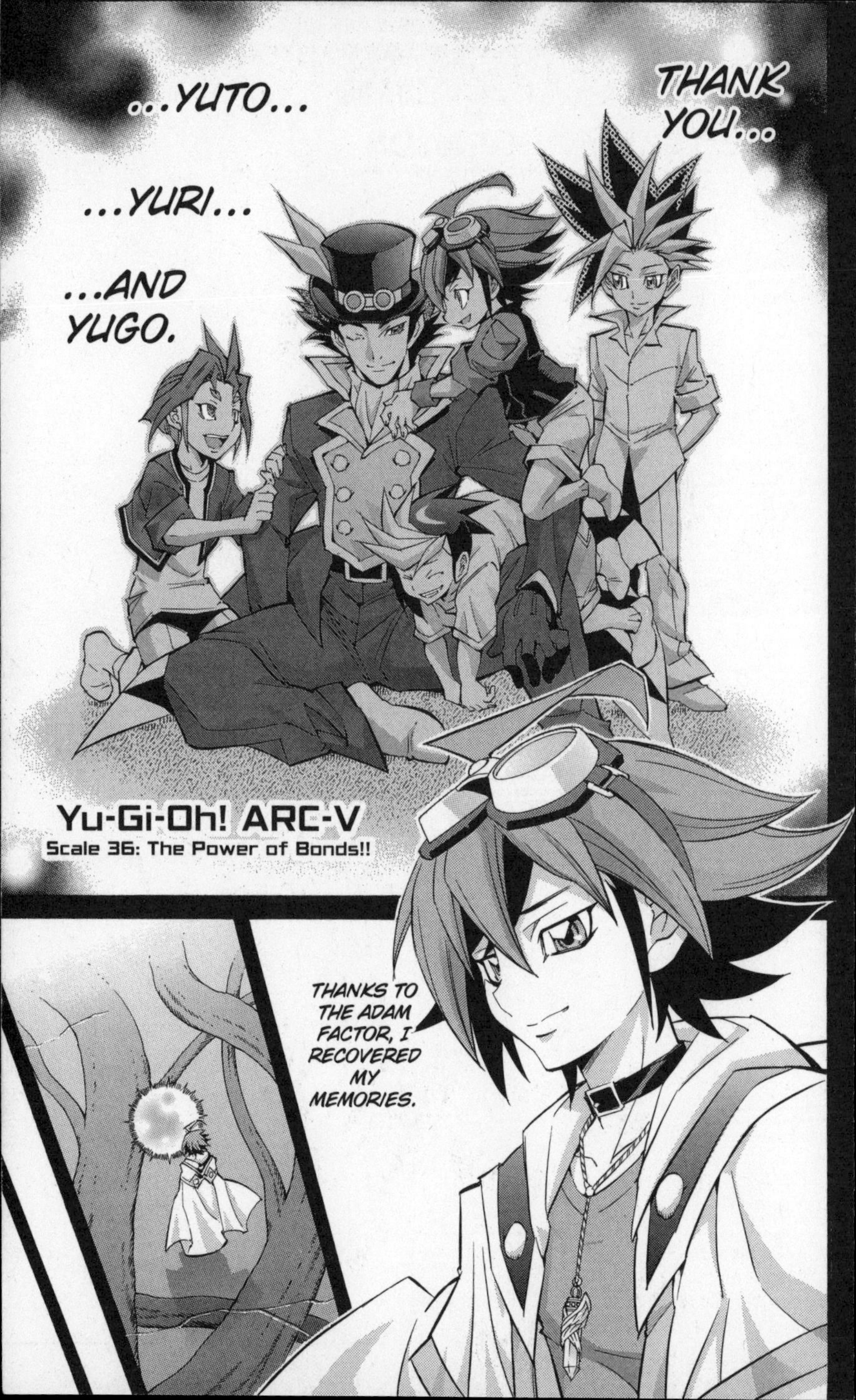
THANK YOU...
...YUTO...
...YURI...
...AND YUGO.
Yu-Gi-Oh! ARC-V
Scale 36: The Power of Bonds!!
THANKS TO THE ADAM FACTOR, I RECOVERED MY MEMORIES.

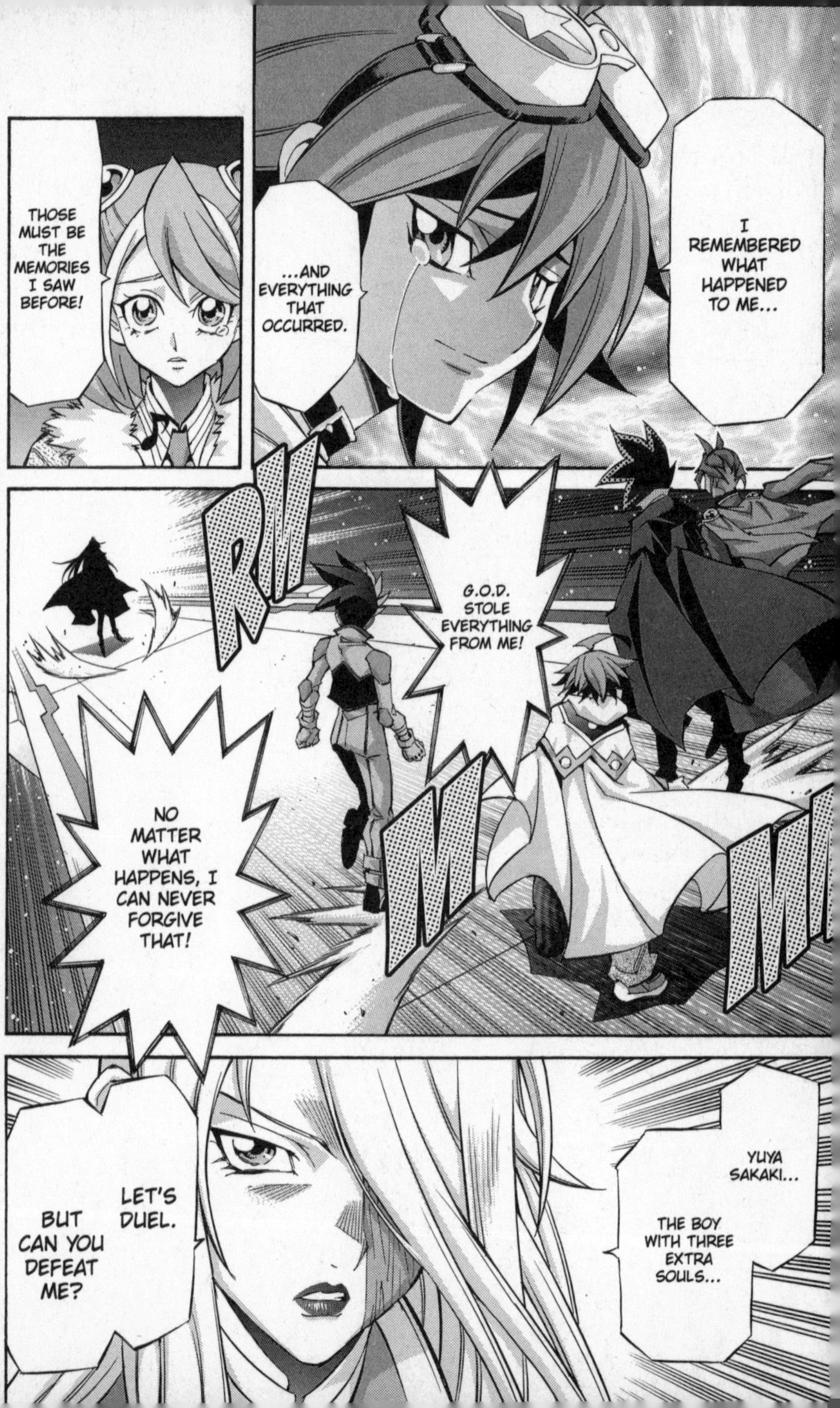
I REMEMBERED WHAT HAPPENED TO ME...
...AND EVERYTHING THAT OCCURRED.
THOSE MUST BE THE MEMORIES I SAW BEFORE!
G.O.D. STOLE EVERYTHING FROM ME!
RMM
NO MATTER WHAT HAPPENS, I CAN NEVER FORGIVE THAT!
YUYA SAKAKI...
THE BOY WITH THREE EXTRA SOULS...
LET'S DUEL.
BUT CAN YOU DEFEAT ME?

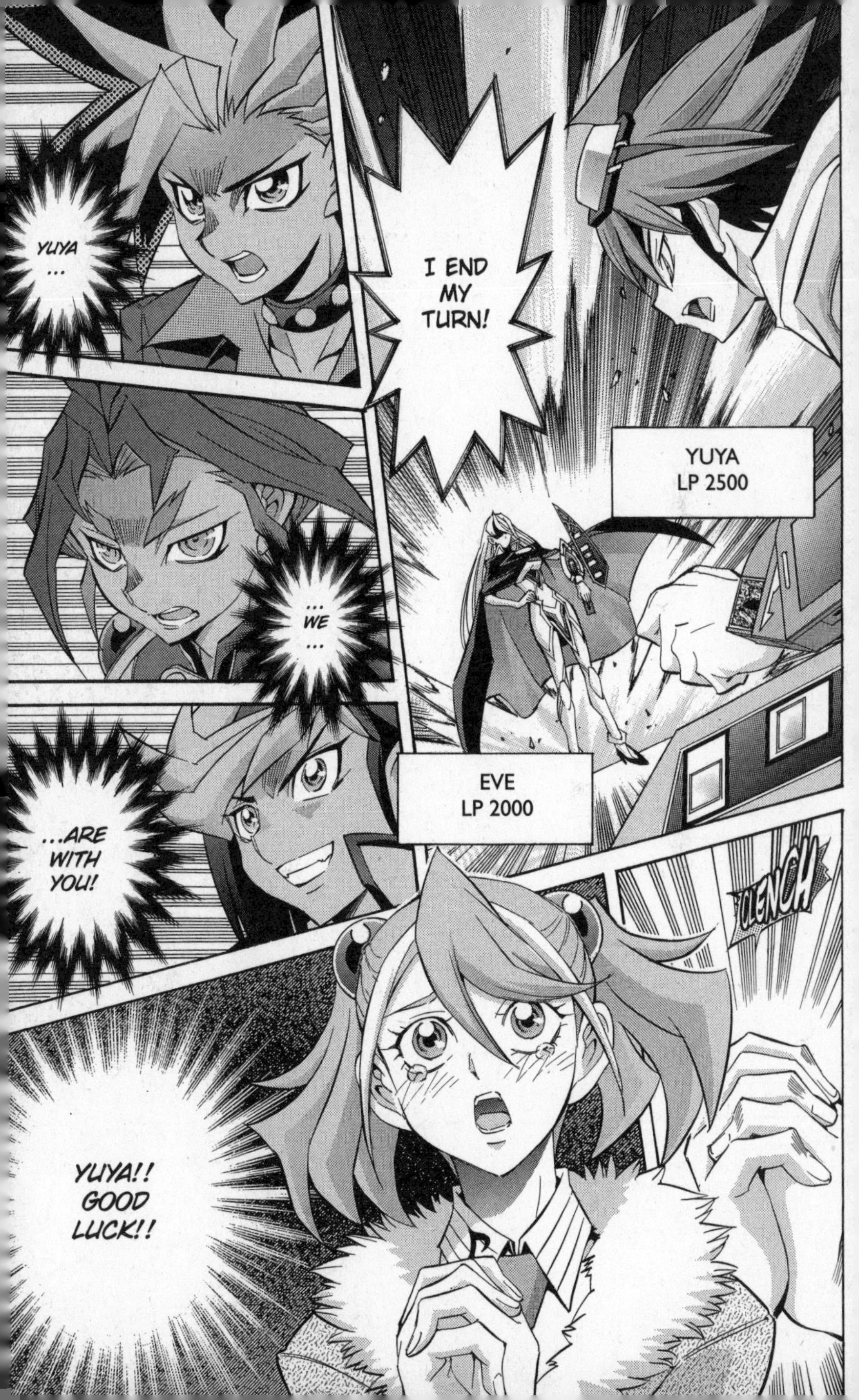
I END MY TURN!
YUYA
LP 2500
EVE
LP 2000
YUYA ...
... WE ...
...ARE WITH YOU!
CLENCH
YUYA!! GOOD LUCK!!

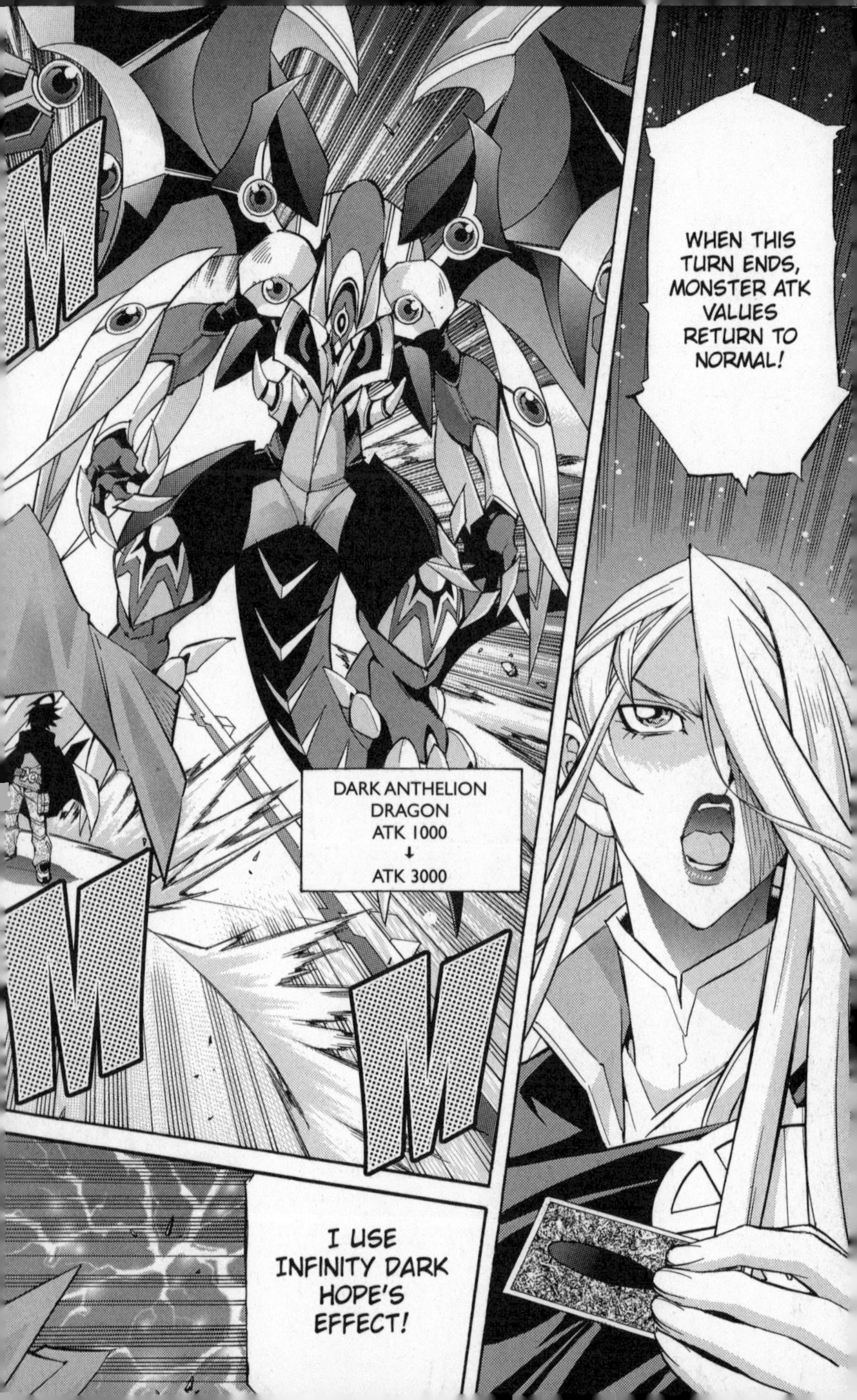
WHEN THIS TURN ENDS, MONSTER ATK VALUES RETURN TO NORMAL!
MMMM
DARK ANTHELION DRAGON ATK 1000 ↓ ATK 3000
I USE INFINITY DARK HOPE'S EFFECT!

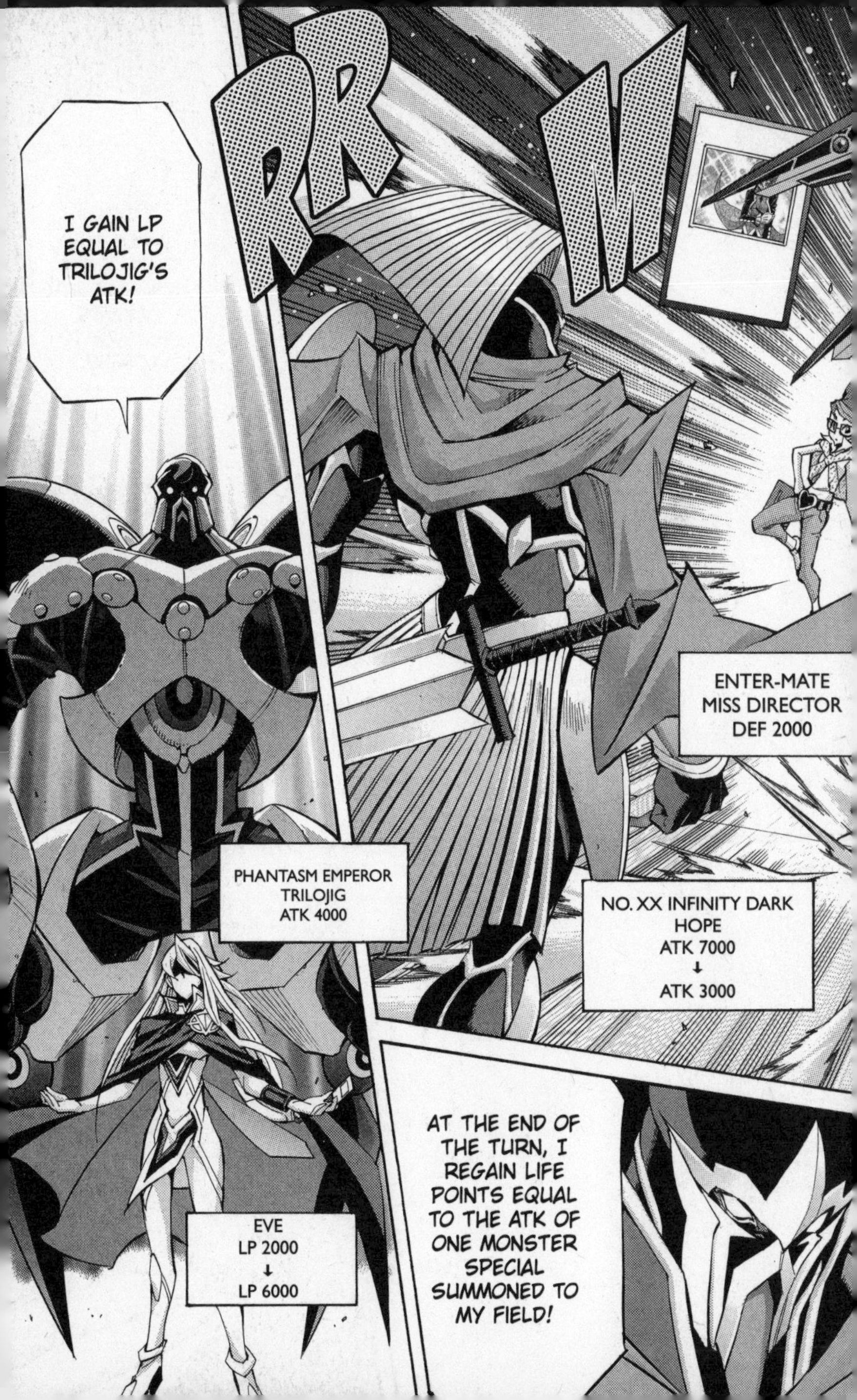
RRM
ENTER-MATE MISS DIRECTOR DEF 2000
NO. XX INFINITY DARK HOPE ATK 7000 ↓ ATK 3000
AT THE END OF THE TURN, I REGAIN LIFE POINTS EQUAL TO THE ATK OF ONE MONSTER SPECIAL SUMMONED TO MY FIELD!
I GAIN LP EQUAL TO TRILOJIG'S ATK!
PHANTASM EMPEROR TRILOJIG ATK 4000
EVE LP 2000 ↓ LP 6000

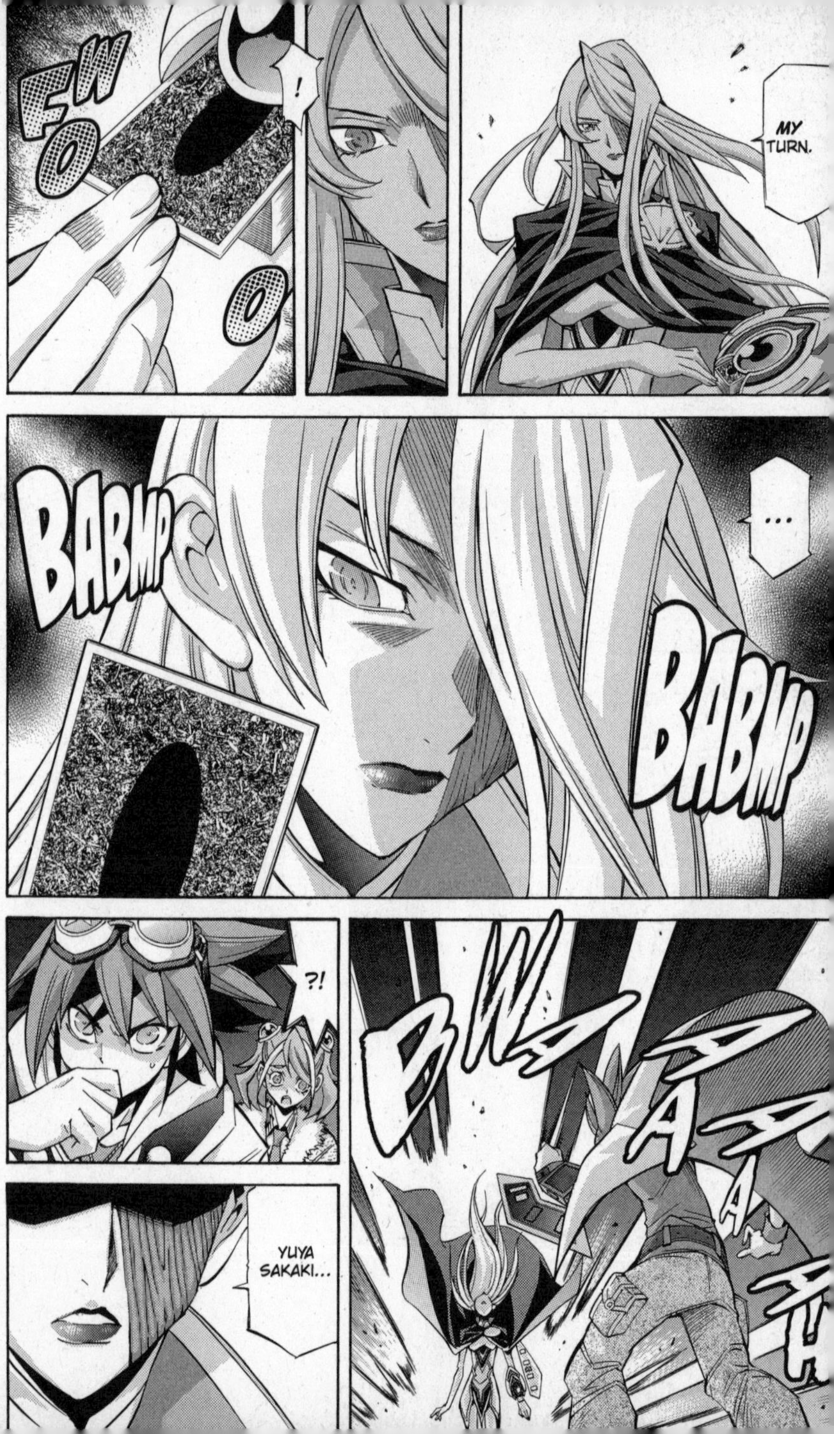
MY TURN.
!
FWOO
...
BABMP
BABMP
BWAHAHAHA
?!
YUYA SAKAKI...

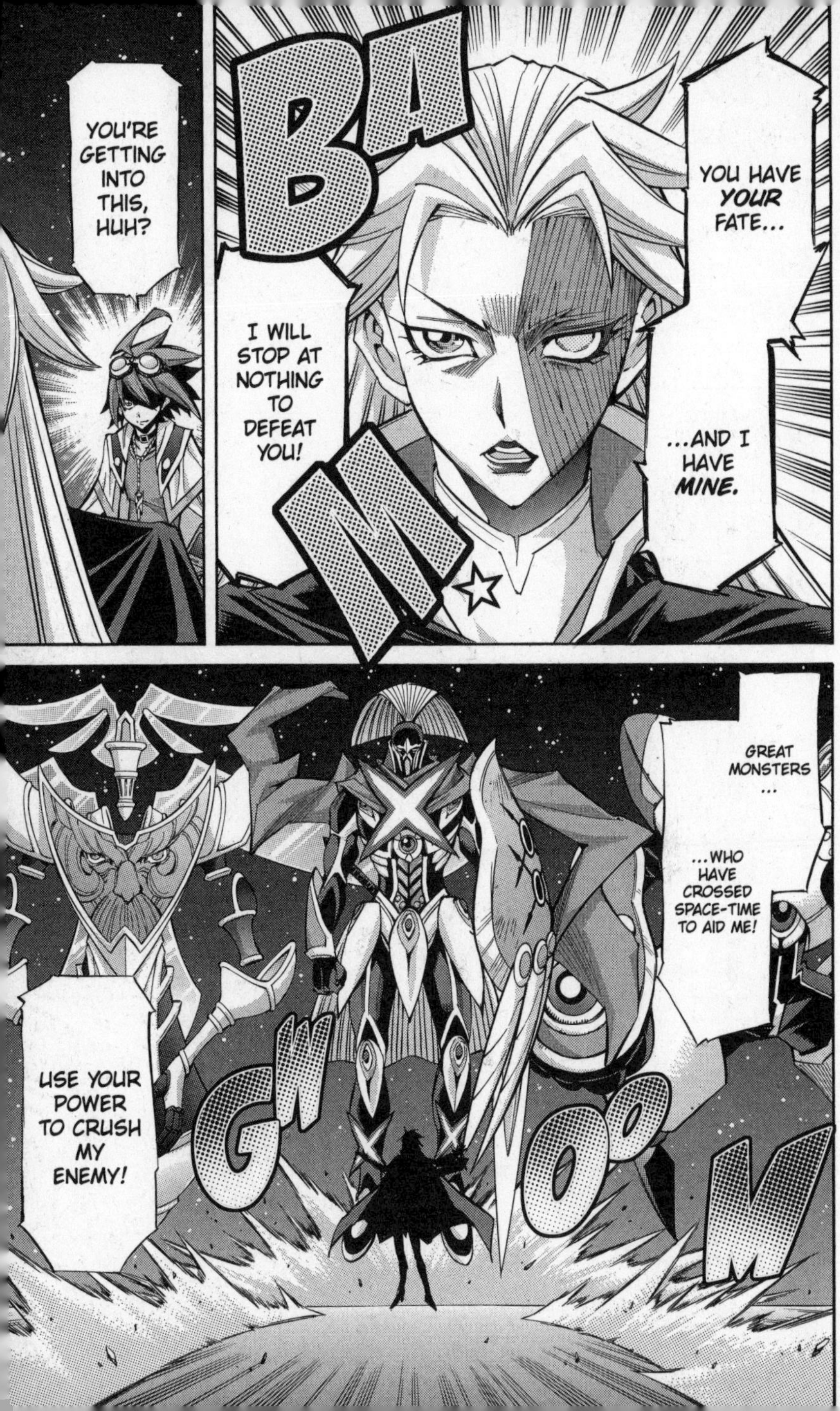
YOU HAVE YOUR FATE...
...AND I HAVE MINE.
BAM
I WILL STOP AT NOTHING TO DEFEAT YOU!
YOU'RE GETTING INTO THIS, HUH?
GREAT MONSTERS...
...WHO HAVE CROSSED SPACE-TIME TO AID ME!
GWOOOM
USE YOUR POWER TO CRUSH MY ENEMY!

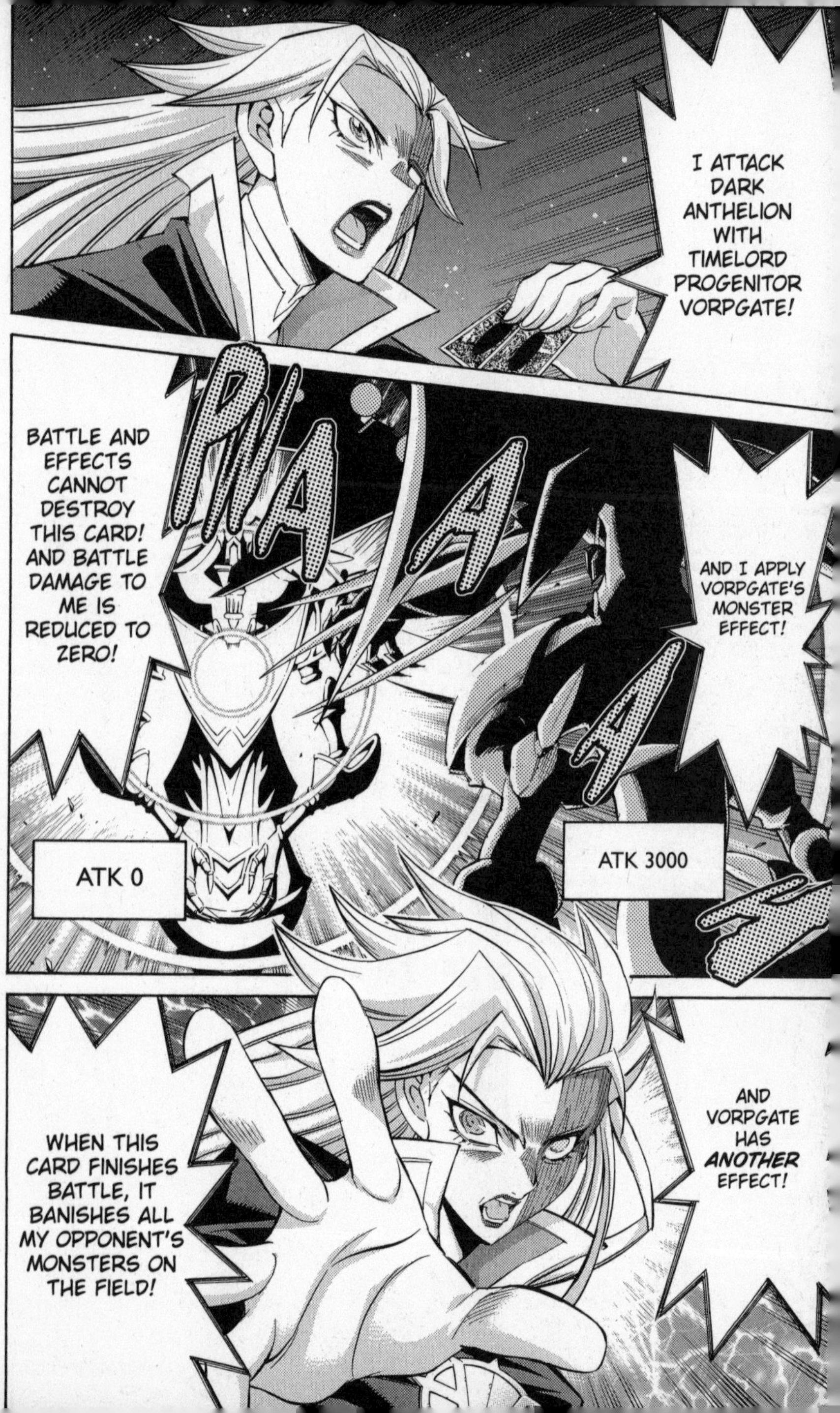
I ATTACK DARK ANTHELION WITH TIMELORD PROGENITOR VORPGATE!
AND I APPLY VORPGATE'S MONSTER EFFECT!
PHAAA
BATTLE AND EFFECTS CANNOT DESTROY THIS CARD! AND BATTLE DAMAGE TO ME IS REDUCED TO ZERO!
ATK 3000
ATK 0
AND VORPGATE HAS *ANOTHER* EFFECT!
WHEN THIS CARD FINISHES BATTLE, IT BANISHES ALL MY OPPONENT'S MONSTERS ON THE FIELD!

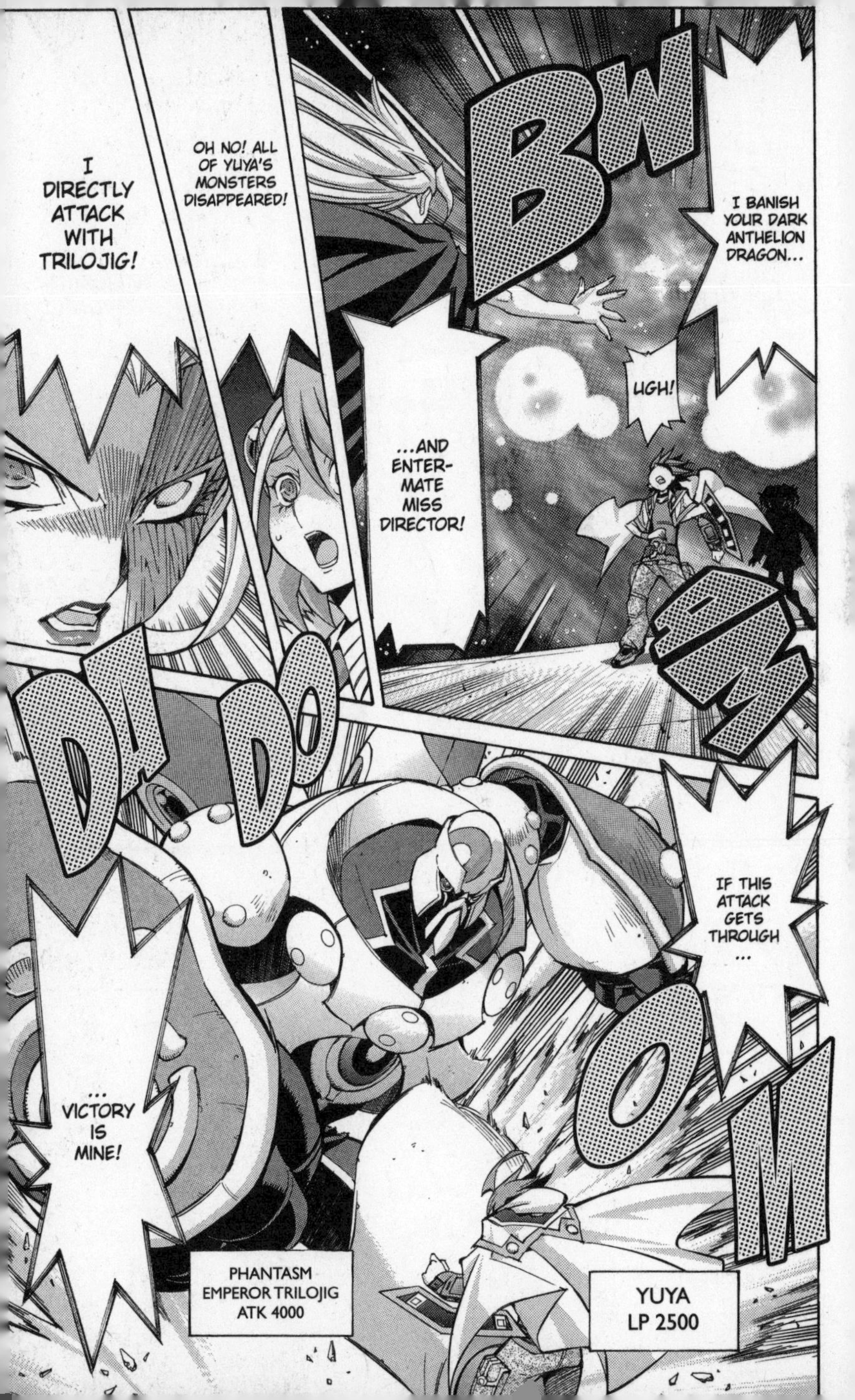
BW
I BANISH YOUR DARK ANTHELION DRAGON...
UGH!
...AND ENTER-MATE MISS DIRECTOR!
OM
OH NO! ALL OF YUYA'S MONSTERS DISAPPEARED!
I DIRECTLY ATTACK WITH TRILOJIG!
IF THIS ATTACK GETS THROUGH...
DA
DO
OOM
YUYA LP 2500
PHANTASM EMPEROR TRILOJIG ATK 4000
...VICTORY IS MINE!

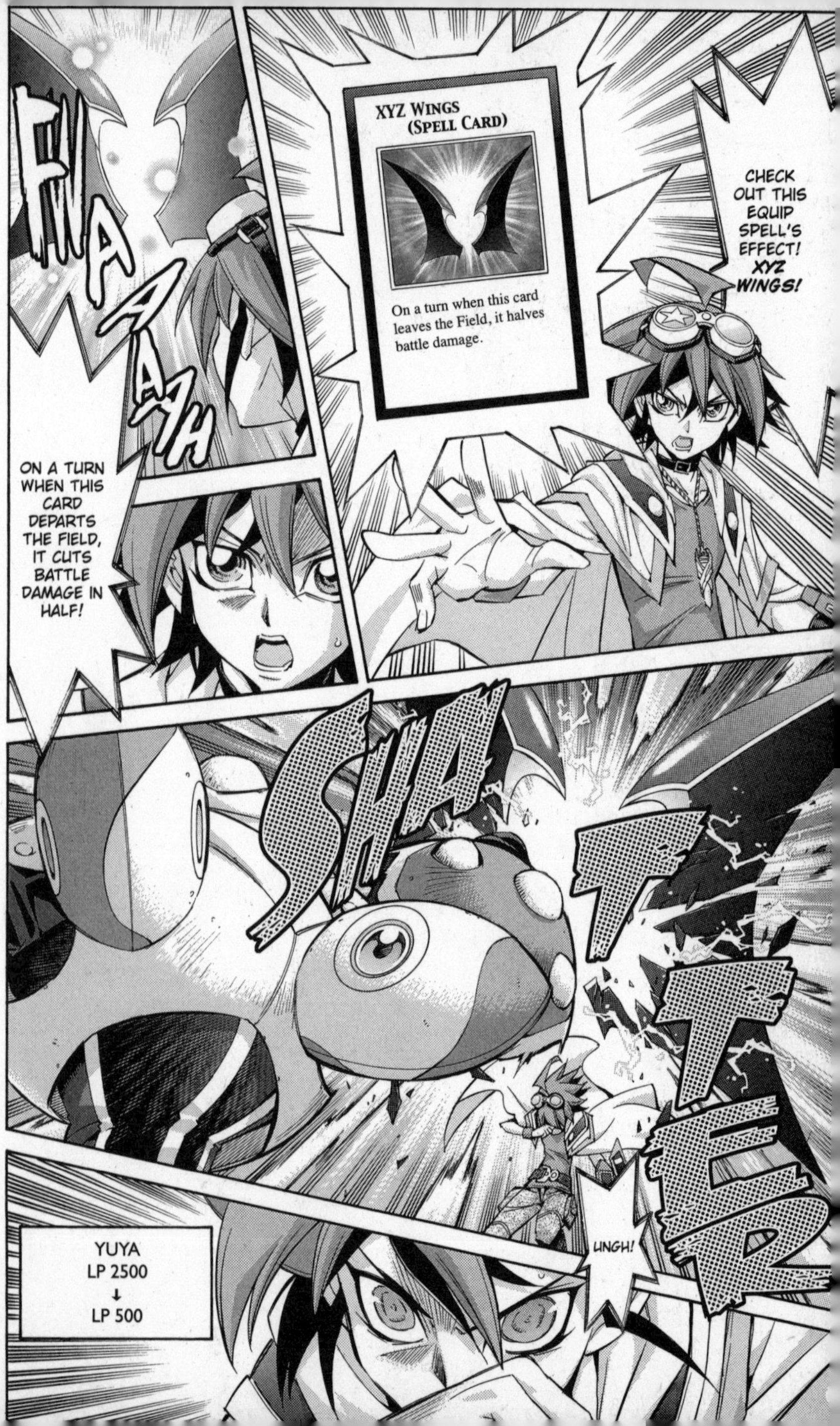
CHECK OUT THIS EQUIP SPELL'S EFFECT! XYZ WINGS!
XYZ Wings (Spell Card)
On a turn when this card leaves the Field, it halves battle damage.
FWAAAAH
ON A TURN WHEN THIS CARD DEPARTS THE FIELD, IT CUTS BATTLE DAMAGE IN HALF!
SHATTER
UNGH!
YUYA LP 2500 ↓ LP 500

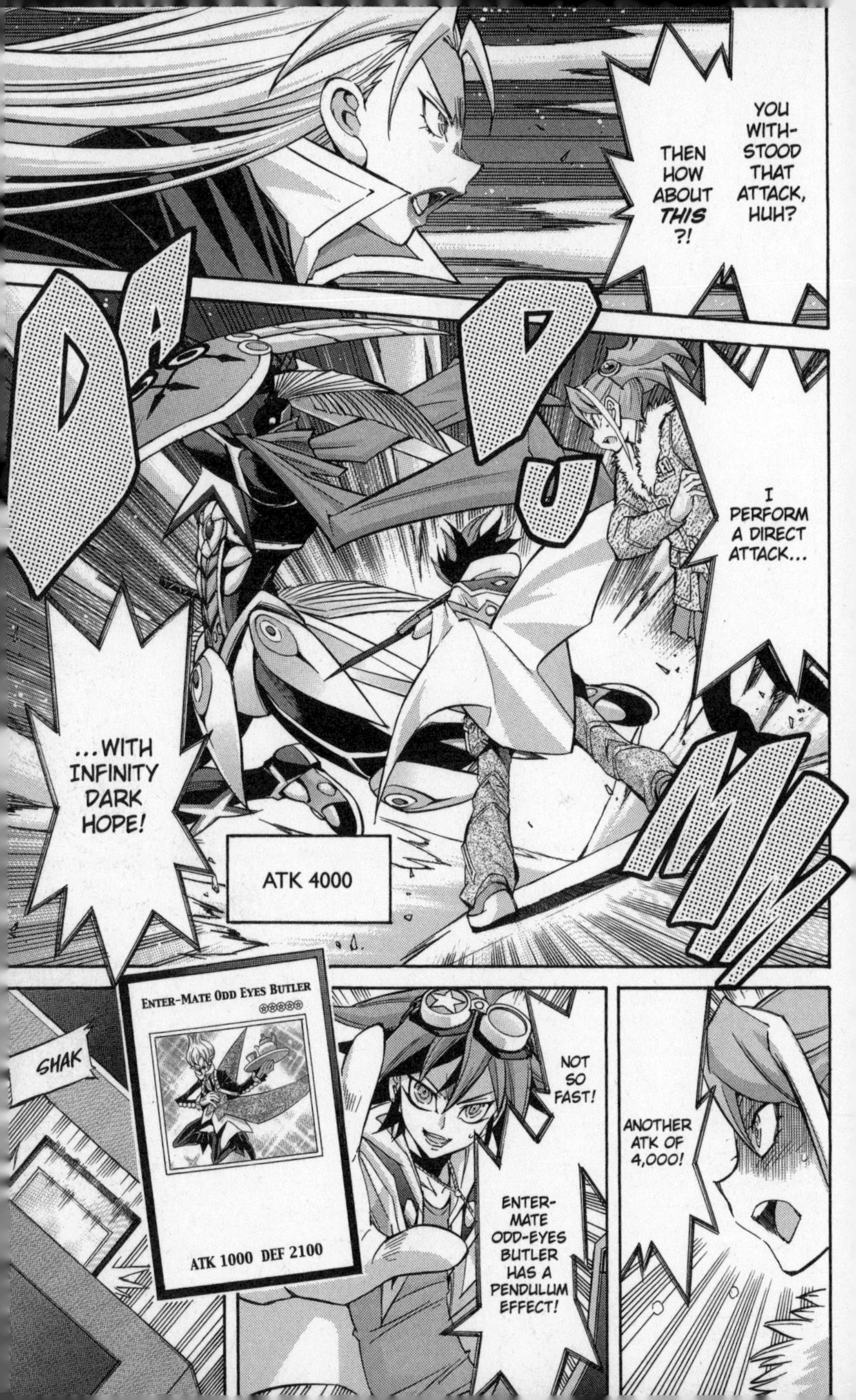
YOU WITH-STOOD THAT ATTACK, HUH?
THEN HOW ABOUT *THIS* ?!
I PERFORM A DIRECT ATTACK...
...WITH INFINITY DARK HOPE!
ATK 4000
ANOTHER ATK OF 4,000!
NOT SO FAST!
ENTER-MATE ODD-EYES BUTLER HAS A PENDULUM EFFECT!
ENTER-MATE ODD EYES BUTLER
ATK 1000 DEF 2100
SHAK

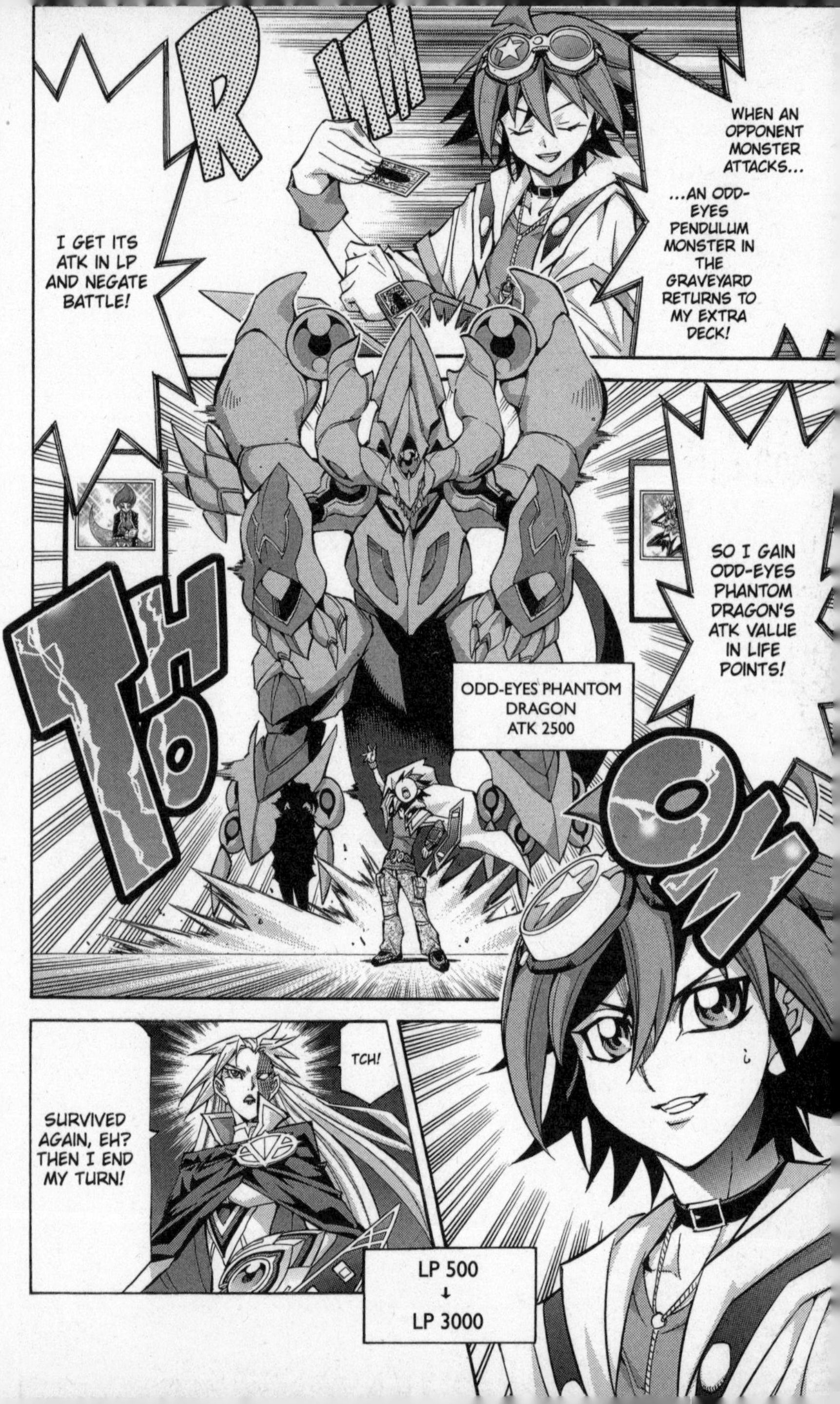
WHEN AN OPPONENT MONSTER ATTACKS...
...AN ODD-EYES PENDULUM MONSTER IN THE GRAVEYARD RETURNS TO MY EXTRA DECK!
I GET ITS ATK IN LP AND NEGATE BATTLE!
SO I GAIN ODD-EYES PHANTOM DRAGON'S ATK VALUE IN LIFE POINTS!
ODD-EYES PHANTOM DRAGON ATK 2500
LP 500 ↓ LP 3000
TCH!
SURVIVED AGAIN, EH? THEN I END MY TURN!

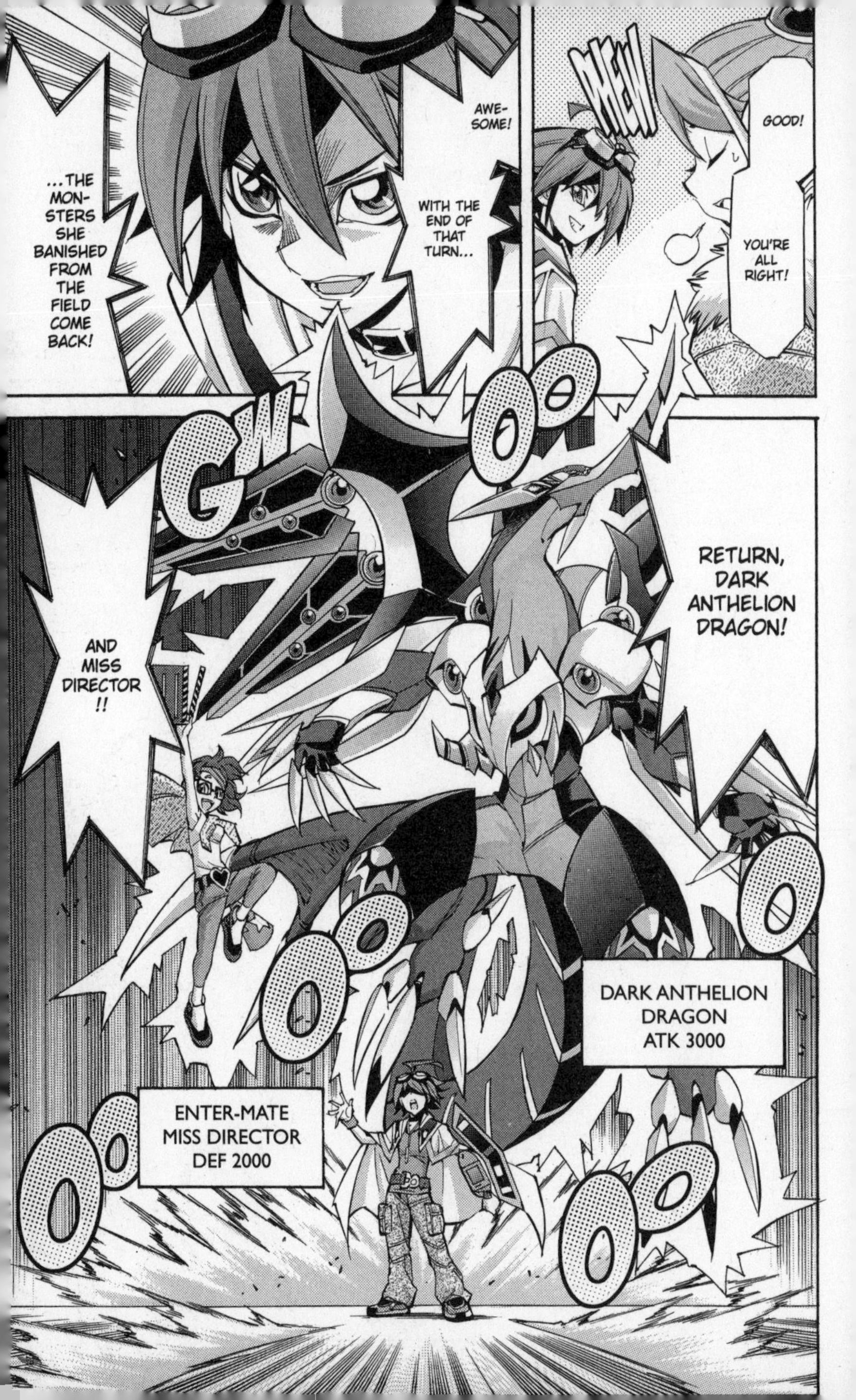
PWEW
GOOD!
YOU'RE ALL RIGHT!
AWE-SOME!
WITH THE END OF THAT TURN...
...THE MON-STERS SHE BANISHED FROM THE FIELD COME BACK!
GW
RETURN, DARK ANTHELION DRAGON!
AND MISS DIRECTOR!!
DARK ANTHELION DRAGON ATK 3000
ENTER-MATE MISS DIRECTOR DEF 2000

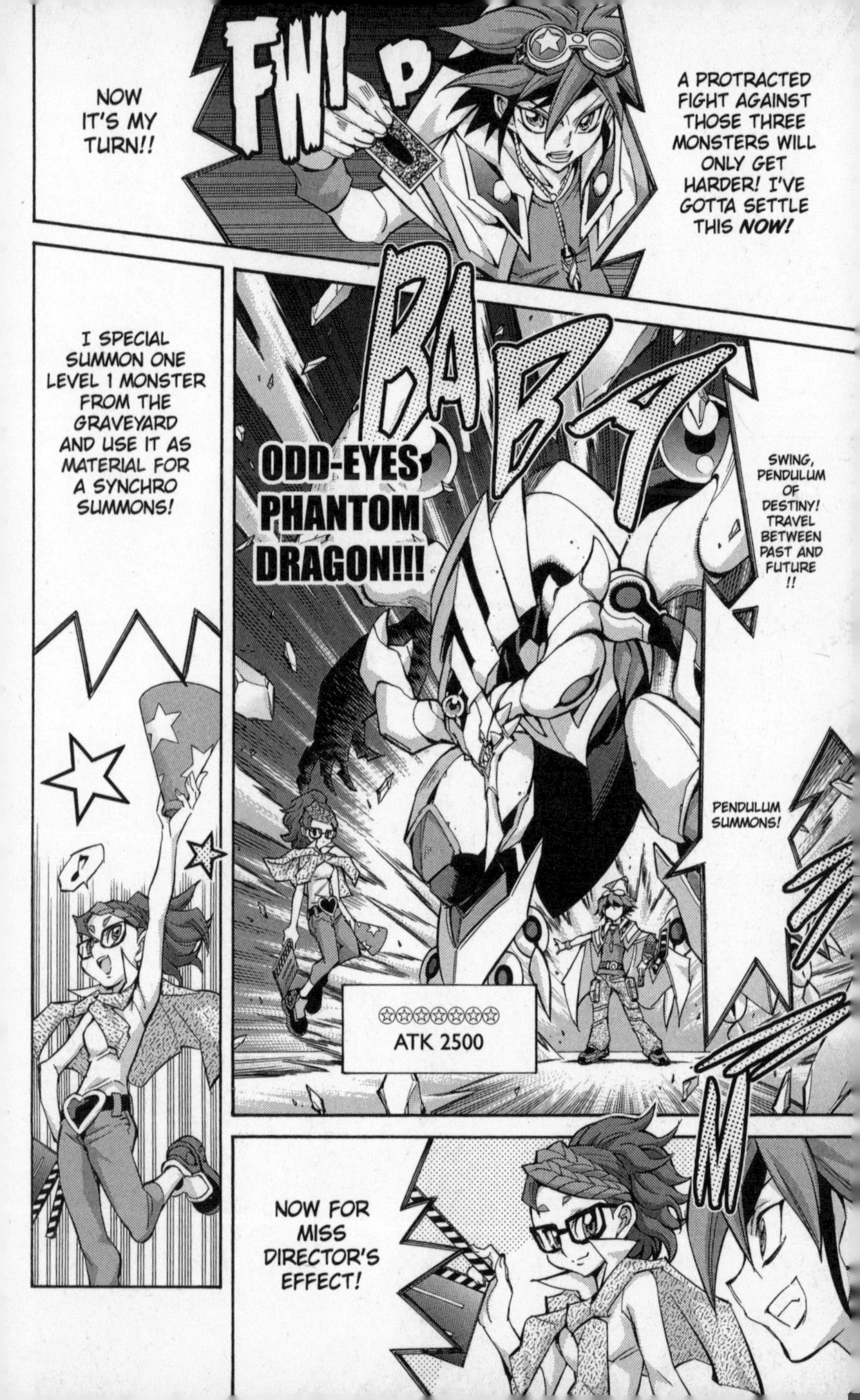

A PROTRACTED FIGHT AGAINST THOSE THREE MONSTERS WILL ONLY GET HARDER! I'VE GOTTA SETTLE THIS NOW!
FWIP
NOW IT'S MY TURN!!
SWING, PENDULUM OF DESTINY! TRAVEL BETWEEN PAST AND FUTURE!!
BABA
PENDULUM SUMMONS!
ODD-EYES PHANTOM DRAGON!!!
ATK 2500
NOW FOR MISS DIRECTOR'S EFFECT!
I SPECIAL SUMMON ONE LEVEL 1 MONSTER FROM THE GRAVEYARD AND USE IT AS MATERIAL FOR A SYNCHRO SUMMONS!

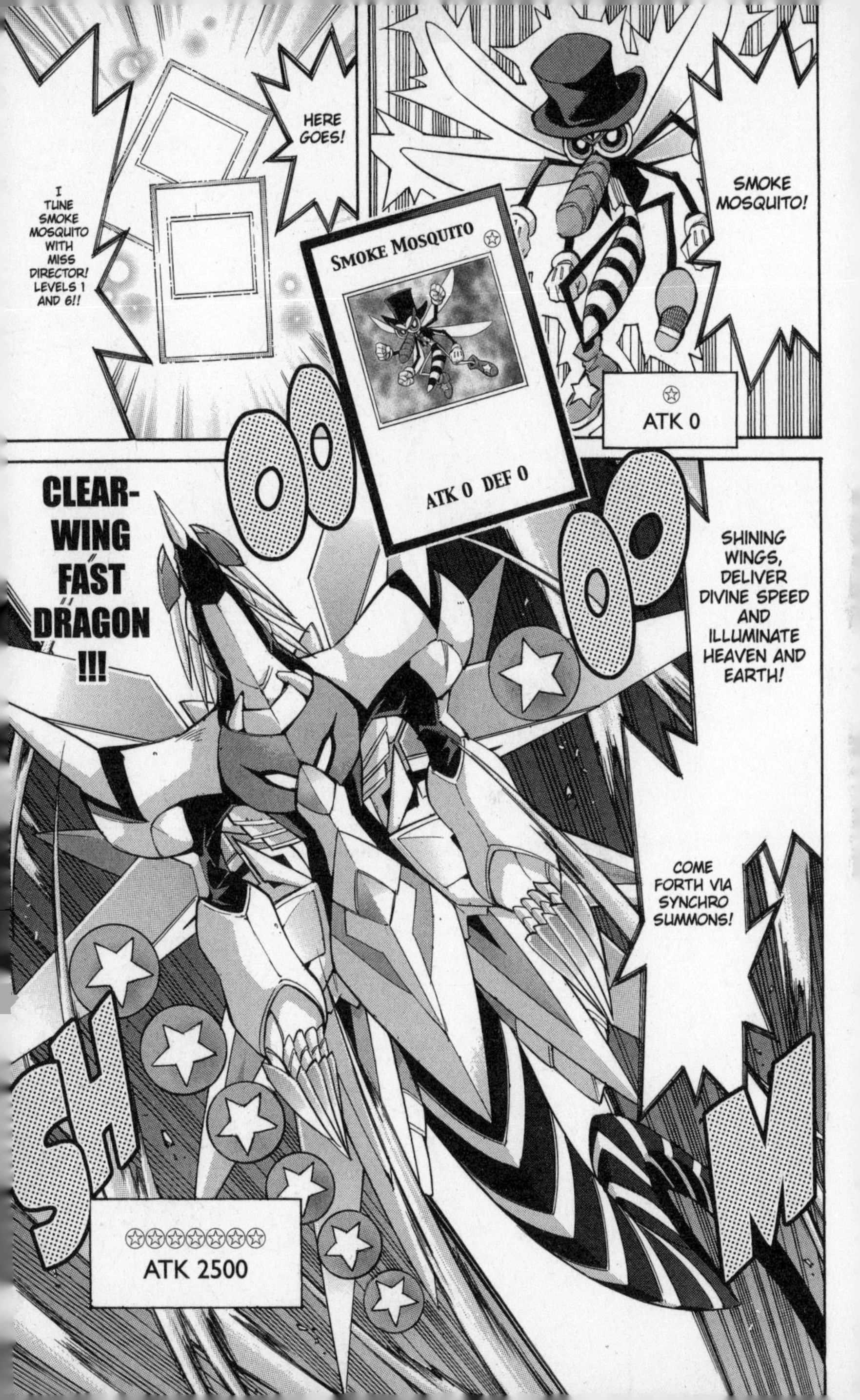
SMOKE MOSQUITO!
Smoke Mosquito
ATK 0 DEF 0
ATK 0
HERE GOES!
I TUNE SMOKE MOSQUITO WITH MISS DIRECTOR! LEVELS 1 AND 6!!
SHINING WINGS, DELIVER DIVINE SPEED AND ILLUMINATE HEAVEN AND EARTH!
COME FORTH VIA SYNCHRO SUMMONS!
CLEAR-WING "FAST" DRAGON!!!
ATK 2500

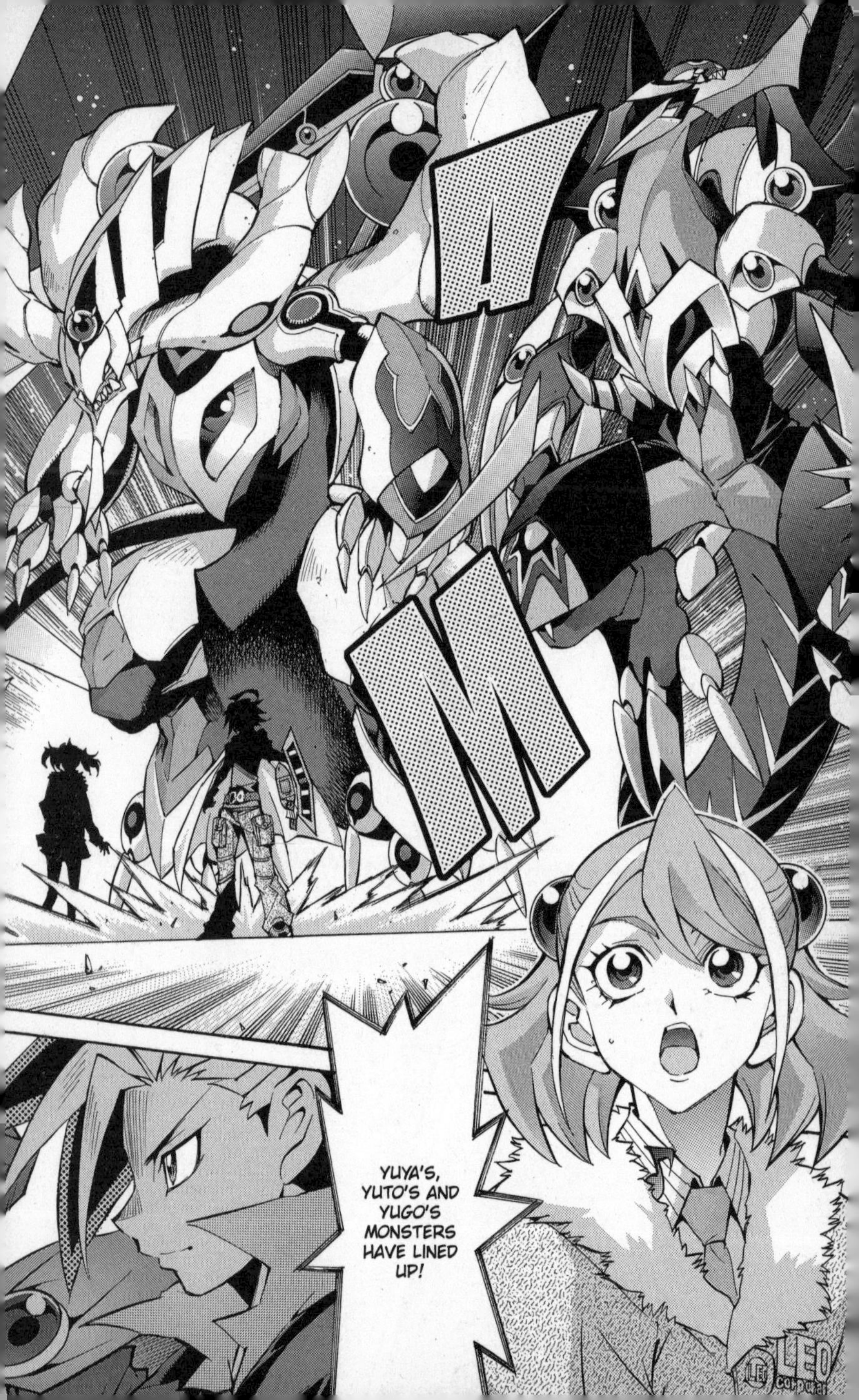
YUYA'S, YUTO'S AND YUGO'S MONSTERS HAVE LINED UP!

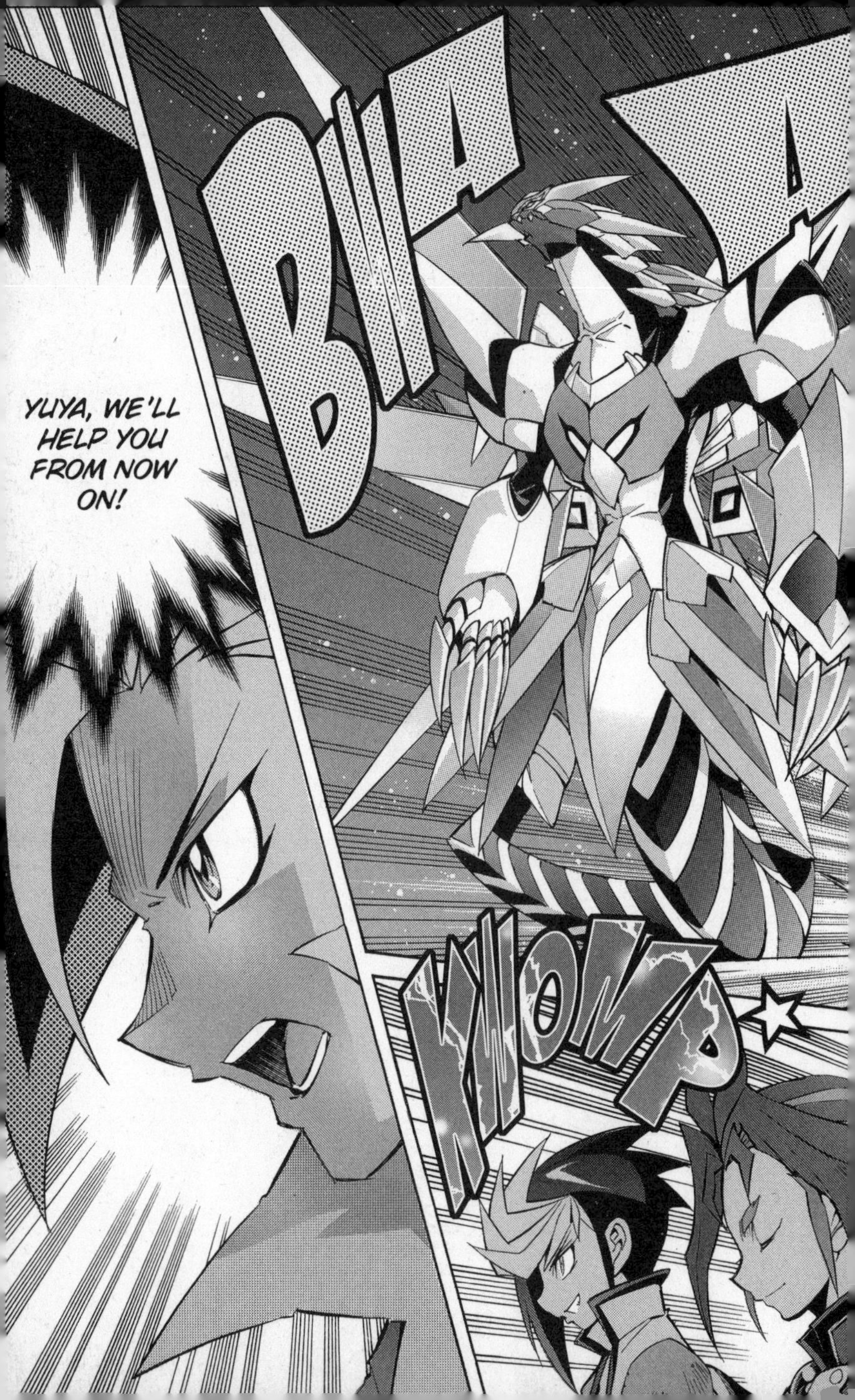
BWA
YUYA, WE'LL HELP YOU FROM NOW ON!
WHOMP

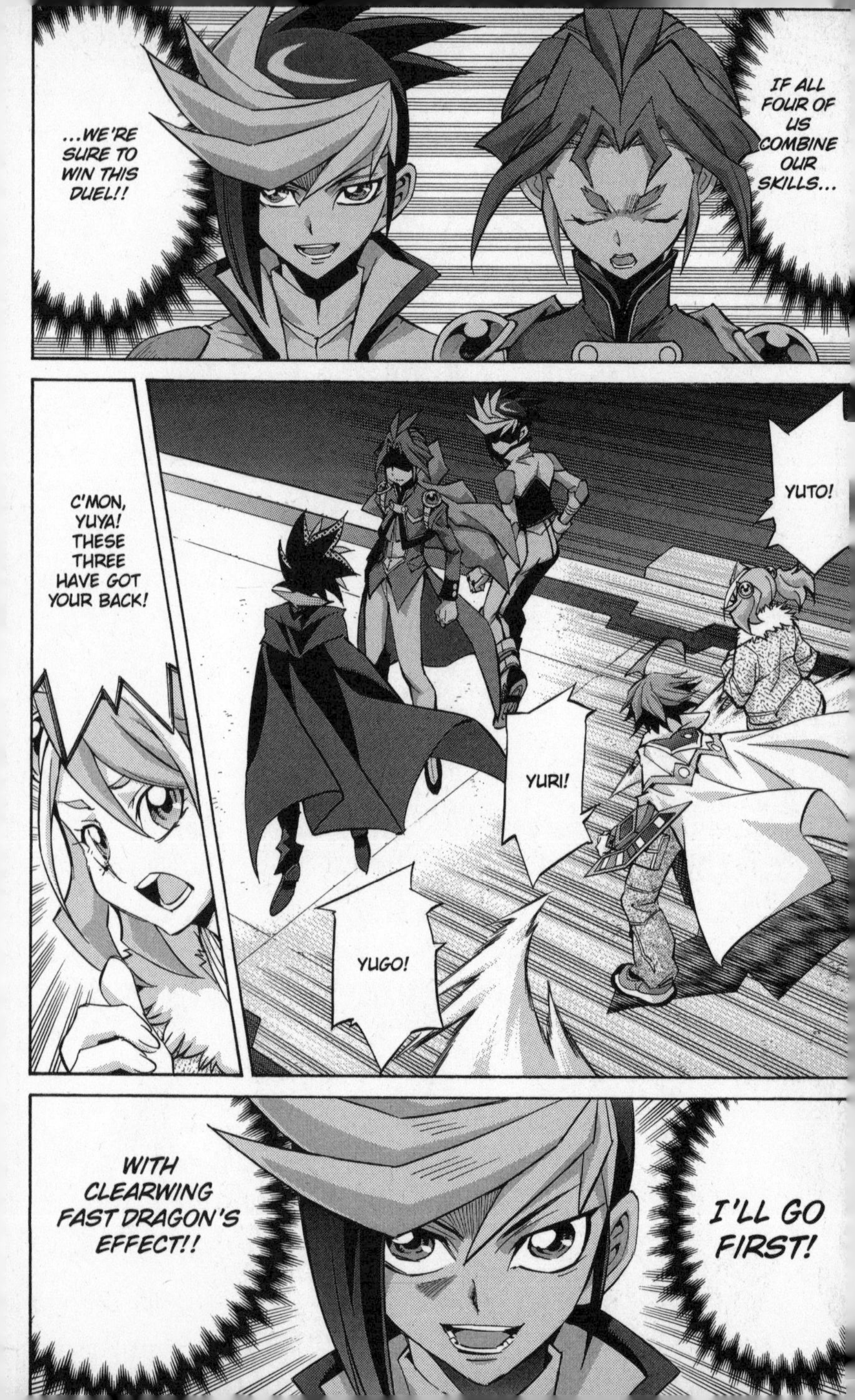
IF ALL FOUR OF US COMBINE OUR SKILLS...
...WE'RE SURE TO WIN THIS DUEL!!
YUTO!
YURI!
YUGO!
C'MON, YUYA! THESE THREE HAVE GOT YOUR BACK!
I'LL GO FIRST!
WITH CLEARWING FAST DRAGON'S EFFECT!!

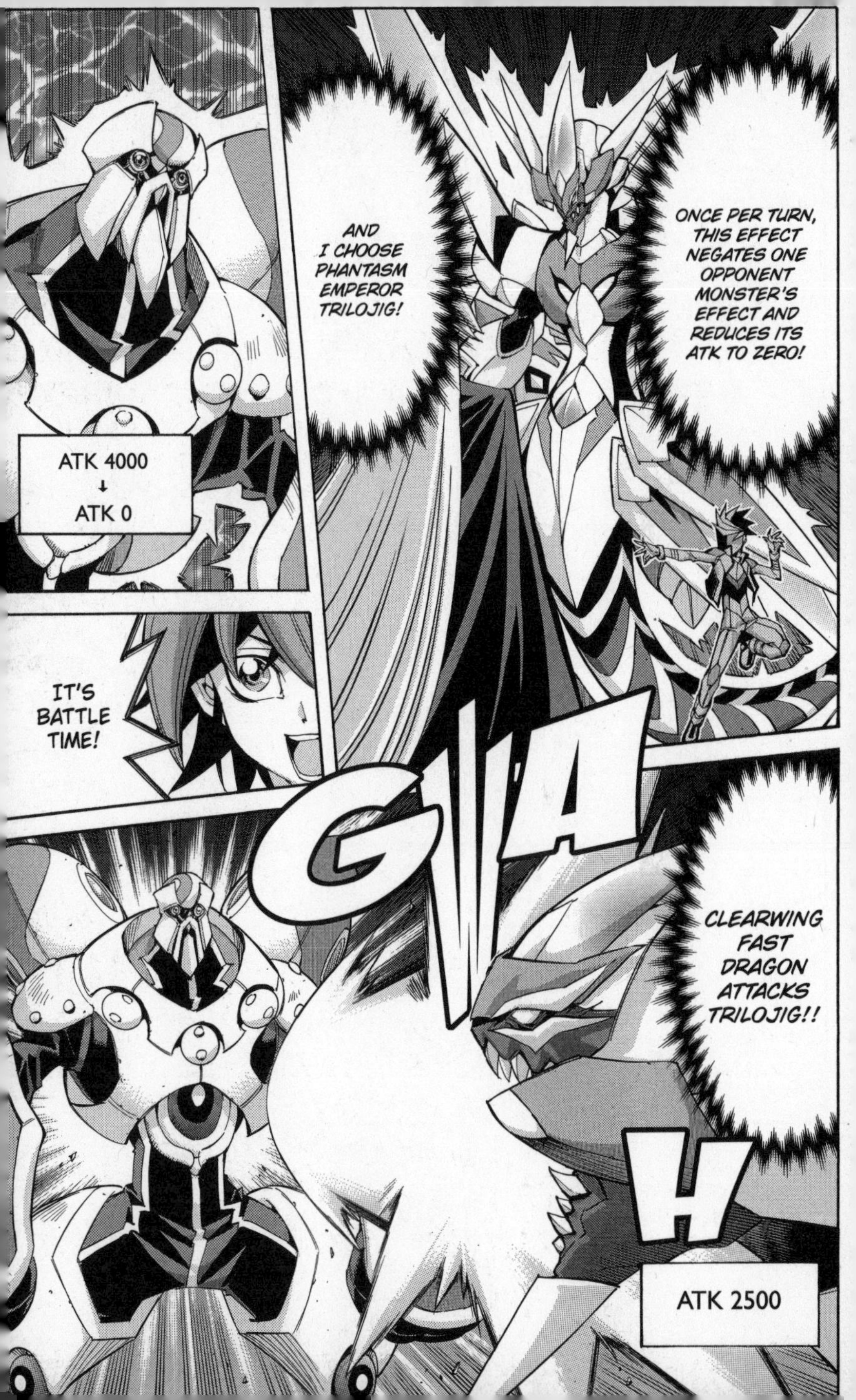
ONCE PER TURN, THIS EFFECT NEGATES ONE OPPONENT MONSTER'S EFFECT AND REDUCES ITS ATK TO ZERO!
AND I CHOOSE PHANTASM EMPEROR TRILOJIG!
ATK 4000 → ATK 0
IT'S BATTLE TIME!
GWAH
CLEARWING FAST DRAGON ATTACKS TRILOJIG!!
ATK 2500

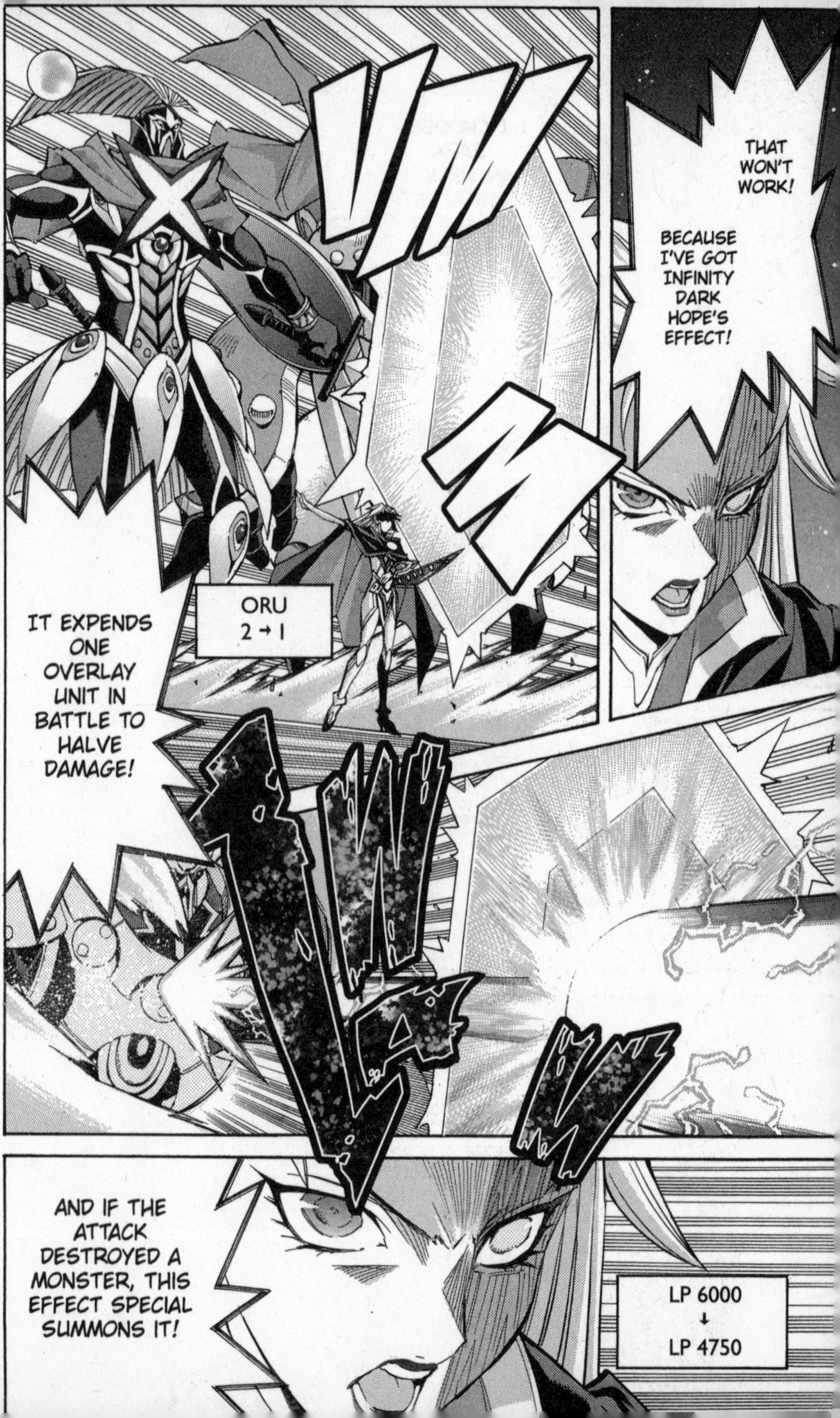
THAT WON'T WORK!
BECAUSE I'VE GOT INFINITY DARK HOPE'S EFFECT!
ORU 2 → 1
IT EXPENDS ONE OVERLAY UNIT IN BATTLE TO HALVE DAMAGE!
AND IF THE ATTACK DESTROYED A MONSTER, THIS EFFECT SPECIAL SUMMONS IT!
LP 6000 ↓ LP 4750

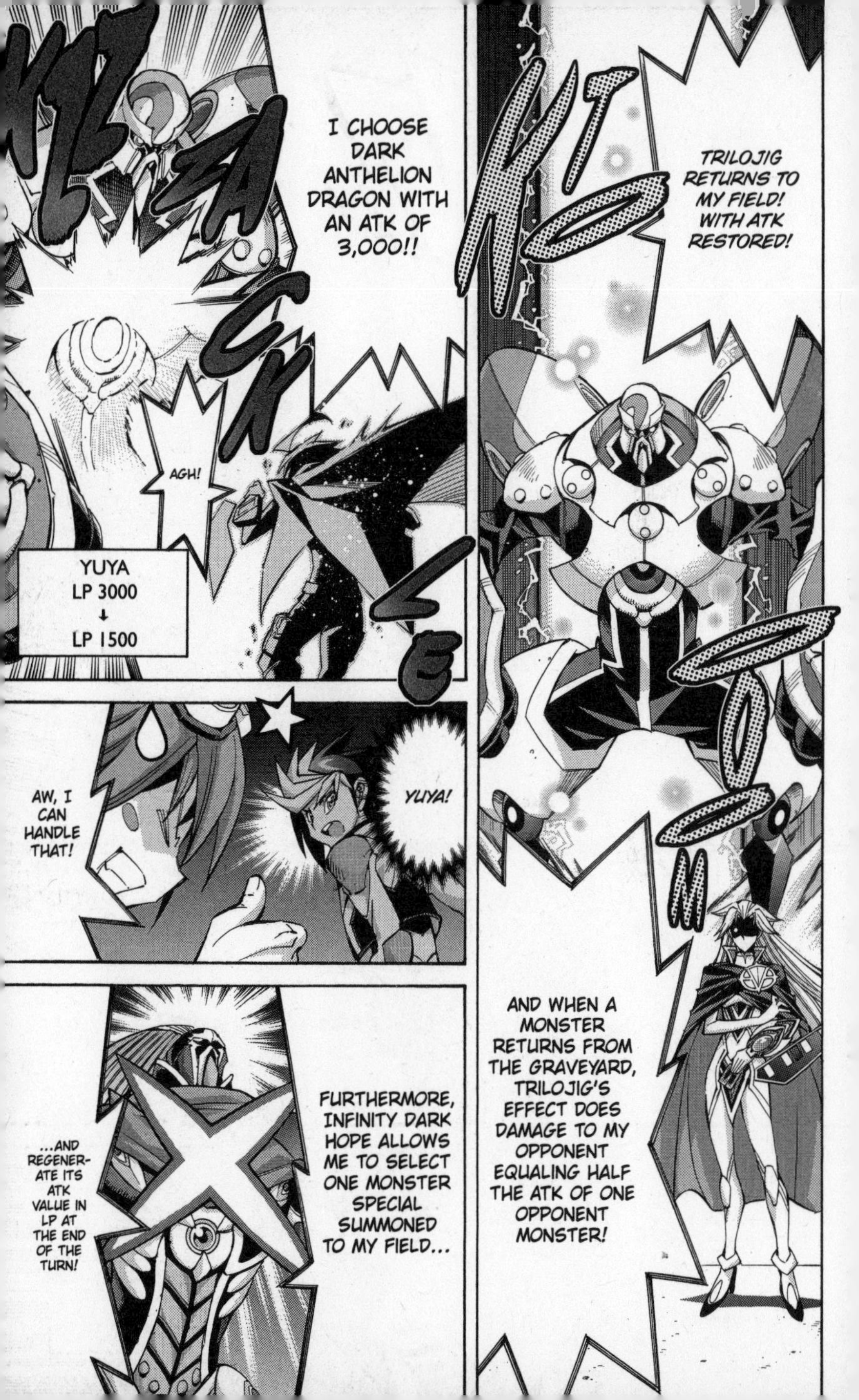
TRILOJIG RETURNS TO MY FIELD! WITH ATK RESTORED!
AND WHEN A MONSTER RETURNS FROM THE GRAVEYARD, TRILOJIG'S EFFECT DOES DAMAGE TO MY OPPONENT EQUALING HALF THE ATK OF ONE OPPONENT MONSTER!
I CHOOSE DARK ANTHELION DRAGON WITH AN ATK OF 3,000!!
AGH!
YUYA
LP 3000
↓
LP 1500
YUYA!
AW, I CAN HANDLE THAT!
FURTHERMORE, INFINITY DARK HOPE ALLOWS ME TO SELECT ONE MONSTER SPECIAL SUMMONED TO MY FIELD...
...AND REGENER-ATE ITS ATK VALUE IN LP AT THE END OF THE TURN!

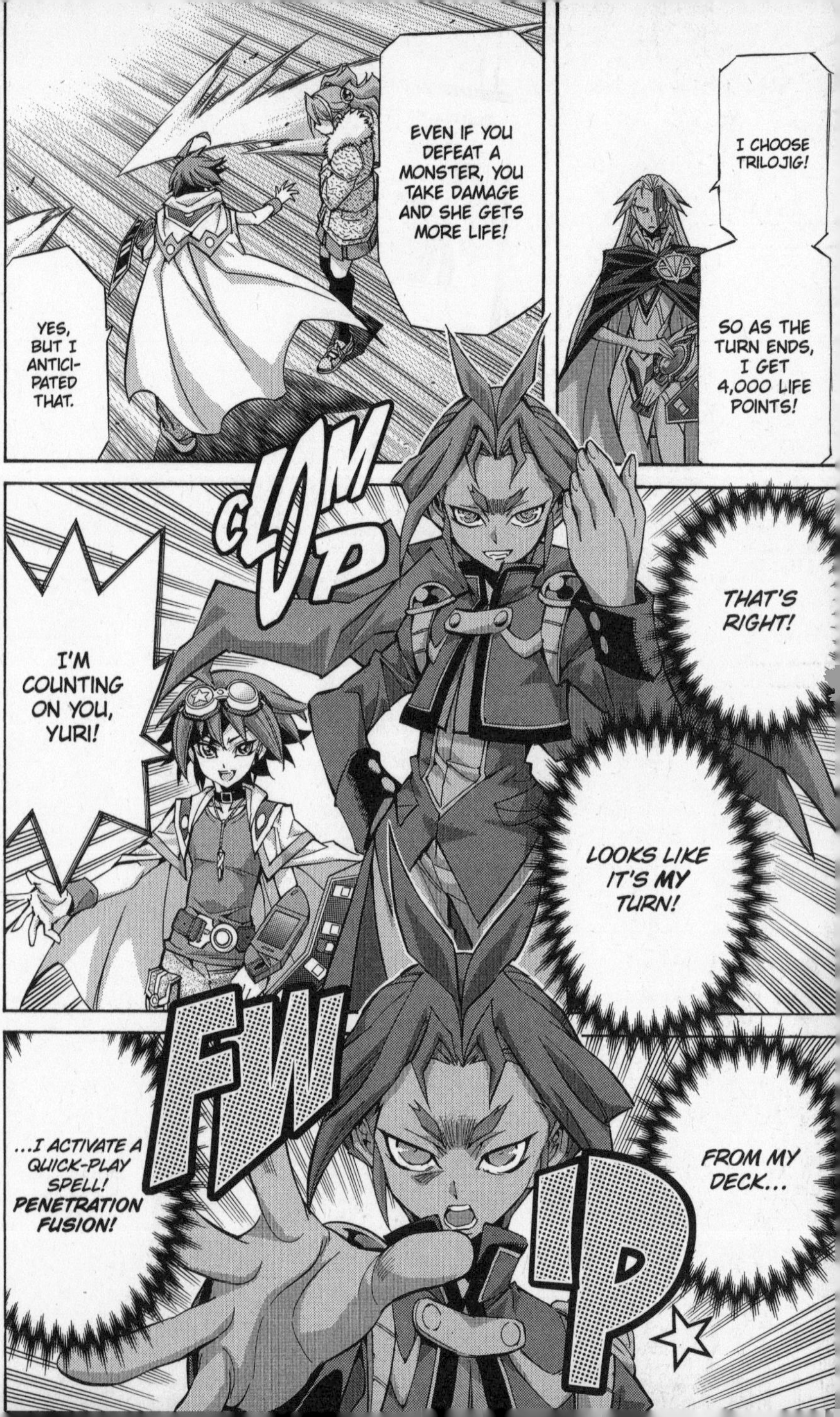
I CHOOSE TRILOJIG!
SO AS THE TURN ENDS, I GET 4,000 LIFE POINTS!
EVEN IF YOU DEFEAT A MONSTER, YOU TAKE DAMAGE AND SHE GETS MORE LIFE!
YES, BUT I ANTICIPATED THAT.
CLOMP
I'M COUNTING ON YOU, YURI!
THAT'S RIGHT!
LOOKS LIKE IT'S MY TURN!
FROM MY DECK...
FWIP
...I ACTIVATE A QUICK-PLAY SPELL! PENETRATION FUSION!

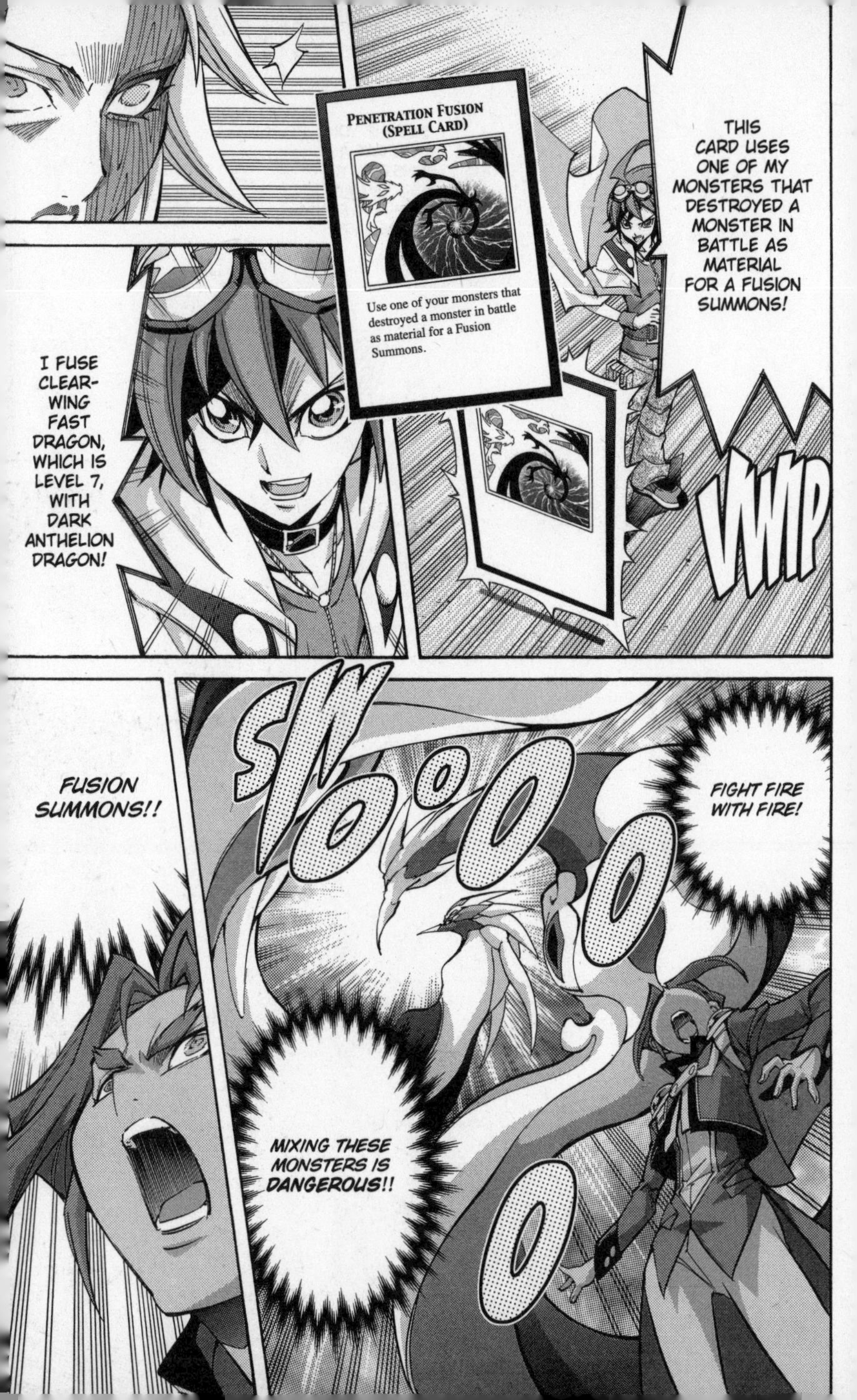
THIS CARD USES ONE OF MY MONSTERS THAT DESTROYED A MONSTER IN BATTLE AS MATERIAL FOR A FUSION SUMMONS!
VWIP
PENETRATION FUSION
(SPELL CARD)
Use one of your monsters that destroyed a monster in battle as material for a Fusion Summons.
I FUSE CLEAR-WING FAST DRAGON, WHICH IS LEVEL 7, WITH DARK ANTHELION DRAGON!
FIGHT FIRE WITH FIRE!
SHOOOOO
FUSION SUMMONS!!
MIXING THESE MONSTERS IS DANGEROUS!!

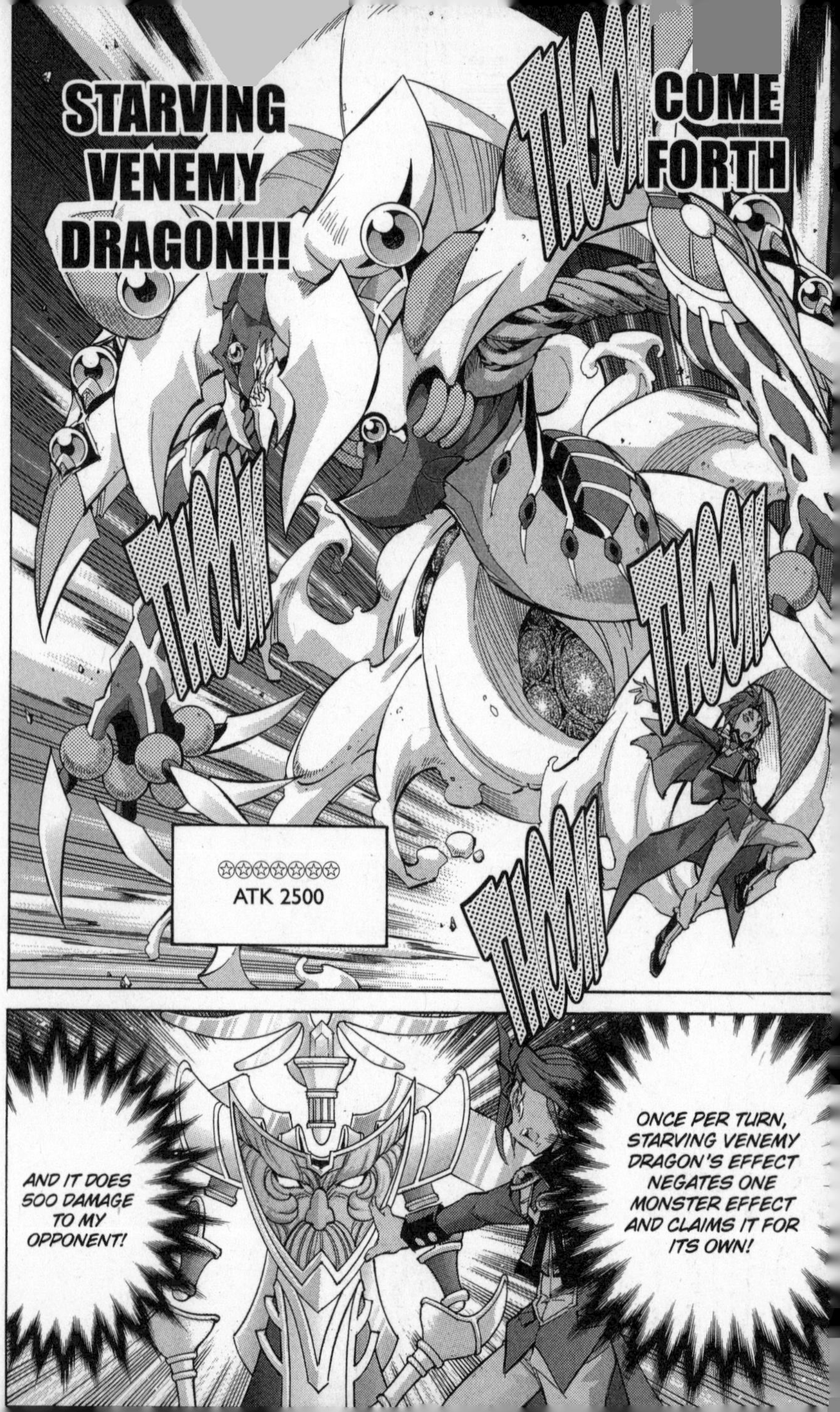
COME FORTH
THOOM
STARVING VENEMY DRAGON!!!
THOOM
THOOM
THOOM
ATK 2500
ONCE PER TURN, STARVING VENEMY DRAGON'S EFFECT NEGATES ONE MONSTER EFFECT AND CLAIMS IT FOR ITS OWN!
AND IT DOES 500 DAMAGE TO MY OPPONENT!

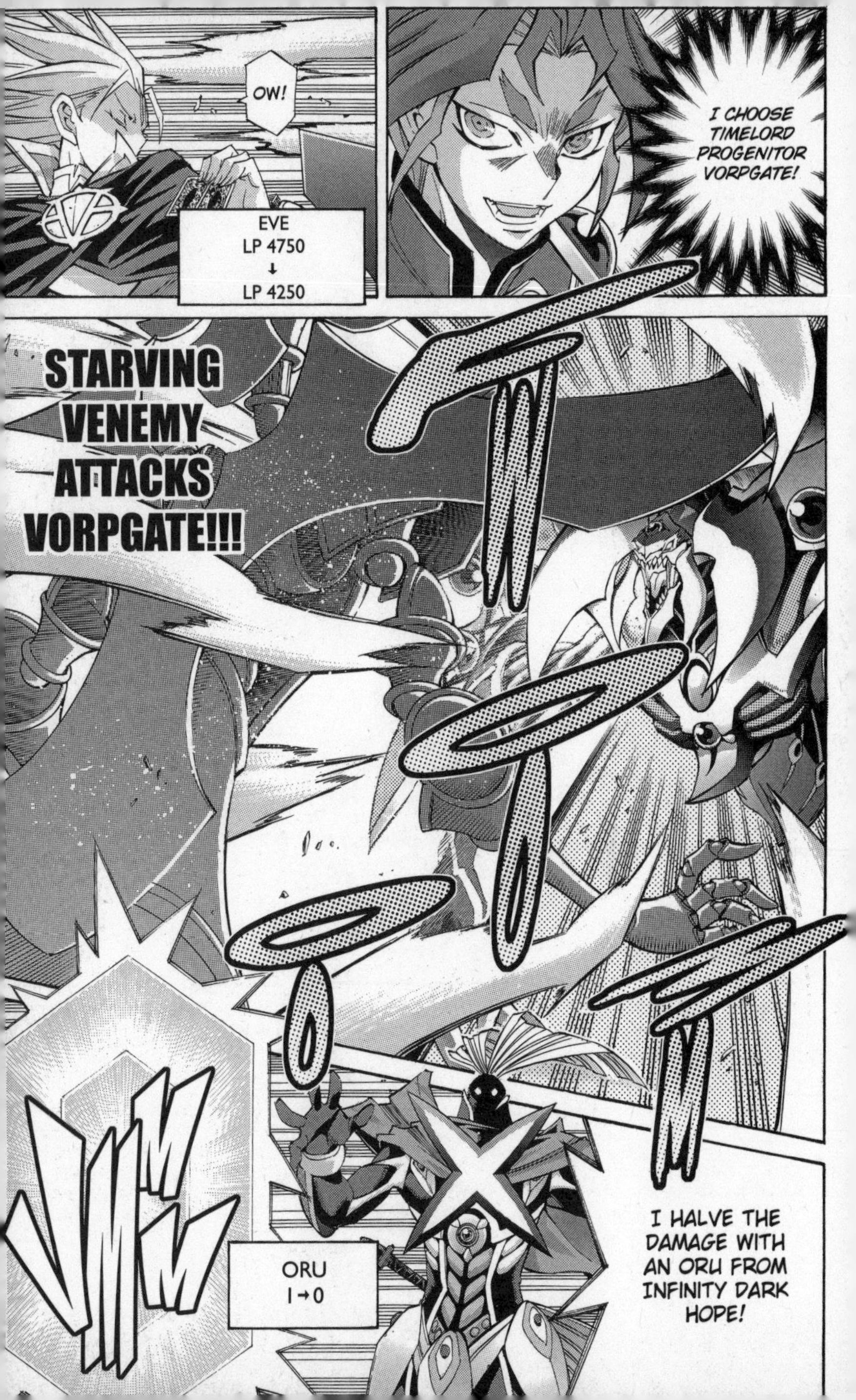
I CHOOSE TIMELORD PROGENITOR VORPGATE!
OW!
EVE
LP 4750
↓
LP 4250
STARVING VENEMY ATTACKS VORPGATE!!!
I HALVE THE DAMAGE WITH AN ORU FROM INFINITY DARK HOPE!
ORU
1→0

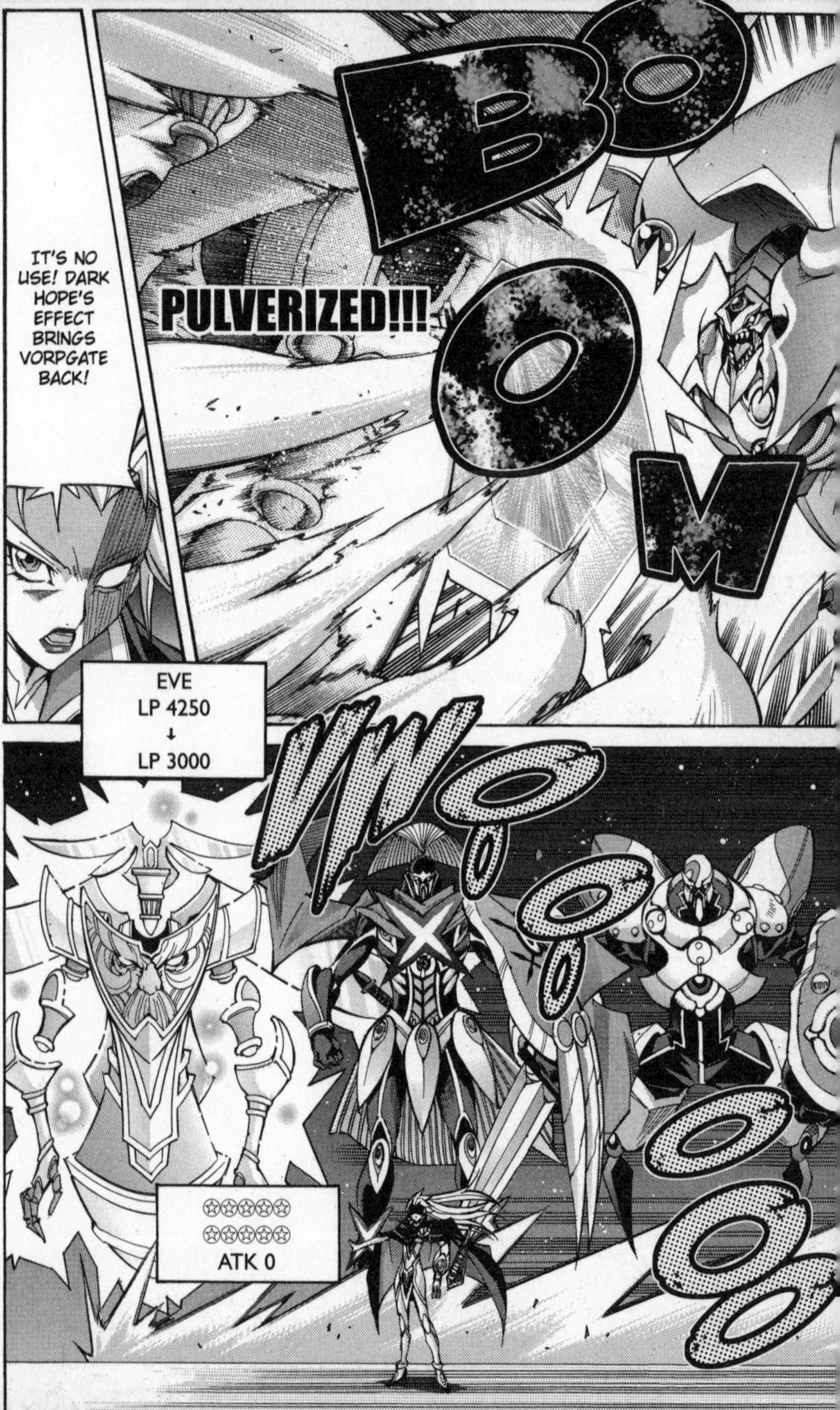
BOOM
PULVERIZED!!!
EVE
LP 4250
↓
LP 3000
IT'S NO USE! DARK HOPE'S EFFECT BRINGS VORPGATE BACK!
WHOOOOOOO
☆☆☆☆☆
☆☆☆☆☆
ATK 0

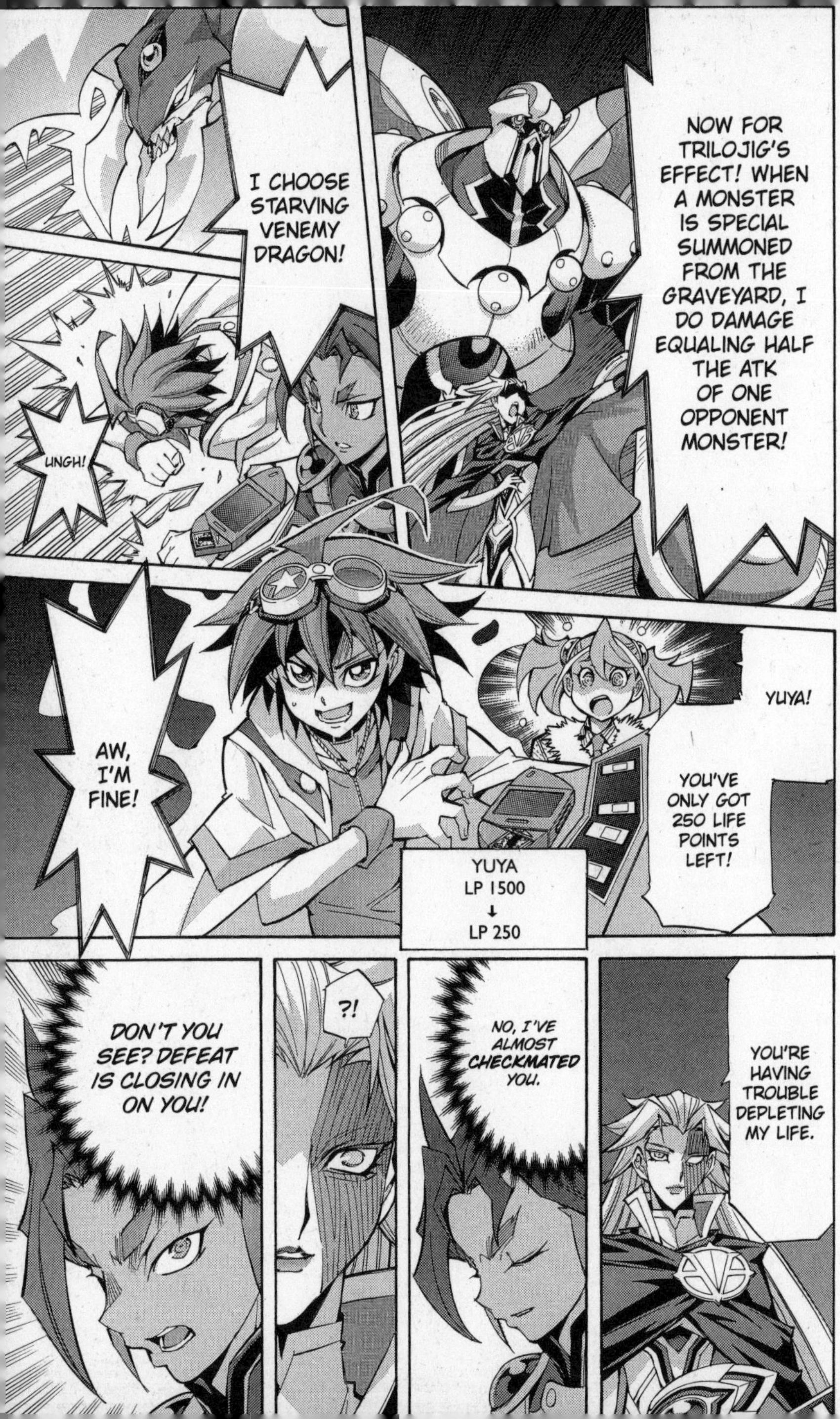
NOW FOR TRILOJIG'S EFFECT! WHEN A MONSTER IS SPECIAL SUMMONED FROM THE GRAVEYARD, I DO DAMAGE EQUALING HALF THE ATK OF ONE OPPONENT MONSTER!
I CHOOSE STARVING VENEMY DRAGON!
UNGH!
YUYA!
YOU'VE ONLY GOT 250 LIFE POINTS LEFT!
YUYA LP 1500 ↓ LP 250
AW, I'M FINE!
YOU'RE HAVING TROUBLE DEPLETING MY LIFE.
NO, I'VE ALMOST CHECKMATED YOU.
?!
DON'T YOU SEE? DEFEAT IS CLOSING IN ON YOU!

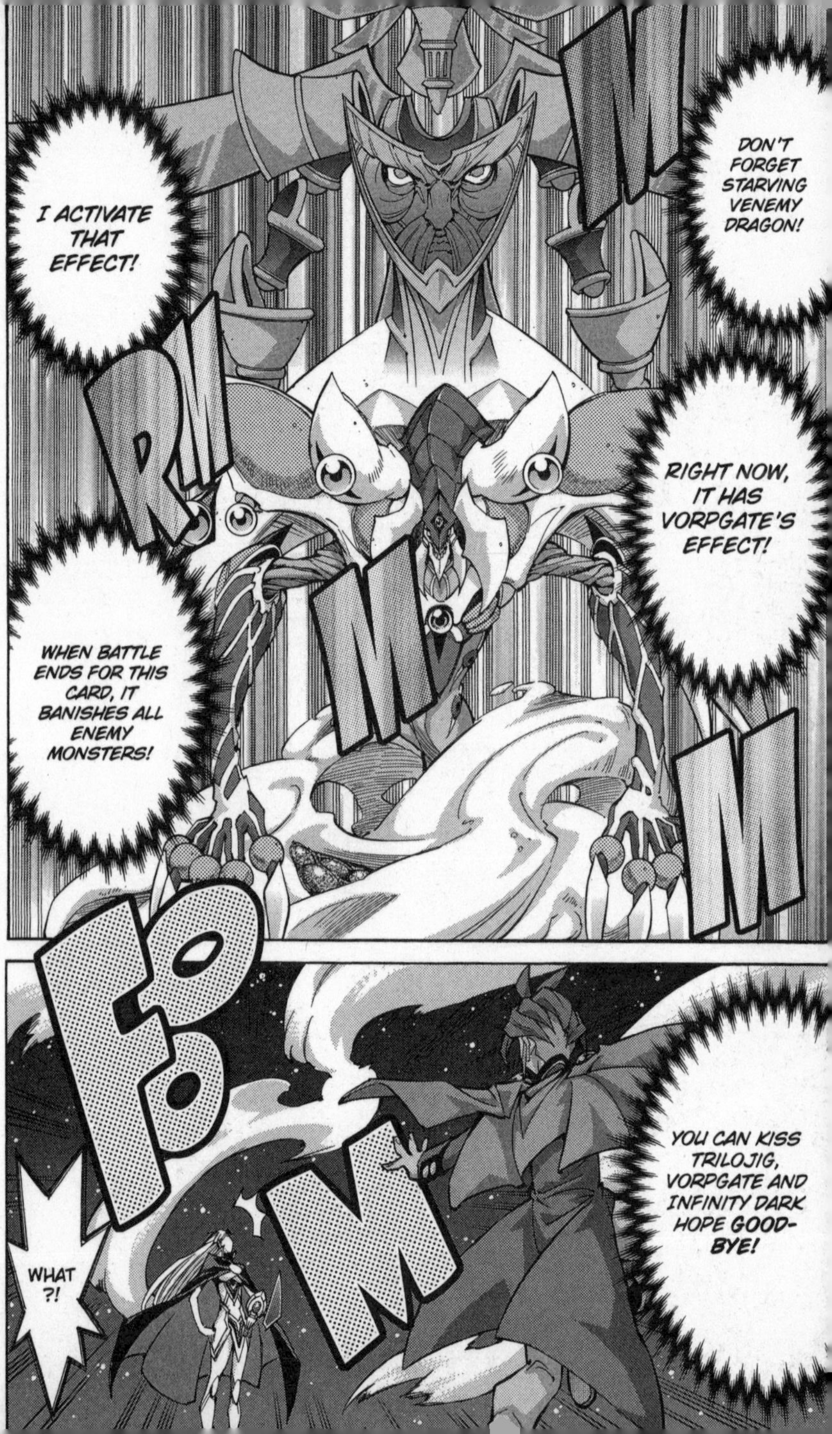
DON'T FORGET STARVING VENEMY DRAGON!
RIGHT NOW, IT HAS VORPGATE'S EFFECT!
WHEN BATTLE ENDS FOR THIS CARD, IT BANISHES ALL ENEMY MONSTERS!
I ACTIVATE THAT EFFECT!
YOU CAN KISS TRILOJIG, VORPGATE AND INFINITY DARK HOPE GOOD-BYE!
FOOM
WHAT ?!

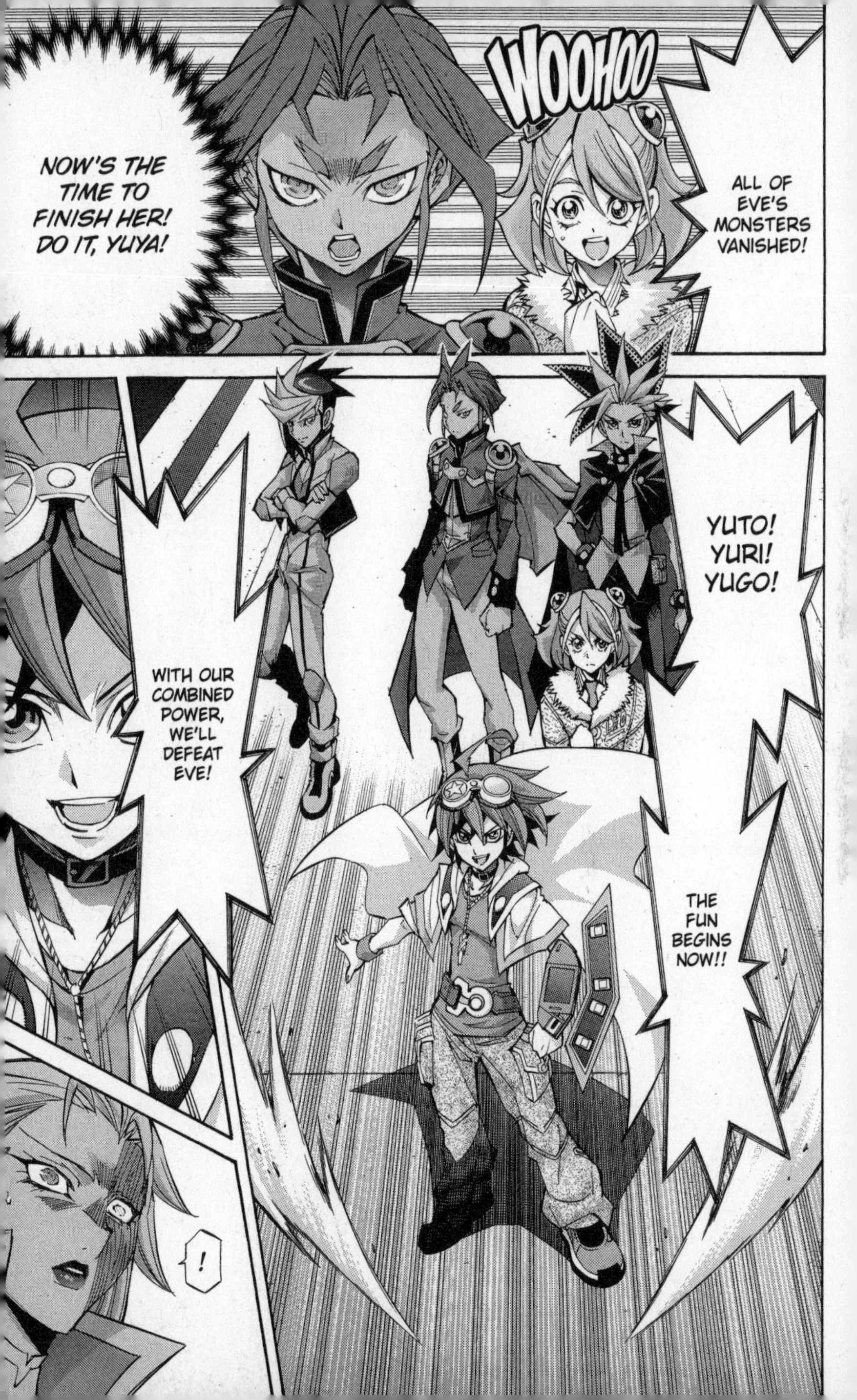
WOOHOO
ALL OF EVE'S MONSTERS VANISHED!
NOW'S THE TIME TO FINISH HER! DO IT, YUYA!
YUTO! YURI! YUGO!
WITH OUR COMBINED POWER, WE'LL DEFEAT EVE!
THE FUN BEGINS NOW!!
!

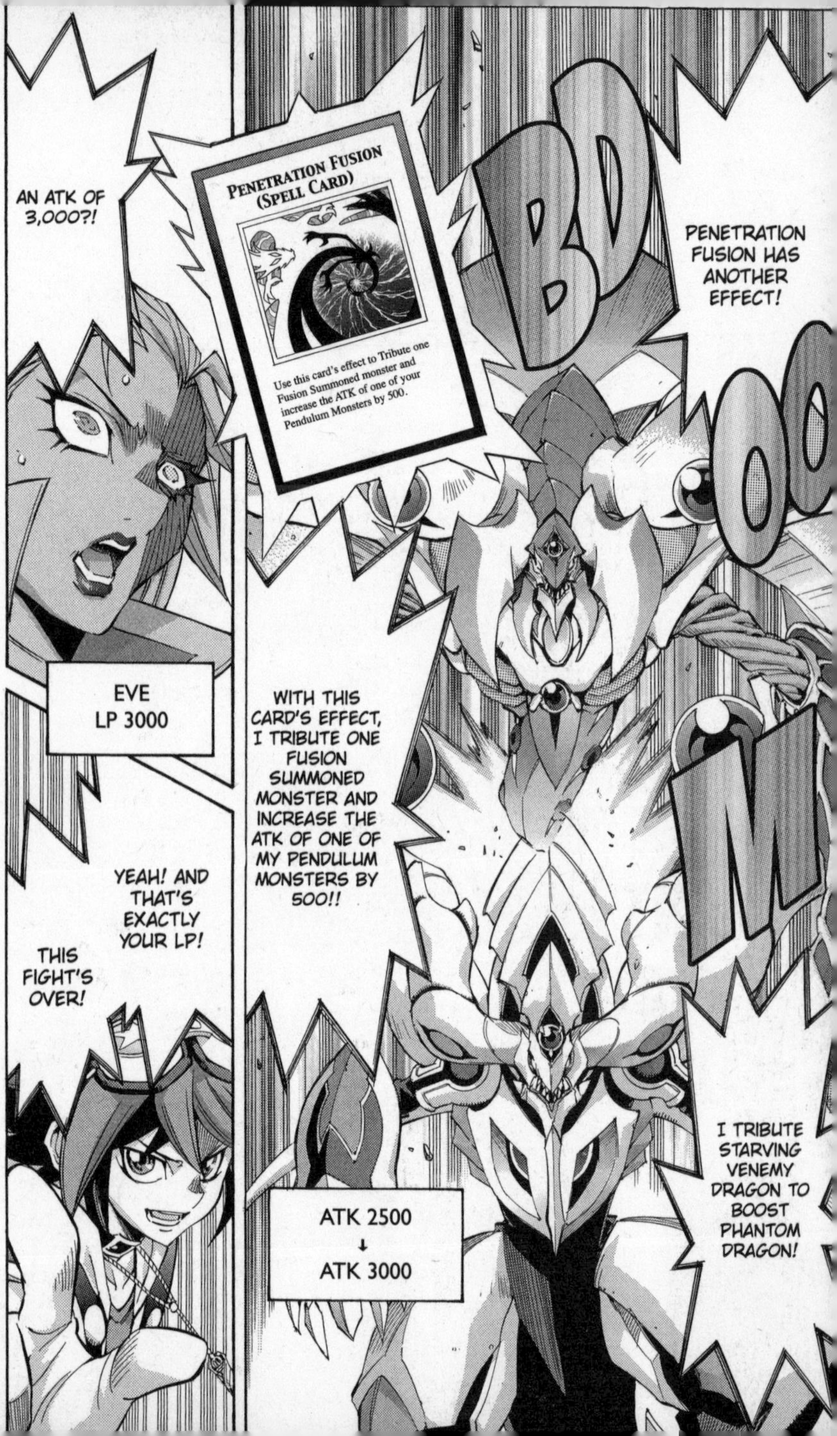

BOOOM
PENETRATION FUSION HAS ANOTHER EFFECT!
PENETRATION FUSION (SPELL CARD)
Use this card's effect to Tribute one Fusion Summoned monster and increase the ATK of one of your Pendulum Monsters by 500.
WITH THIS CARD'S EFFECT, I TRIBUTE ONE FUSION SUMMONED MONSTER AND INCREASE THE ATK OF ONE OF MY PENDULUM MONSTERS BY 500!!
I TRIBUTE STARVING VENEMY DRAGON TO BOOST PHANTOM DRAGON!
ATK 2500
↓
ATK 3000
AN ATK OF 3,000?!
EVE
LP 3000
YEAH! AND THAT'S EXACTLY YOUR LP!
THIS FIGHT'S OVER!

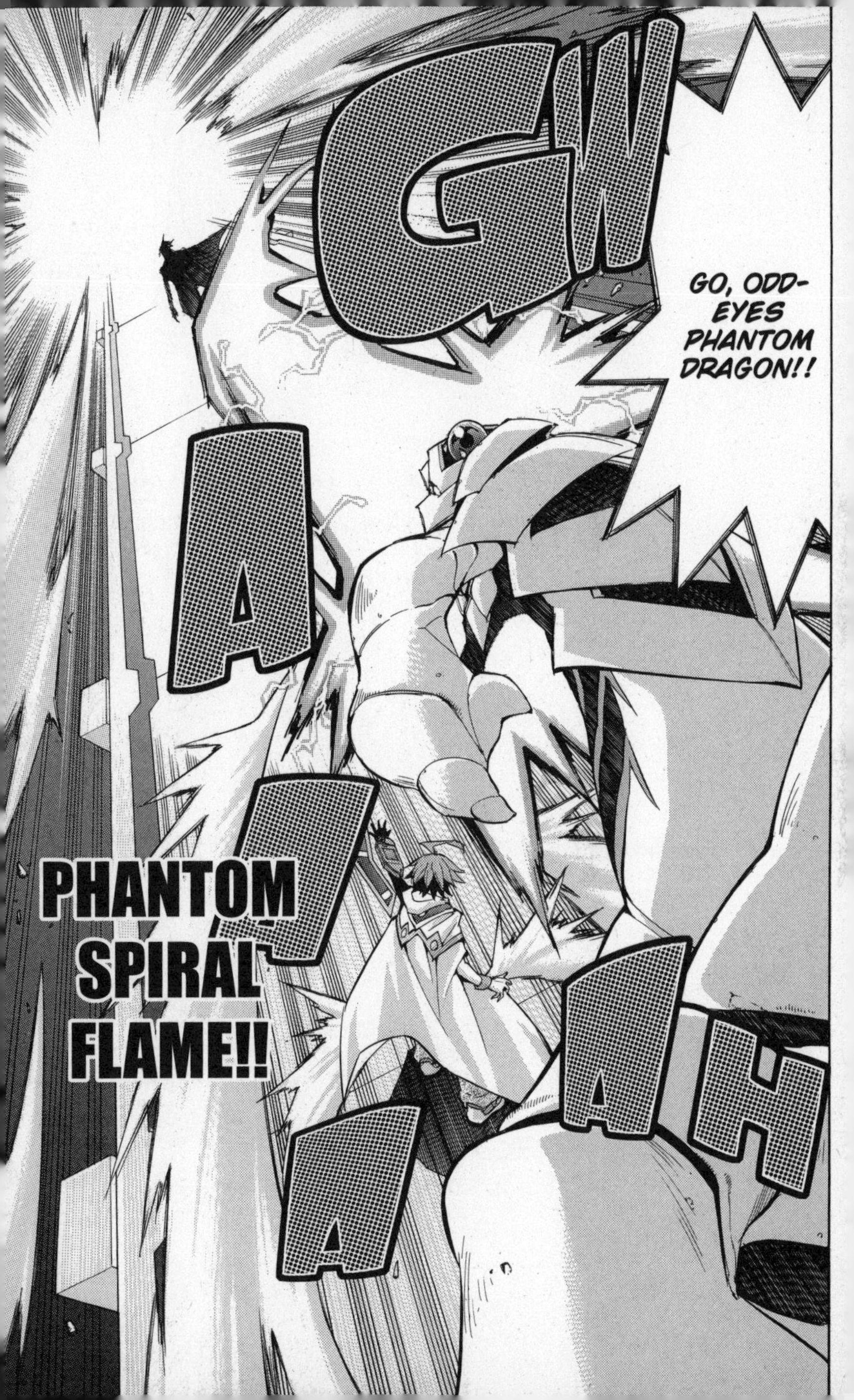
GO, ODD-EYES PHANTOM DRAGON!!
GWAAAAAH
PHANTOM SPIRAL FLAME!!

Yu-Gi-Oh! ARC-V

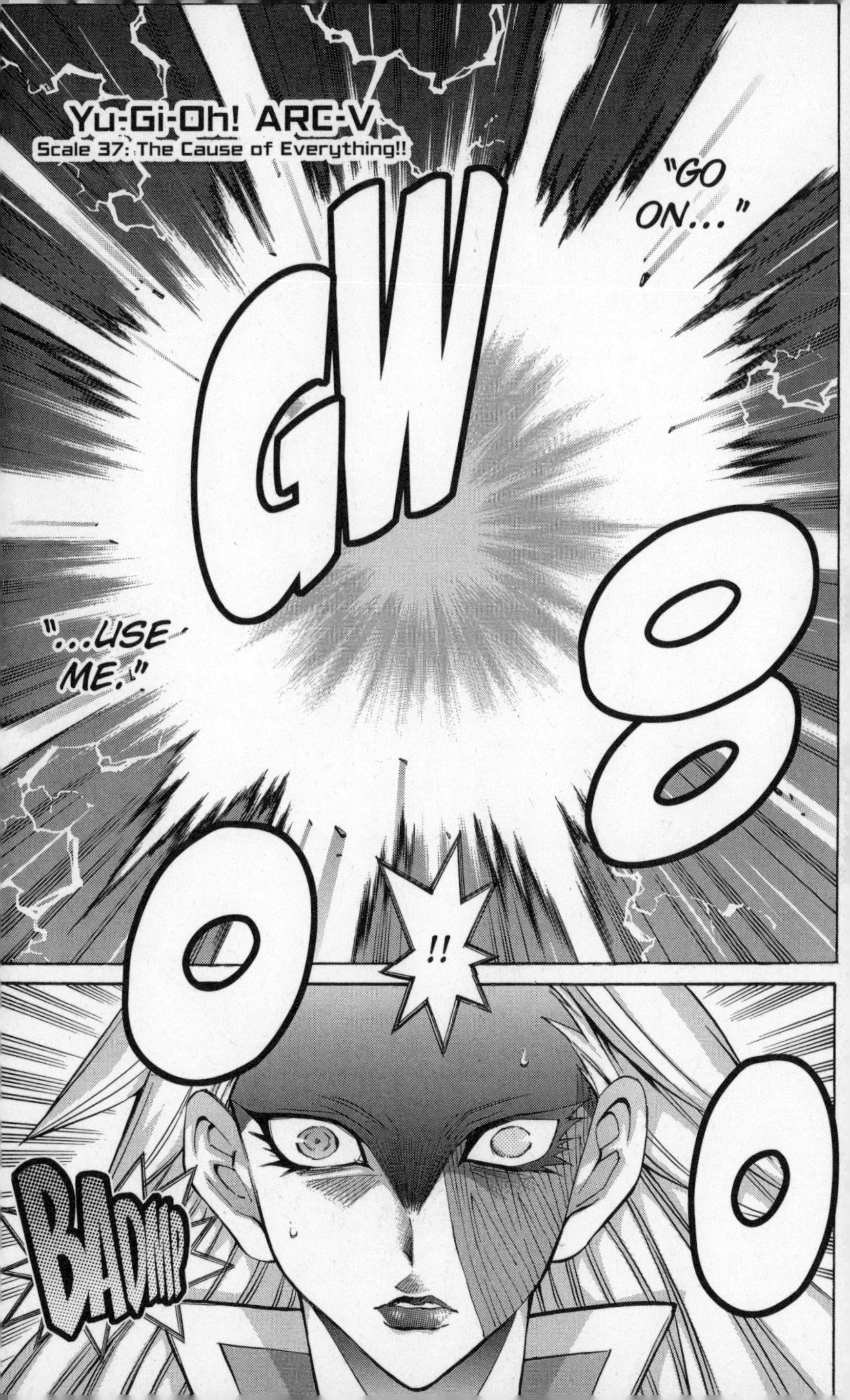
Yu-Gi-Oh! ARC-V
Scale 37: The Cause of Everything!!
"GO ON..."
GWOOOO
"...USE ME."
!!
BADMP

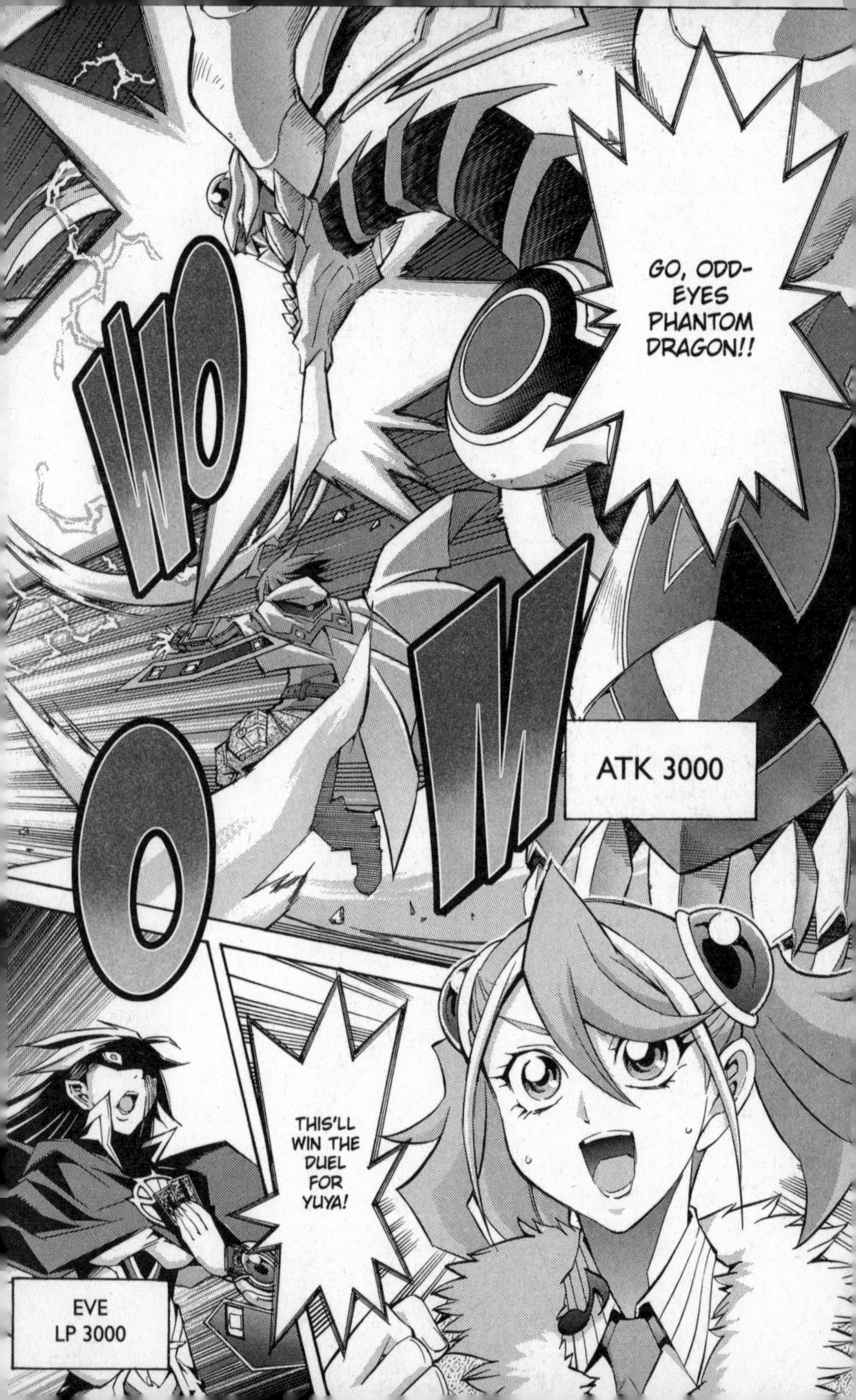
GO, ODD-EYES PHANTOM DRAGON!!
WOOM
ATK 3000
THIS'LL WIN THE DUEL FOR YUYA!
EVE LP 3000

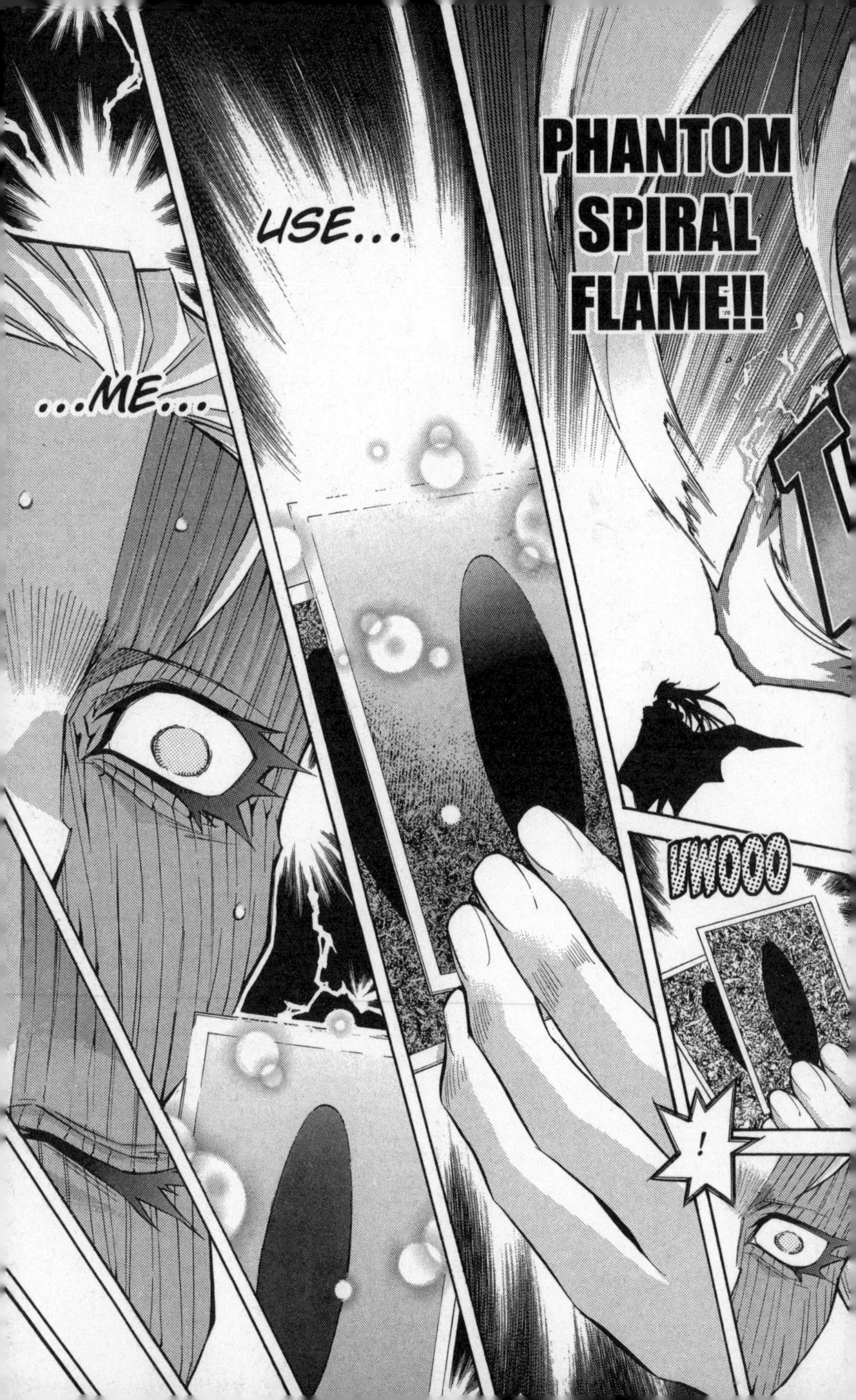
PHANTOM SPIRAL FLAME!!
VWOOO
!
USE...
...ME...

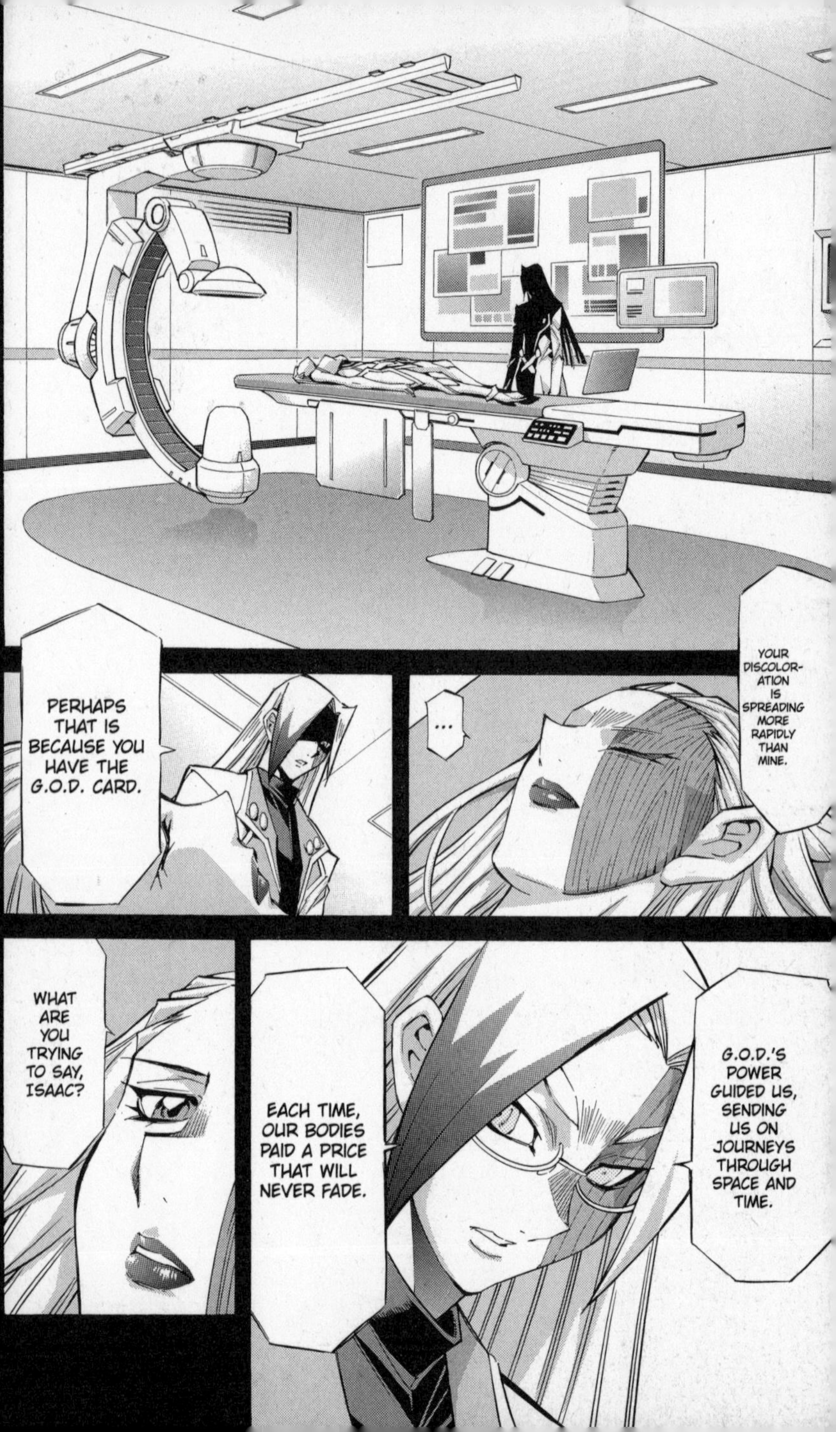
YOUR DISCOLORATION IS SPREADING MORE RAPIDLY THAN MINE.
...
PERHAPS THAT IS BECAUSE YOU HAVE THE G.O.D. CARD.
G.O.D.'S POWER GUIDED US, SENDING US ON JOURNEYS THROUGH SPACE AND TIME.
EACH TIME, OUR BODIES PAID A PRICE THAT WILL NEVER FADE.
WHAT ARE YOU TRYING TO SAY, ISAAC?

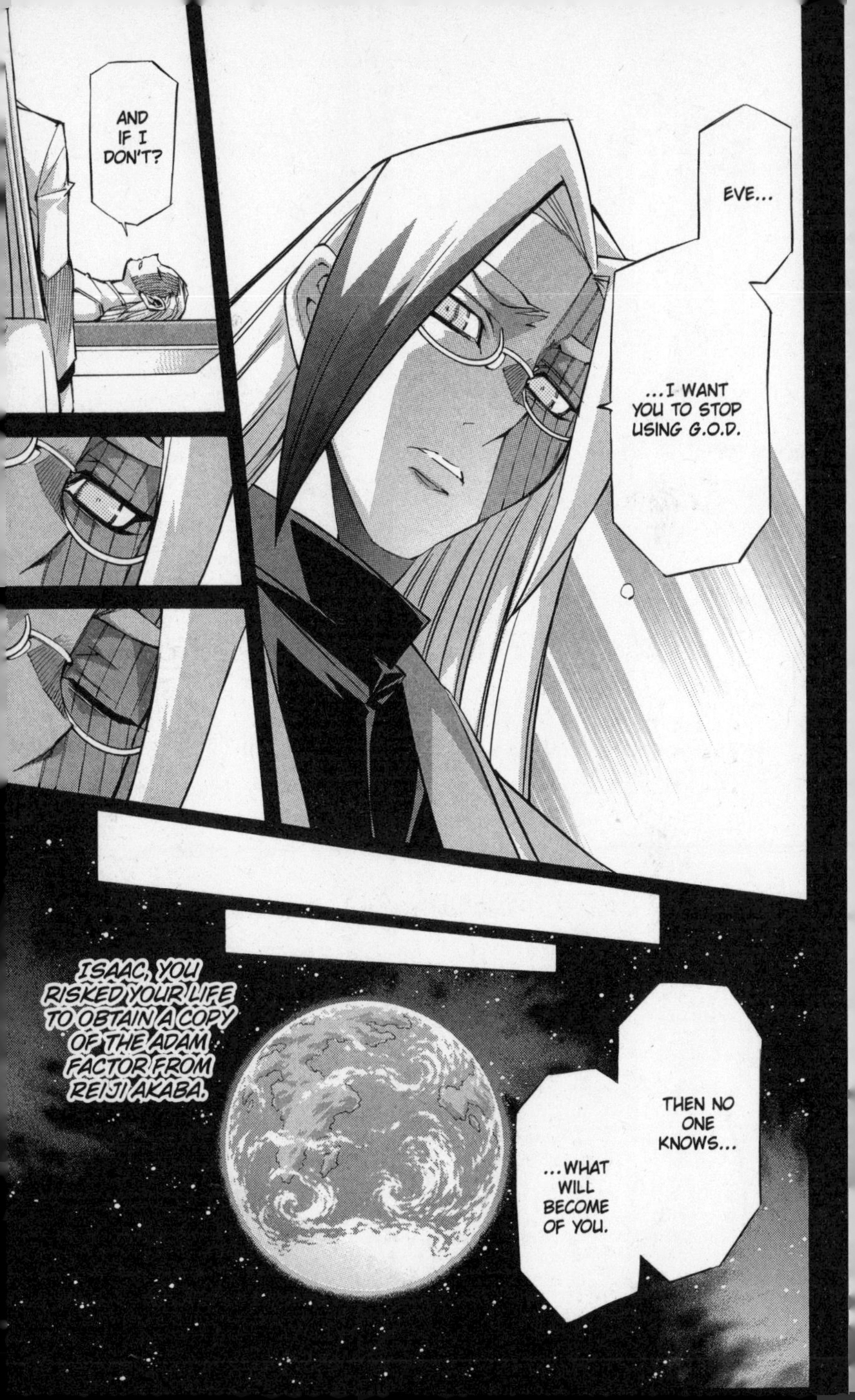
EVE...
...I WANT YOU TO STOP USING G.O.D.
AND IF I DON'T?
THEN NO ONE KNOWS...
...WHAT WILL BECOME OF YOU.
ISAAC, YOU RISKED YOUR LIFE TO OBTAIN A COPY OF THE ADAM FACTOR FROM REIJI AKABA.

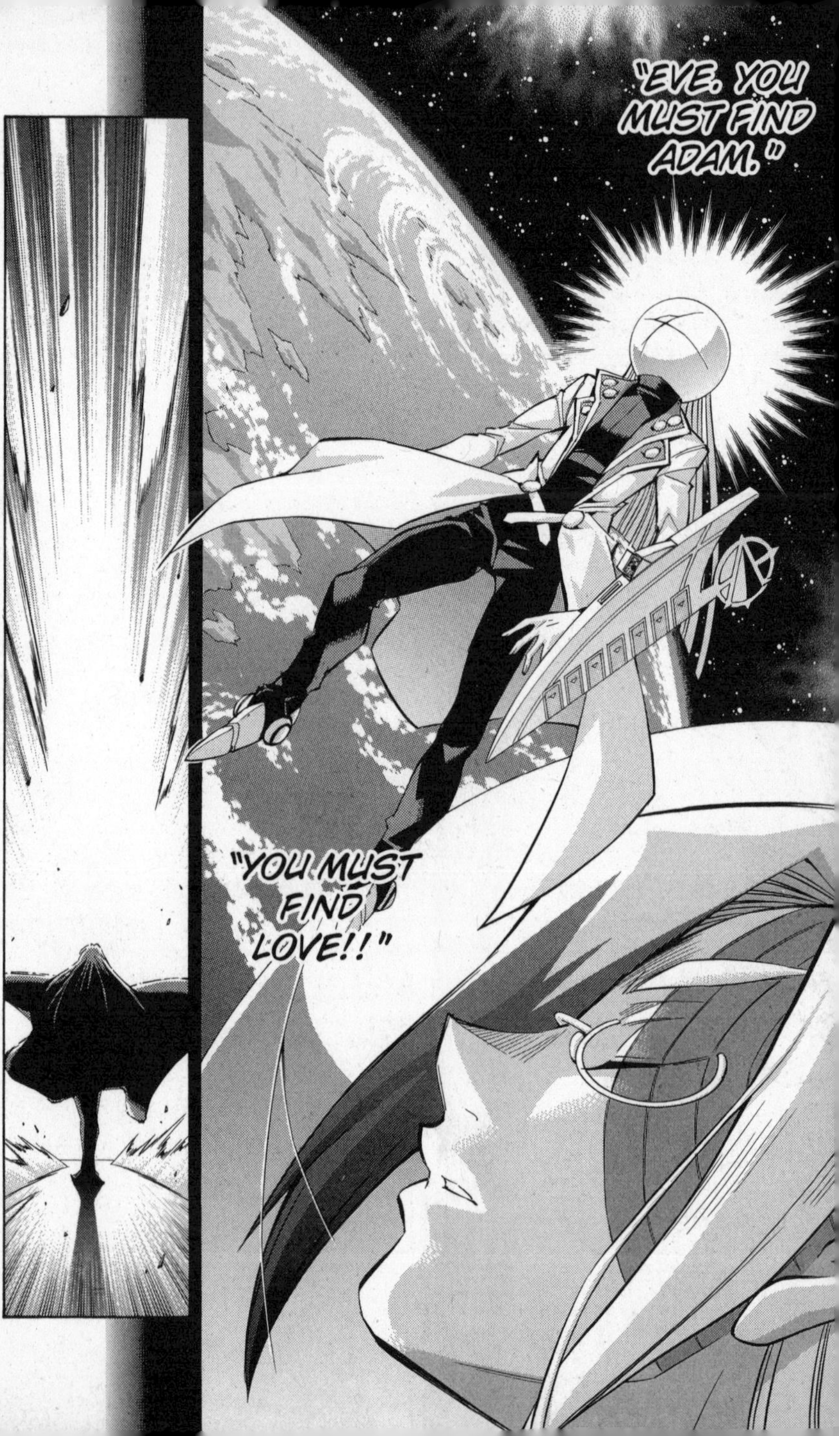
"EVE. YOU MUST FIND ADAM."
"YOU MUST FIND LOVE!!"

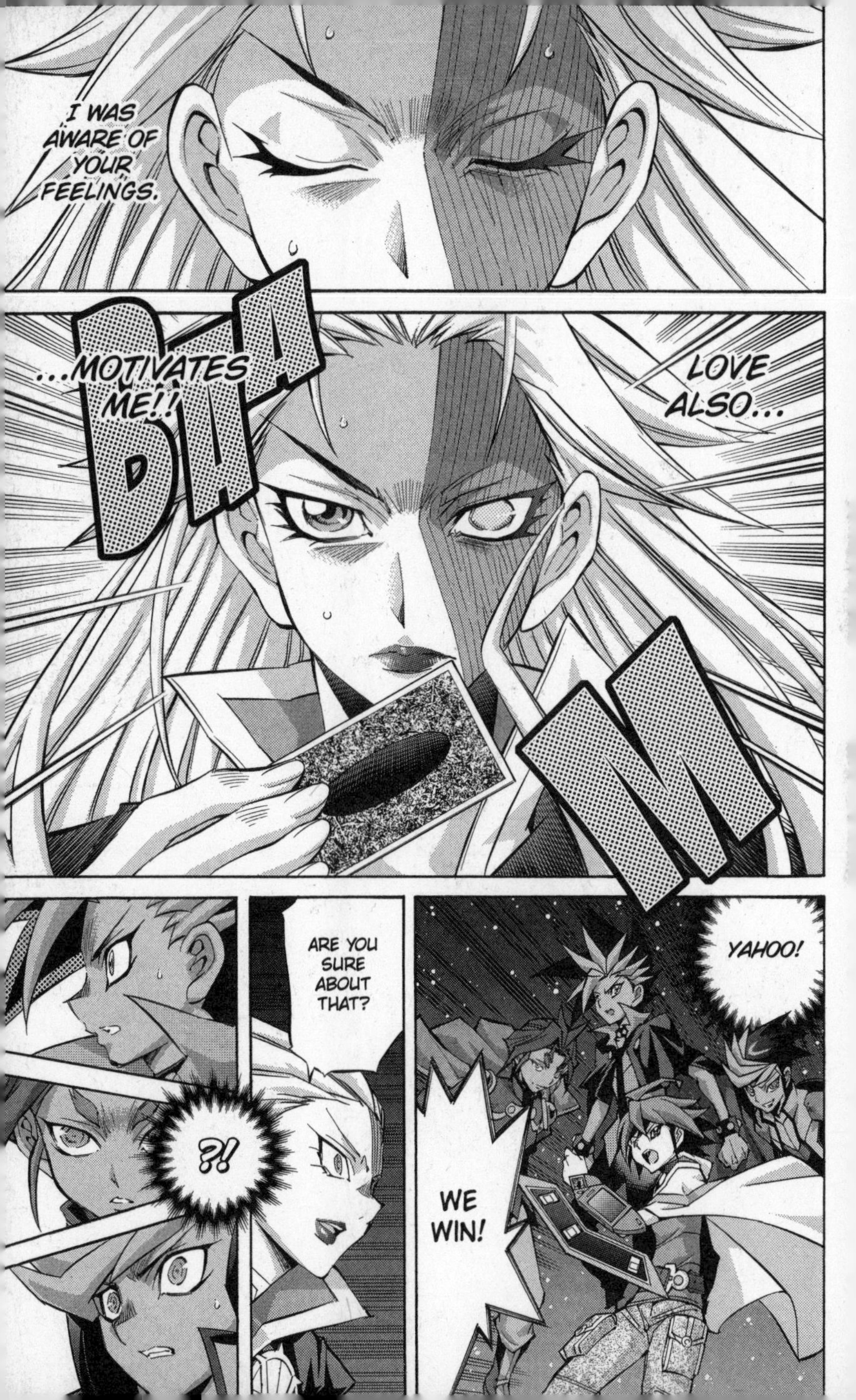
I WAS AWARE OF YOUR FEELINGS.
LOVE ALSO...
...MOTIVATES ME!!
YAHOO!
WE WIN!
ARE YOU SURE ABOUT THAT?
?!

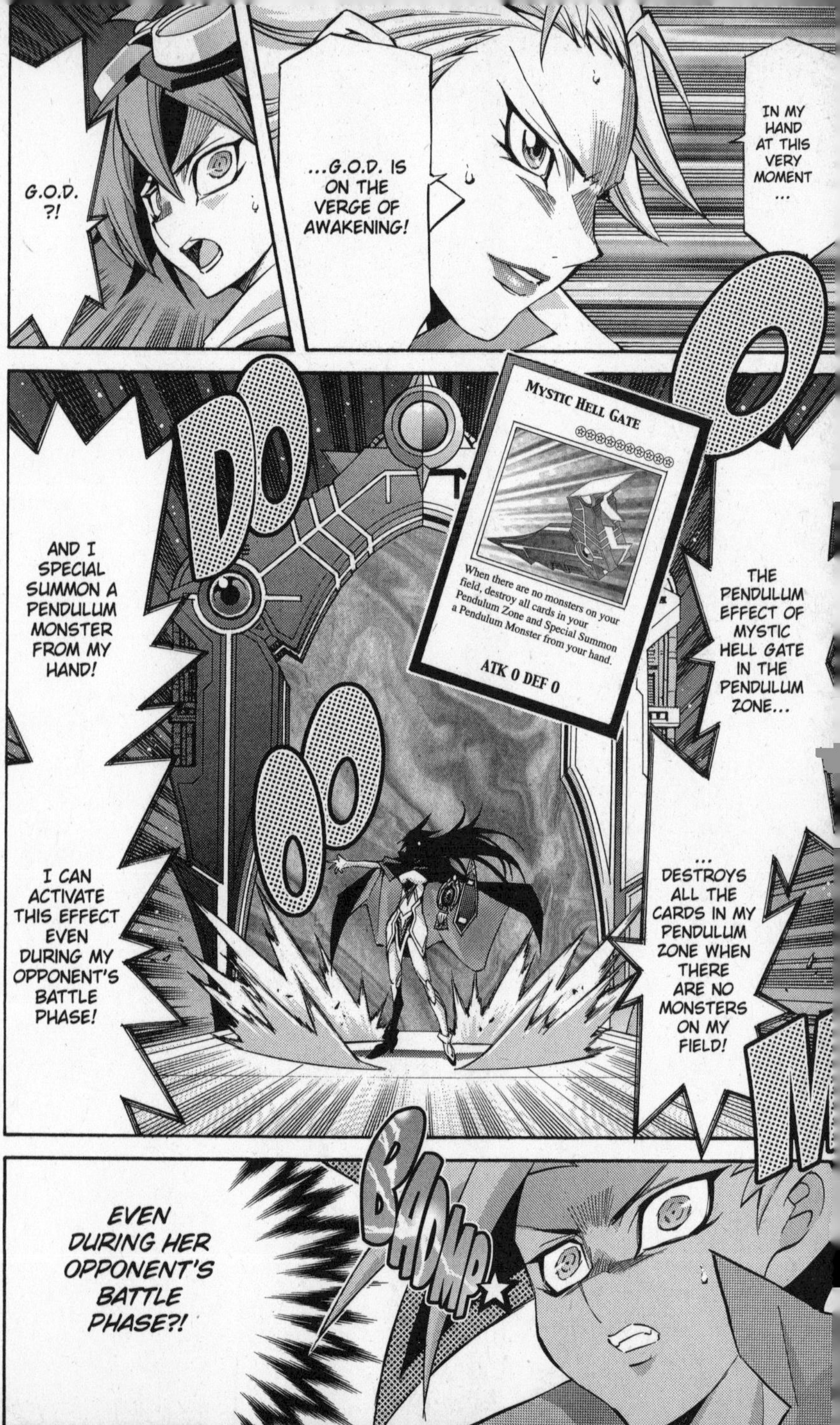
IN MY HAND AT THIS VERY MOMENT...
...G.O.D. IS ON THE VERGE OF AWAKENING!
G.O.D. ?!
MYSTIC HELL GATE
When there are no monsters on your field, destroy all cards in your Pendulum Zone and Special Summon a Pendulum Monster from your hand.
ATK 0 DEF 0
THE PENDULUM EFFECT OF MYSTIC HELL GATE IN THE PENDULUM ZONE...
...DESTROYS ALL THE CARDS IN MY PENDULUM ZONE WHEN THERE ARE NO MONSTERS ON MY FIELD!
AND I SPECIAL SUMMON A PENDULUM MONSTER FROM MY HAND!
I CAN ACTIVATE THIS EFFECT EVEN DURING MY OPPONENT'S BATTLE PHASE!
BADUMP★
EVEN DURING HER OPPONENT'S BATTLE PHASE?!

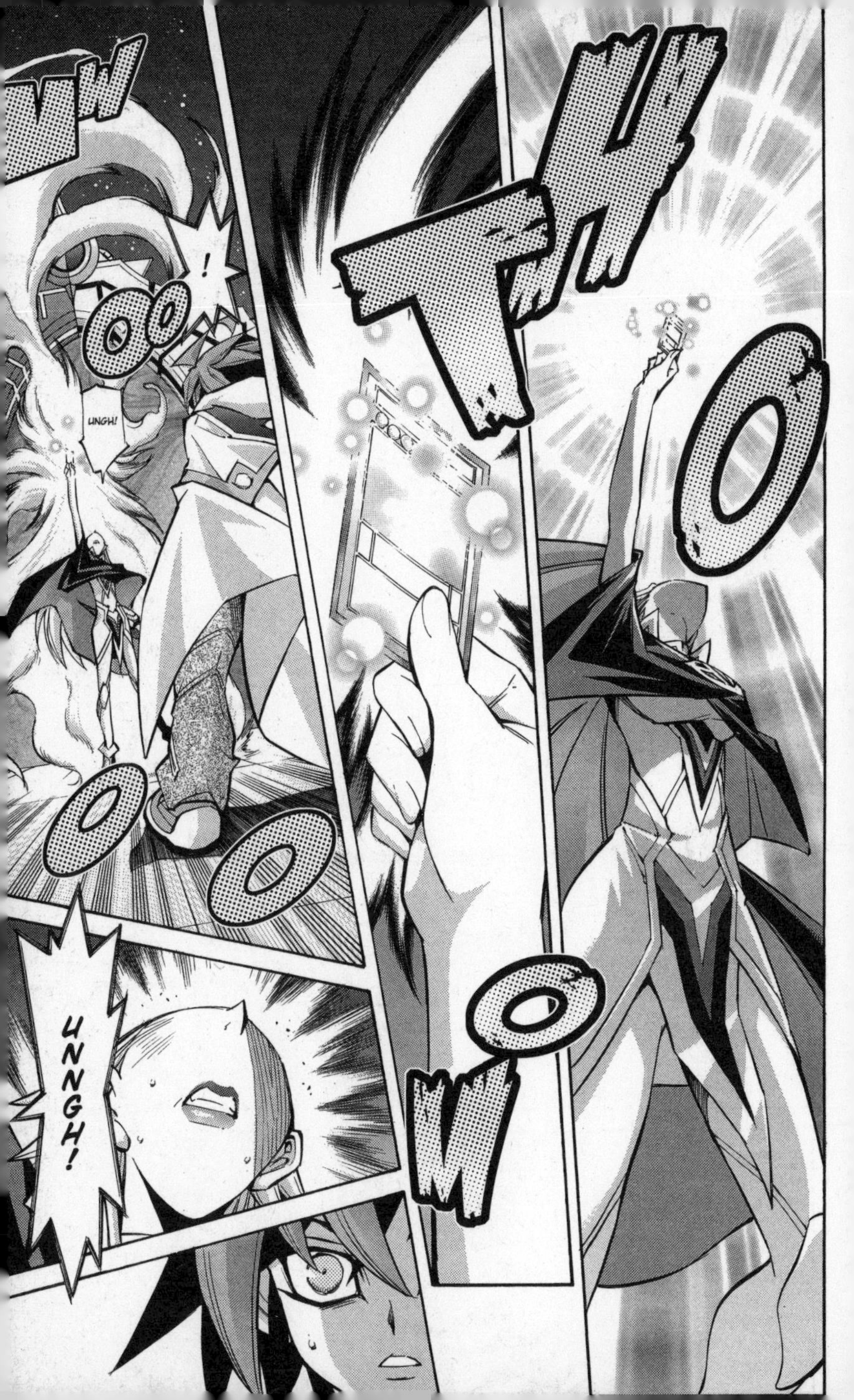
!
UNGH!
UNNNGH!

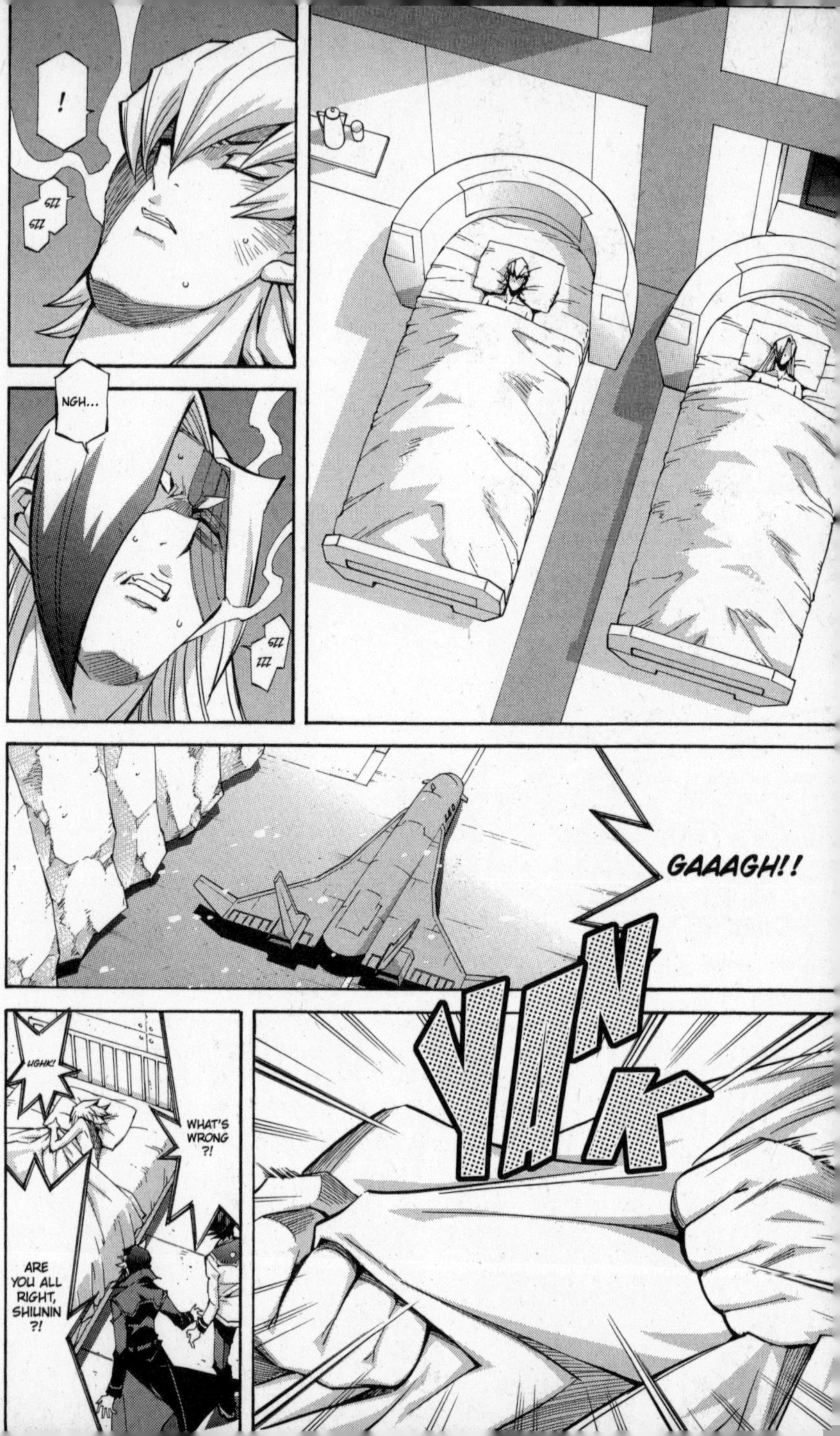
!
SZZ SZZ
NGH...
SZZ ZZZ
GAAAGH!!
YANK
UGHK!
WHAT'S WRONG?!
ARE YOU ALL RIGHT, SHIUNIN?!

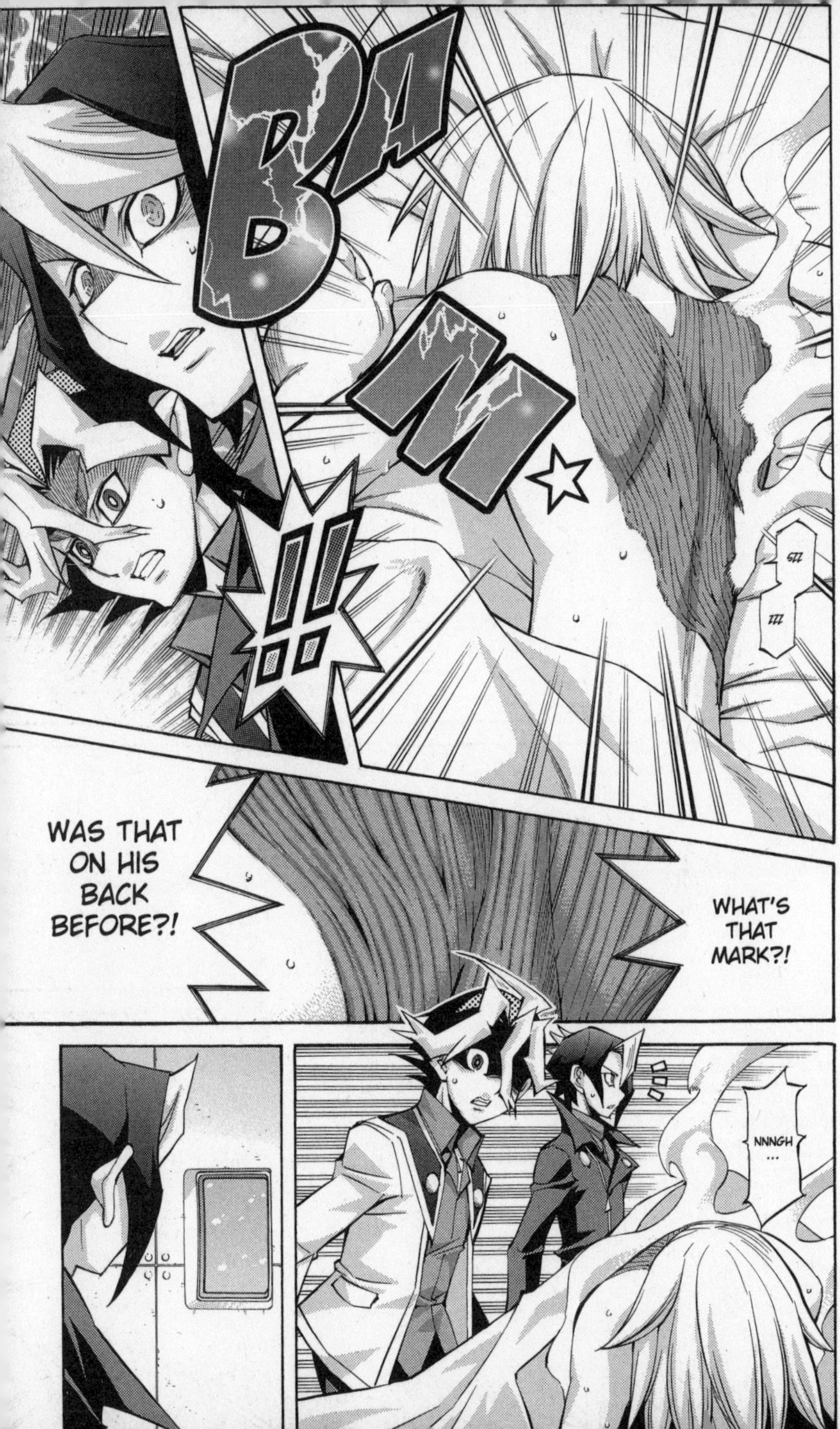
BAM
!!
SZZ
ZZZ
WHAT'S THAT MARK?!
WAS THAT ON HIS BACK BEFORE?!
NNNGH...

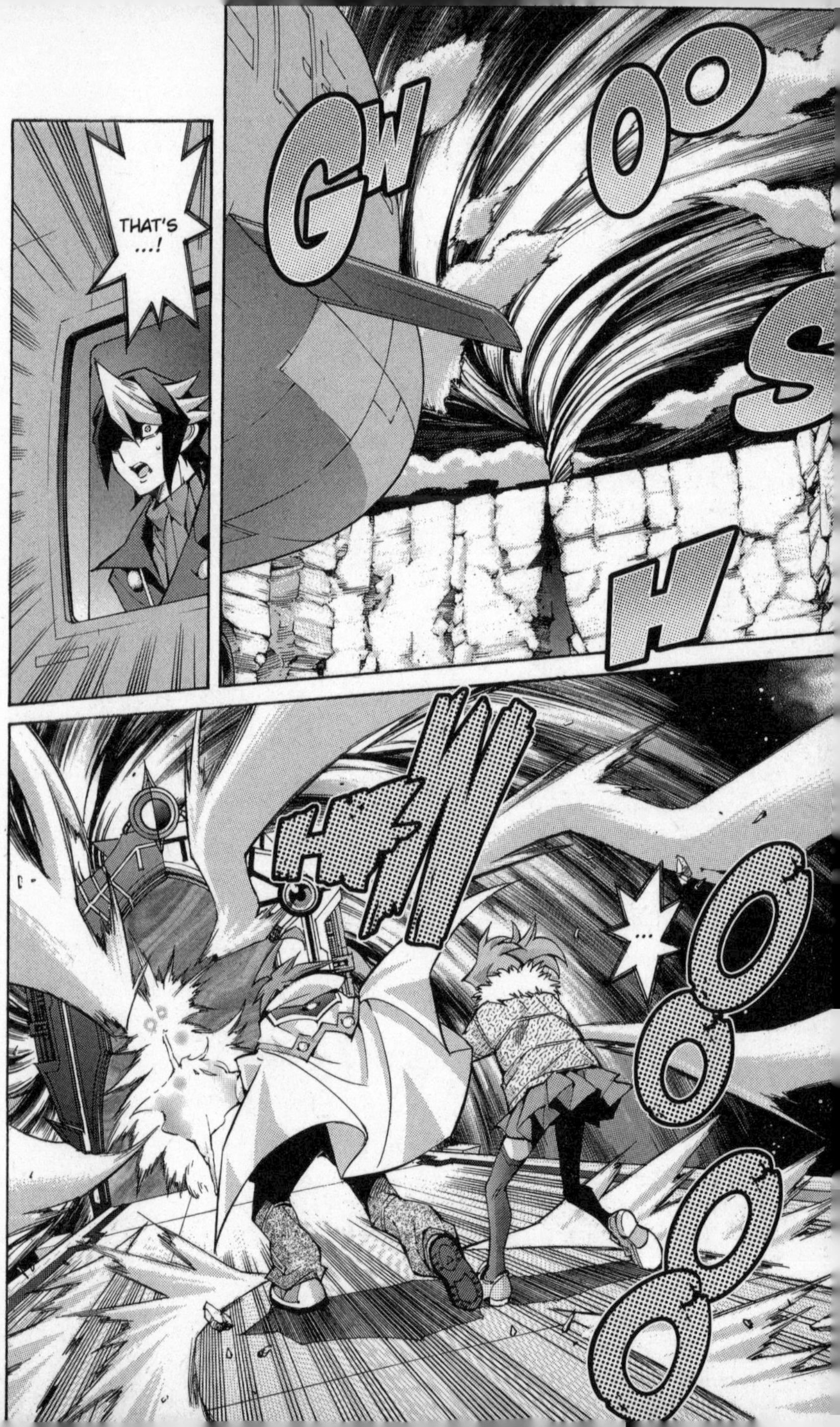
GWOOOSH
THAT'S ...!
GWOOOOO
...

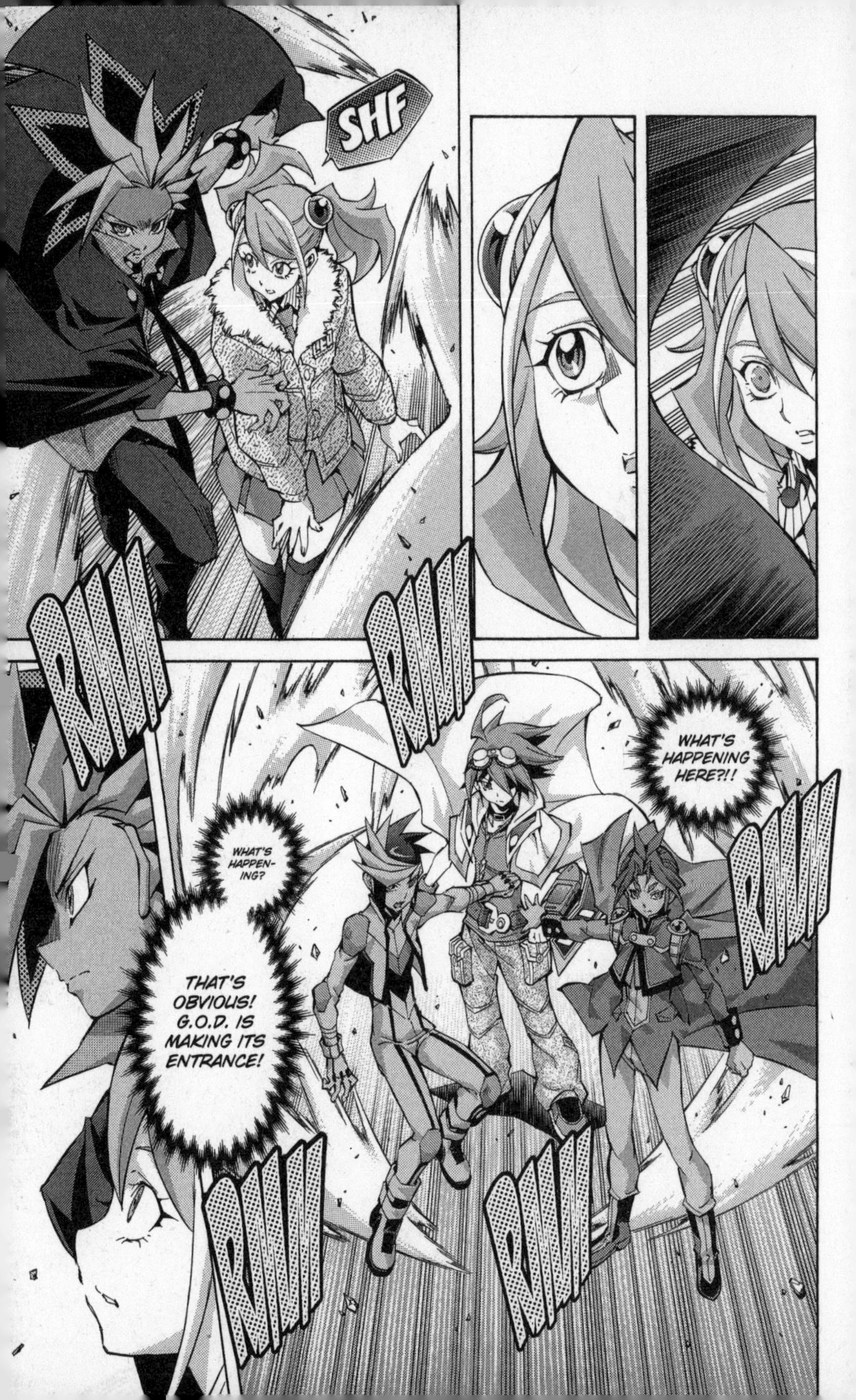
SHF
WHAT'S HAPPENING HERE?!!
WHAT'S HAPPEN-ING?
THAT'S OBVIOUS! G.O.D. IS MAKING ITS ENTRANCE!

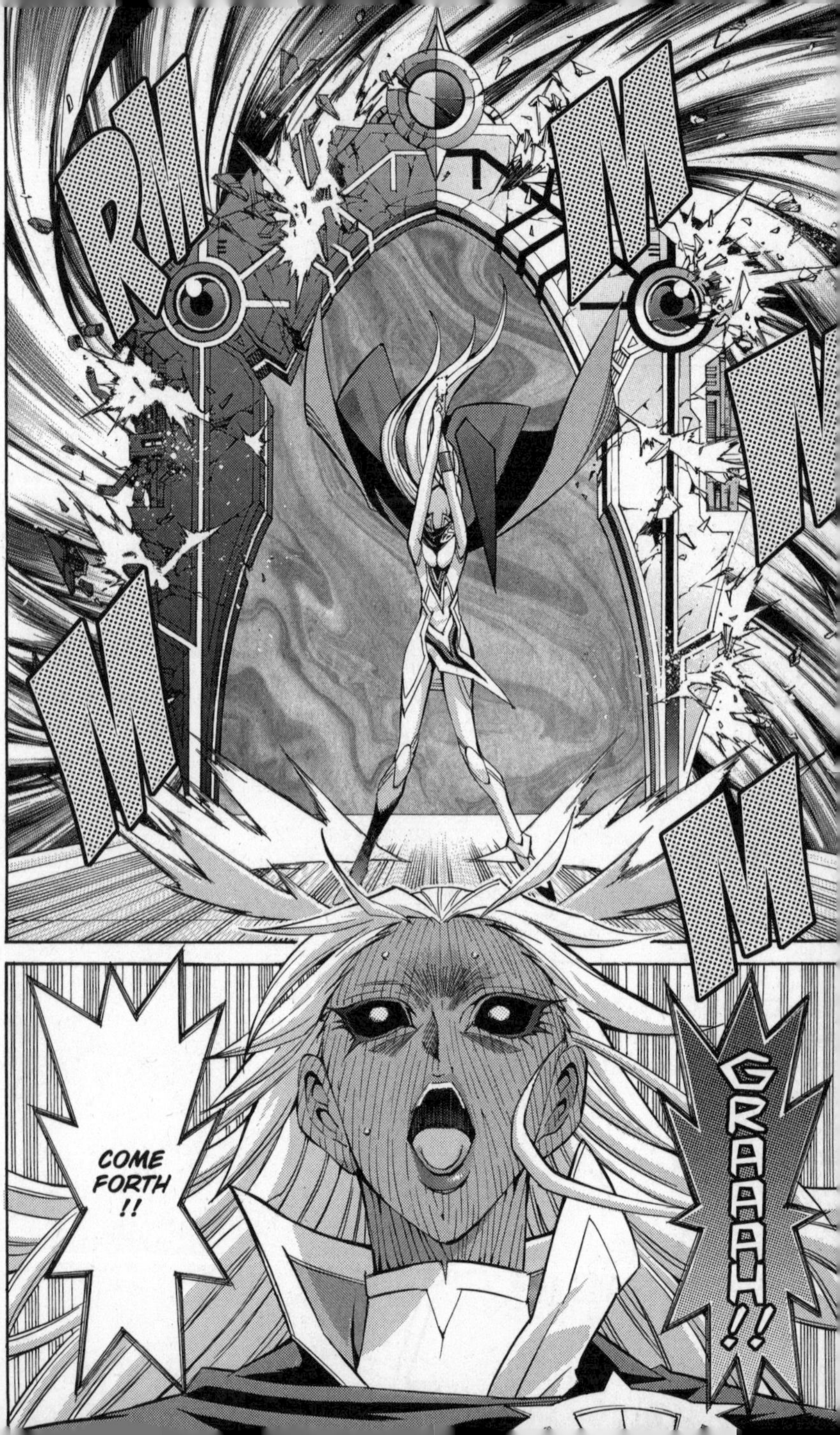

RMMMMM
GRAAAAH!!
COME FORTH !!

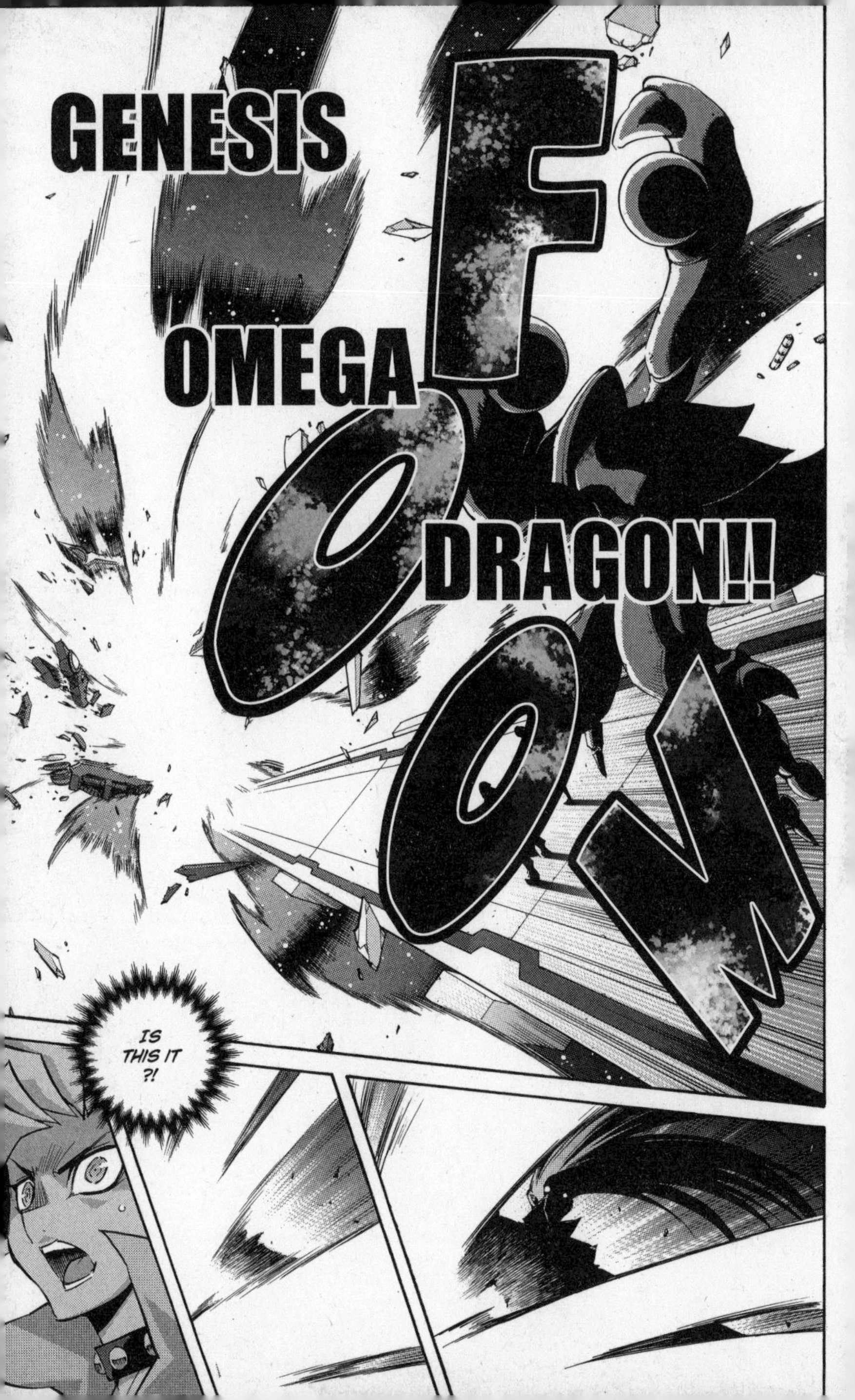
GENESIS OMEGA DRAGON!!
FOOM
IS THIS IT ?!

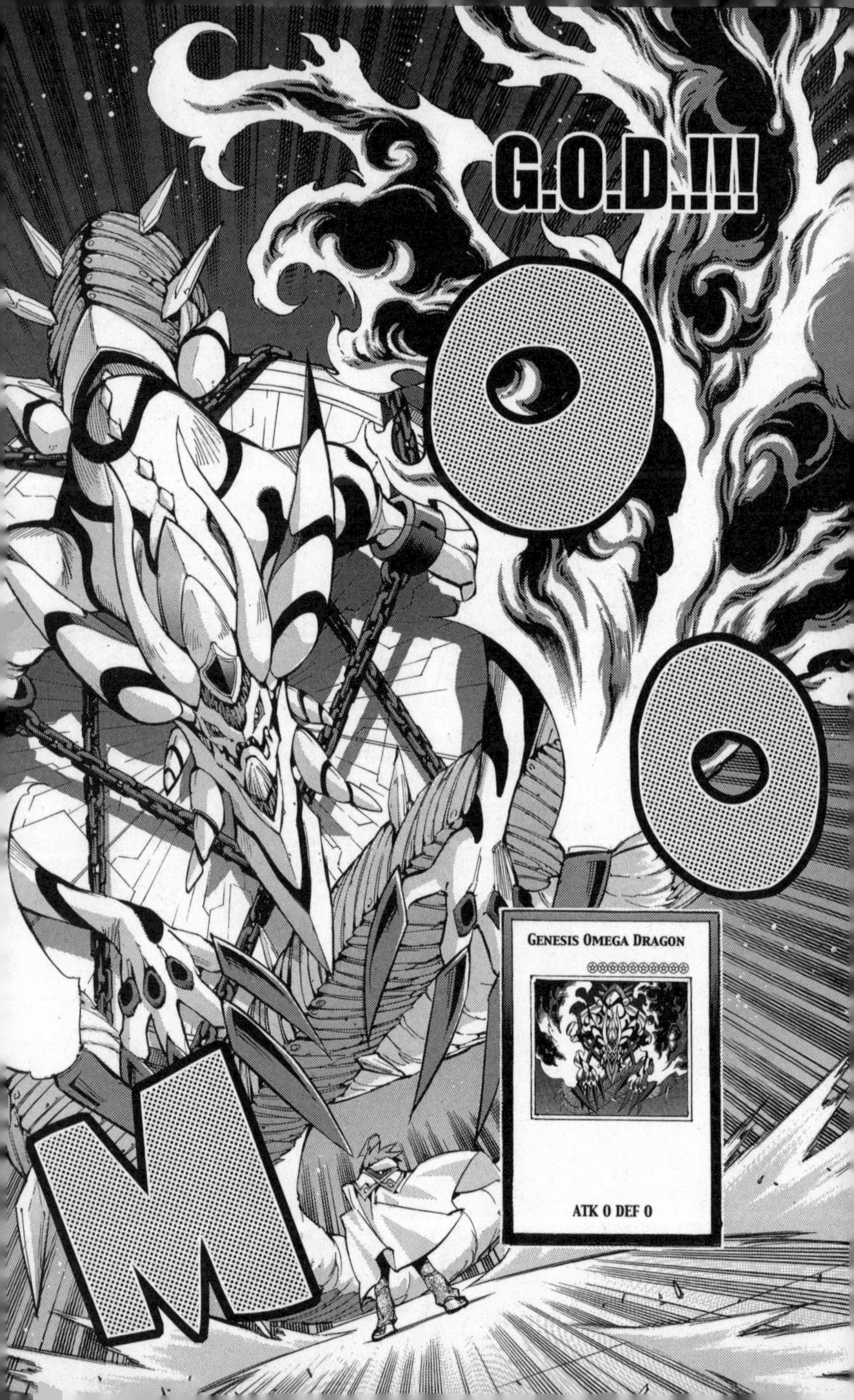
G.O.D.!!!
OOOM
GENESIS OMEGA DRAGON
ATK 0 DEF 0

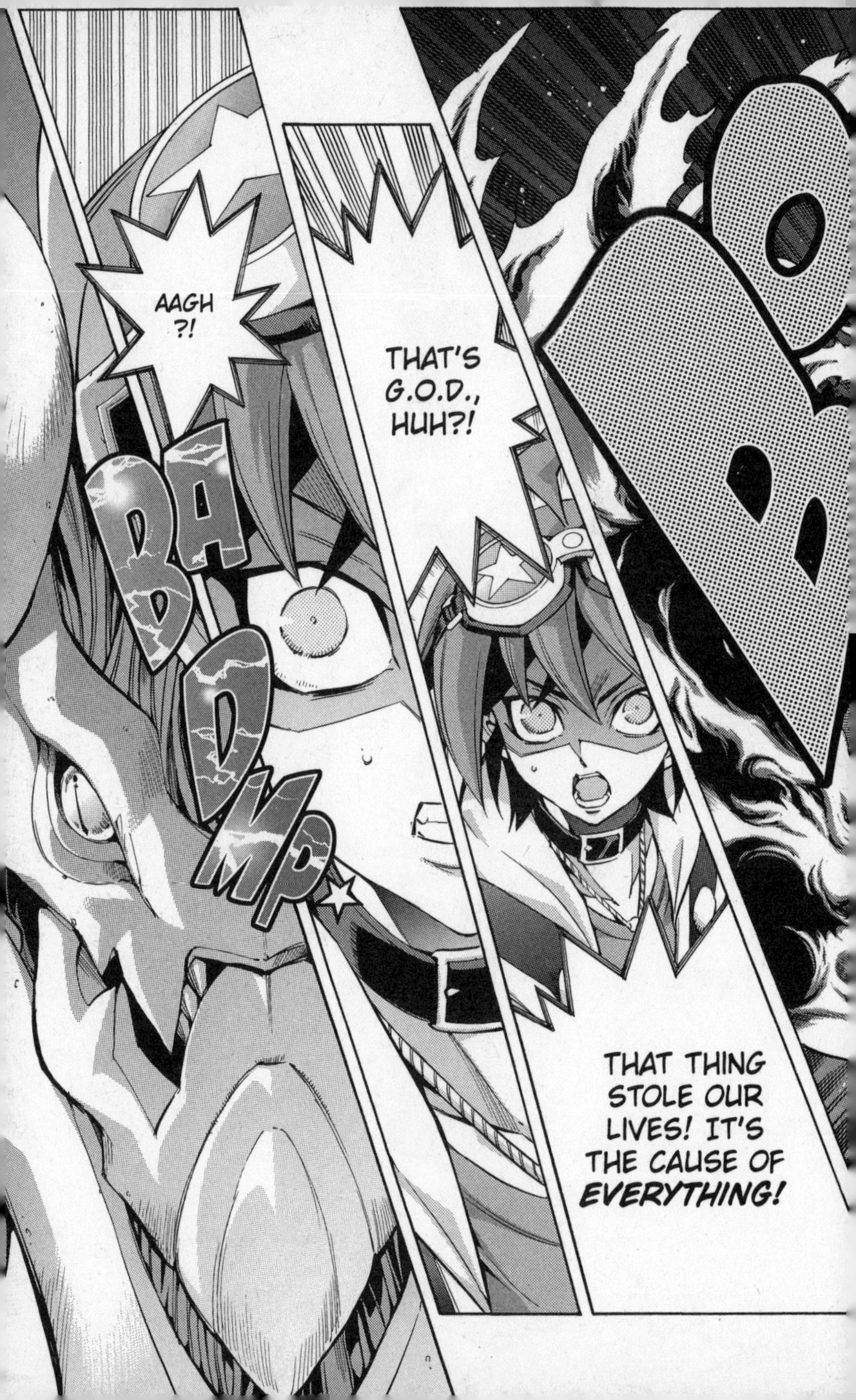
THAT'S G.O.D., HUH?!
THAT THING STOLE OUR LIVES! IT'S THE CAUSE OF *EVERYTHING!*
AAGH ?!
BA DUMP

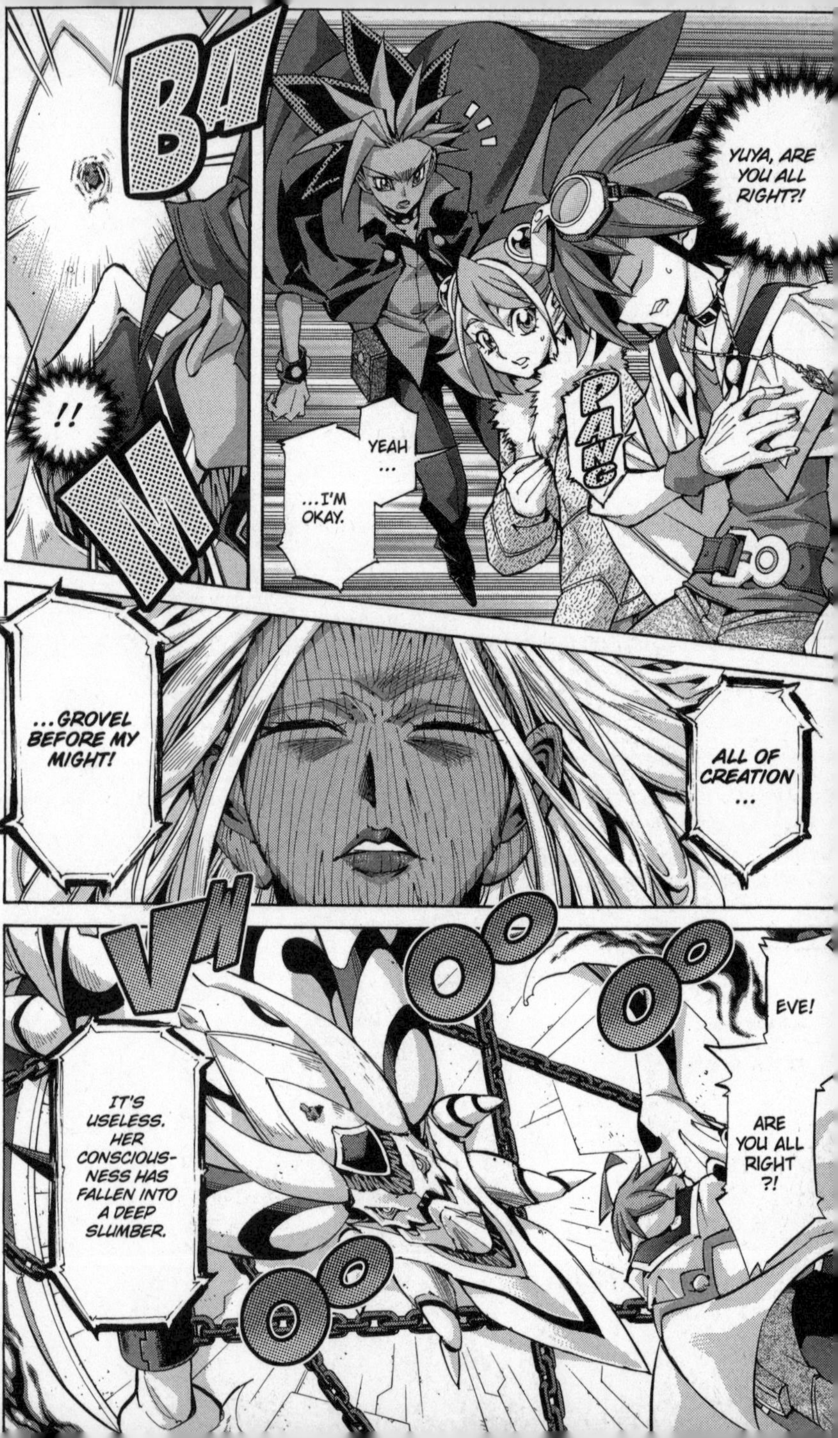
YUYA, ARE YOU ALL RIGHT?!
PANG
YEAH ...
...I'M OKAY.
BA
!!
M
ALL OF CREATION ...
...GROVEL BEFORE MY MIGHT!
EVE!
ARE YOU ALL RIGHT ?!
VOOOOO
IT'S USELESS. HER CONSCIOUS-NESS HAS FALLEN INTO A DEEP SLUMBER.

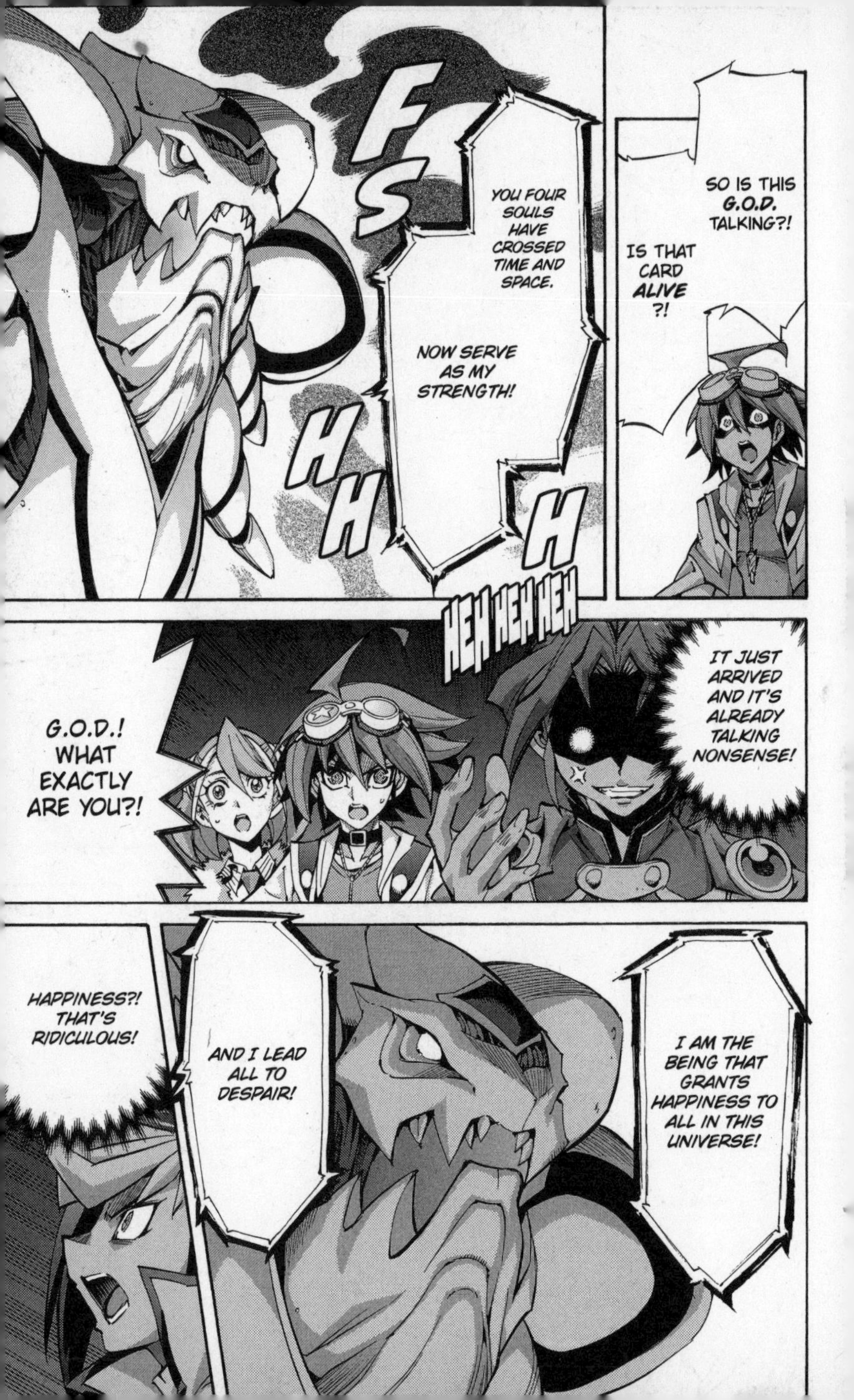

SO IS THIS G.O.D. TALKING?!
IS THAT CARD ALIVE?!
FS
YOU FOUR SOULS HAVE CROSSED TIME AND SPACE.
NOW SERVE AS MY STRENGTH!
HHH
HEH HEH HEH
IT JUST ARRIVED AND IT'S ALREADY TALKING NONSENSE!
G.O.D.! WHAT EXACTLY ARE YOU?!
I AM THE BEING THAT GRANTS HAPPINESS TO ALL IN THIS UNIVERSE!
AND I LEAD ALL TO DESPAIR!
HAPPINESS?! THAT'S RIDICULOUS!

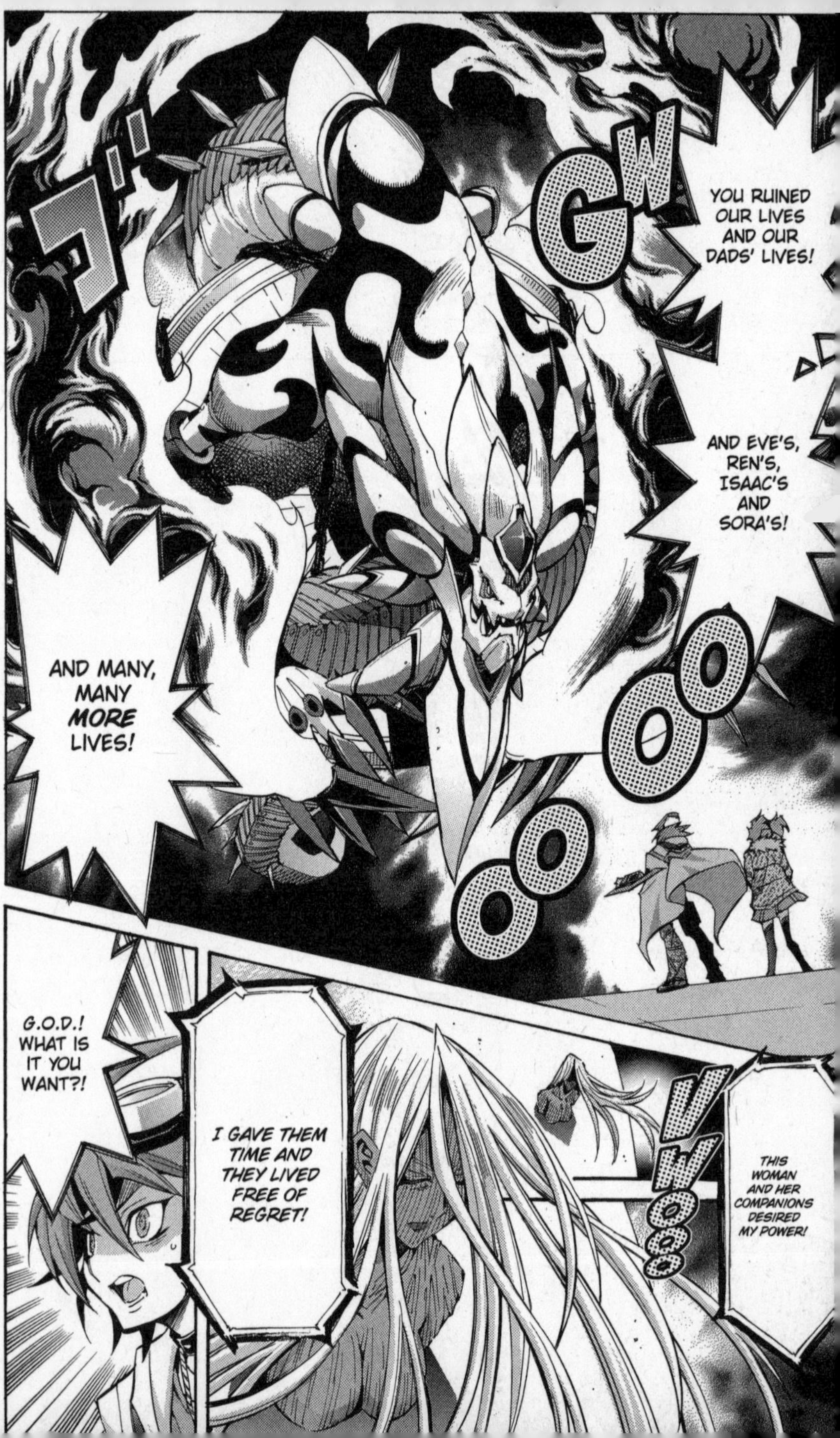
YOU RUINED OUR LIVES AND OUR DADS' LIVES!
AND EVE'S, REN'S, ISAAC'S AND SORA'S!
AND MANY, MANY MORE LIVES!
THIS WOMAN AND HER COMPANIONS DESIRED MY POWER!
I GAVE THEM TIME AND THEY LIVED FREE OF REGRET!
G.O.D.! WHAT IS IT YOU WANT?!

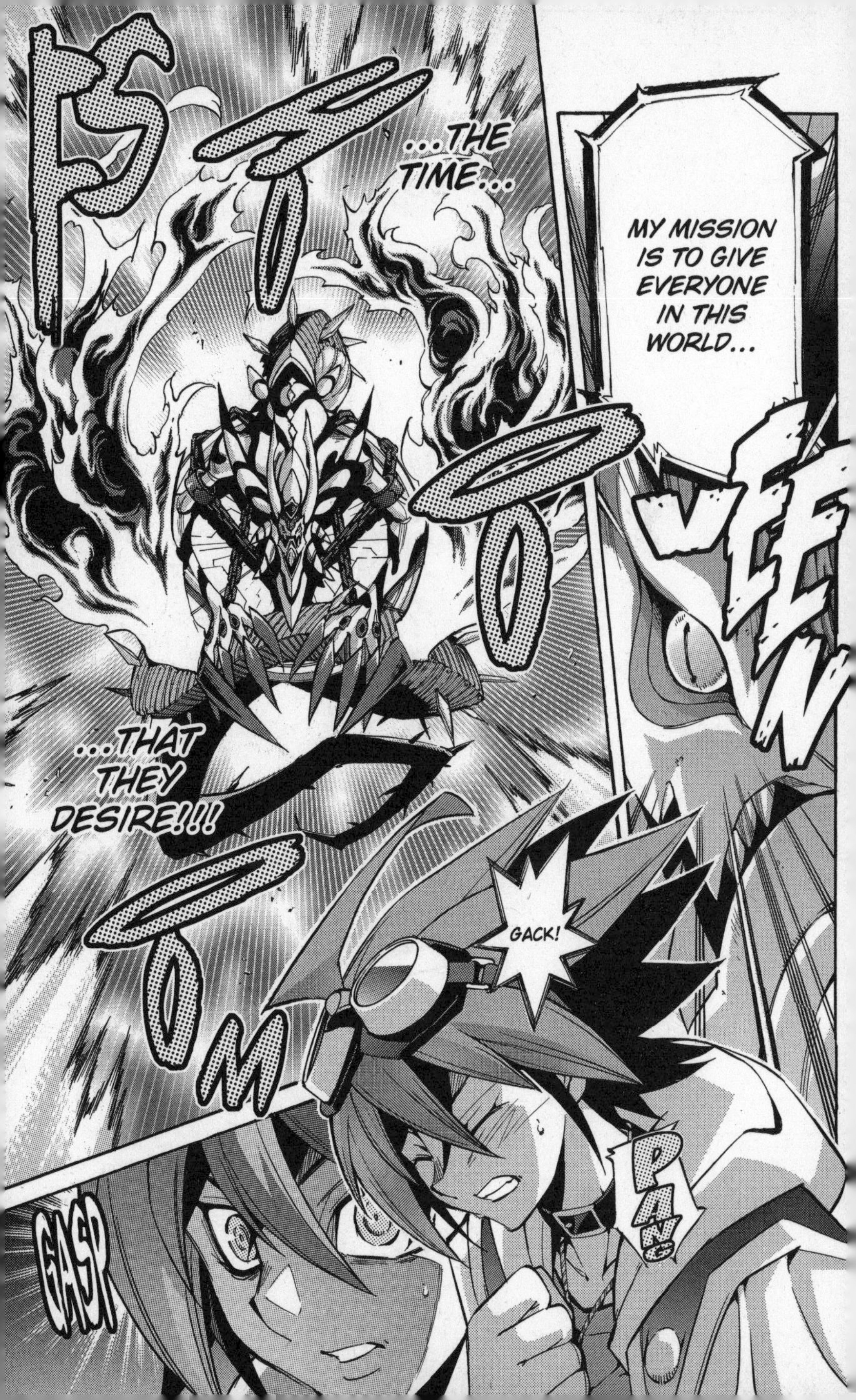
MY MISSION IS TO GIVE EVERYONE IN THIS WORLD...
...THE TIME...
...THAT THEY DESIRE!!!
VEEN
GACK!
PANG
GASP

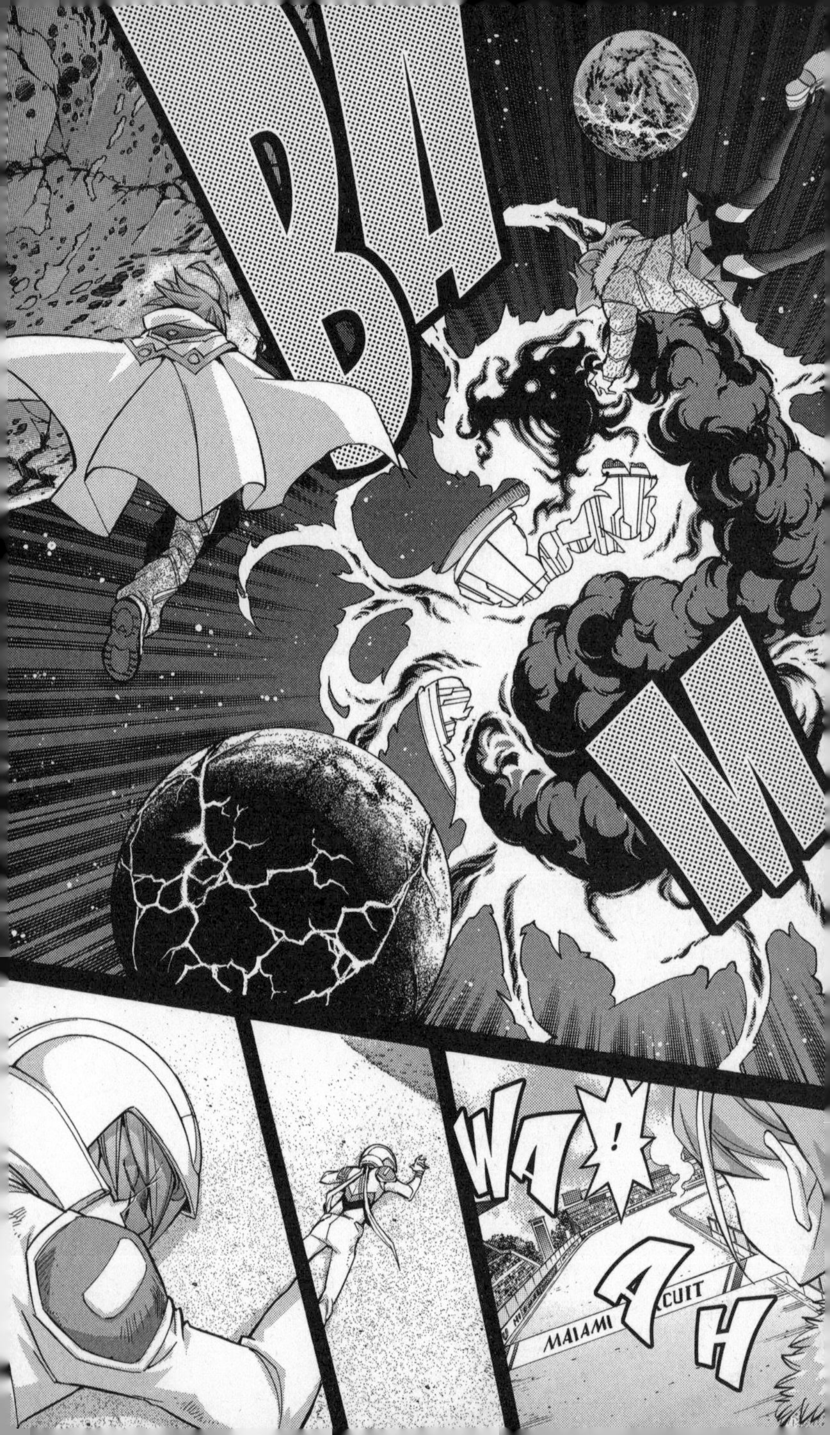
BA
M
WA!
A H
MAIAMI
CUIT

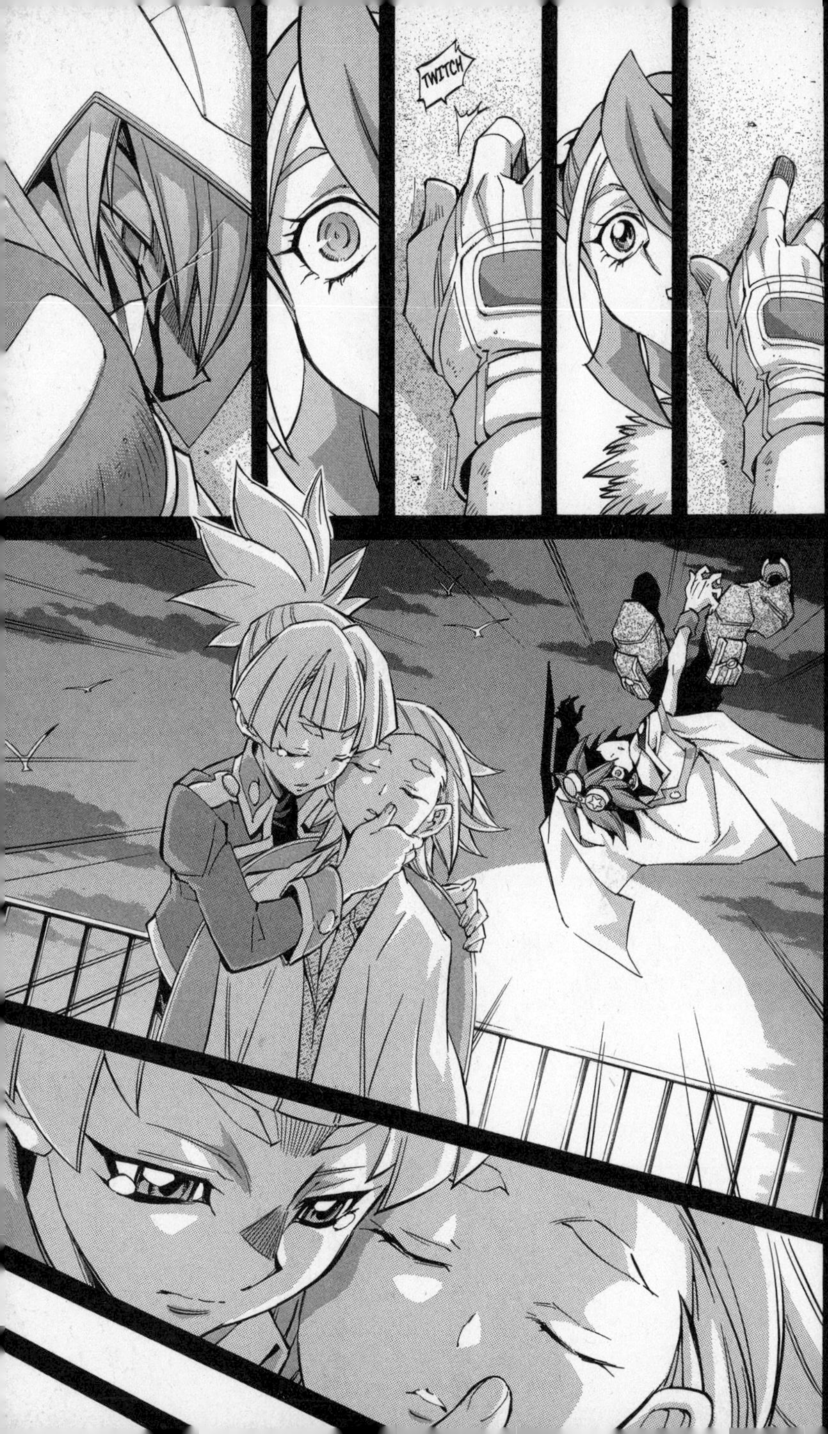
TWITCH

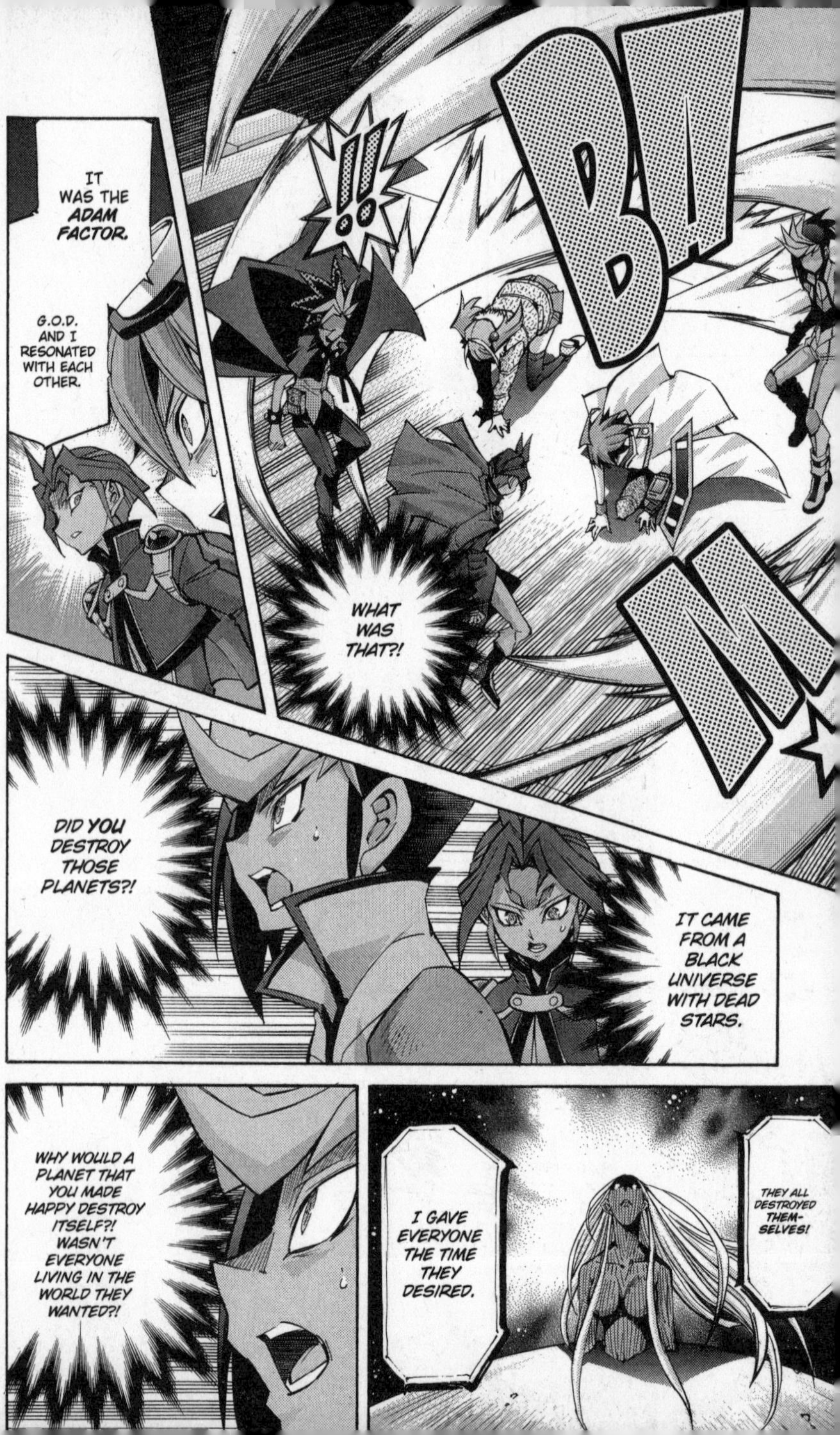
!!
WHAT WAS THAT?!
IT WAS THE ADAM FACTOR.
G.O.D. AND I RESONATED WITH EACH OTHER.
IT CAME FROM A BLACK UNIVERSE WITH DEAD STARS.
DID YOU DESTROY THOSE PLANETS?!
THEY ALL DESTROYED THEM-SELVES!
I GAVE EVERYONE THE TIME THEY DESIRED.
WHY WOULD A PLANET THAT YOU MADE HAPPY DESTROY ITSELF?! WASN'T EVERYONE LIVING IN THE WORLD THEY WANTED?!

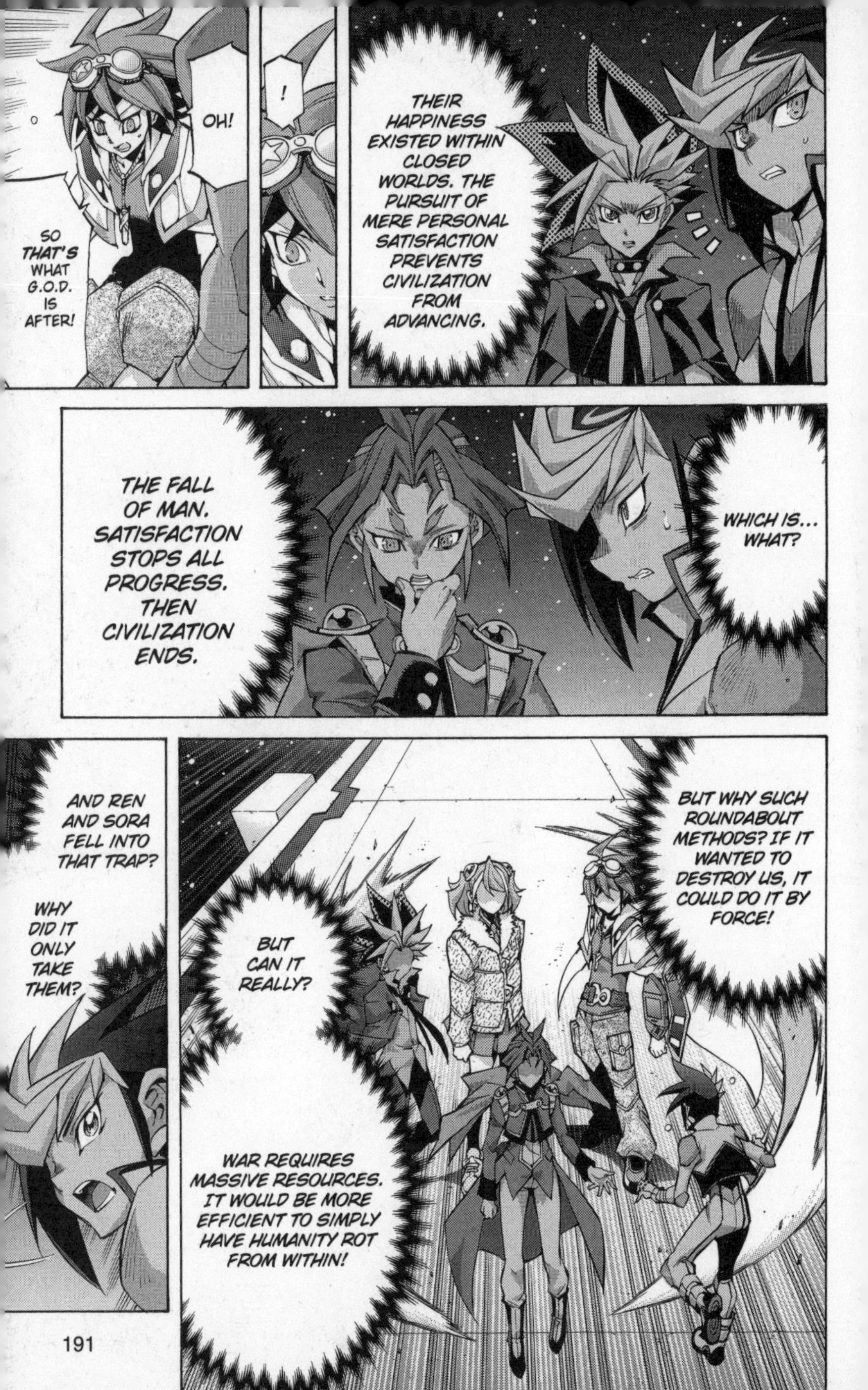
THEIR HAPPINESS EXISTED WITHIN CLOSED WORLDS. THE PURSUIT OF MERE PERSONAL SATISFACTION PREVENTS CIVILIZATION FROM ADVANCING.
!
OH!
SO THAT'S WHAT G.O.D. IS AFTER!
WHICH IS... WHAT?
THE FALL OF MAN. SATISFACTION STOPS ALL PROGRESS. THEN CIVILIZATION ENDS.
BUT WHY SUCH ROUNDABOUT METHODS? IF IT WANTED TO DESTROY US, IT COULD DO IT BY FORCE!
BUT CAN IT REALLY?
WAR REQUIRES MASSIVE RESOURCES. IT WOULD BE MORE EFFICIENT TO SIMPLY HAVE HUMANITY ROT FROM WITHIN!
AND REN AND SORA FELL INTO THAT TRAP?
WHY DID IT ONLY TAKE THEM?

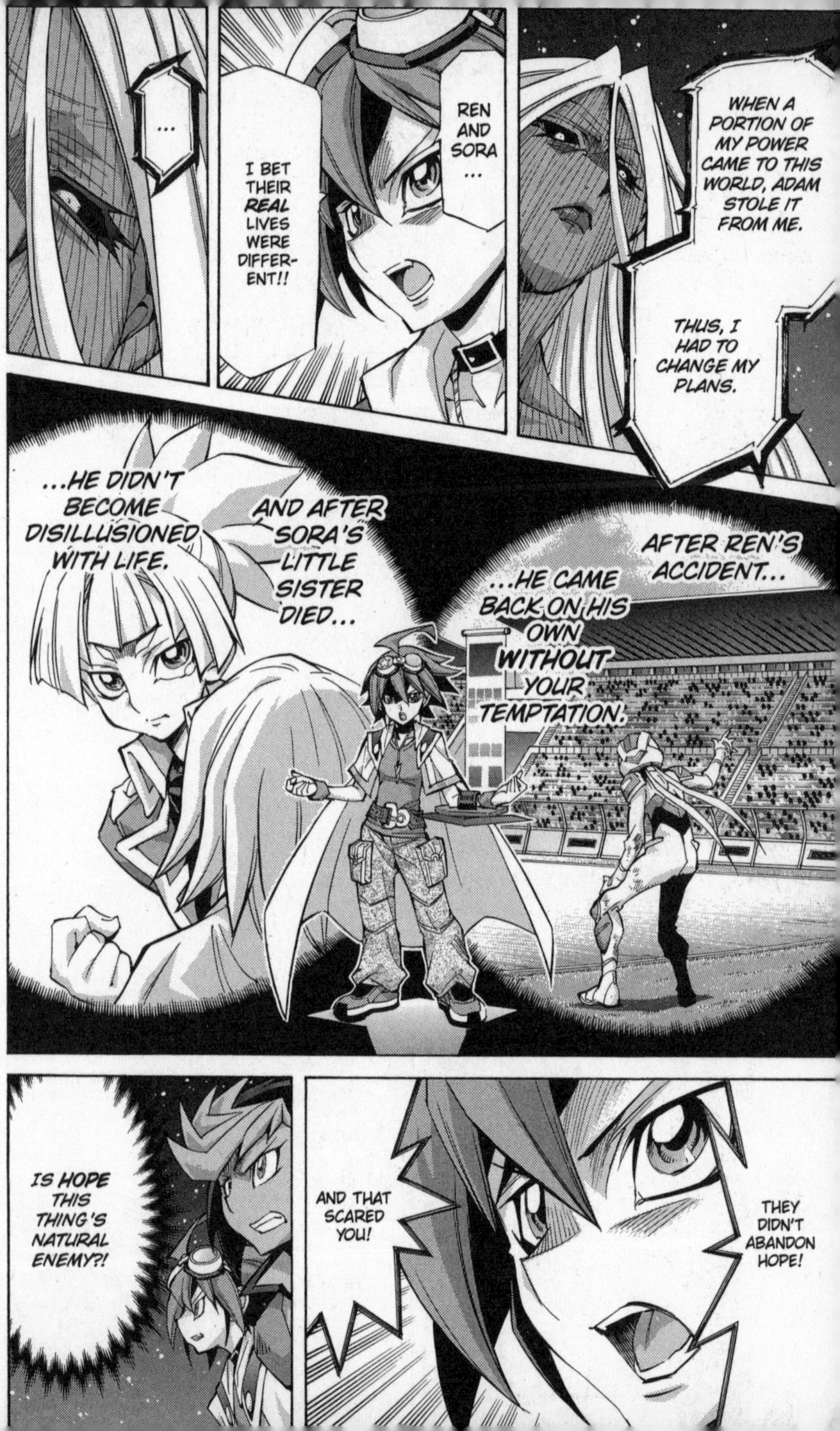
WHEN A PORTION OF MY POWER CAME TO THIS WORLD, ADAM STOLE IT FROM ME.
THUS, I HAD TO CHANGE MY PLANS.
REN AND SORA...
I BET THEIR REAL LIVES WERE DIFFERENT!!
...
AFTER REN'S ACCIDENT...
...HE CAME BACK ON HIS OWN WITHOUT YOUR TEMPTATION.
AND AFTER SORA'S LITTLE SISTER DIED...
...HE DIDN'T BECOME DISILLUSIONED WITH LIFE.
THEY DIDN'T ABANDON HOPE!
AND THAT SCARED YOU!
IS HOPE THIS THING'S NATURAL ENEMY?!

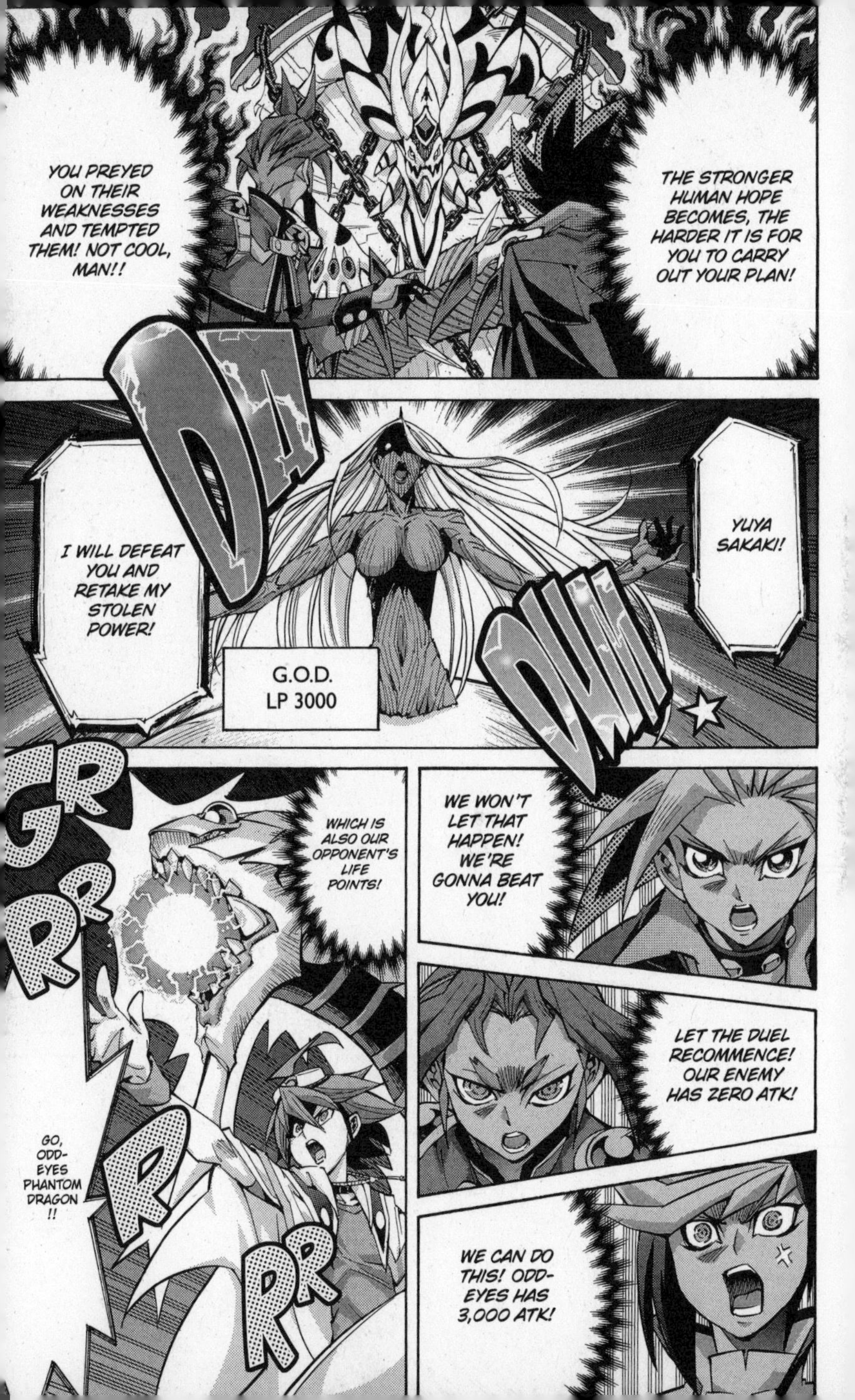
THE STRONGER HUMAN HOPE BECOMES, THE HARDER IT IS FOR YOU TO CARRY OUT YOUR PLAN!
YOU PREYED ON THEIR WEAKNESSES AND TEMPTED THEM! NOT COOL, MAN!!
YUYA SAKAKI!
DA
I WILL DEFEAT YOU AND RETAKE MY STOLEN POWER!
DUM
G.O.D.
LP 3000
WE WON'T LET THAT HAPPEN! WE'RE GONNA BEAT YOU!
LET THE DUEL RECOMMENCE! OUR ENEMY HAS ZERO ATK!
WE CAN DO THIS! ODD-EYES HAS 3,000 ATK!
WHICH IS ALSO OUR OPPONENT'S LIFE POINTS!
GRRRR
GO, ODD-EYES PHANTOM DRAGON!!
RRR

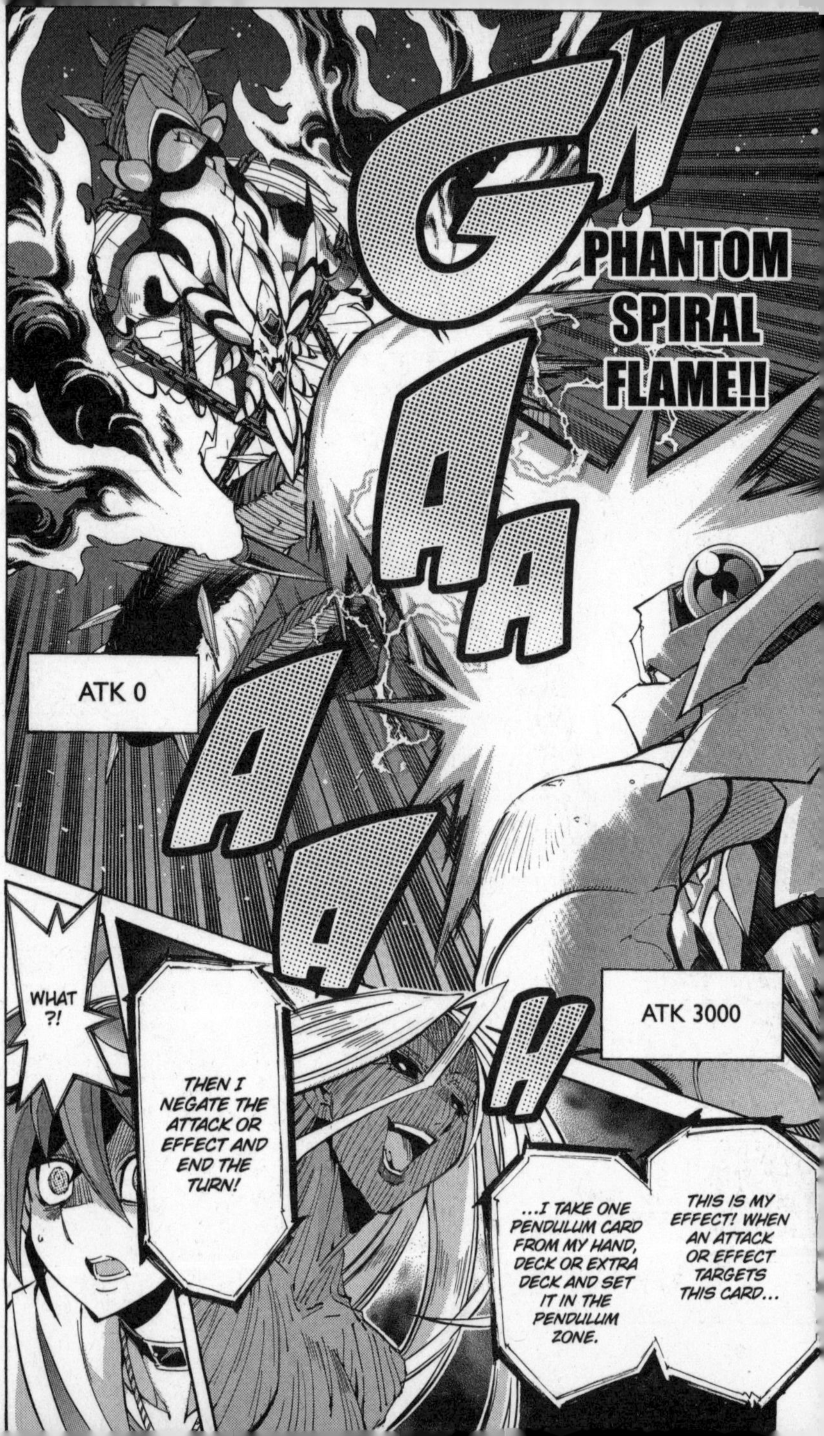
GWAAAAAH
PHANTOM SPIRAL FLAME!!
ATK 0
ATK 3000
THIS IS MY EFFECT! WHEN AN ATTACK OR EFFECT TARGETS THIS CARD...
...I TAKE ONE PENDULUM CARD FROM MY HAND, DECK OR EXTRA DECK AND SET IT IN THE PENDULUM ZONE.
THEN I NEGATE THE ATTACK OR EFFECT AND END THE TURN!
WHAT?!

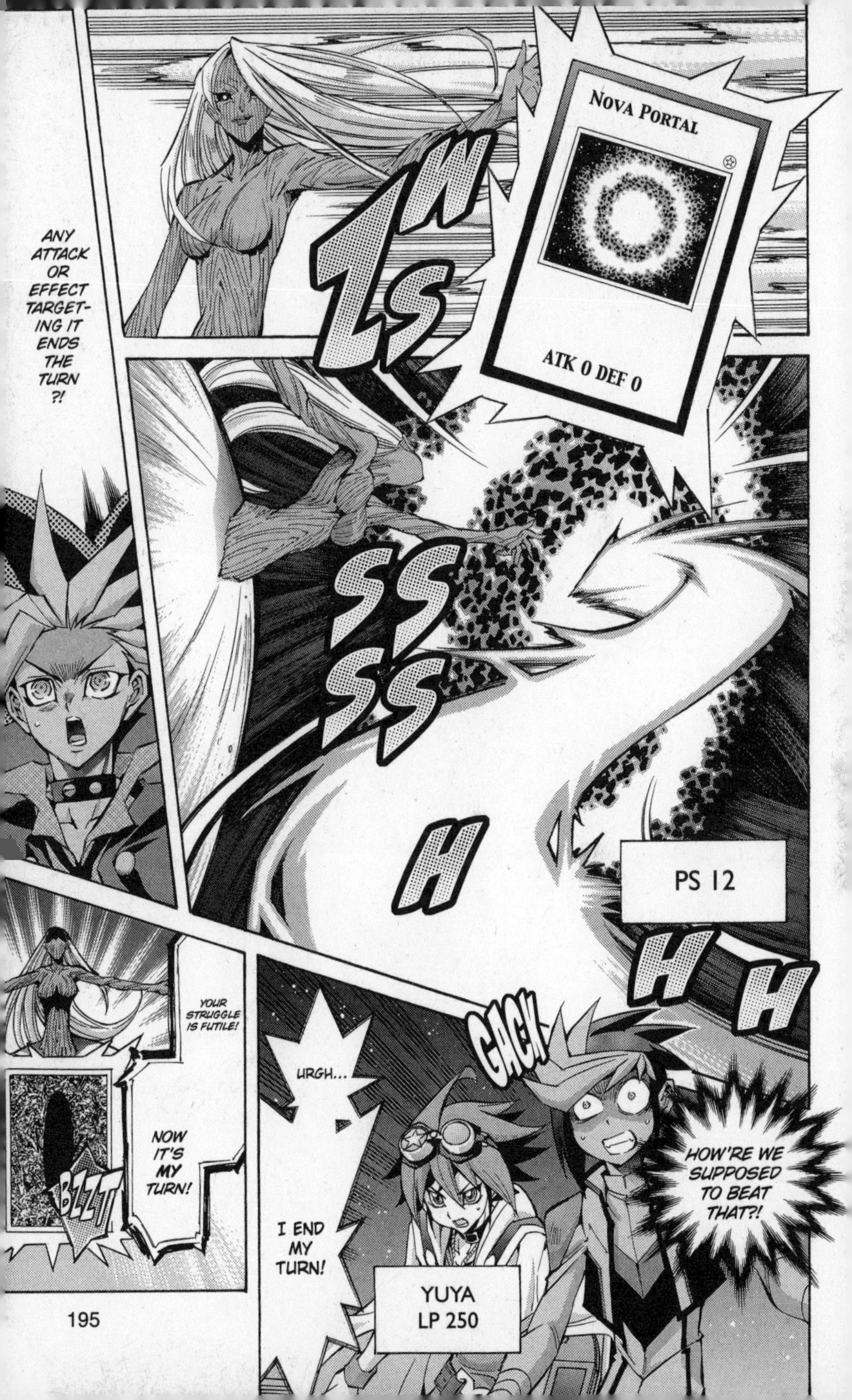
Nova Portal
ATK 0 DEF 0
ANY ATTACK OR EFFECT TARGETING IT ENDS THE TURN ?!
SS
SS
H
PS 12
H H
GACK
HOW'RE WE SUPPOSED TO BEAT THAT?!
URGH...
I END MY TURN!
YUYA
LP 250
YOUR STRUGGLE IS FUTILE!
NOW IT'S MY TURN!
BZZT

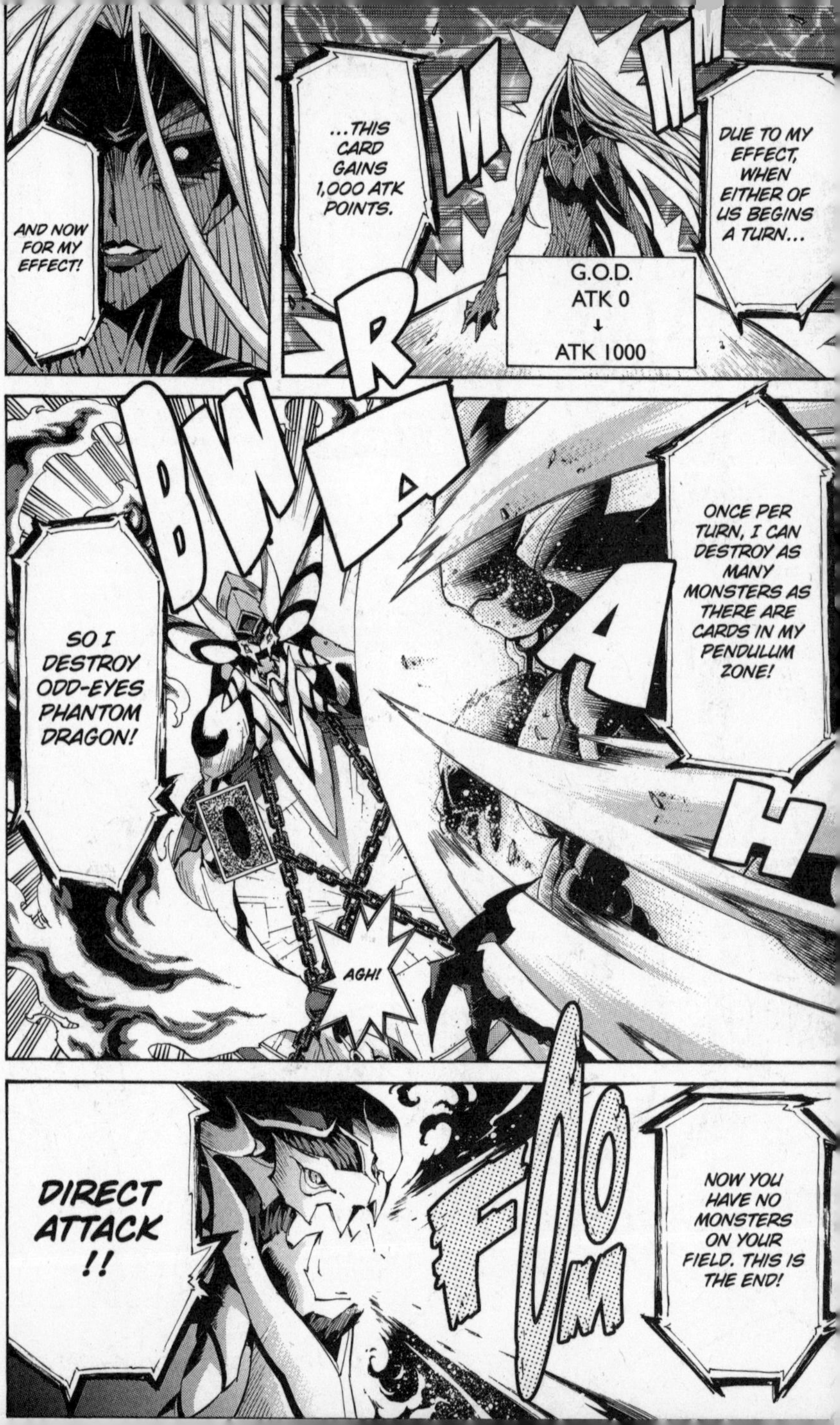
DUE TO MY EFFECT, WHEN EITHER OF US BEGINS A TURN...
...THIS CARD GAINS 1,000 ATK POINTS.
G.O.D.
ATK 0
↓
ATK 1000
AND NOW FOR MY EFFECT!
ONCE PER TURN, I CAN DESTROY AS MANY MONSTERS AS THERE ARE CARDS IN MY PENDULUM ZONE!
SO I DESTROY ODD-EYES PHANTOM DRAGON!
AGH!
NOW YOU HAVE NO MONSTERS ON YOUR FIELD. THIS IS THE END!
FOOOM
DIRECT ATTACK !!

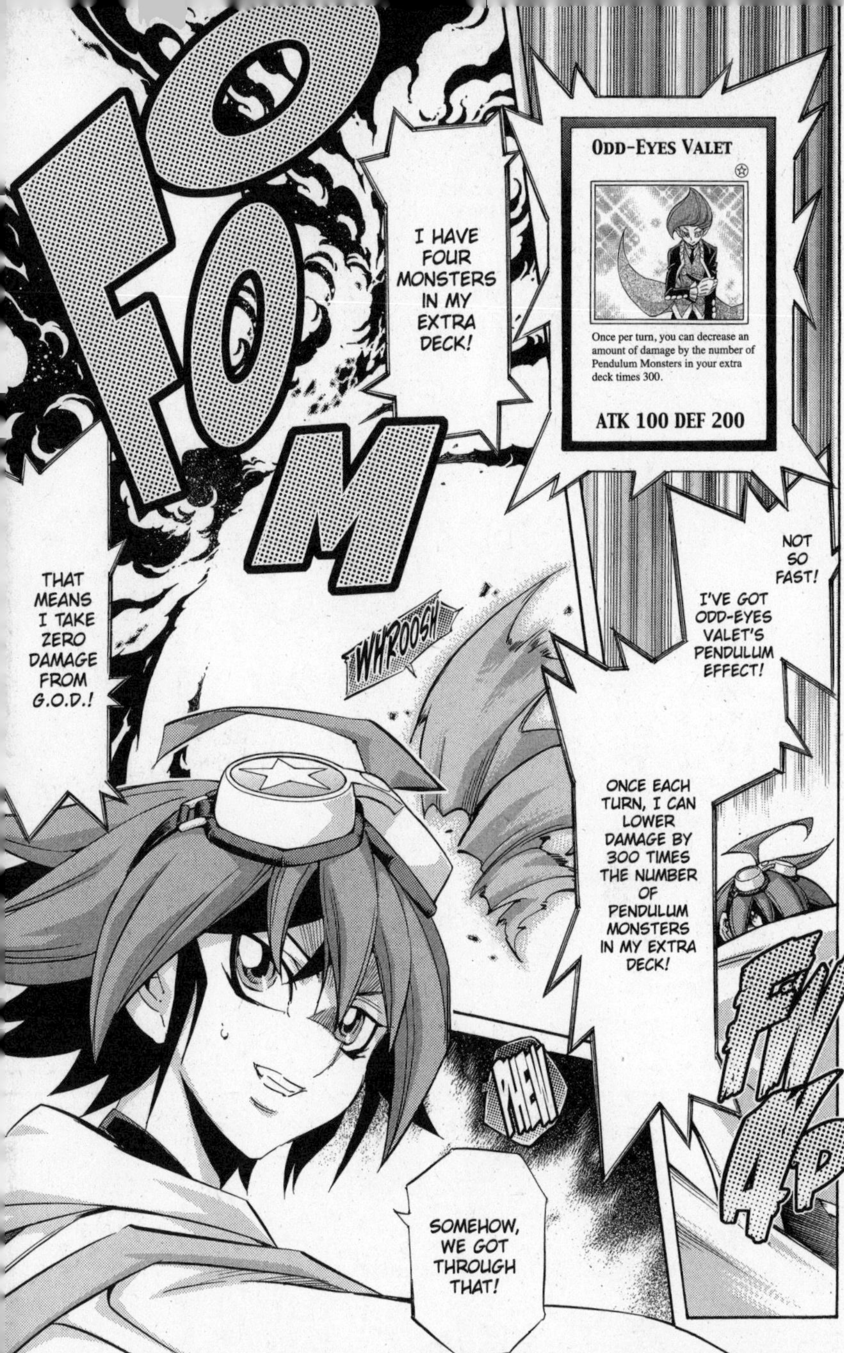
FOOM
NOT SO FAST!
I'VE GOT ODD-EYES VALET'S PENDULUM EFFECT!
ONCE EACH TURN, I CAN LOWER DAMAGE BY 300 TIMES THE NUMBER OF PENDULUM MONSTERS IN MY EXTRA DECK!
ODD-EYES VALET
Once per turn, you can decrease an amount of damage by the number of Pendulum Monsters in your extra deck times 300.
ATK 100 DEF 200
I HAVE FOUR MONSTERS IN MY EXTRA DECK!
THAT MEANS I TAKE ZERO DAMAGE FROM G.O.D.!
WHROOSH
FWHAP
PHEW
SOMEHOW, WE GOT THROUGH THAT!

YU-GI-OH! ARC-V—VOL. 6—THE END

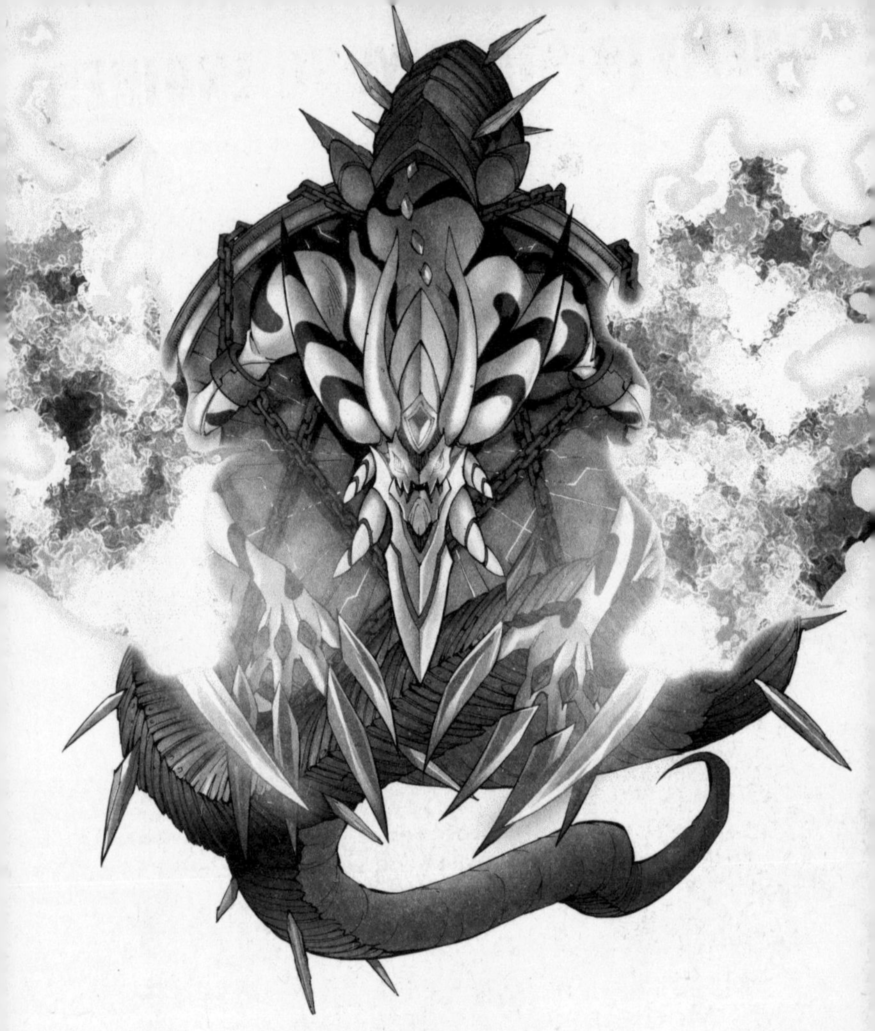

Staff	Junya Uchino Kazuo Ochiai
Coloring	Toru Shimizu
Editing	Takahiko Aikawa
Support	Gallop Wedge Holdings

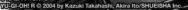

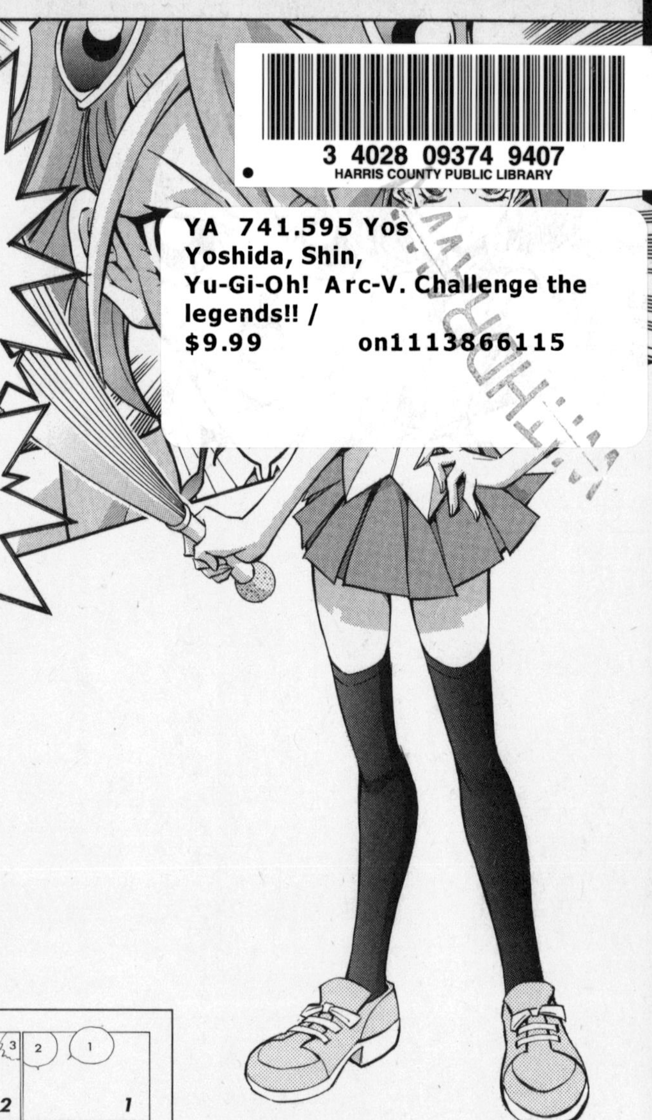

STOP!

YOU'RE READING THE WRONG WAY!

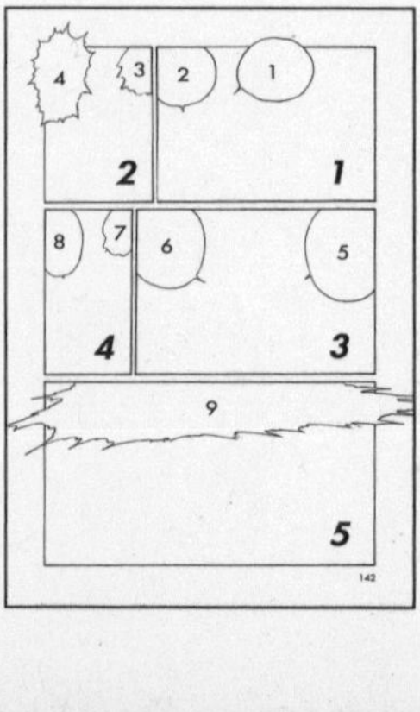

Yu-Gi-Oh! ARC-V

reads from right to left, starting in the upper-right corner. Japanese is read from right to left, meaning that action, sound effects and word-balloon order are completely reversed from English order.